Native Bush, Rainbow Springs, Rotorua

The third edition of the TRAVELwise Guide is dedicated to the many hosts who continuously provide the New Zealand unique style of Bed & Breakfast hospitality.

For all enquiries please contact Uli or Brian at Travelwise
Ph 0064-3-476 1515.   Fax 0064-3-4761514
e-mail: welcome@travelwise.co.nz

The TRAVELwise Guide to

BED & BREAKFAST
in
NEW ZEALAND

"Welcome"

year 2001 edition

TRAVEL*wise* LTD.

Waterfront, Russell, Northland.

The TRAVELwise Guide to

BED & BREAKFAST
in
NEW ZEALAND

*Presenting New Zealand's
Rich World of
Bed & Breakfast Hospitality*

First published 1998.
Copyright © 2000 Uli and Brian Newman.

The authors assert their moral rights in this work.

This book is copyright. Except for the purposes of fair reviewing, no part of this publication may be reproduced or transmitted in any form or by any means, electronic or mechanical, including photocopying, recording or any information storage and retrieval system, without permission in writing from the publisher.
Infringers of copyright render themselves liable to prosecution.

ISBN 0-9582094-1-3

Published by TRAVELwise Ltd.
P.O.Box 6226, Great King Street, Dunedin, New Zealand.
Production and design by TRAVELwise Ltd.

Printed by PrintLink, Wellington, New Zealand.

Distributed by Nationwide Distributors, Christchurch.
Front Cover Photo:
Photography, **Bill Nichol**.
Furnished by '**MacKenzie & Willis**' Dunedin.
Accessories provided by the following Dunedin businesses:
Acquisitions, Dimensions, MacKenzie & Willis, The Victorian Room.

All listings in this publication rely on the provision of information supplied by third parties. Accordingly the publisher expressly disclaims all and any liability and responsibility to any person, whether a purchaser or reader of this publication or not, in respect of damages arising out of any reliance, in full or in part, upon any contents of this publication for any purpose.

Prices listed herein, and availability of accommodation and services, may change without prior notice. Please confirm all details with your host when you make your booking.

Table of Contents

Introduction 9
Bed and Breakfast Categories 12

How to use this guide - "at a glance" 14
How to use this guide - guestroom details 15

General information 16
Practical travel information: On the Road 18
Practical travel information: Banking 20
Practical travel information: Telephones 21
Practical travel information: Post Services 22
Natural New Zealand 24

Map of North Island Accommodation 26
North Island Accommodation Listings 30

Map of South Island Accommodation 128
South Island Accommodation Listings 132

Introduction to translated sections 237
German language section 238
Japanese language section 248
Mandarin (Chinese) language section 258

Credits 266
Alphabetical Index 267

Visit our Web site http://www.travelwise.co.nz

Introduction

"*Experience the real New Zealand – its people*"

Welcome to the rich world
of
Hosted Accommodation in New Zealand.

And what a rich choice it is – from cottages to castles, from budget accommodation to luxurious lodges. You will stay with hosts ranging from those who simply love meeting people to those who have taken hospitality to great entrepreneurial heights. Under the umbrella of Bed & Breakfast you will find: Homestays, Farmstays, Guest Houses, Inns, Boutique Accommodation, Countrystays. Bed & Breakfast in New Zealand, where you can get to know the real New Zealand – its people. Stay with teachers, farmers, retired professionals, orchardists, artists, healers and writers. Share the same interests, hobbies or professional background as your hosts. Enjoy unique Bed & Breakfast experiences at a fishing lodge or a high country sheep farm, or at a riding or weaving school, or just find a "home away from home" in town or country. While both hosts and styles of accommodation vary widely, they all reflect the genuine warmth and friendly hospitality that New Zealanders are known for. Wherever you stay, you will be a welcome guest and your stay a pleasant and memorable one.

Introduction

What to Expect

Bed & Breakfast in New Zealand has a fine reputation for its standard of services. Guests can expect cleanliness, comfortable beds, a good substantial breakfast and warm, generous hospitality. In addition, your hosts can provide you with first-hand in-depth information about their area. They take pleasure in helping you with your pursuits and travel plans. Their invaluable knowledge can enrich your stay immensely.

What is Expected of You

Your hosts will do everything in their power to make your stay an enjoyable and memorable one. However, it is important to remember that in most cases you are a guest in a private home. So please consider the little things, like arranging to have a house-key if returning late at night, or asking about the tariffs for toll calls prior to using the telephone. Please let your hosts know in time if you will be late. Thoughtfulness on your part will contribute to a satisfying experience for both host and guest.

What to Do – Hints

You will avoid any disappointment by booking ahead, especially during the high summer season. It is also advisable to call your hosts one day in advance to confirm your booking and let them know about your expected time of arrival. Some hosts offer a complimentary pick-up service from coach, plane or train if guests don't have their own transport. Please give your hosts one day's notice if you would like to have an evening meal.

Most holiday memories are mere snapshots – images we treasure, but that fade with any passing year. But the people we meet – they become a part of us. They live in us. They travel with us.

PAM BROWN, b 1928

Bed & Breakfast Categories

Bed & Breakfast

Bed & Breakfast is the umbrella term for the variety of hosted accommodations that include a comfortable bed for the night and a substantial breakfast in the morning. The hosts offer warm and generous hospitality throughout your stay.

Homestay

Homestay is the popular Bed & Breakfast accommodation that offers warm and friendly hospitality in a private home. The hosts love meeting people, they enjoy providing their guests with that "home away from home" feeling, knowing that they arrive as strangers but will leave as friends.

Countrystay

Countrystays are often like Homestays. They offer accommodation in a private home. Being in a rural setting, they are associated with all the features and attractions of the countryside. Many Countrystays are close to popular country attractions which offer you the chance to experience rural New Zealand life.

Farmstay

Farmstays are an ideal way to experience real farm life in New Zealand. An opportunity for you to have hands-on contact with the animals and daily life on a farm. A farm tour may be included. Breakfast is usually taken with the family. Many Farmstays offer lunch and evening meals, as restaurants are often not close by.

Bed & Breakfast Categories

Guesthouse/Inn

Guest Houses and Inns are usually larger establishments that cater for more guests, but still offer that personalised style of hospitality. They might have several lounge areas and a breakfast room. Guest Houses do not usually offer an evening meal.

Boutique Accommodation

Within the Bed & Breakfast world Boutique Accommodation has been adopted by those hosts whose unique property features reflect a special ambience - period elegance, grace and charm, romance, art, etc. These features are usually enhanced by the hosts' flair for entertainment and hospitality.

Luxury Accommodation

Luxury Accommodation symbolizes superb facilities, excellent food and an exceptional level of service. Many properties within this category have spectacular settings and offer various additional top class attractions. They represent outstanding accommodation and hospitality.

Self-contained Accommodation

Self-contained accommodation usually includes a separate entrance, own bathroom facilities and an independent lounge area. Kitchen and laundry facilities may be included. It can be a self-contained part of the family home or a separate cottage. Breakfast is either served in the hosts' home, delivered to the doorstep or breakfast provisions provided on the premises.

How to use this guide – "at a glance"

"at a glance"
Easy Contact Panel
Your hosts: who they are, where they are, and how to make quick contact.

"at a glance"
Tariff Panel
Each tariff indicates the nightly rate. **Double** indicates the cost for two people sharing one room. **Single** indicates the cost for one person occupying a room. A deposit may be required when booking. Tariffs include breakfast unless otherwise stated. **All prices quoted are in NZ$ – GST inclusive.**
Please confirm details with your host.

"at a glance"
Category Symbols
These quick-to-spot symbols are designed to make selecting your preferred accommodation easy. Particularly helpful for travellers with a limited knowledge of the English language.

"at a glance"
Category Panel
Your hosts' personal description of their category.

"at a glance"
Features & Attractions
Highlighting the main features and attractions in and around this accommodation and locality.

"at a glance"
Location Map
Your hosts' property is indicated by a red dot. Property name is displayed in white box. Maps may be accompanied by a direction panel outlining easy directions.

Clear Address Details
Clear address panel displays essential information, including property address, telephone and fax numbers, e-mail and Internet address. **NOTE:** *When calling from overseas dial New Zealand's international code, 0064, then drop the 0 off the area code (03), for example "Whispering Pines" 0064-3-443-1448.*

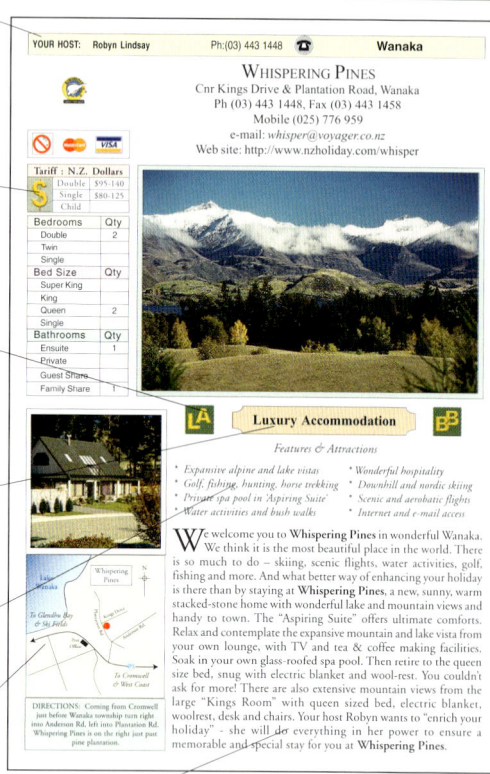

"A Personal Warm Welcome"
These words of welcome have been written personally by your hosts. They describe the features of the accommodation and portray their personality and lifestyle.

 No Smoking

Abbreviations		
SH	–	State Highway
h.p.	–	half price
N.A.	–	not applicable
neg.	–	negotiable
Qty	–	Quantity
Tce	–	Terrace

Book direct – Reduce costs
By booking direct with your Bed & Breakfast host in New Zealand, you make the personal connection right from the start and avoid many additional costs.

How to use this guide – Guest room details

Bedrooms

Double = Room with bed for two people
Twin = Room with two beds for two people
Single = Room with bed for one person

Bathrooms

Ensuite = Bathroom adjoining bedroom
Private = Separate bathroom for your use only
Guest Share/Family Share = Bathroom shared with other guests or host family

Bedrooms	Qty
Double	
Twin	
Single	
Bed Size	**Qty**
Super King	
King	
Queen/Double	
(King-) Single	
Bathrooms	**Qty**
Ensuite	
Private	
Guest Share	
Family Share	

Bed Size

Super King
180 x 200cm

King
165 x 200cm

Queen
150 x 200cm

Double
135 x 190cm

Single
90 x 190cm

King Single
90 x 200cm

How to use this guide – Category Symbols

  Bed & Breakfast

  Boutique Accommodation

  Countrystay

  Farmstay

  Guest House / Inn

  Homestay

  Luxury Accommodation

  Self-contained Accom. & Cottages

How to use this guide – Credit Cards Accepted by Hosts

  Amex – American Express

  Japanese Credit Card

  VISA

  Diners

  Bankcard

MasterCard

Maestro

Eftpos

How to use this guide – Hosts' Associations & Affiliations

  Historic Places Trust

  Hospitality Hosts

  New Zealand Association Farm & Home Hosts

  Superior Inns of New Zealand

  Auckland Home & Farmstay

  Heritage Inns of New Zealand

  Hostlink-Network of Fine Hosts

  New Zealand's Federation *of* Bed & Breakfast Hotels

  This logo assures you of a warm Kiwi welcome, friendly attention and good service. Kiwihost is New Zealand's award winning customer service training programme, a sure sign that we value you as a visitor everywhere you go.

General Information

Dairies and Supermarkets

Dairies, a long-established feature of the New Zealand landscape, are usually open 7 days a week, from early to late. Like the old general country stores, dairies stock a wide variety of goods. You can normally expect to obtain basic foods and commodities, such as bread, milk, newspapers, confectionery and grocery items.

Because of the extended trading hours, and the benefits of convenient locations, prices are normally slightly higher than those at the supermarket. Some dairies, especially in small communities, also offer Post Shop services.

Supermarkets

Nearly all towns and cities have supermarkets. Supermarkets provide a wider range of goods for one-stop grocery shopping, and have more competitive prices. Free parking is normally provided, but only for genuine customers - you may be asked to show your receipt. Some supermarkets now have extended trading hours, and most are open 7 days a week.

The New Zealand Dairy – so much a part of New Zealand's daily life.

Petrol Stations

Also known as 'service stations', these provide basic commodities for motor vehicles. You can expect to obtain fuel, oil, air and water, and general motoring accessories. Although petrol stations do not normally provide repair or maintenance services - these are provided by 'garages' - those that do may have a sign saying 'Mechanic on duty' or 'Repairs carried out'.

Tourist Radio

Tourist Information FM is a service established to provide information to visitors to New Zealand 24 hours a day, and is available in most tourist areas. For English-language broadcasts, tune to 88.2 FM on your radio. For German-language broadcasts, tune to 100.4 FM, and for Japanese-language broadcasts, tune to 100.8 FM on your radio.

The **New Zealand Automobile Association** (*AA*) offers an excellent service. *AA* centres around the country provide maps, guides and touring information to local members and to members of affiliated overseas motoring clubs. For more information, call the freephone 0800 500 444 at any time.

General Information

Emergency Services

**If you require the police, ambulance or fire service, dial 111.
There is no charge for making a 111 call from a public phone box.**

Visitor Information Network

Visitor Information Centres are identified by the distinctive green italic *i* logo in conjunction with the Visitor Information logo.
Over 80 of them are located throughout New Zealand. They offer a wide range of services including travel bookings, tours and accommodation. The staff, who have unparalleled local and national knowledge are trained and committed to providing accurate and appriorate information to visitors.

Dunedin Visitor Information Centre

| On the Road | Practical Travel Information |

*Driving in New Zealand can be a pleasure,
the ever changing scenery is superb.*

On the Road

Driving in New Zealand is a pleasure; the scenery is superb, the roads are generally of a high standard and New Zealanders are helpful and courteous. However, for your safety and that of other motorists, we urge you to take a little time (New Zealand is patient, it will wait for you) and read the following before you begin driving.

The *New Zealand Road Code* is the definitive guide to correct and lawful driving in New Zealand. It is available at a small cost from the Land Transport Safety Authority. Look in the local telephone directory for the nearest office. A useful leaflet, with English, German and Japanese sections, is *Driving Safely in New Zealand*, also available free of charge from the Land Transport Safety Authority.

An excellent leaflet - *Budget's Guide to Safe Driving in New Zealand* - is available in English, German, Japanese and Chinese editions from Budget Rental Car offices throughout New Zealand.

| Practical Travel Information | On the Road |

Driving : Some Basic Points

Keep Left: In New Zealand we drive on the **left**. Overseas visitors may find this difficult. – We suggest you take time to adjust and plan your journeys accordingly.

Speed Limit: In general, the maximum speed limit on the open road or motorway / freeway, identifiable by this sign, is 100 kilometres per hour.

In cities and towns, it is 50km per hour. There are exceptions, so watch out for signs (positioned on the left of the road) which may indicate a lower specified speed limit.

Road Signs at Intersections:
Stop: Stop completely, then give way to all traffic.

Give way - Drive slowly. Stop if drivers are approaching from left or right, and give way to all traffic, including those opposite if you are turning left.

Seatbelts: The driver and all passengers (adults and children) - including those sitting in rear seats - must use seatbelts or approved child restraints.

*If you are one of the more adventurous travellers,
many outstanding sights await you in New Zealand.*

Money Matters | Practical Travel Information

Money and Banks

Currency
New Zealand has been operating on the decimal currency system with the NZ Dollar as its base since 10 July 1967. Coins in use are: 5c, 10c, 20c, 50c, $1 and $2. Bank notes are available in denominations of $5, $10, $20, $50 and $100.

Changing Money
Money exchange facilities exist at all banks and at most New Zealand international airports. New Zealand banks buy and sell all major currencies and offer competitive exchange rates which are updated daily.

Travellers' Cheques
Travellers' cheques can also be cashed at Bureaux de Change and hotels or large stores in resorts and larger cities.
Import or export of foreign currency is not subject to any restrictions.
All banks are listed in the Yellow Pages at the back of the local telephone directory.

Credit cards
Payment by any of the international credit cards including Visa, Master Card, American Express, Diners Club and JCB (Japanese credit card) is widely accepted. Most shops display the card signs in their windows. If in doubt, please check with a sales person before you start shopping.

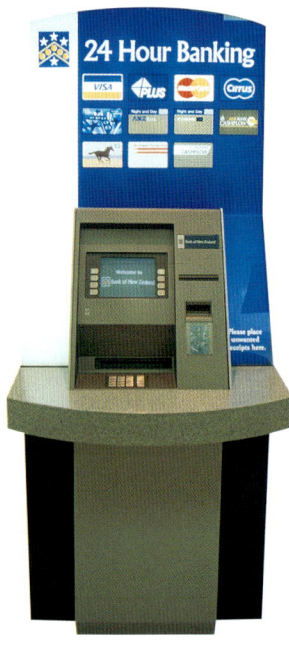

Automatic Teller Machine, 24 hours access.

Banks
All trading banks are open for business between the hours of 9:30am and 4:30pm. Monday to Friday inclusive, with the exception of public holidays. Automatic Teller Machines (ATMs), operate on a card and pin number system. Cash can be withdrawn 24 hours a day.

EFTPOS (Electronic Transfer of Funds at Point of Sale) is a highly used way of cash payments, which is being used all over New Zealand. You will find operating EFTPOS machines in shops, museums, supermarkets, petrol stations, to name only a few. Instead of a cash payment, the cash amount is transferred directly from the customer's into the selling company's bank account. The transaction takes place at the counter or check out, where customers swipe their EFTPOS card through the machine and type in their pin number. This convenient way of cash payment can be very handy in remote places or after hours. Many stores with EFTPOS facilities also allow you to withdraw cash when making purchases.

Practical Travel Information | Telephone

Using the Telephone

The phone system in New Zealand is of a high technical standard and performs efficiently. There are two main service providers, **Telecom** and **Clear**. You will find public telephones throughout the entire country. The majority of public telephones in NZ operate the pre-paid phone card system. Telecom **PhoneCards** are available in NZ$5, NZ$10, NZ$20 and NZ$50 denominations. These can be purchased from many outlets including **NZ Post Shops**, supermarkets, dairies, newsagents, **Visitor Information Centres** and petrol stations. You may find it helpful to purchase a **PhoneCard** even if it is only for emergencies. Increasing numbers of credit card operated phones are now being established which accept major international credit cards. Some public telephones are still coin operated, using 10c, 20c, 50c, NZ$1 and NZ$2 coins. When dialling **Freephone** numbers (commencing with 0800) from public phones you will not require any cards or coins.

Typical public phone booths. Coloured for easy recognition, Yellow for Credit card, Green for PhoneCard, and Blue for Coin.

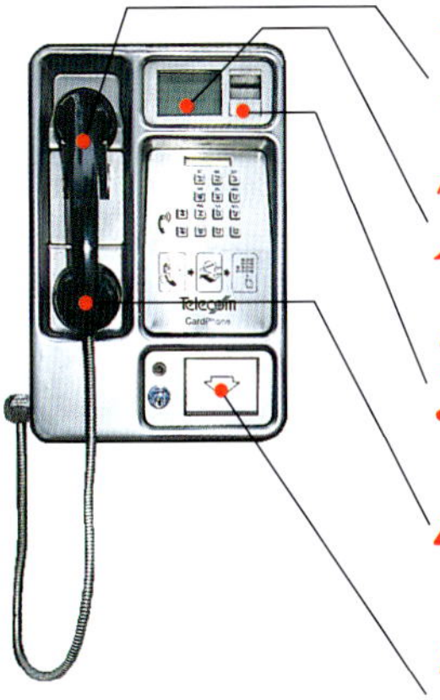

1. Lift handset, do not insert coins.

2. Dial the number you require. The price per minute or part minute will show on screen.

3. Insert coins. Usable coins: 10c, 20c, 50c, NZ$1, and NZ$2.

4. Once call is finished replace handset.

5. Unused coins returned, partly used coins not returned.

Telecom PhoneCards available : NZ$5, NZ$10, NZ$20, and NZ$50. They can be easily obtained at many outlets such as Dairies, Post Offices, and Petrol Stations.

Using the PhoneCard
1. Lift handset. 2. Insert Card. 3. Dial number.
4. After call, replace handset. 5. Remove card (Don't forget!)

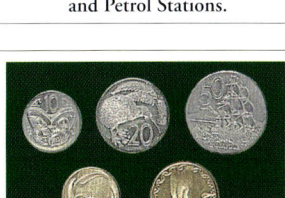

Coins acepted by Coin Phones:–
10c, 20c, 50c, NZ$1 and NZ$2.

e-Phone Maxi-Save Toll Card

The ***e*-Phone Toll Card** is an easy and convenient way to use almost any touch tone phone at your own expense. It can be used from a private phone, card phone, credit card phone, cellphone, **Your Yost's Phone**, etc.
Using these prepaid phone cards will make you and your host feel less apprehensive when you use their phone. ***e*-Phone Toll Cards** can be purchased in many dairies, super markets and shopping malls.
For detailed information, just call Free Phone 0800-437 4663.

EMERGENCY CALLS......111
Police, Fire, Ambulance
Useful Telephone Numbers

Operator 010
International Operator 0170
National Enquiries 018
International Enquiries 0172
International Access Code 00
Australia dialling code 0061
Germany dialling code 0049
Japan dialling code 008
USA dialling code 001

Post Services | Practical Travel Information

Posting a Letter

New Zealand's main postal operator is New Zealand Post with a network of 1000 Post Shops and Post Centres covering the whole country, and 5,000 post boxes where you can post letters. Some outlets combine their normal retail activities with providing New Zealand Post services, especially in smaller towns. Look for the red New Zealand Post logo displayed outside shops.

New Zealand Post Shop

Post Shops

Post Shops offer a wide range of products and services including:
- stamps
- protective packaging
- sending letters and parcels
- sending faxes and telegrams, couriering items overseas or around New Zealand
- stationery, greeting cards, phone cards, gifts (e.g. calendars) and more

Post Shop staff can help you decide which type of packaging will get your parcels delivered as cheaply as possible. A handy Parcel Packaging Guide is also available which contains advice on ways to ensure your parcel arrives safely. Post Shops accept cash, cheque, EFTPOS, MasterCard and VISA for most products and services.

If you need help and cannot get to a Post Shop, you can call New Zealand Post on freephone 0800 NZPOST (0800 697 678), 8am to 7pm weekdays, or 9am to 1pm Saturdays.

Postal Costs

For Sending letters and packages within New Zealand. A standard size letter (maximum 129mm x 235mm) costs 40 cents and takes 2-4 days to be delivered. If you want to get it there faster, FastPost costs 80 cents for a standard size letter which is then delivered by the next working day between major towns and cities. (Rural and remote areas may take a little longer.) You can send parcels from $3.40, depending on size and weight. Items can also be couriered from a Post Shop.

For sending letters and packages overseas. You can ask at the local Post Shop about the best way to package and send items overseas. Options include first class air mail, sea post, registered post and courier. By paying an additional $8 and sending your parcel as a customs parcel, New Zealand Post extends cover for loss or damage from NZ$250 to NZ$1,500.

For sending packages to Japan, there is a special Kiwi Yu Pack for items up to 5kg, and for delivery within 2-4 working days.

The rural mailbox, a roadside feature throughout New Zealand's countryside.

A rather "Unique Stay"?

| Natural New Zealand |

Magnificent Contrasts and Colourful Variety

New Zealand's landscapes are as colourful and diverse as its people. No other country can offer such variety of magnificent scenery in such a comparatively small area. In both islands evergreen native bush abounds. In the North Island there are also exotic forests of huge Kauri trees. A wonderland of hot springs, geysers and boiling mud pools is situated near Rotorua in the centre of the North Island. Therapeutic hot springs are located in parts of both islands, and spectacularly beautiful National Parks with their unspoiled scenery and nature will delight the traveller. The South Island offers scenery on the grand scale: mountains, glaciers, lakes and sweeping coastal beaches. Deep-water fiords slice into the south-west coast, with virgin mountain country in the background. One of the most famous fiords - Milford Sound - is accessible by road as well as by the famed Milford Track, the "most beautiful walk in the world". New Zealand has an abundance of aquatic scenery. Take your pick of spectacular waterfalls, raging torrents, broad rivers, lakes big and small, surfing beaches and rocky coast lines.

South Island West Coast - Native bush.

Waitangi Golf Course - *one of the many superb golf courses you will find in New Zealand.*

Most New Zealanders love sport and the outdoors. Their country's natural features support an abundance of outdoor activities: yachting, golf, rugby and mountaineering, to name only a few. All types of winter sports are practised in both islands and wild game and fish provide excellent hunting and fishing.

Tane Mahuta, Waipoua Forest, Northland.

North Island

26

NORTH ISLAND HOSTS

NORTHLAND – BAY OF ISLANDS – WHANGAREI

- 30 Beach Abode, *Ahipara – Kaitaia*
- 30 Fernbrook, *Kerikeri*
- 31 Wai-Tui Lodge, *Kerikeri*
- 31 Raemere Homestead, *Kerikeri*
- 32 The Summer House, *Kerikeri*
- 33 RiverPark, *Paihia*
- 34 Fairlight River Lodge, *Paihia*
- 35 Villa Casablanca, *Paihia*
- 36 Ounuwhao B&B Homestead, *Russell*
- 37 Arcadia Lodge, *Russell*
- 38 Anchorage Bed & Breakfast, *Russell*
- 39 Ten on One Home/Farmstay, *Kaikohe*
- 40 Jarvis Family Farmstay, *Pakaraka*
- 41 Lewood Farm Park, *Okaihau*
- 42 Brookers Bay Olive Grove, *Whananaki*
- 43 Chelsea House, *Whangarei*
- 43 Graelyn Villa, *Whangarei*
- 44 Channel Vista, *Whangarei*
- 44 Tide Song, *Whangarei*
- 45 Parua House, *Whangarei*
- 46 Kauri House Lodge, *Dargaville*
- 46 Flower Haven, *Waipu*

AUCKLAND REGION

- 47 Belvedere Homestay, *Warkworth*
- 48 Bayview Manly Quality B&B, *Whangaparaoa*
- 48 Albany Country Home, *Albany*
- 49 Stafford Villa, *Birkenhead Point*
- 50 Amberley Bed & Breakfast, *Devonport*
- 50 Buchanan's of Devonport, *Devonport*
- 51 Amersham House, *Parnell*
- 51 Villa 536, *Mt.Eden*
- 52 Sealladh, *Orakei*
- 52 Woodlands, *Remuera*
- 53 Omahu House, *Remuera*
- 54 Cockle Bay Homestay, *Howick*
- 55 Fishers - Above the Beach, *Howick*
- 55 Whitfords Country Villa, *Howick*
- 56 Airport Pensione, *Mangere*
- 56 Mountain View Bed & Breakfast, *Airport*
- 57 Top of the Hill, *Brookby – Manurewa*
- 58 Ardern's Fine Accommodation, *Waiheke Island*
- 59 Tatu Orchards, *Waiuku – Franklin*

COROMANDEL PENINSULA

- 59 Cotswold Cottage, *Thames*
- 60 Te Mata Bay Country Homestay, *Te Mata Bay*
- 61 Karamana (1872) Homestead, *Coromandel*
- 62 Cosy Cat Cottage, *Whitianga*
- 62 Harbour Lights Guesthouse, *Whitianga*
- 63 Halcyon Heights, *Whitianga*
- 63 The White House, *Whitianga*
- 64 Il Casa Moratti Homestay, *Whangamata*

HAMILTON REGION

- 65 Parnassus Farm & Garden, *Huntly*
- 65 Waingaro Palms, *Huntly*

NORTH ISLAND HOSTS

PAGE

66	Beaumere Lodge, *Hamilton*
67	Matangi Oaks, *Hamilton*

BAY OF PLENTY

68	Cotswold Lodge, *Katikati*
68	Glen Sheiling, *Katikati*
69	Taiparoro House 1882, *Tauranga*
70	Charlemagne, *Tauranga*
71	The Palms Bed & Breakfast, *Tauranga*
71	Markbeech Homestay, *Papamoa*
72	Sandtoft, *Papamoa*
72	Papamoa Homestay, *Papamoa*
73	Pohutukawa Farmhouse B&B, *Matata*
74	Tirohanga Farmstay, *Opotiki*

ROTORUA REGION

75	Bush Haven Cottage, *Okere Falls*
75	Lakeside Bed & Breakfast, *Okere Falls*
76	Woodbery Lodge B&B Countrystay, *Hamurana*
77	Clover Downs Estate, *Kaharoa*
78	Deer Pine Lodge, *Ngongotaha*
79	Alraes Lakeview Homestay, *Ngongotaha*
80	Ngongotaha Lakeside Lodge, *Ngongotaha*
81	Kahilani Farm, *Ngongotaha*
82	Emandee Farm Bed & Breakfast, *Paradise Valley*
82	Lynmore Homestay, *Rotorua*

TAUPO REGION

83	Brackenhurst, *Oruanui*
83	Minarapa, *Oruanui*
84	Kinloch Lodge, *Kinloch*
85	Twynham at Kinloch, *Kinloch*
85	Pariroa Homestay, *Acacia Bay*
86	Kooringa, *Acacia Bay*
87	Paeroa Lakeside Homestay, *Acacia Bay*
88	Te Moenga Farmstay, *Acacia Bay*
89	Catley's Homestay, *Taupo*
89	Fairviews, *Taupo*
90	Jensen's Homestay, *Taupo*
90	Lochinver Homestay, *Taupo*
91	Pataka House, *Taupo*
91	Yeoman's Lakeview Homestay, *Taupo*
92	Kotiri Lodge, *Taupo*
93	Richlyn, *Taupo*
94	The Pillars, *Taupo*
95	Five Mile Bay Homestay, *Five Mile Bay*

GISBORNE REGION

95	Reomoana, *Mahia Peninsula*

TARANAKI

96	Birdhaven, *New Plymouth*
97	Balconies Bed & Breakfast, *New Plymouth*
97	93 By the Sea, *New Plymouth*
98	Anderson's Alpine Residence, *Stratford*

TONGARIRO NATIONAL PARK

98	Al & Julie's Garden & Gallery, *Owhango*
99	Horopito Lodge, *Ohakune*

NORTH ISLAND HOSTS

AGE

HAWKES BAY

- 100 Cornucopia Lodge, *Napier*
- 101 Eskview Heights, *Napier*
- 102 A Room With A View, *Napier*
- 103 Twinpeak, *Napier*
- 104 Jervois Road Bed & Breakfast, *Napier*
- 105 Mynthurst Farmstay, *Waipukurau*
- 105 The Hermytage, *Dannevirke*
- 106 Plaisted Park Homestay, *Hunterville*

WANGANUI – MANWATU

- 107 Arles, *Wanganui*
- 107 Operiki, *Wanganui*
- 108 Larkhall, *Palmerston North*
- 109 Ro Nali, *Palmerston North*
- 110 The Fantails, *Levin*

WELLINGTON REGION – WAIRARAPA

- 111 Naumai Otaki Gracious Lady, *Otaki*
- 111 Kapiti Vistas, *Waikanae*
- 112 Country Patch, *Waikanae*
- 113 Burnard Gardens, *Waikanae*
- 115 Terracotta Lodge, *Carterton*
- 116 Froggy Cottage, *Greytown*
- 116 Southey Manor, *Greytown*
- 117 The Ambers, *Greytown*
- 118 Whispering Pines, *Upper Hutt*
- 119 Braebyre, *Pauatahanui*
- 120 Black Fir Lodge, *Lower Hutt*
- 121 Homestay Wellington, *Ngaio*
- 122 Shalimares, *Khandallah*
- 122 Top O' T'ill, *Hataitai*
- 123 Matai House, *Hataitai*
- 124 Seaview Homestay, *Seatoun*
- 125 Francesca's Homestay, *Seatoun*
- 126 Edgewater, *Seatoun*
- 127 Saltaire, *Island Bay*

Ahipara - Northland

YOUR HOSTS: **Susan and Ned Pyne**   Ph: (09) 409 4070

BEACH ABODE
11 Korora Street, P.O.Box 134
Ahipara, Northland
Ph/Fax: (09) 409 4070
Mobile: 025 574 963

Features & Attractions

- *Absolute beachfront*
- *Links golf course*
- *World class surfing*
- *Quad bike hire*
- *Horseback riding/fishing*
- *Breakfast/dinner availab[le]*

Double	$85-115
Single	$75-85
Child	$15

Self-contained Beachside Accommodation

Bedrooms	Qty
Double	2
Twin	2
Single	

Bed Size	Qty
King	
Queen	2
Single	4

Bathrooms	Qty
Ensuite	
Private	2
Guest Share	
Family Share	

'Organic food available"

Ned and I were living in Tauranga and came to Ahipara for a holiday with friends from Hawaii. That was in November 1998. It was rainy sub-tropical night when we arrived, reminiscent of Hawaii. The following day the weather became sunny and we spent our time in the warm sun, surfing and swimming in the Tasman Sea. What struck me was the stunning beauty of the green hills meeting the sea, the warm water and the expansiveness of 90 Mile Beach. After our holiday, we decided to make the move up north and build a new home and business. We found an ideal beach front property. The contemporary interior design of the purpose-built units in earth and sea tones reflects the natural environment. We love our **Beach Abode** and our little seaside village of Ahipara.

DIRECTIONS: Please phone for easy directions.

Kerikeri - Bay of Islands

YOUR HOSTS: **Margaret and Robert Cooper**   Ph: (09) 407 8570

FERNBROOK
Kurapari Road, Rangitane
Kerikeri R.D.1.
Ph (09) 407 8570, Fax (09) 407 8572
e-mail: tfc@igrin.co.nz

Features & Attractions

- *Kiwi sanctuary*
- *Historic sites*
- *Magnificent views*
- *Bush walks*
- *Bay of Islands Tranquility*

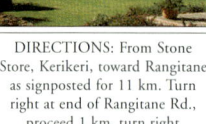

Boutique Holiday Accommodation

Double	$175-200
Single	$85-100
Child	Free u/7

DIRECTIONS: From Stone Store, Kerikeri, toward Rangitane as signposted for 11 km. Turn right at end of Rangitane Rd., proceed 1 km, turn right into unsealed Kurapari Rd. **Fernbrook** is on right.

Fernbrook is a comfortable hillside country house, set in 27 hectares overlooking the Kerikeri Inlet - 12 minutes drive from the town of Kerikeri and 35 min. flying time from Auckland. It offers magnificent views, a secluded beach, bush walks and a wide variety of bird life including the rare North Island Brown Kiwi.
The house has an extensive library, large garden, croquet lawn and petanque court. Dinner is by arrangement and comprises the best of New Zealand food and wine. Tariff includes laundry service and collection from the airport if required. The wide variety of recreational activities includes golf, horse riding, charter sailing, big game fishing and exploring ancient kauri forests and historic sites. In this idyllic rural setting you can enjoy New Zealand's northern region for its fascinating history and magnificent coastal scenery.

Bedrooms	Qty
Double	3
Twin	1
Single	

Bed Size	Qty
King	
Queen	3
Single	

Bathrooms	Qty
Ensuite	1
Private	2
Guest Share	
Family Share	

OUR HOSTS: **Jean and Ian Dunn**   Ph: (09) 407 9033   **Kerikeri**

Wai-Tui Lodge
Yacht Drive, Opito Bay RD 1
Kerikeri, Bay of Islands
Ph (09) 407 9033. Fax (09) 407 7176
e-mail: *estuary@igrin.co.nz*

Features & Attractions
- Tea/coffee, TV in rooms
- Sea and rural views
- Kiwi habitat
- Safe swimming beaches
- Bush walks
- Fishing

A Relaxing Homestay In A Busy World

	Double	$110
	Single	$90
	Child	NA

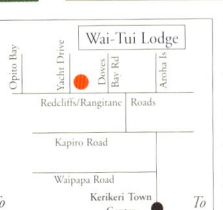

By day the gardens are alive with native birds. By night hear the call of the morepork and kiwi.
Wai-Tui Lodge is nestled in a peaceful bush-clad valley, overlooking the Kerikeri Inlet and twelve minutes from Kerikeri shops, restaurants and golf course. We are close to safe swimming beaches, Aroha Island Ecological Centre, bush walks, boat ramps and kayak hire.
Catering for a maximum of four guests, our priority is your comfort and relaxation. The spacious rooms have queen beds, luxurious ensuites with heated floors and towel rails. Enjoy our spa and swimming pool, private decks and gardens. Self catering available.
Ours is a stress-free environment – relax and enjoy!

Bedrooms	Qty
Double	2
Twin	
Single	
Bed Size	Qty
King	
Queen	2
Single	
Bathrooms	Qty
Ensuite	2
Private	
Guest Share	
Family Share	

YOUR HOSTS: **Dorothy and Bill Fletcher**   Ph: (09) 407 7787   **Kerikeri - Bay of Islands**

Raemere Homestead
Cnr SH 10 & Wiroa Road, Kerikeri,
Postal: P.O. Box 560, Kerikeri, Bay of Islands
Ph (09) 407 7787, Fax (09) 407 6797
e-mail: *willdot@xtra.co.nz*

Features & Attractions
- Lovely gardens
- Arts and crafts abound
- Great golfing
- Tourist tours arranged
- Kayaking
- Horse treks

	Double	$90
	Single	$55
	Child	

Homestay Bed & Breakfast

Bedrooms	Qty
Double	1
Twin	2
Single	
Bed Size	Qty
King	
Double	1
Single	4
Bathrooms	Qty
Ensuite	
Private	1
Guest Share	1
Family Share	

Situated just 3 minutes from Kerikeri and 20 min. from Paihia, this lovely old homestead was built in the early 1930's by one of the ex-patriot British immigrant families who settled here from China at the start of the civil war. Set in one acre of gardens and trees and surrounded by citrus orchards, the park-like setting in the centre of the Bay of Islands is within easy access to all Northland and Bay tourist attractions as well as two of the finest golf courses in the country. We are happy to book you in for any of these activities. Your hosts, Dorothy and Bill, have travelled extensively and 'homestayed' in the UK and France - a most enjoyable experience, which we now offer to visitors both international and domestic. We are happy to pick up guests from either the bus depot or the airport. Dinner is optional by prior arrangement. Try us! You are assured of a warm welcome.

DIRECTIONS: At Pakaraka turn right off SH 1 onto SH 10 towards KERIKERI. We are situated 15km along SH 10 at the Kerikeri crossroads.

Kerikeri - Bay of Islands YOUR HOSTS: **Christine and Rod Brown**   Ph: (09) 407 4294

THE SUMMER HOUSE
Kerikeri Road, Kerikeri
Ph (09) 407 4294, Fax(09) 407 4297
Mobile (025) 409 288
e-mail: *summerhouse@xtra.co.nz*
http://www.thesummerhouse.co.nz

Tariff : N.Z. Dollars		
	Double	$145-16
	Single	$115-12
	Child	n/a

Bedrooms	Qty
Double	3
Twin	
Single	
Bed Size	**Qty**
Super King	
King	
Queen/Double	2
King/Single	1
Bathrooms	**Qty**
Ensuite	2
Private	1
Guest Share	
Family Share	

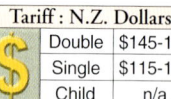

 Self-contained Boutique Accommodation

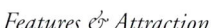

Special rates for off-season and longer stays.

Features & Attractions
- 1.5 kms from Kerikeri village
- Cafés, craft shops, vineyards
- Historic sites
- Forests, beaches, Bay of Islands
- Striking design and decor
- Fruit and juice from orchard
- Tranquil garden and pond
- Kauri Cliffs golf course

The setting is idyllic, the accommodation exquisite, and the company convivial at **The Summer House**, a French Provincial inspired Bed and Breakfast. This is the perfect retreat for relaxation, to experience Kerikeri's vineyards, cafés and craft shops and to explore the Bay of Islands and the beaches, Kauri forests and historic sites of the Far North.

This architecturally designed home is set in a tranquil hectare of citrus orchard and beautifully landscaped sub-tropical garden. Enjoy gourmet breakfasts, warm hospitality and inspiring surroundings. One self-contained, semi-detached suite and two rooms both with ensuites and guest lounge.

We can help with your itinerary and can arrange: sailing, diving, fishing, golf, bush walks, tours etc and even to see a kiwi in its habitat.

French and German spoken. Unsuitable for children.

DIRECTIONS: From State Highway 10, **The Summer House** is 1.7 km along Kerikeri Rd on the left, just two minutes drive from Kerikeri Village. Pick up from the airport would be a pleasure.

YOUR HOSTS: **Noelle and Graham** Ph: (09) 402 8067 **Paihia - Bay of Islands**

RiverPark

Puketona Road, RD 1
Paihia, Bay of Islands
e-mail: *RiverPark@xtra.co.nz*

Features & Attractions

- *Rural riverside setting*
- *Two acres gardens/lawns*
- *Paihia 5 min. drive*
- *Beaches & Golf 5 min. drive*
- *Cruises/dolphin trips 5 min.*
- *Wheelchair - friendly*

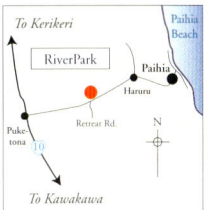

Double	$ 90-120
Single	
Child	

Bed & Breakfast
Self-contained Unit

Bedrooms	Qty
Double	
Twin	2
Single	

Bed Size	Qty
King	
King - Single	2
Single	2

Bathrooms	Qty
Ensuite	2
Private	
Guest Share	
Family Share	

DIRECTIONS: Opposite Retreat Rd. on Puketona Road. 5.7 km from SH 10 on left. 6.5 km from Paihia Beach on right. Stone walls at entrance.

RiverPark is Noelle and Graham's modern riverside home with carefully landscaped gardens of trees, shrubs and evergreen lawns. **RiverPark's** self-contained unit is exclusively yours. Enjoy a microwave kitchen with fridge/freezer, fan oven, pantry, a TV lounge and a comfortably appointed bedroom with tiled bathroom ensuite. To freshen your wardrobe an electric steam iron is included in your own laundry with dryer.

Noelle and Graham invite you to enjoy your generous continental breakfast in the sunny dining alcove. Or set your table outside on tiled verandah decks beside the tidy herb garden. A delightful idea! If you take pleasure from spacious gardens and lawns, lush sub-tropical growth, natural surroundings and sensible home comforts, neat and clean – welcome to **RiverPark!**

Paihia township and wharf.

Paihia - Bay of Islands   YOUR HOSTS: **Anna and Michael Jones**   Ph: (09) 402 8004

FAIRLIGHT RIVER LODGE
107B Yorke Road, Haruru Falls
Ph (09) 402 8004. Fax (09) 402 8048
e-mail: *fairlight@bay-of-islands.co.nz*
http://www.bay-of-islands.co.nz/accomm/fairlite.html

Tariff : N.Z. Dollars	
Double	$100-145
Single	$70-90
Child	

Bedrooms	Qty
Double	3
Twin	1
Single	
Bed Size	**Qty**
Super King	3
King/Twin	1
Queen	
Single	
Bathrooms	**Qty**
Ensuite	2
Private	
Guest Share	1
Family Share	

   Riverside Retreat

Features & Attractions
- Nature walks
- Haruru Falls
- Cape Reinga Tours
- Island cruises
- Waitangi Golf Course
- Dinner River Cruise
- Bird watchers' paradise
- 2 acres landscaped gardens

Are you looking for something special and restful away from noise yet easily accessible on major highways?
Located close to Paihia and the Bay of Islands, **Fairlight River Lodge**, one of Paihia's fine country homes is nestled in a beautiful rural environment on the Waitangi River and is surrounded by two acres of landscaped gardens. You will love the peace and tranquility of the native bush reserve, the river and the bird life. Enjoy our spacious grounds with an evening stroll on the river's edge and listen to the sounds of kiwis, owls and fish splashing. Watch the ducks, herons and shags settle for the night.
We have been hosting for four years and being well travelled ourselves enjoy the experience of hearing about our guests' travels. We offer single/twin/double rooms with ensuites and magnificent river, bush and garden views with all day sun.
Bookings can be made for Cape Reinga, Hole in the Rock, Cream trip, Waitangi golf course, dolphin and whale cruises. The river boat dinner cruise departs close by at Haruru Falls.

DIRECTIONS:
Travelling north on SH 1 turn left at Kawakawa, go through Moerewa, turn right onto SH 10 at Pakaraka, go through Oromahoe, turn right at Puketona Junction. Travel 10 km, go past Haruru Falls Road and turn left onto Yorke Road. Follow signs downhill to **Fairlight** on right. Look for blue letterbox.

YOUR HOSTS: Barbara and Derek	Ph: (09) 402 6980		**Paihia**

VILLA CASABLANCA
18 Goffe Drive, Haruru Falls, Paihia
Postal: P.O. Box 73, Paihia, Bay of Islands
Ph/Fax (09) 402 6980, Mobile 021- 666 567
e-mail: *derek@bestprice.co.nz*
http://www.bestprice.co.nz

Tariff : N.Z. Dollars	
Double	$95-250
Single	$75-220
Child	neg.

Bedrooms	Qty
Double	4
Twin	3
Single	
Bed Size	**Qty**
Super King	1
King	
Queen/Double	3
King/Single	6
Bathrooms	**Qty**
Ensuite	4
Private	2
Guest Share	
Family Share	

      **Luxury Bed & Breakfast Inn**

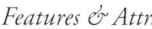

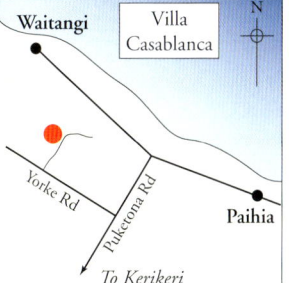

Features & Attractions

- *Private hilltop position*
- *Self-contained garden apartments*
- *Vegetarian-friendly meals*
- *Dinner by arrangement*
- *Spectacular views over Bay of Islands*
- *Traditional Bed & Breakfast in guest wing*
- *Walk to restaurants and brewhouse*
- *Sailing, golf, kayaking, swimming*

Imagine a Spanish-style hacienda, surrounded by a sub-tropical garden of flowering shrubs, palms and fern trees, enjoying the most spectacular views over Waitangi and the Bay of Islands! Barbara and I found this place a year ago and we were so impressed by its location and ambience that we decided to convert it to a guesthouse and share the privacy and tranquility with visiting friends.

Enjoy the Northland sunshine as you sip a glass of wine on our shady verandahs, watching fishing boats and sailing ships in the bay below. Or let us arrange an exciting trip to explore the Bay, swim with dolphins or catch a year's supply of seafood from a single day's fishing.

Villa Casablanca makes an ideal base for your stay in Northland and is within easy driving or coach distance from all the main sites. We offer a choice of traditional homestay in our in-house guest wing or the privacy of self-contained accommodation in our self-contained garden apartments.

DIRECTIONS: Paihia is 3° hours north of Auckland by car. Follow the Coast Road from Paihia to the Waitangi roundabout, turn left, drive up the hill for 3 km and turn right into Yorke Road, then next right into Goffe Drive.

Russell - Bay of Islands   YOUR HOSTS: **Marilyn and Allan Nicklin**   Ph: (09) 403 7310

OUNUWHAO B & B HOMESTEAD

Matauwhi Bay, Russell, Bay of Islands
Ph (09) 403 7310, Fax (09) 403 8310
e-mail: *thenicklins@xtra.co.nz*
http://www.bay-of-islands.co.nz/ounuwhao.com

Tariff : N.Z. Dollars		
	Double	$135-150
	Single	$100-120
	Child	$35 (u/12)

Bedrooms	Qty
Double	2
Twin	3
Single	
Bed Size	**Qty**
Super King	
King	1
Queen/Double	4
Single	4
Bathrooms	**Qty**
Ensuite	4
Private	2
Guest Share	
Family Share	

 Boutique Accommodation & Self-contained Accommodation

Features & Attractions

- *Detached garden suite*
- *Safe, sandy swimming beaches*
- *Swimming with the dolphins*
- *Hearty, healthy gourmet breakfasts*
- *Historic Russell Village*
- *Sea and island excursions*
- *Coastal and bush walks*
- *Historic homestead*

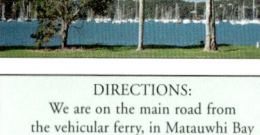

DIRECTIONS:
We are on the main road from the vehicular ferry, in Matauwhi Bay 1 km from Russell Village.

When visiting Historic Russell take a step back into a bygone era. Spend some time with us in our delightful nostalgic, immaculately restored villa (circa 1894). Enjoy wrap-around verandahs in summer and the large guest lounge with open fire in winter. Each room has traditional wallpapers and paint work with handmade patchwork quilts and fresh flowers to create a lovingly detailed, traditional romantic interior. Breakfast is served in our farmhouse kitchen around the large kauri dining table. It is an all homemade affair, from the fresh baked bread to the yummy daily special and the jam conserves. Our 1930's self-contained cottage is set in park-like grounds for your privacy and enjoyment. With two double bedrooms, large lounge and sunroom and fully self-contained kitchen, it is ideal for people wanting peace and time out. Breakfast is available if required. We look forward to meeting you soon. EXPERIENCE OUR HISTORIC BED & BREAKFAST, ENJOY A WORLD OF DIFFERENCE. *We are closed June and July.

YOUR HOSTS: Jolene and Peter   Ph: (09) 403 7756   **Russell - Bay of Islands**

ARCADIA LODGE HISTORIC GUESTHOUSE
10 Florance Ave or Brind Road extension
Russell Village, Bay of Islands (P.O.Box 23)
Ph (09) 403 7756, Fax (09) 403 7657
e-mail: *arcadialodge@xtra.co.nz*
http://www.bay-of-islands.co.nz/accomm/arcadia.html

Tariff : N.Z. Dollars	
Double	$125-155
Single	$ 95-155
Child	

Bedrooms	Qty
Double	8
Twin	3
Single	
Bed Size	**Qty**
Super King	
King	
Queen	8
Single	3
Bathrooms	**Qty**
Ensuite	3
Private	
Guest Share	2
Family Share	

**Boutique Accommodation
Bed & Breakfast**

Features & Attractions

- *Healthy, fresh, great breakfasts*
- *All tours/excursions arranged*
- *5 min. stroll to village*
- *Expansive gardens*

- *Circa 1899 Tudor*
- *Glorious bay views*
- *5 restaurants nearby*
- *Large guest lounge*

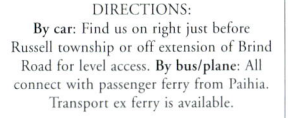

DIRECTIONS:
By car: Find us on right just before Russell township or off extension of Brind Road for level access. **By bus/plane**: All connect with passenger ferry from Paihia. Transport ex ferry is available.

This historic, faithfully restored Tudor building, overlooking the anchorage in Russell's Matauwhi Bay, was built with hospitality in mind and has operated variously, as a private hotel, lodge and private dwelling for almost 100 years.

Full of character, antiques, nooks and crannies and oozing charm and comfort, **Arcadia** is surrounded by an acre of lawns, orchards and olde English gardens, and there are magnificent views from almost every room. - Bedrooms and suites are decorated in Victorian style. The dining room and lounges are expansive and comfy – in all seasons.

From here the Russell shops, cafes and restaurants are a mere 5 min. flat stroll away and all tours, cruises and ferries depart from the nearby wharf.

The Arcadian Bay Breakfasts include homemade baking, fresh fruits, a muesli to die for and bottomless cup "Old Russell" blend coffee.

Arcadia is best suited to discerning peace-seekers who appreciate history, romance and some of the finer things in life in pampered comfort.

Russell

YOUR HOSTS: Janey and David Horrell Ph: (09) 403 8410

ANCHORAGE B & B

43 Tapeka Road, Russell, Bay of Islands
Ph (09) 403 8410, Fax (09) 403 8410
Mobile 021-751 921
e-mail: *anchorage.boi@xtra.co.nz*
www.bay-of-islands.co.nz/accomm/anchorage.htm

Features & Attractions

- *Beach front setting*
- *Safe, sandy swimming beach*
- *Continental breakfast buffet*
- *Tour/excursions arranged*
- *Good local restaurants*
- *Historic sites*

Double	$100-150	
Single	$95-120	
Child		

Homestay Bed & Breakfast

Bedrooms	Qty
Double	2
Twin	
Single	

Bed Size	Qty
King	
Queen	2
Single	

Bathrooms	Qty
Ensuite	2
Private	
Guest Share	
Family Share	

DIRECTIONS: Travel through Russell Village, up Flagstaff Hill to Tapeka Point.

Step out of your new suite onto Tapeka Beach – the undiscovered gem of the Bay of Islands. Romantic Russell is a two minute drive and here you may experience early European settlement, New Zealand's oldest church, Russell Museum or Flagstaff Hill. Russell offers a wide range of culinary experiences, the ambience of a small picturesque sea-side town, coastal walkways and from here all boat tours of the Bay depart. We your hosts Janey, David and our dog Greta, have had a long involvement in the accommodation industry and offer the very best of Kiwi hospitality in our idyllic beachside location. Gourmet continental breakfast is served on our deck or in your suite, the call is yours. Your suite is complete with tea, coffee, fridge, TV, stereo and cane furniture. Please come and share our slice of heaven - make this your "**Anchorage**" where the only sound is the lap of waves.

Typical New Zealand café scene.

YOUR HOSTS: Jude and Art Hansen   Ph: (09) 405 9460   **Pakaraka - Bay of Islands**

TEN ON ONE HOME/FARMSTAY

Ludbrook Road, RD 2, Kaikohe, Bay of Islands
Ph (09) 405 9460, Fax (09) 405 9460
Mobile 025-886 618
e-mail: *farm.accommodation@xtra.co.nz*
www.hokiangatours.co.nz/homestay.html

Tariff : N.Z. Dollars	
Double	$75
Single	$45
Child	half price

Bedrooms	Qty
Double	4
Twin	
Single	1

Bed Size	Qty
Super King	
King	
Queen	4
Single	1

Bathrooms	Qty
Ensuite	4
Private	1
Guest Share	
Family Share	

**Affordable & Relaxing
Farm – Homestay Accommodation**

Features & Attractions

- *Hearty breakfast*
- *Clean towels daily*
- *Complimentary tea/coffees*
- *Laundry service/iron avail.*
- *Evening meals available*
- *Laundry service,*
- *Courtesy airport and coach pick-up and return*

DIRECTIONS:
At intersection of SH. 10 and SH.1 travel 80m north on SH.1. We are first house on left (use Ludbrook Rd. entrance).

"Good morning" - to all our visitors a warm and friendly greeting. The Bay of Islands awaits you. Visit New Zealand's true sub-tropical region for that unforgettable and friendly experience. We have a shower of exciting things to keep you occupied, here **are a few suggestions:** Would you like to visit Cape Reinga (top of New Zealand), cruise to Cape Brett (*hole in the rock*), visit a 2000 year old kauri tree (*Tane Mahuta*) enjoy a 14 km vintage train ride, visit the famous Waitangi Treaty House, visit historic Russell Town, glow worm caves, chocolate factory, water falls, steam saw mill, visit hokianga to meet Louis (*the gentle giant*) in his amazing craft shop, swimming, paragliding, tramping or milk a cow? Hey - the list goes on and on. **Why visit anywhere else?** Our modern farmstay is central to all activities with clean swimming pool and full Fire Safety Regulation standards. We have both been in the tourist business for many years, and our home meets all fire and safety regulations (1992). **Try us with our positive and caring attitude and you won't be disappointed.** Smoking area available.
Try a completely new tour experience, exclusive day Coach Tours to giant boulders, hot mud pools, petrified kauris.

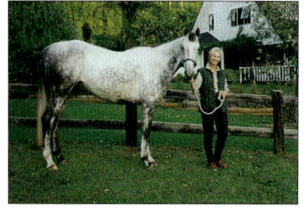

Pakaraka - Bay of Islands YOUR HOSTS: Douglas and Fredi Jarvis   Ph: (09) 405 9606

JARVIS FAMILY FARMSTAY
Pakaraka, State Highway One, Ohaeawai
Bay of Islands
Ph (09) 405 9606 Fax (09) 405 9607
e-mail: *baystay@igrin.co.nz*

Tariff : N.Z. Dollars		
$	Double	$90 -110
	Single	$45
	Child	neg

Bedrooms	Qty
Double	2
Twin	1
Triple	1
Bed Size	**Qty**
Super King/twin	
King	
Queen/Double	2
Single	5
Bathrooms	**Qty**
Ensuite	
Private	4
Spa Bath	1
Guest Share	

Countrystay Boutique Accommodation

VISA MasterCard AMERICAN EXPRESS

Features & Attractions

- Unique accommodation
- Four poster bedroom suites
- English antiques & paintings
- Spa bath & swimming pool
- Landscaped subtropical & water gardens
- Horse and pony riding in orchard setting
- A bird lover's paradise
- Cross roads to Far North & Bay of Islands

For a comfortable and relaxing break, look no further!
As you travel down our orchard road, emus and ostriches line the driveway paddocks. Closer to home family ponies and thoroughbred horses complete the picture.
Our four poster bedroom suite includes its own lounge with two single beds, tv/video, plus a private deck in the "wishing well" garden. Upstairs boasts the "Scottish Room" (3 singles) and an extra double overlooking the cascading water gardens.
Our home enjoys the choice of indoor and outdoor dining - either in the conservatory or on the spacious deck, with its many palms and comfortable outdoor furniture. Here guests can enjoy being hosted to a BBQ or self cater. Dinner parties can be arranged in advance.
Douglas and Fredi emigrated from the UK 10 years ago, where they ran one of England's Top Country Inns, so they are no strangers to hospitality. Guests may also wish to ride on the well-schooled horses and ponies at our adjoining Equestrian Centre - riding by arrangement.
We are centrally based for touring the Bay and West and North Coasts with all the popular tourist and marine activities.
We look forward to hearing from you - a warm welcome awaits you.

Directions:
Just off SH1 - 1.5 km past SH 10
T- junction travelling towards
Ohaeawai and the historical
Pakaraka Mission Church.
We are well signed with flag
poles on the right.

YOUR HOSTS: Patricia and Ronald Lewis   Ph: (09) 401 9290   **Okaihau - Bay of Islands**

LEWOOD FARM PARK
Mangataraire Road, RD 1,
Okaihau, Bay of Islands
Ph (09) 401 9290, Fax (09) 401 9290
Mobile 025-277 7305
e-mail: myles.taylor@xtra.co.nz

Tariff : N.Z. Dollars

Double	$80
Single	$40
Child	$10

Bedrooms	Qty
Double	2
Twin	
Single	

Bed Size	Qty
Super King	
King	1
Queen/Double	1
Single	1

Bathrooms	Qty
Ensuite	
Private	
Guest Share	1
Family Share	

**Farmstay
Bed & Breakfast**

Features & Attractions

- *New millennium sunrise*
- *Peacock and turkey hunting*
- *Stream and bush walks*
- *Home-grown meats/game foods*
- *Black sheep*
- *Shearing and wool handling*

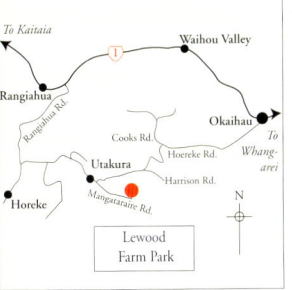

Welcome to the hidden valley of Utakura, originally purchased from the Crown in 1896 by three Lewis brothers. It has remained in the Lewis family ever since.

We are central to both Bay of Islands and historic Hokianga. Visit nearby Mangungu Mission House, site of the largest signing of the Treaty of Waitangi.

We farm sheep, beef and forestry on 1000 acres of land. Our home is furnished with family heirlooms. The guest area is private and opens onto a patio. Stroll through our garden park with exotic trees from around the world. After dinner Ron will take you to visit our glow worm display. Pat has a small cottage industry making, speciality preserves, available to guests at a moderate charge. We specialise in home-grown meats and game food. Your generous continental breakfast is served on antique china.

Our interests are travel, gardening, local and family history and beekeeping, amongst others. We are NZKC registered breeders of Australian Cattle Dogs (Blue and Red Heelers). We have a pet sheep called Daffodil. Tea and coffee available from the tea wagon.

Whananaki - Northland YOUR HOSTS: Chris and Faith Nathan Ph: (09) 433 8304

BROOKERS BAY OLIVE GROVE
Brookers Bay, Rockell Road, R.D.1
Whananaki North, Hikurangi, Northland
Ph: (09) 433 8304 Fax: (09) 433 8305
e-mail: *bbog@ihug.co.nz*

Tariff : N.Z. Dollars	
2-4 people	$225

Bedrooms	Qty
Double	1
Twin	1
Single	
Bed Size	**Qty**
Super King	
King	
Queen	1
Single	2
Bathrooms	**Qty**
Ensuite	
Private	1
Guest Share	
Family Share	

Luxury Self-contained Accommodation

Features & Attractions

- On the water's edge
- Fantastic sea views
- Fully equipped kitchen
- Wheelchair friendly
- Swimming, fishing, diving
- Complimentary kayaks
- Private tennis court
- Hot tub, private gardens

Set in a secluded location on the east coast close to many off-shore islands, just 45 minutes drive from Whangarei. This is a prime position, right on the water's edge of a beautiful sheltered bay. The famous Poor Knights Islands are on the horizon and diving is spectacular in our waters.

The guest villa is separated fom the main house by an adjoining conservatory, a perfect setting for alfresco dining. Lounge and main bedroom areas open onto spacious patios facing the beach. A private hot tub is set outside the twin bedroom, amongst the gardens and olive grove. The kitchen is fully equipped for self-catering, an optional grocery package is offered, with catered meals available by prior arrangement only.

Breakfast is not included in tariff. Breakfast charge $20 per person.

DIRECTIONS: SH1 north to Whangarei, from Kamo drive 15km, turn right at the Whananaki North turn-off. (Or, coming from Bay of Islands, continue south on SH1, past Whakapara drive 1km to the Whananaki turn-off). Drive through countryside 23km until reaching Whananaki North Village, continue 7km along the coastline to Brookers Bay.

YOUR HOSTS: Cathy and Mel Clarke   Free Ph: 0508 243 573

Whangarei

CHELSEA HOUSE
83 Hatea Drive, Whangarei
Free Ph: (0508) 243 573
e-mail: *mel.clarke@clear.net.nz*

Features & Attractions

- *Central convenient location*
- *Double room with own kitchen*
- *Delicious breakfast menu*
- *Off-street parking*
- *1 km from city centre*
- *Opposite Mair Park*

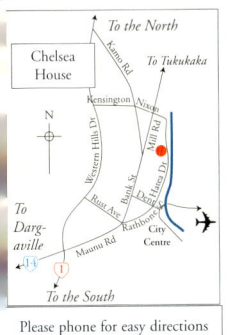

Chelsea House Bed & Breakfast

Double	$70-90
Single	$40
Child	$20

Please phone for easy directions

Welcome to **Chelsea House**, the most convenient B & B in Whangarei. Our home is a double gable villa built in 1910 and close to the central city, Town Basin, restaurants and heated pools. Across the road is the entrance to Mair Park which features walkways through beautiful native bush to the summit of Parahaki, the site of the largest Maori Pa in New Zealand. Let us drive you to the top for spectacular views and a leisurely walk down to **Chelsea House**. Our double guest room has a fully equipped kitchen and ensuite, the twin room has tea and coffee making facilities and ensuite. A cooked breakfast of your choice can be served in our family kitchen or outside in the delightful cottage garden. Laundry available.

Bedrooms	Qty
Double	1
Twin	1
Single	
Bed Size	**Qty**
King	
Queen/Double	1
King/Single	2
Bathrooms	**Qty**
Ensuite	2
Private	
Guest Share	
Family Share	

YOUR HOSTS: Linda and Grace   Ph: (09) 437 7532

Whangarei

GRAELYN VILLA
166 Kiripaka Road, Whangarei
Ph (09) 437 7532. Fax (09) 437 7533
e-mail: *graelyn@xtra.co.nz*

Features & Attractions

- *Tranquil gardens*
- *Bush walks nearby*
- *Choice of golf courses*
- *Adjacent Whangarei Falls*
- *Close to city centre*
- *25 min. to Tutukaka Coast*

Bed & Breakfast Boutique Accommodation

Double	$80
Single	$55
Child	

DIRECTIONS:
5km from City Centre, north-east towards Whangarei Falls. Please call for further directions.

Come into our home and be our guest for a while. You'll receive a very warm welcome. Beautifully presented in a tranquil setting, **Graelyn** is a turn of the century villa, which has been lovingly restored to offer comfort and luxury. Three guest rooms all have ensuite bathrooms, superbly comfortable beds, TV, tea and coffee, electric blankets and heaters. Breakfast is continental, or for a small extra charge your choice of cooked breakfasts, other meals by arrangement. **Graelyn Villa** is only 25 min. from the Tutukaka Coast. Also handy to golf courses, horse riding, bush walks and the spectacular Whangarei Falls. The centre of Whangarei City is only 5 km, with many top class restaurants, cafés, shops, museums and the popular town basin marina. Courtesy transport available from bus or airport. Pets welcome. Mother and daughter team, Grace and Linda, look forward to offering you an escape from your everyday hustle and bustle to our haven of peace and tranquillity.

Bedrooms	Qty
Double	2
Twin	1
Single	
Bed Size	**Qty**
King	
Queen/Double	2
Single	2
Bathrooms	**Qty**
Ensuite	3
Private	
Guest Share	
Family Share	

Whangarei

YOUR HOSTS: **Jenny and Murray Tancred**   Ph: (09) 436 5529

CHANNEL VISTA
254 Beach Road, Onerahi, Whangarei
Ph (09) 436 5529, Fax (09) 436 5529
Mobile 025 973 083
e-mail: *tancred@igrin.co.nz*
http://www.northland.org.nz

Features & Attractions

- Only 1 hour to Bay of Islands
- Many golf courses handy
- Restaurant, shopping centre 5 min.
- Many interesting walks
- Sandy, safe beaches nearby
- Top diving, fishing 30 min.

Harbourside, handy Luxury self-contained

DIRECTIONS: Follow signs to Onerahi Airport, go past gates to Pah Road, go down Pah Road to roundabout and turn left into Beach Road - No 254.

	Double	$100-$130
	Single	$80-$90
	Child	

Bedrooms	Qty
Double	2
Twin	
Single	
Bed Size	**Qty**
King	
Queen	2
Single	
Bathrooms	**Qty**
Ensuite	2
Private	
Guest Share	
Family Share	

Channel Vista is a modern purpose-built luxury self-contained Bed & Breakfast situated on the interesting Whangarei Harbour, 9 km from Whangarei Central and very handy to the Onerahi shopping complex and sports centres (golf, swimming, walks, pools) and only 5 min. walk along the waterfront to a top restaurant. Bay of Islands, Kerikeri and the West Coast are only one hour away. Poor Knight's Diving and deep sea fishing at Tutukaka is 30 minutes away and lovely Whangarei Heads beaches are also handy. You can see, we are a very handy base for your Northland Holiday.
Both self-contained units have lovely decks where you can sit and relax or view the garden or watch superb sunsets. We have a cat called Pepi and a very friendly dog called Salty. We offer a smoke-free environment and a tantalising breakfast menu.
Murray and Jenny look forward to hosting you in their home.

Whangarei

YOUR HOSTS: **Ros and Hugh Cole-Baker**   Ph: (09) 436 1959

TIDE SONG
Beasley Road, RD 1, Onerahi,
Whangarei, Northland
Ph (09) 436 1959
e-mail: *stay@tidesong.co.nz*
http://www.tidesong.co.nz

Features & Attractions

- Quiet privacy
- Bush setting
- Farm animals
- Spectacular walks
- Choice of ocean beaches
- Safe estuary for boating

Countrystay Self-contained Accom.

Double	$85
Single	$60
Child	

Bedrooms	Qty
Double	2
Twin	
Single	
Bed Size	**Qty**
King	
Queen/Double	2
Single	1
Bathrooms	**Qty**
Ensuite	
Private	1
Guest Share	
Family Share	

From Whangarei drive east for 25 minutes to our 8 acres on the Taiharuru Estuary. With a bush and seaside setting, there is a small jetty, and a variety of small craft to use on the estuary. Spots for fishing and shellfish are close. There is a variety of wonderful walks, with Pacific views and peaks, available to differing levels of fitness. A choice of ocean and surf beaches 10 to 20 minutes away. Our animals include sheep, dogs and cattle. We have a farming and teaching background and are interested in sailing, cycling, conservation, gardening, home-cooking and music. With only one of our four children still living at home, we enjoy having company and looking after guests. Our accommodation is a separate upstairs flat with its own bathroom, kitchen and T.V. We can provide extra home-cooked meals if you wish, or there are restaurants 20 minutes away. We appreciate people not smoking indoors. Looking forward to showing you Northland hospitality.

YOUR HOSTS: **Pat and Peter Heaslip**   Ph: (09) 436 5855   **Whangarei**

PARUA HOUSE

Parua Bay, Whangarei Heads Road, RD 4
Postal: Parua Bay, RD 4, Whangarei, Northland
Ph (09) 436 5855, Fax (09) 436 3419
e-mail: paruahomestay@clear.net.nz
http://www.paruahouse.co.nz

Tariff : N.Z. Dollars

Double	$90-110
Single	$60
Child	half price

Bedrooms	Qty
Double	2
Twin	1
Single	1
Bed Size	**Qty**
Super King	
King	
Queen	2
Single	3
Bathrooms	**Qty**
Ensuite	2
Private	1
Guest Share	
Family Share	

Farmstay - Boutique Accommodation

Features & Attractions

- *Outstanding panoramic views*
- *Peaceful setting*
- *Homegrown fruit & produce*
- *Golf course nearby*
- *Superb swimming beaches*
- *Spa pool*
- *Featured on TV: "Ansett NZ-Time of Your Life" & "Corban's Taste NZ"*

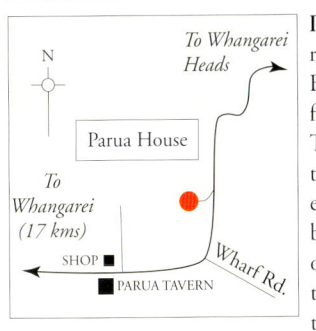

Parua House is a classical colonial house built in 1883, comfortably restored and occupying an elevated site with panoramic views of Parua Bay and Whangarei harbour. The property covers 29 hectares of farmland with lush valleys leading into steep slopes of native bush. Two protected reserves on the property are rich in a variety of native trees (including kauri) and native birds abound. Guests are welcome to explore the farm, milk the Jersey house cow, track through the bush beside the Kohinui stream, explore the olive grove and sub-tropical orchard or just relax in the spa-pool or on the verandah overlooking the marina. A safe swimming beach ajoins the farm with a short walk to a fishing jetty. Two marinas and an excellent golf course are nearby. We have travelled extensively and especially welcome overseas guests. Our interests are wide including travel, photography, patchwork-quilting and horticulture. The house is attractively appointed with antique furniture and a rare collection of spinning wheels. We enjoy good food, wine and conversation. Fresh home-grown produce is used where possible along with home-baked bread and freshly squeezed orange juice. Vegetarian food is provided if requested. A warm welcome awaits you.

Dargaville

YOUR HOSTS: Doug Blaxall Ph: (09) 439 8082

KAURI HOUSE LODGE

Bowen Street, Dargaville, P.O.Box 382
Ph (09) 439 8082, Fax (09) 439 8082
Mobile 025-547 769
e-mail: *kauri@infomace.co.nz*

Features & Attractions

- *Kauri villa over 5000 sq"*
- *Farm bush walk included*
- *Set in private location*
- *Beach, lakes, bush walks*
- *Breakfast included*
- *Summer swimming pool*

Luxury Bed & Breakfast

Double	$150-175	
Single	$140-150	
Child		

Bedrooms	Qty
Double	2
Twin	1
Single	
Bed Size	**Qty**
Super King	1
King	1
King/Single	1
Bathrooms	**Qty**
Ensuite	3
Private	
Guest Share	
Family Share	

Original features of this 1880s style villa include the detailed verandah balustrading, stained glass, pressed ceilings, sash windows and native Kauri panelling. Completed in 1910 by a leading bushman as a spacious family residence, **Kauri House** now offers three private ensuite guest rooms and three lounge rooms – a billiard room, library and television lounge – furnished with antiques. Only three kilometres from the township of Dargaville, with many nice restaurants. **Kauri House** is set in three hectares of garden with abundant native birdlife including fantails, wood pigeons and seasonal tui. A swimming pool provides relaxation and exercise in summer only. Nearby is Doug's 40 hectare farm on which he runs steers and donkeys. This land includes 16 hectares of protected native bush.

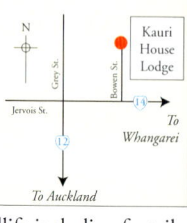

Waipu

YOUR HOSTS: Shirley and Brian Flower Ph: (09) 432 0421

FLOWER HAVEN

53 St Ann Road, Waipu Cove, Northland
Ph (09) 432 0421, Mobile 025-287 2418
e-mail: *flowerhaven@xtra.co.nz*

Features & Attractions

- *Panoramic ocean view*
- *Garden retreat*
- *Surf patrol in summer*
- *Extensive beach walks*
- *Walk to bird sanctuary*
- *Golf courses & fishing*

Bed & Breakfast Self-contained Accom.

Double	$70-90	
Single	$45-65	
Child	neg.	

Bedrooms	Qty
Double	2
Twin	
Single	
Bed Size	**Qty**
King	
Queen/Double	2
Single	
Bathrooms	**Qty**
Ensuite	
Private	1
Guest Share	
Family Share	

At **Flower Haven** we enjoy an elevated position with panoramic views of the sweep of Bream Bay and off-shore islands and are developing the quarter acre grounds as a garden retreat. We are retired with interests in gardening, genealogy and meeting people. Our accommodation is a self-contained downstairs two bedroom flat with separate access, fridge/freezer, stove, microwave, washing machine, radio and TV. Linen, duvets, blankets and bath towels are provided. Reduced tariff applies if continental breakfast not required. We are a 5 minute walk to shop, sandy surf beach and rocks – restaurants handy. We are near many places of interest such as bird sanctuary, museums, golf courses, horse riding treks, chartered fishing trips, limestone caves, walking tracks, Marsden Point Oil Refinery Visitors Centre. Auckland is 1° hours away.

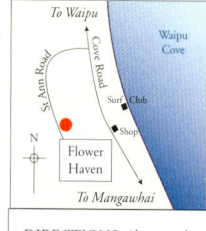

DIRECTIONS: 8km south of Waipu on Cove Road, right into St Ann Road, Flower Haven is the last house on left.

YOUR HOSTS: Margaret and Ron Everett   Ph: (09) 425 7201   **Warkworth - Sandspit**

BELVEDERE HOMESTAY

38 Kanuka Road, RD 2, Sandspit, Warkworth
Ph (09) 425 7201, Fax (09) 425 7201
Mobile: 025 284 4771

Tariff : N.Z. Dollars	
Double	$90
Single	$50
Child	

Bedrooms	Qty
Double	2
Twin	1
Single	
Bed Size	**Qty**
Super King	
King	
Queen	2
Single	2
Bathrooms	**Qty**
Ensuite	1
Private	1
Guest Share	
Family Share	

Quality Homestay Bed & Breakfast

Features & Attractions

- Panoramic sea views
- Airconditioned home
- Dinner an occasion
- Warm, friendly hospitality
- Home produce for breakfast
- Glassed spa pool & games room
- "Goat Island" marine reserve
- Beaches, wineries, pottery

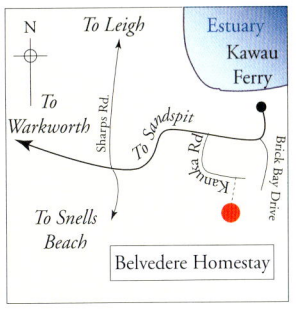

Warkworth Sandspit is the perfect stop going to and from the Bay of Islands. **Belvedere Homestay** is sited on top of the hill with 360° views overlooking the spit where the ferries leave for Kawau Island and Governor Grey's restored mansion. The view is awesome which you will enjoy while relaxing on our spacious decks and terraces. Stroll around our 11 acre property with sunken barbecue, rose garden, orchards, lawns, native birds and bush and 2 lilly ponds and enjoy a friendly game of Petanque (boule).

Fishing off the beach or boat, golf, tennis, swimming etc. are all within 7 km. Our house is for your comfort and enjoyment and as "Roger Hall" (NZ/English stage and televison playwright) wrote about **Belvedere Homestay:** "It is no wonder people come for one day and stay a week." Margaret's flair with cooking is a great way to relax after an adventurous day - with pre-drinks, 3 course meal and wine. Come and enjoy a stay with Margaret, Ron and our friendly dog "Nicky".

Auckland Region

YOUR HOSTS: Wendy and Eddie Hewlett Ph: (09) 428 0990

BAYVIEW MANLY QUALITY B & B

1 Beach Road, Manly, Hibiscus Coast,
Whangaparaoa, Auckland
Ph/Fax: (09) 428 0990
e-mail: *bayviewmanly@xtra.co.nz*
http://www.bayview-manly.co.nz

Features & Attractions

- *Panoramic seaviews*
- *Great breakfasts*
- *Adjacent to restaurants*
- *Tiritiri Matangi Island*
- *Check your e-mail*
- *Stroll to sandy beaches*

Quality Homestay Bed & Breakfast

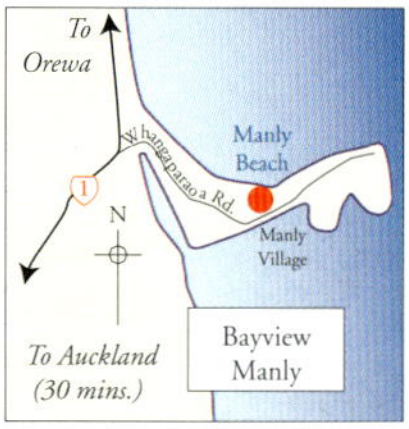

Double	$110-135
Single	$100-125
Child	N/A

Bedrooms	Qty
Double	2
Twin	1
Single	
Bed Size	**Qty**
Queen	1
Double	1
Single	2
Bathrooms	**Qty**
Ensuite	2
Private	1
Guest Share	
Family Share	

At **Bayview** we welcome you with drinks and nibbles to the ultimate in "Home Away from Home" accommodation. We are on the fabulous **Whangaparaoa Peninsula** just 30 min. drive north of Auckland. Comfortable beds, queen and twin rooms with balconies and panoramic sea views, quality guest lounge with TV, video and sunny deck, superb breakfast, cooked and continental, tea/coffee anytime, complimentary laundry. Adjacent to Manly Palms Village – shops and six restaurants. **Gulf Harbour** is 4 km for ferries to **Tiritiri Matangi Island** open bird sanctuary; fishing and diving trips. Other attractions include golf courses, regional parks, walks, swimming, thermal pools, cinemas, and a steam railway, our Peninsula has it all. Relax at **Bayview** - your first choice for exceptional **Quality**, **Hospitality** and **Value**. Ideal arrival/departure point. Airport one hour.

YOUR HOSTS: Patricia and Bruce Fordham Ph: (09) 413 9580 **Albany - Auckland**

ALBANY COUNTRY HOME

"Birethanti", 57 Ngarahana Avenue,
Albany 1331, Auckland
Ph (09) 413 9580, Fax (09) 413 9583
Mobile 025-745 898
e-mail: *patricia.fordham@xtra.co.nz*

Features & Attractions

- *Satisfaction guaranteed*
- *Tranquil retreat*
- *Ideal stopover going north or south*
- *Special breakfast included*
- *Free bottle of wine with dinner at "The Wine Box" Café*

Countrystay Boutique Accommodation

Double	$100-130
Single	$80-110
Child	neg.

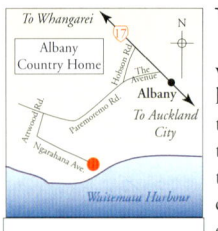

Bedrooms	Qty
Double	2
Twin	
Single	
Bed Size	**Qty**
King	
Queen/Double	2
Single	
Bathrooms	**Qty**
Ensuite	1
Private	1
Guest Share	
Family Share	

DIRECTIONS:
Turn opposite Albany Inn, 7km, then left into Attwood Road, 1km left into Ngarahana Avenue.

When you arrive to awesome river views you will be greeted with a warm welcome, be offered refreshments with freshly baked muffins or slice. You will sleep in luxurious linen, have plenty of soft fluffy towels and all the little extras that will make your day special! You will awake to birdsong, the smell of freshly baked bread. You could amble down to the jetty before breakfasting on fresh tropical fruit, your choice of oaty pancakes, French toast with bacon, poached egg with smoked salmon, English or continental breakfast. "We never think of staying anywhere else" say Barry and Dorothy of Cambridge England (after their third stay). Bruce and I look forward to your call. 7 min. from Albany, North Harbour Stadium and University. 19 min. from Auckland.

48

YOUR HOSTS: Chris and Mark   Ph: (09) 418 3022   **Birkenhead - Auckland**

STAFFORD VILLA

2 Awanui Street, Birkenhead Point, Auckland
Ph:(09) 418 3022, Fax (09) 419 8197
e-mail: *rest@staffordvilla.co.nz*
http://www.staffordvilla.co.nz

Tariff : N.Z. Dollars	
Double	$190-225
Single	$165-195
Child	neg.

Bedrooms	Qty
Double	2
Twin	
Single	

Bed Size	Qty
Super King	
King	2
Queen	
Single	2

Bathrooms	Qty
Ensuite	2
Private	
Guest Share	
Family Share	

**Historic Elegant Luxury
Bed & Breakfast Accommodation**

Features & Attractions

- *Heritage listed house*
- *Designer décor*
- *Perfect central location*
- *Warm and friendly hosts*
- *Private setting, gourmet food*
- *Bridal package*
- *Gateway to "Twin Coast Discovery Route"*

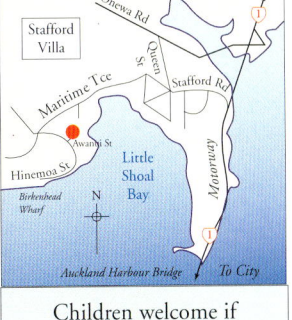

Children welcome if both rooms taken.

Welcome to **Stafford Villa**, located on the North Shore of Auckland City, in the historic harbour suburb of Birkenhead Point. Built in the late 1800's Stafford Villa is luxuriously interior designed in the grand elegance of yesteryear. Every effort is made so your stay is one to remember.

From the private and exquisitely furnished guest rooms – **China Blue**: with magnificent four poster bed, antique furniture, original paintings, luxurious ensuite facilities and dressing room with access to private verandah. **Tuscany Summer**: with large bay window, looking out onto the remaining Victorian orchard, furnishings in antique cream and terracotta, Victorian brass beds and armoire plus natural aromatherapy fragrances and bath oils – to the fine food and wines New Zealand is famous for.

Our family – 4th generation New Zealanders – can assist you with whatever you may wish to do from day trip fishing, the best golf courses or sailing on the harbour. As seasoned world travellers ourselves, Mark and I welcome you to our home and the beautiful harbour city of Auckland.

North Shore - Auckland
YOUR HOSTS: Mary and Michael Burnett Ph: (09) 446 0506

AMBERLEY BED & BREAKFAST
3 Ewen Alison Avenue, Devonport, Auckland
Ph/Fax (09) 446 0506
Mobile 025-2880161
e-mail: *amberley@xtra.co.nz*

Features & Attractions
- Quiet, peaceful surroundings
- Delicious breakfasts
- Cafés and antique shops
- Handy to golf course
- Safe swimming beaches
- Friendly helpful hosts

Homestay Bed & Breakfast

Double	$100-130
Single	$70-100
Child	neg

Bedrooms	Qty
Double	3
Twin	1
Single	

Bed Size	Qty
King	
Queen/Double	3
Single	2

Bathrooms	Qty
Ensuite	
Private	
Guest Share	2
Family Share	

DIRECTIONS: Turn right at Mt Victoria roundabout, go 200m then first right at Superette Corner

Nestled at the base of Mt Victoria, our charming Edwardian Villa is within easy walking distance of Devonport's numerous cafés, shops, golf course, safe swimming beaches, and the ferry terminal (a 10 min. ride to downtown Auckland). It is the ideal base for Auckland and the Hauraki Gulf. Spectacular panoramic views are enjoyed from the summit of Mt. Victoria. Our spacious bedrooms are charmingly furnished with exceedingly comfortable beds! Double spa bath in one bathroom; bathrobes provided.
Early a.m. flight guests welcome. Door-to-door airport shuttle available. Large guest lounge with sky TV, complimentary tea/coffee making facilities, fridge and home baking. Laundry facilities available on request. Our delicious breakfasts are served in our spacious dining room with city views. We have travelled extensively both here and overseas. We look forward to meeting you and to making your stay with us in our beautiful country an enjoyable and unforgettable experience.

Devonport - Auckland
YOUR HOSTS: Cecille and Eric Charnley Ph: (09) 445 3333

BUCHANAN'S OF DEVONPORT B&B
22 Buchanan Street, Devonport,
North Shore City, Auckland
Ph (09) 445 3333. Fax (09) 445 3333
e-mail:*info@buchanansofdevonport.co.nz*
http://www.buchanansofdevonport.co.nz

Features & Attractions
- Friendly, helpful host family
- Outstanding location w/views
- 24-hr security/safety deposit box
- Strictly smoke-free home
- Ample off-street parking
- Guests' spa-in-gazebo

Luxury Boutique Bed & Breakfast

Double	$170-230
Single	$140-180
Child	n/a

Bedrooms	Qty
Double	3
Twin	1
Single	

Bed Size	Qty
Super King	
Queen/Double	3
King/Single	2

Bathrooms	Qty
Ensuite	4
Private	
Guest Share	
Family Share	

Please phone for easy directions.

Welcome to the luxury and "olde-worlde" elegance of Buchanan's of Devonport, our gracious Edwardian home in the heart of Devonport village. Immaculately restored and furnished throughout with genuine NZ and colonial antiques and artworks, we offer luxurious, comfortable guest rooms, all with balconies and ensuites with complimentary toiletries. Each room is colour-themed and furnished with an antique wooden bed and furnishings, finest imported beddings, plush Egyptian cotton towels, electric blanket, heater, TV, CD player, hairdryer, ironing facilities, tea/coffee-making facilities, fresh flowers, complimentary biscuits and sherry. We also have a very spacious Honeymoon Suite with angels and cupids décor throughout for that truly romantic touch. Your delicious, hearty, full breakfast can be served either at our formal dining room or in our sunny back garden with the water fountain and native trees with their resident birds! Just a 5-minute stroll to the Devonport ferry wharf and a stone's throw away from Devonport's numerous attractions and amenities.

YOUR HOSTS: Jill and Robin Stirling   Ph: (09) 303 0321   **Parnell - Auckland**

AMERSHAM HOUSE

Corner Gladstone Road & Canterbury Place,
Parnell, Auckland
Ph (09) 303 0321, Fax (09) 303 0621
e-mail: *info@amershamhouse.co.nz*
http://www.amershamhouse.co.nz

Features & Attractions

- Spectacular views
- Five minutes to the city
- In-room spa or sauna
- "AT HOME" atmosphere
- Free in-room 24 hour internet and e-mail service

Luxury Accommodation Bed & Breakfast

$		
Double	$230-330
Single	
Child	

Our guests like **Amersham House** as much as we do. "Felt just like home", "Absolutely exceeded all our expectations". Enjoy total privacy or relax with your NZ-born hosts in their luxury home in central Parnell. Our "oasis in the city" has a 10m gas-heated pool with illuminated palms and orchids and a private outdoor spa. Bedrooms are sunny and spacious with Sky TV, phone and office, original art and top quality beds and linen. All ensuites are unique and stylish, so select a room that has an ensuite with a spa bath and double shower or choose one with a private sauna. The bedrooms all have 180° views, some with city and harbour views as does our guest lounge/library.
Amersham House is within safe and easy walking distance to shops, restaurants, malls, parks and historic homes. We are only a 5 min. drive to downtown Auckland. The hop-on hop-off city or tourist buses leave regularly.
In the evening relive the day with us and experience true "Kiwi" hospitality.

Bedrooms	Qty
Double	4
Twin	
Single	
Bed Size	**Qty**
Super King	1
King	1
Queen	1
Double	1
Bathrooms	**Qty**
Ensuite	4
Private	
Guest Share	
Family Share	

YOUR HOSTS: Anna Watson   Ph: (09) 630 5258   **Mt Eden - Auckland**

VILLA 536

536 Mt Eden Road, Mt Eden, Auckland
Ph (09) 630 5258, Fax (09) 630 5258
e-mail: *annasvilla@hotmail.com*

Features & Attractions

- "Quality" plus
- City bus at door. Parking
- Easy to find
- Close to city and airport
- Complimentary cookies, teas, coffees
- Stroll around village cafés/shops

$		
Double	$125-145
Single	$115-135
Child	

Superior Bed & Breakfast

Bedrooms	Qty
Double	1
Twin	1
Triple	1
Bed Size	**Qty**
King	
Queen	2
Single	3
Bathrooms	**Qty**
Ensuite	2
Private	1
Guest Share	
Family Share	

DIRECTIONS: On Mt Eden Road between Windmill Road and Disraeli Street.

Villa 536 is a beautifully extended and restored early Auckland home situated in the heart of Mt Eden, a long-established central city suburb. The home is light and airy, comfortable and cheerful. Spacious bedrooms have excellent beds and bedding, a heater, cool-fan and television. The bathrooms boast high water-pressure showers, heated towel-rails, hair dryers and toiletries. Great breakfasts include fresh fruit, yoghurt and home-made muffins. You can relax in the pleasant lounge, casual living area or during summer on the wooden deck from where the view includes "One Tree Hill", Auckland's famous landmark. Guests like to stroll around popular Mt Eden Village with its many speciality shops and cafés. Downtown, motorways, airport, tourist attractions, Eden Park, Expo Centre, shopping centres, race courses, main hospitals and tertiary institutions are all easily and quickly reached. Guests say: "Excellent hospitality, conversation, breakfast and travel advice.", "Simply superb. Cheers!", "A truly relaxing stay.", "A great source of local knowledge."

Auckland

YOUR HOSTS: Heather and Bill Nicholson Ph: (09) 522 2836

SEALLADH

2/9 Rewiti Street, Orakei, Auckland
Ph: (09) 522 2836, Fax:(09) 522 9666
Mobile 025-211 7186
e-mail: sealladh@xtra.co.nz

Features & Attractions

- *Spacious modern home*
- *Near tourist attractions*
- *Secure parking*
- *City and sea views*
- *Exclusive guest lounge*
- *Restaurants close by*

Double	$140-160
Single	$100
Child	

Homestay Bed & Breakfast

Bedrooms	Qty
Double	1
Twin	1
Single	
Bed Size	**Qty**
King	1
Queen/Double	
Single	2
Bathrooms	**Qty**
Ensuite	2
Private	
Guest Share	
Family Share	

Welcome to our modern sunny and spacious home. Enjoy the views from the king bedroom which has TV and a large ensuite. The exclusive guest lounge has views, stereo, TV, video, piano, library and mini kitchen including complimentary tea and coffee. A full breakfast is served in the sunny dining room or "al fresco". We have plenty of secure off street parking and laundry facilities are available. Close to amenities in a quiet residential area, we are five minutes to restaurants, cafés, theatres, CBD and casino. Five minutes to parks, beaches, Kelly Tarlton's Underwater World, harbour cruises, Viaduct Harbour and many other tourist attractions. Ten minutes to race courses and northern and southern motorways. Enjoy many local scenic walks. A short stroll to post office and bus stops.

We have travelled extensively in NZ and overseas and warm and friendly hospitality is assured. No smoking indoors please. From the airport, taxi or shuttle will deliver you to our door.

Auckland Central

YOUR HOSTS: Jude and Roger Harwood Ph: (09) 524 6990

WOODLANDS

18 Waiatarua Road, Remuera
Auckland
Ph: (09) 524 6990, Fax:(09) 524 6993
e-mail: woodlands@ake.quik.co.nz

Features & Attractions

- *Secluded peaceful setting*
- *Dinner by arrangement*
- *Close to Ericsson Stadium*
- *Woodland views*
- *Wonderful full breakfasts*
- *Handy to Auckland Airport*

Double	$110-120
Single	$90
Child	n/a

Homestay Bed & Breakfast

Bedrooms	Qty
Double	2
Twin	
Single	
Bed Size	**Qty**
King	1
Double	1
Single	
Bathrooms	**Qty**
Ensuite	1
Private	1
Guest Share	
Family Share	

Our two guest bedrooms overlook the solar heated swimming pool and lush native greenery. The ensuite king-size bedroom is very large and has french windows opening out into a sunny private conservatory. The **Pink Room** has a double bed and private bathroom. Each room has coffee/tea making facilities, coloured TV, and heated towel rails. Both rooms are very quiet and peaceful. There is safe off street undercover carparking. Our breakfasts are very special, starting with an individual platter of seasonal fruits, followed by a cooked breakfast of your choice, homemade preserves and jams, assorted teas or percolated coffee. In the evening, join us for an Advanced Cordon Bleu candlelit dinner. We delight in using fresh NZ produce and serving good NZ wines. Bookings essential. Guest Book comments - "superb hospitality with delectable food" - "Divine breakfasts" - "Incredible dinner - wow" - "we have found paradise". We are close to motorways - north and south, cafés and bistros, Ericsson Stadium, Expo Centre, Ellerslie Racecourse.

YOUR HOSTS: **Keith and Shirley Mossman**　　Ph: (09) 524 9697　　**Auckland - Remuera**

OMAHU HOUSE

35 Omahu Road, Remuera, Auckland
Ph: (09) 524 9697, Fax:(09) 524 9997
Mobile (025) 208 0469
e-mail: *omahu@voyager.co.nz*

Tariff : N.Z. Dollars	
Double	$150-165
Single	$140-150
Child	$20

Bedrooms	Qty
Double	3
Twin	3
Single	1
Bed Size	**Qty**
King	
King/Single	3
Queen	1
Single	
Bathrooms	**Qty**
Ensuite	4
Private	
Guest Share	
Family Share	

**Boutique Accommodation
Bed & Breakfast**

Features & Attractions

- Easy to find - city location
- Off-street parking
- Frequent bus service - 200 m
- Fax - email - telephone
- Large, relaxing garden, big pool
- Quiet city living, country style
- 10 min. - city, shops and attractions
- Walk to café, Remuera, Newmarket

Whether you visit us on business, as an overseas visitor, on holiday or require an exclusive conference venue, we offer our guests hospitality and privacy in an atmosphere of absolute comfort. Relaxing in the guests' lounge by the fire, in the garden or by the pool, take time to enjoy casually elegant **Omahu House**. Omahu House provides country-style hospitality, set in peaceful surroundings, on a quiet street, within an easy walk to a selection of cafés, fine restaurants, retail therapy locations and a short distance from Auckland's main attractions. Offstreet parking available. City transport nearby. Spacious King Size or Twin Rooms with ensuites. Pleasant surprises await you at Omahu House, where small extra details provide for your comfort, including quality linen, feather duvets, electric blankets, bathrobes, hairdryers, fruit, flowers and magazines. Also ironing and laundry facilities available. Complimentary breakfast provided. Complimentary glass of sherry or port. Complimentary tea, coffee and biscuits available. Evening meal by arrangement. We look forward to sharing our home with you at **Omahu House**, the quintessential Bed and Breakfast!

DIRECTIONS: Exit Market Road off ramp. Travel and right turn at Remuera Road, next right to 35 Omahu Road.

Howick - Auckland

YOUR HOSTS: Jill and Richard Paxman   Free Ph: 0800 159 837

COCKLE BAY HOMESTAY

81 Pah Road, Cockle Bay, Howick, Auckland
Ph/Fax (09) 535 0120, Mobile (021) 685 638
e-mail: *cocklebay.homestay@clear.net.nz*
http://www.bnbnz.co.nz

Tariff : N.Z. Dollars	
Double	$100-120
Single	$85-100
Child	

Bedrooms	Qty
Double	1
Twin	1
Single	

Bed Size	Qty
Super King	
King	1
Queen	1
Single	2

Bathrooms	Qty
Ensuite	1
Private	1
Guest Share	
Family Share	

Homestay Bed & Breakfast

Features & Attractions

- *Breathtaking sea views*
- *Warm welcome*
- *Quiet location*
- *Historical Village Museum*
- *Gateway to Pacific Coast Highway*
- *Walk to beach & historic restaurant*
- *Auckland Airport/City 20 min.*
- *Golf courses(4) within easy reach*

DIRECTIONS: Please phone for directions.

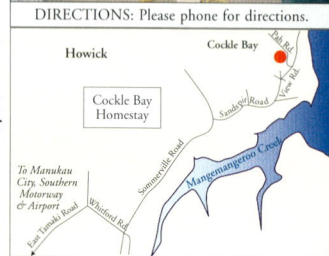

COCKLE BAY is one of several beaches in the Howick area, an eastern suburb of Auckland on the edge of rural and coastal reserve areas. It is a beautiful safe swimming beach, tree-lined with pohutukawa trees. Howick is one of the oldest settlements in NZ being one of the original four settlements established around 1847. Our elevated home has breath taking sea views looking towards Little Barrier Island, Waiheke Island and many other islands. Howick village is 3 kilometres away and has many restaurants/cafés with excellent food. A ferry ride to the City (35 min.) is a delightful way to see the harbour, or use the bus stop end of our driveway (45 min.). Guest rooms are spacious and comfortable with sea views. Both rooms are well appointed. Off-street parking. Laundry facilities available. We can suggest rental car companies, help you with cell phone requirements, and with any travel arrangements you may require. Transport to and from the airport can be arranged. Feel relaxed with us and enjoy your holiday. We look forward to meeting you.

YOUR HOSTS: Marjorie and Max Fisher   Ph: (09) 534 2245   ☎   **Howick - Auckland**

Fishers. "Above the Beach"

141 Mellons Bay Road, Howick, Auckland
Ph (09) 534 2245. Fax (09) 534 2245
e-mail: *kea.nz@attglobal.net*

Features & Attractions

- Lovely sea and bush views
- Handy to Auckland Airport
- Beach 100 metres
- Six beaches, 2 golfcourses nearby
- Close to delightful village
- Auckland Ferry close by

Bed & Breakfast Homestay

Double	$85-100
Single	$55
Child	

DIRECTIONS: In Howick turn into Mellons Bay Road by Stockade Hill. We are well down Mellons Bay Road just 100 yards above the beach.

Welcome to our comfortable home – 100 yards "Above the Beach", with kauri trees growing through our decks, lovely sea views to Waiheke Island, Rangitoto and Coromandel in the background. We are about 25 minutes from the International Airport, 16 kilometres to Auckland by road and just a 35 minute ferry ride to and from downtown Auckland. Howick is a delightful village on the eastern side of Auckland. We have at least 14 restaurants, a historic church, colonial village and six beaches, two golf courses and the Auckland Ferry – all within a two mile radius. Our double rooms have feather duvets, electric blankets, heaters and individual decks looking onto bush and sea. Tea and coffee facilities, easy chairs, lounge suite, fridge and TVs for your convenience. We can advise you on places of interest. We offer a "Home away from Home" and – super breakfasts. We look forward to meeting you. Come and relax with us. Marjorie and Max.

Bedrooms	Qty
Double	2
Twin	
Single	2
Bed Size	**Qty**
King	
Queen/Double	2
Single	2
Bathrooms	**Qty**
Ensuite	1
Private	1
Guest Share	1
Family Share	

YOUR HOSTS: Wendy and Ian Hanna   Ph: (09) 530 8981   ☎   **Howick - Auckland**

Whitfords Country Villa

367 Whitford Road, Howick, Auckland
Ph (09) 530 8981, Fax (09) 530 8981
e-mail: *wendy39@attglobal.net*

Features & Attractions

- Historic Homestead
- Dinner by arrangement
- Full silver service breakfast
- Restaurants, golf clubs, beaches close
- Large English rose garden
- Auckland Airport/city 20 minutes

Homestay Bed & Breakfast

Double	$100
Single	$80
Child	

Bedrooms	Qty
Double	1
Twin	1
Single	
Bed Size	**Qty**
King	
Double	1
Single	2
Bathrooms	**Qty**
Ensuite	
Private	1
Guest Share	
Family Share	

Wendy and Ian invite you to come and enjoy the ambience of our genuine early colonial grand villa. Relax in our beautiful private rose filled garden or laze in front of an open fire. **Whitfords Country Villa** is one of Auckland's original homes, built in 1868 by Captain Springs and renovated meticulously over the last 20 years.
Each bedroom has tea and coffee making facilities, bathrobes, electric blankets, hair dryer, TV etc.
Enjoy our scrumptious breakfast on our rose and wisteria-clad verandah.
We love sharing our beautiful home and warmly welcome all our visitors and guests.
Please phone for bookings or easy directions.

Directions: On Whitford Road between Howick and Whitford.

Auckland - Airport

YOUR HOSTS: Gleny Philips   Ph: (09) 275 0533

Airport Pensione Bed & Breakfast

Cnr Kirkbride/Westney Road, Mangere,
1 Westney Road, Auckland Airport
Ph (09) 275 0533, Fax(09) 275 0533
Mobile (025) 296 9329
e-mail: pensione@paradise.net.nz

Features & Attractions

- 5 min. Auckland Airport
- Sky TV lounge
- 5 minutes to restaurants
- 10 min. walk to Town Centre
- Laundry & e-mail available
- Car storage while away

	Double	$65-80
	Single	$30-65
	Child	neg

Guest House Bed & Breakfast

Bedrooms	Qty
Double	10
Twin	10
Single	10
Bed Size	**Qty**
King	
Queen/Double	10
Single	10
Bathrooms	**Qty**
Ensuite	2
Private	1
Guest Share	4
Family Share	1

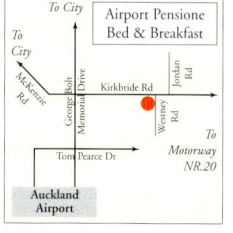

When arriving or leaving Auckland we are 5 minutes from the Airport, where we transport you by courtesy coach to/from our Lodge. Free Phone at Airport Information No.28. We are 5 minutes walk from restaurants, supermarkets and liquor stores, and 10 minutes walk to Mangere Shopping Mall. City bus 100 metres. We can advise you if you need a rental car, restaurant, places to go and see in Auckland and the best ways to do this.

We have a large dining room/lounge with Sky TV. If you are leaving Auckland and need to leave your car behind, we do have car storage available. If you need to use the kitchen/laundry/microwave, please make yourself at home. Please phone/fax/e-mail us for any information. Don't worry - be happy! - Gleny.

Auckland - Airport

YOUR HOSTS: Jenny and Ian Davis   Ph: (09) 636 6535

Mountain View Bed & Breakfast

85A Wallace Road, Mangere Bridge, Auckland
Ph (09) 636 6535, Fax (09) 636 6126
e-mail: mtviewbb@voyager.co.nz

Features & Attractions

- 5 minutes from airport
- Expansive harbour views
- Quiet locality on 1/2 acre
- Public transport at gate
- Modernised kauri villa
- Friendly helpful hosts

Homestay Bed & Breakfast

Double	$75+
Single	$65+
Child	neg.

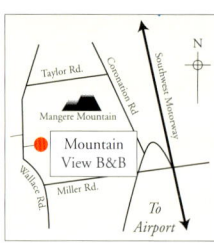

Bedrooms	Qty
Double	4
Twin	1
Single	
Bed Size	**Qty**
King	
Queen/Double	4
Single	3
Bathrooms	**Qty**
Ensuite	3
Private	
Guest Share	1
Family Share	

If you are looking for a quiet, restful place with quality décor and wonderful views handy to both the airport and Auckland City, you have found it at **Mountain View Bed and Breakfast**. Situated on the lower slopes of Mangere Mountain, a leisurely 30 minute walk to the top gives an even more spectacular panorama. You will have the choice of a TV lounge to relax in with home-baked cookies and refreshments or sit upstairs and enjoy the view and chat to your hosts. We offer delicious choices of continental or cooked breakfasts - dinners by prior arrangement.

Our interests centre around gardening, travel and aircraft with Ian having three custom-built aircraft on the go. Together we have travelled extensively around New Zealand in the GY20 Minicab custombuilt aircraft.

YOUR HOSTS: Pat and Trevor Simpson   Ph: (09) 530 8576   ☎ **Auckland Brookby Clevedon**

TOP OF THE HILL COUNTRY HOMESTAY

183 Fitzpatrick Road, Brookby, Manurewa
Postal: Fitzpatrick Rd., Brookby, RD 1, Manurewa, Auckland
Ph/Fax (09) 530 8576, Mobile 025-288 0835
e-mail: topofthehill@xtra.co.nz
http://www.geocities.com/topofthehill_nz

Tariff : N.Z. Dollars	
Double	$110
Single	$75
Child	n/a

Bedrooms	Qty
Double	2
Twin	2
Single	

Bed Size	Qty
Super King	
King	
Queen	2
King Single	4

Bathrooms	Qty
Ensuite	4
Private	
Guest Share	
Family Share	

Luxury Countrystay

Features & Attractions

- *Amazing expansive views*
- *Beautiful bush – glow worms*
- *Gateway to Pacific Coast Highway*
- *Auckland Airport/City 20 min.*
- *Luxurious new home*
- *Tiled ensuite bathrooms*
- *10 minutes S H One*
- *42 acres to explore*

Brookby-Clevedon – a beautiful rural area, 20 minutes from Auckland Airport and City. Abounding with country attractions, polo, craft shops, vineyards, golfing, horse riding, excellent restaurants, with unspoiled beaches nearby. The Pacific Coast Highway meanders south to the popular Coromandel. High on the hill overlooking the twin valleys is our spacious new home with its landscape windows, taking full advantage of the 360° views. Wonderful tranquillity, clean air and a lifestyle only millions dream about.

Our purpose-built home designed by us accommodates the international traveller and the Kiwi holidaymaker. The luxurious large guest bedrooms each with ensuite bathrooms have floor to ceiling landscape windows, encompassing scenes of calendar beauty. Sit and enjoy panoramic views from our guest lounge. We love to show our guests around the farm. The pristine native bush with its colony of glow worms is an unforgettable evening experience. Sample Pat's scrumptious home baking and enjoy our warm hospitality. Dinner if required is $30 pp. We can help with any travel arrangements and provide a courtesy pick up from Auckland Airport.

DIRECTIONS;
From Auckland take the Manurewaturn-off.
From Hamilton take the Takanini turn-off.

Waiheke Island - Auckland

YOUR HOSTS: Bryce and Julie Ardern

Ph: (09) 372 5487

ARDERN'S FINE ACCOMMODATION
241 Church Bay Road, Oneroa, PO Box 193
Waiheke Island, Auckland
Ph (09) 372 5487, Fax (09) 372 5489
Mobile 025-291 5882
e-mail: *ardern@ihug.co.nz*

Tariff : N.Z. Dollars	
Double	$175-250
Single	
Child	

Bedrooms	Qty
Double	3
Twin	
Single	

Bed Size	Qty
Super King	
King	
Queen/Double	3
Single	

Bathrooms	Qty
Ensuite	3
Private	
Guest Share	
Family Share	

**Luxury Accommodation
Bed & Breakfast**

Features & Attractions
- *Tranquil peaceful setting*
- *22 acres native bush*
- *Equisitly decorated rooms*
- *Wharf and Oneroa 5 min.*
- *Spectacular sea views*
- *Olive grove and gardens*
- *Mudbrick Restaurant 3 min.*
- *Vineyards/art tours/golf*

DIRECTIONS:
Please phone for easy directions

ADVANCE BOOKING
RECOMMENDED

Celebrating something special? Need a little pampering? Then **Ardern's** is the place for you! Our luxuriously appointed homestead offers a traditional friendly environment in a tranquil country setting. You are welcome to wander through the gardens and olive grove or explore the beautiful native bush abundant with birdlife. We encourage you to make **Ardern's** your home away from home. Hideaway in the reading room with a book, sip on a glass of wine in the lounge listening to your favourite music, snuggle up to one of the two open log fires, or just sit and marvel at the awe inspiring view - the choice is yours. We have three beautifully decorated rooms, each with fine linen, tea/coffee making facilities, TV, juliet balconies, fresh flowers and ensuites. In the morning you will be served the renowned **Ardern's** breakfast - a selection of cereals, nuts, fresh fruits, tea/coffee, toast and a sumptuous farmstyle cooked breakfast. Waiheke has many activities such as golf, vineyard/art tours, kayaking, bush walks and horse riding. The Mudbrick Restaurant is only 3 minutes away and Oneroa Village 5 minutes. Come and experience this Island Paradise - you will not be disappointed!

YOUR HOSTS: Miriam and Chris Glyde   Ph: (09) 235 7924   **Waiuku - Auckland**

TATU ORCHARDS
McGowan Road, RD 3,
Waiuku, Franklin
Ph/Fax (09) 235 7924, Mobile 025-216 2301
e-mail: tatu@zfree.co.nz

Features & Attractions
- Peaceful setting
- Beautiful scenery
- Garden tours
- Farmhouse breakfast
- Dinner by arrangement
- Activities to suit all

Double	$80-140
Single	$40-70
Child	$40-50

Farmstay Bed & Breakfast

Bedrooms	Qty
Double	2
Twin	1
Single	

Bed Size	Qty
King	
Queen/Double	2
King/Single	2

Bathrooms	Qty
Ensuite	
Private	2
Guest Share	1
Family Share	

Enjoy the tranquility of a peaceful citrus orchard only 45 minutes from Auckland's international airport. A great place to start or end your New Zealand holiday or just take time out from the noisy metropolis. We offer traditional farm house accommodation with all modern conveniences. Three guest bedrooms with private bathrooms and all those little touches to make your stay comfortable. There are activities in the immediate area to suit all tastes. Sedate garden visits and bush walks, a stroll on a golden beach. For the more adventurous there is horse trekking, caving, abseiling and paragliding. Step back in time with a sail on the restored sailing scow 'Jane Gifford' or take a trip on the Glenbrook Vintage Steam Railway. We offer full farmhouse breakfast and our home-grown juice has been described by one visitor as "the best OJ in New Zealand"! A delicious three-course dinner is available with prior notice. We aim to make your stay relaxing and enjoyable. Why not come and have some fun in the country?

YOUR HOSTS: Heather and Bruce   Ph: (07) 868 6306   **Thames - Coromandel**

COTSWOLD COTTAGE
46 Maramarahi Road, PO Box 152
Totara, Thames
Ph (07) 868 6306, Fax (07) 868 6306
e-mail: NZH_COTSWOLD.COTTAGE@xtra.co.nz

Features & Attractions
- Picturesque view
- Quiet and comfortable
- 5 minutes from Thames
- Gateway to Coromandel Penins.
- Cooked breakfast included
- Private entrance & ensuites

Double	$80-100
Single	$50
Child	$12

Homestay Bed & Breakfast

Bedrooms	Qty
Double	2
Twin	1
Single	

Bed Size	Qty
King/Single	2
Queen/Double	2
Single	1

Bathrooms	Qty
Ensuite	3
Private	
Guest Share	
Family Share	

Just one hour drive from Auckland and five minutes from Thames, **Cotswold Cottage** is the perfect place to stop over before seeing the Coromandel Peninsula. Shifted from Epsom in 1990, our gracious old villa was re-sited at Totara overlooking Thames and the Kauaeranga River/Valley. Initially a restaurant, the guest wing was added in 1995. Now, three sunny well appointed rooms with private ensuites, offer guests stunning views and a private entrance to come and go as they please. The lounge, conservatory and terrace offer a choice of places to read, write or simply relax. Tea and coffee making facilities. Sky Digital available.
We offer dinner by arrangement.

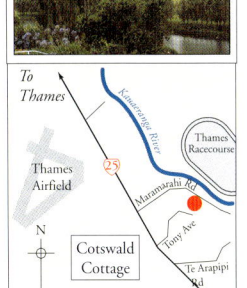

Thames Coast

YOUR HOSTS: Helen and Charles

Free Ph: (0800) 368 550

TE MATA BAY COUNTRY HOMESTAY

29 Eames Crescent, Te Mata Bay
Thames Coast, Coromandel
Ph (07) 868 4754, Fax (07) 868 4757
Mobile (025) 233 0656
e-mail: *temata.hstay@xtra.co.nz*

Tariff : N.Z. Dollars

Double	$80
Single	$40
Child	

Bedrooms	Qty
Double	1
Twin	1
Single	1
Bed Size	**Qty**
Super King	
King	1
Queen	1
Single	2
Bathrooms	**Qty**
Ensuite	
Private	
Guest Share	1
Family Share	

TE MATA BAY COUNTRY HOMESTAY

Country Homestay

Features & Attractions

- *Panoramic sea & mountain views*
- *Complimentary wine & juice*
- *Pianola, music for everyone*
- *Guest lounge with open fire*
- *Breakfast - great choice*
- *Peaceful - no traffic noise*
- *Excellent evening meal*
- *Bush or beach walks*

Come and stay with us at **Te Mata Bay**, any day of the year. You won't be disappointed!
Good beds, excellent home-cooked meals, great company too! Enjoy the peace and the wonderful sea and mountain views from the balcony, which surrounds our large comfortable home. Guest's bedrooms are pleasantly furnished and have sea and mountain views. We have a pianola and pool table for your enjoyment, also a comfortable lounge with a log fire.
Visit our local water garden and square kauri – 15 min. drive, or Coromandel's Driving Creek Railway – 35 min. away, or the famous Hot Water Beach – 50 min. by car, or enjoy good fishing at **Te Mata Bay.**
Hot bread, croissants, cappuccino and fresh percolated coffee along with fresh eggs from our chickens and a large choice of cereals and fruit are offered for breakfast. Complimentary wine with evening meals. Make our day – come and stay. **We are a non smoking family.**

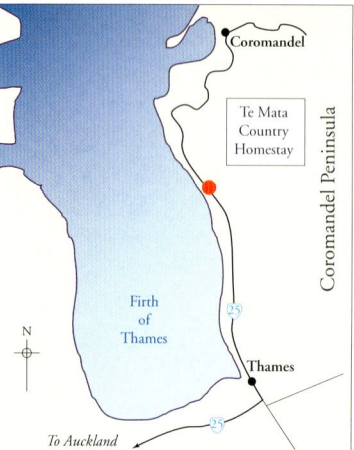

Directions: Please phone for easy directions

YOUR HOSTS: Richard and Virginia Endean   Ph: (07) 866 7138

Coromandel

KARAMANA (1872) HOMESTEAD
84 Whangapoua Road, Coromandel
Ph (07) 866 7138, Fax (07) 866 7477
Mobile 025-735 707
e-mail: karamana@xtra.co.nz

Tariff : N.Z. Dollars	
Double	$125
Single	$90
Child	

Bedrooms	Qty
Double	3
Twin	1
King Single	

Bed Size	Qty
Super King	1
King	
Queen/Double	2
Single	2

Bathrooms	Qty
Ensuite	4
Private	
Guest Share	
Family Share	

Boutique Accommodation

Features & Attractions

- *Spectacular coastal walks*
- *Driving Creek Railway*
- *Craft Trail*
- *Fishing and scenic tours*
- *Charming golf course*
- *Garden tours*
- *One hour from Cathedral Cove walk*

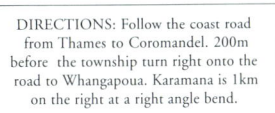

DIRECTIONS: Follow the coast road from Thames to Coromandel. 200m before the township turn right onto the road to Whangapoua. Karamana is 1km on the right at a right angle bend.

Karamana is one of New Zealand's unique Bed&Breakfast experiences. Set in a quiet rural valley in beautiful Coromandel, the Homestead is one of the oldest working buildings, built in 1872 for the well known Cadman family. **Karamana** has been lovingly restored in keeping with the Victorian era, but lacks nothing in guest comfort with all rooms having ensuite facilities. Your hosts, Richard and Virginia Endean, will ensure that you have a complete Coromandel experience and that you leave the region, having enjoyed its rugged beauty and hospitality. You will be welcomed with afternoon tea and at the 'happy hour" in the evening you may choose to sample some of New Zealand's best wines or even try Richard's legendary homebrew. Happy hour has become an institution at the Homestead, providing guests with the opportunity to meet each other and to catch up on the day's activities in a relaxed and laid back environment. For those who choose to dine in, Virginia's cuisine will delight you. We specialise in a wide range of local seafoods, which are in abundance, but also cater for all tastes with traditional New Zealand dishes and vegetarian meals as required. Dining **Karamana** style is a treat. Coromandel provides the visitor with the opportunity to relax and unwind in a different world and yet is only just over two hours by car or ferry from Auckland.

Whitianga

YOUR HOSTS: Lisa Anwander and Brian Pope   Ph: (07) 866 2408

HARBOUR LIGHTS GUESTHOUSE

9 Harbour Lights Terrace, Whitianga
Coromandel Peninsula
Ph (07) 866 2408, Fax (07) 866 2108
e-mail: harbourlights@xtra.co.nz

Features & Attractions

- Spa pool for 4 people
- Sea views from all rooms
- BBQ area
- Big decks
- Candlelit dinner available
- German & French spoken

Boutique Accom. Bed & Breakfast

DIRECTIONS: Take SH 25 to Whitianga. Through township along Buffalo Beach Rd, for 5km. At top of hill turn left into Harbour Lights Tce. We are at the end on the left.

Double	$125-150
Single	$90
Child	half price

Bedrooms	Qty
Double	4
Twin	2
Single	
Bed Size	Qty
King	1
Queen/Double	1/2
King Single	4
Bathrooms	Qty
Ensuite	2
Private	2
Guest Share	2
Family Share	

Harbour Lights Guesthouse was designed to look like an old New Zealand Villa, but has all the modern features that a top quality Bed & Breakfast needs. Nestled into a tree-covered hill, has fabulous views of Mercury Bay and its deck is a vantage point for connoisseur of fine sunsets! Inside, Lisa's good taste is reflected in the décor. Four charming double rooms are available for guests. All have sea views and ensuites or private bathrooms. A spacious lounge opens onto the balcony and there is a well-equipped kitchen. A spa pool and barbecue complete the facilities. The property is in a private residential area. Lisa and Brian live in a separate house of similar standard, where homestay accommodation is also available. We assure you that you will feel welcome and at "home" in this very comfortable house. Nothing is very far away. It is a short drive to the town with its restaurants and shops and **Harbour Lights** is within easy reach of many of Coromandel's fantastic beaches.

Whitianga

YOUR HOSTS: Gordon Pearce   Ph: (07) 866 4488

COSY CAT COTTAGE

41 South Highway, Whitianga, Mercury Bay
Coromandel Peninsula
Ph (07) 866 4488, Fax (07) 866 4488
e-mail: cosycat@whitianga.co.nz

Features & Attractions

- Picturesque cottage
- Amusing catty decor
- A-la-carte breakfast
- Large shaded verandah
- Comfortable guest lounge
- Helpful, friendly service

Boutique Accom. Bed & Breakfast

Double	$80-95
Single	$50-60
Child	

DIRECTIONS: 1 km south of the town centre on Highway 25.

Bedrooms	Qty
Double	2
Twin	1
Single	1
Bed Size	Qty
King	
Queen	2
Single	2
Bathrooms	Qty
Ensuite	2
Private	1
Guest Share	
Family Share	

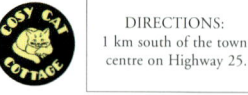

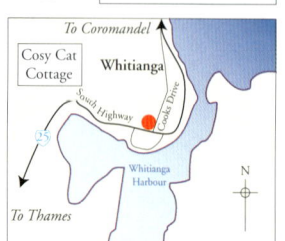

Welcome to our picturesque cottage and enjoy the amusing catty décor and unique feline ambience!
Cosy queen/double/twin/single bedrooms with ensuite/private bathrooms are available all year.
Delicious a-la-carte breakfasts are complimentary and teas or coffees can be served when required.
An easy drive may take you to "Hot Water Beach" "Cathedral Cove" and other fascinating places.
Friendly and helpful service is assured and you will probably like to meet the playful Tonkinese cat.
A self-contained cottage is also available.

OUR HOSTS: **Hisae and David Lynch** Ph: (07) 866 0166

HALCYON HEIGHTS

Whitianga

365 Mill Creek Road, RD 1, Whitianga
Ph (07) 866 0166, Fax (07) 866 5399
Mobile 025-846 873
e-mail: *hisae@aikido.co.nz*
http://www.aikido.co.nz/farmstay

Features & Attractions

- *Tranquil setting*
- *65 acres of bush*
- *Large kauri*
- *Beautiful gardens*
- *Glow-worms*
- *Waterfalls*

Countrystay Bed & Breakfast

Double	$90
Single	$60
Child	$40

Set in a beautiful valley, **Halcyon Heights** is the dream of David Lynch, who lived in Tokyo for many years as Manager, Japan of New Zealand Tourist & Publicity Dept., and his Japanese wife Hisae. They wanted something somewhere far from the pressures of the big city, that had the essence of the Real New Zealand, and found it in this magic spot.

Familiar with the needs of international visitors, David and Hisae delight in sharing their piece of Paradise. Hisae's delicious meals have an international appeal. (Dinner by arrangement for $30 p.p.) plan on staying more than one night and using **Halcyon Heights** as your base for exploring the fantastic Coromandel Peninsula.

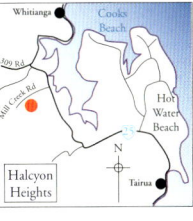

DIRECTIONS:
3.6 km along
Mill Creek Road off
State Highway 25.
Just south of Whitianga.

Bedrooms	Qty
Double	
Twin	2
Single	
Bed Size	**Qty**
King/Single	2
Queen/Double	
Single	2
Bathrooms	**Qty**
Ensuite	
Private	
Guest Share	1
Family Share	1

YOUR HOSTS: **Murray and Jessie** Ph: (07) 866 5116

THE WHITEHOUSE B&B

Whitianga

129 Albert Street
Whitianga, Coromandel Peninsula
Ph (07) 866 5116, Fax (07) 866 5116
Mobile 025-341 029
e-mail: *whitehousebb@paradise.net.nz*

Features & Attractions

- *Tasty, hearty breakfast*
- *Central to beaches*
- *Golf course nearby*
- *2¼ hrs from Auckland Airport*
- *Complimentary tour of area*
- *Shops & fine dining nearby*

Homestay Bed & Breakfast

Double	$100-120
Single	$70
Child	neg.

"When only the best will do".

Welcome to **The White House** which overlooks the inner harbour. We offer a friendly comfortable stay in our modern purpose built home. We are happy to share local knowledge and folklore with you over breakfast. Feast on a continental, traditional or Murray's special of pan-fried fish and Pipi fritters. Whitianga is an excellent base to explore the Coromandel Peninsula. It is the closest town to the internationally recognised Cathedral Cove and Hot Water Beach. Try some of the many activities such as bone carving, deep sea fishing, watch the dolphins play, visit a kauri grove, or just enjoy our beautiful beaches. We can even arrange an intimate wedding for couples on holiday in New Zealand. We aim to make your stay memorable.

Bedrooms	Qty
Double	2
Twin	1
Single	
Bed Size	**Qty**
King	
Queen/Double	2
Single	2
Bathrooms	**Qty**
Ensuite	1
Private	
Guest Share	1
Family Share	

Whangamata

YOUR HOSTS: Bev and George Moratti Ph: (07) 865 6164

IL CASA MORATTI HOMESTAY

313 Mary Road, Whangamata, Coromandel
Ph (07) 865 6164, Fax (07) 865 6164
Mobile 021-685 027
e-mail: *ilcasamoratti@xtra.co.nz*
www.thepeninsula.co.nz/moratti

Features & Attractions

- *Beautiful safe surf beach*
- *Two golf courses 9 & 18 holes*
- *Guest lounge - tea/coffee*
- *Comfortable beds*
- *Seven day shopping*
- *Magnificent scenery*

Homestay Bed & Breakfast

Double	$95
Single	$70
Child	

Bedrooms	Qty
Double	1
Twin	1
Single	

Bed Size	Qty
King	
Queen/Double	1
Single	2

Bathrooms	Qty
Ensuite	
Private	
Guest Share	1
Family Share	

DIRECTIONS: Please phone for bookings and directions.

Experience genuine Kiwi hospitality with your friendly hosts George and Bev who welcome you to their comfortable, clean modern smokefree home, where guests have their own TV, lounge, tea and coffee making facilities, microwave and fridge. Laundry facilities available for small charge. Dinner is available by prior arrangement - $25 pp. Our magnificent surf beach only minutes away, handy to town, park, surf club and golf course. We have travelled extensively and enjoy swapping experiences with fellow travellers. Our other interests include gardening, sport, fishing, tramping and conservation. Whangamata has plenty to offer visitors - surfing, swimming, boating, fishing, and tramping through beautiful native bush. The area abounds with history of Kauri Gum Digging, gold mining and timber milling. Whangamata is known as the cafe capital of the Coromandel with many outdoor cafes and restaurants. Our aim is to ensure our guests have an enjoyable hassle free holiday.

Outdoor dining - Cherry Island, Waikato River.

YOUR HOSTS: **Sharon and David Payne** Ph: (07) 828 8781 **Huntly**

Parnassus Farm & Garden
191 Te Ohaki Road, Huntly
Ph/Fax (07) 828 8781, Mobile 021-458 525
e-mail: *parnassus@xtra.co.nz*

Features & Attractions
- Rural tranquility
- Only minutes off SH1
- Auckland less than 1 hour
- Working farm
- Glorious gardens
- Families welcome

Bed & Breakfast Farmstay on "Real Working Farm"

Double	$80
Single	$45
Child	neg.

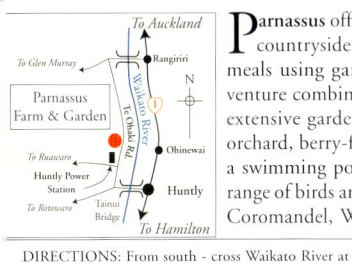

DIRECTIONS: From south - cross Waikato River at Huntly turn right into Harris St, proceed 2km to Huntly power station, right into Te Ohaki Rd, we are 1.9km on left. From north - cross Waikato River at Rangiriri south along Te Ohaki Rd. 12km, we are on right.

Parnassus offers you all the calm and beauty of the New Zealand countryside only minutes off SH1 and wonderful farmhouse meals using garden-fresh produce. We are a successful farming venture combining dairying, forestry, sheep and beef and have an extensive garden incorporating formal rose bed, woodland area, orchard, berry-fruit courtyard and kitchen gardens. We have both a swimming pool and heated spa. Children enjoy our delightful range of birds and small animals. Auckland, Raglan, Hamilton, the Coromandel, Waitomo, Rotorua and Taupo are all easy day trip destinations. Courtesy pick-up is available from Huntly, bus or rail. We offer a delicious cooked breakfast and picnics, luncheons and dinners are available by arrangement. Be assured of a warm country welcome at **Parnassus**.

Bedrooms	Qty
Double	2
Twin	1
Single	
Bed Size	**Qty**
King	
Double	2
Single	4
Bathrooms	**Qty**
Ensuite	
Private	1
Guest Share	1
Family Share	1

YOUR HOSTS: **Sally and Kevin** Ph: (07) 825 4580 **Ngaruawahia - Waikato**

Waingaro Palms
1955 Waingaro Road, RD 1, Ngaruawahia
Ph (07) 825 4580, Fax (07) 825 4586
Mobile (025) 268 6985
e-mail: *sally.kevin.emily@xtra.co.nz*

Features & Attractions
- Auckland 1½ hours
- Only minutes off SH1
- Farm forestry
- Waingaro Hot Springs 3 km
- Rural views and tranquility
- Laundry facilities available

Homestay Bed & Breakfast

Double	$80
Single	$50
Child	$25

Bedrooms	Qty
Double	1
Twin	1
Single	
Bed Size	**Qty**
King	
Queen	1
King/Single	2
Bathrooms	**Qty**
Ensuite	1
Private	1
Guest Share	
Family Share	

Waingaro Palms Homestay Bed & Breakfast is equidistant from Huntly and Ngaruawahia. We are 3 km from renowned Waingaro Hot Springs including sparkling thermal pools, private spa pools and hot water hydroslides. Enjoy the rural tranquility from the grandeur of our turn of the century hilltop restored kauri villa with floodlit gardens. Enjoy delicious farm to table produce and fine wines. Sky TV in guest lounge. Explore our hilly farm on 4WD bike. Hosts can advise on local walks, theatre, adrenalin adventures. Auckland, Raglan, Hamilton, Coromandel, Waitomo, Rotorua and Taupo are all easy day trip destinations. We also have quality accommodation available at Opoutere on the eastern Coromandel Peninsula. Families are welcome. We have no household pets but quality kennelling is available.

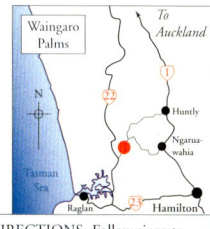

DIRECTIONS: Follow signs to Waingaro Hot Springs from SH1 at Ngaruawahia. We are 20km west of Ngaruawahia, just 3 km from the Hot Springs. Alternatively, take Scenic Route 22 from Auckland.

Hamilton   YOUR HOSTS: Isobel and Peter Wiren   Ph: (07) 829 4556

BEAUMERE LODGE

19 Riverlinks Lane, Horsham Downs,
RD 1, Hamilton
Ph (07) 829 4556, Fax (07) 829 4556
e-mail: *beaumere@wave.co.nz*

FARM & HOME HOSTS

Tariff : N.Z. Dollars	
Double	$120
Single	$95
Child	half-price

Bedrooms	Qty
Double	2
Twin	
Single	
Bed Size	**Qty**
Super King	
King	
Queen/Double	2
Single	
Bathrooms	**Qty**
Ensuite	2
Private	
Guest Share	
Family Share	

Countrystay Bed & Breakfast

Features & Attractions

- *Right on the edge of Golf Course*
- *Country setting on city boundary*
- *Brand new, purpose-built home*
- *Extensive native bush and gardens*
- *Opposite Equestrian Centre*
- *Spa Pool*
- *6 golf courses in the vicinity*
- *Dine with your hosts*

Beaumere Lodge is a golfer's dream, situated on 1¼ acres of native bush and water gardens adjacent to the lovely Horsham Downs Golf Course, on the Waikato River. Every room opens to fabulous views of the golf course - look right down on the fourth green and the fifth tee, against a backdrop of distant hills. Luxury accommodation provided in private guest wing, includes tea-making, TV, underfloor-heating, electric blankets, security surveillance, smoke alarm, security windows. Continental breakfast included. Dinner available on request ($25 pp).
Isobel has had many years experience as an educator and is always delighted to help visitors with the English language.
We are a few minutes drive from Hamilton International Airport (we can pick you up), the city centre and many excellent shops, restaurants, river cruises, famous Museum of Art and History, the the world-renowned Clydesdale Museum and the Mystery Creek Events Centre. One hour from Auckland International Airport. We have home-hosted many overseas visitors and you can be assured of a wonderful overseas experience.

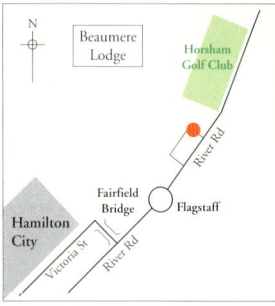

YOUR HOSTS: Clyde and Gloria   Ph: (07) 829 5765   **Hamilton**

MATANGI OAKS
634 Marychurch Road, Matangi RD 4, Hamilton
Ph (07) 829 5765, Fax (07) 829 5765
e-mail: *matangi.oaks@voyager.co.nz*

Tariff : N.Z. Dollars

Double	$120
Single	$100
Child	

Bedrooms	Qty
Double	2
Triple	1
Single	

Bed Size	Qty
Super King	
King	
Queen/Double	2
Single	3

Bathrooms	Qty
Ensuite	1
Private	
Guest Share	1
Family Share	

DIRECTIONS:
Please phone for easy directions.
Advance booking is recommended.

Countrystay - Bed & Breakfast

Features & Attractions

- *Midway Hamilton & Cambridge*
- *Stud tours available*
- *Sports memorabilia nearby*
- *Hamilton Gardens*
- *10 min. to Mystery Creek*
- *Peaceful and relaxing*
- *Waikato River Cruises*
- *Dinner by arrangement*

Matangi Oaks is situated midway between Hamilton and Cambridge on State Highway 1B in a delightful rural setting. Our American Colonial Home, built in 1997, offers peace and tranquillity while being only 12 minutes from the city. An ideal stopover for visits to the National Agricultural Field Days at Mystery Creek or for taking a tour of some of the famous thoroughbred horse studs in the district.

Only 10 minutes from Hamilton Airport. For the golfing enthusiasts there are 12 golf courses within half an hour's drive.

An hour's drive and you can be in Rotorua, Tauranga, Mt Maunganui and Waitomo Caves and only one and a half hours to Lake Taupo and Auckland International Airport.

Cooked and continental breakfasts are provided and tea and coffee making facilities are available. Three-course evening meals are available with your hosts with great home-grown vegetables from Clyde's garden. Pre-dinner drinks and dinner wines are all included at a cost of $40 per person. Complimentary laundry facilities are available. A separate guest lounge is available or visitors are welcome to join their hosts in the evening.

Katikati YOUR HOSTS: Jan and Graham Taylor   Ph: (07) 549 2110

COTSWOLD LODGE

183 Ongare Point Road, RD 1, Katikati
Ph (07) 549 2110, Fax (07) 549 2110
e-mail: cotswold@ihug.co.nz

Features & Attractions

- Ensuite bathrooms
- Large garden
- Dinner available
- Beaches, hot pools nearby
- 4 golf courses nearby
- Murals & open air art

Double	$105
Single	$65
Child	

Country Bed & Breakfast - with a little Luxury

Bedrooms	Qty
Double	2
Twin	1
Single	

Bed Size	Qty
King	
Double	2
Single	2

Bathrooms	Qty
Ensuite	3
Private	
Guest Share	
Family Share	

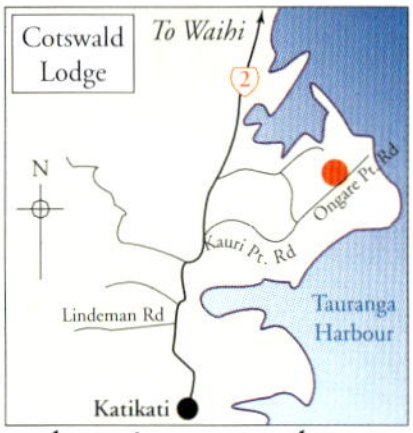

Welcome to **Cotswold Lodge** - come and share our large comfortable home which Graham built in the old colonial style. Wander round the garden and enjoy the flowers and trees, including some natives, in their peaceful setting. Sit on the deck and watch the beautiful sunsets while enjoying a pre-dinner drink. Take a stroll through a kiwifruit and avocado orchard.

Close by are thermal hot pools, beautiful beaches, bush walks to kauri groves, the now famous Murals and open air art in Katikati, and the Ballantyne Golf Course.

Graham restores antiques and makes furniture in his workshop on the premises and takes his boat fishing in the harbour. Jan enjoys working in the garden, making wine, spinning and painting, while Boots, the labrador, watches the world go by!

Katikati YOUR HOSTS: Val and Jim - Rita and Den   Ph: (07) 549 2559

GLEN SHEILING

27 Canon Road, RD 1
Katikati
Ph (07) 549 2559,
e-mail: rchandl@xtra.co.nz

Features & Attractions

- Tranquil, rural surroundings
- Bush or beach walks
- Restaurants & winery nearby
- Golf course 10 mins
- Friendly and comfortable
- Dinner by arrangement

Double	$70
Single	$40
Child	neg

Country Homestay

Bedrooms	Qty
Double	1
Twin	1
Single	

Bed Size	Qty
King	
Queen	1
Single	2

Bathrooms	Qty
Ensuite	
Private	
Guest Share	1
Family Share	

DIRECTIONS
Please phone for booking and easy directions.

A warm welcome awaits you at **Glen Sheiling**, our modern comfortable home set on 3 tranquil acres with a backdrop of hills and bushland. Situated in the Western Bay of Plenty just off State Highway 2, we offer a pleasant stopover for your visit to this beautiful region.

Enjoy breakfast, served at your leisure, relax in one of our two lounges, stroll around the property, make yourself at home. The area is renowned for its arts and crafts, and offers a wide range of activities, from scenic bush walks, safe beaches, hot mineral pools, a winery, an excellent golf course to the Mural Town of Katikati, all within easy reach. The four of us are semi-retired, and between us enjoy a wide range of interests, including meeting people, walking, gardening, fishing, bridge, church activities.

We look forward to welcoming you to our little corner of paradise.

Tauranga

YOUR HOSTS: Lois and Kevin Kelly Ph: (07) 577 9607

TAIPARORO HOUSE 1882
11 Fifth Avenue, Tauranga
Ph (07) 577 9607, Fax (07) 577 9264
Mobile 025-223 5675
e-mail: kl.kelly@clear.net.nz

Tariff : N.Z. Dollars

Double	$150-210
Single	$95
Child	$35

Bedrooms

	Qty
Double	4
Twin	1
Single	

Bed Size

	Qty
Super King	
King	
Queen/Double	4
Single	2

Bathrooms

	Qty
Ensuite	5
Private	
Guest Share	
Family Share	

Historic Homestead Boutique Accommodation

Features & Attractions

- 5 golf courses nearby
- Mt Maunganui Beach 10 min.
- Hot pools
- Rotorua 1 hour
- Sport & leisure fishing
- Swim with dolphins tours
- Sailing on harbour
- 10 min. flat stroll to city

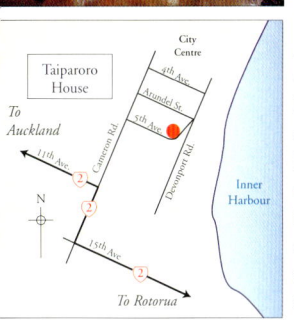

Enjoy a taste of the past in one of Tauranga's oldest and most charming historic homes. In 1882 the Adams family built **Taiparoro** (lapping waters). History and location have created one of Tauranga's landmarks. Surrounded by mature trees and garden, **Taiparoro House** is superbly situated amidst tranquil surroundings overlooking the inner harbour, yet only a short stroll into the city's numerous restaurants, cafés, entertainment and shopping. Colonial furniture and native timber finishings give each guest room a character of its own; firm ther-a-pedic queen beds, crisp white linen, marcella bedcovers and ensuites ensure a comfortable stay. The Harbour View Suite is a favourite. Maybe it's the soothing music while soaking in the original claw foot bath, or relaxing with a wine and a good book in the attached lounge that commands a stunning view across the inner harbour. Or is it the choice of having breakfast served privately in the suite? Why not treat yourself! Relax in the lounge/conservatory in front of the fire with a drink (and Joey the cat). An assortment of teas/coffees is available for self-service at any time. The appetizing aroma of bread baking will draw you downstairs to a leisurely breakfast of fresh fruits, mueslis, yoghurt, fresh baked croissants, quality coffee/teas and home-made jams. With your health and tastes in mind we endeavor to serve organic foods when possible. We look forward to meeting you.

Tauranga YOUR HOSTS: **Brenda and Peter Meadows** Ph: (07) 552 5775

CHARLEMAGNE LODGE
2 Loop Road, Te Puna, Tauranga
Ph (07) 552 5775, Fax (07) 552 5772
Mobile 025-983 255
e-mail: info@purecoromandel.com
http://www.purecoromandel.com

Tariff : N.Z. Dollars

Double	$130-210
Single	$95-150
Child	neg

Bedrooms	Qty
Double	4
Twin	
Single	

Bed Size	Qty
Super King	
King	4
Queen	
Single	

Bathrooms	Qty
Ensuite	2
Private	1
Guest Share	1
Family Share	

Countrystay Boutique Accommodation

Features & Attractions

- Scenic flights
- Luxury boat cruise
- River canoeing
- New Zealand hospitality
- 5 golf courses
- Excellent restaurants
- Top NZ wineries
- Jet boating

A unique experience awaits you in this Heritage Home, with the *Sword of Charlemagne* on display with all the mystique that surrounds it. Just 8 minutes from Tauranga Centre with fine bars and restaurants, nestled between the world's renown vineyards of Morton Estate and Mills Reef, deep within the New Zealand Kiwi Fruit and Avocado region.

The Lodge has a magnificently preserved kauri kitchen and lead light windows throughout. You will enjoy the opportunity to experience the Victorian era with all the modern conveniences. We can offer all our own activities, be it scenic flights to White Island or Rotorua and the Bay of Plenty. We have our own boat for scenic cruises and picnics, water-skiing, canoes to explore the local river with all its wildlife and horsetrekking nearby – just to name a few activities available to you. At the bottom of the garden we have a lovely scenic reserve with native wildlife and a beautiful lake which is surrounded by a path. The Lodge is ideally situated to explore the Coromandel, Rotorua and Bay of Plenty areas.

YOUR HOSTS: **Don and Jackie Brebner**   Ph: (07) 576 7687   **Tauranga**

THE PALMS BED AND BREAKFAST
241 Beach Road, Matua, Tauranga
Ph (07) 576 7687, Fax (07) 576 7627
e-mail: *donbrebs@xtra.co.nz*
www.angelfire.com/oh/the_palms

Features & Attractions

- *Every room has sea view*
- *Only 6 min. from city*
- *Complim. airport pickup*
- *Wake to the lapping of waves*
- *On lovely harbour walkway*
- *Relax on sun-drenched balconies*

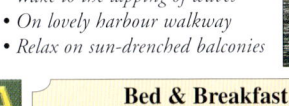

Double	$90-110	
Single	$65-70	
Child		

Bed & Breakfast
"to the sound of the waves"

Bedrooms	Qty
Double	1
Twin	2
Single	1

Bed Size	Qty
King	
Queen	1
Single	5

Bathrooms	Qty
Ensuite	1
Private	1
Guest Share	1
Family Share	

Stay right on Tauranga's magnificent harbour! **The Palms** is situated at the end of a quiet cul-de-sac, with a lovely planted reserve as its eastern neighbour, and only the width of a roadway from the water. All rooms have unobstructed views across the harbour to famous Mt Maunganui and Matakana Island. Stroll Tauranga's favourite harbour walkway, which goes right past the front door and offers a peaceful relaxation in "another world". You'll find the rooms comfortable and welcoming, with the guest wing separated from the host's. Relax at night in the guest's TV lounge, and if you're feeling adventurous during the summer months, talk to Don: if the moon is right, an evening of shallow water harbour fishing could be on!

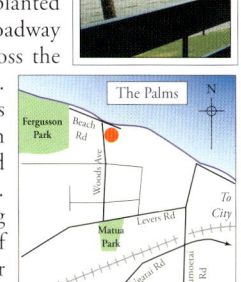

YOUR HOSTS: **Joan and Jim Francis**   Free Ph: 0800 168 791   **Papamoa - Mt. Maunganui**

MARKBEECH HOMESTAY
274 Dickson Road, Papamoa, Bay of Plenty
Ph (07) 542 0815, Fax (07) 542 0815
Mobile 025-318 132

Features & Attractions

- *4 min. walk to ocean beach*
- *Dinner by arrangement $20*
- *Will meet public transport*
- *Relaxing and quiet*
- *Surfcasting*
- *Off-street parking*

Homestay
Bed & Breakfast

Double	$70	
Single	$40	
Child	half price	

Retired and in our late 60's, we have been hosting for 11 years. With family and friends in several countries, our hobbies are gardening, travel, entertaining and collecting memorabilia. A high level of personal service in quiet surroundings will, we hope, make you feel comfortable and relaxed. Full size bath and shower - free laundry - electric blankets on all beds - children welcome. Excellent restaurants nearby. Ten to twenty minutes drive to tourist attractions, shopping and scenic walks. Our motto is "Arrive as a guest but leave as a friend" - many of whom pay frequent return visits!

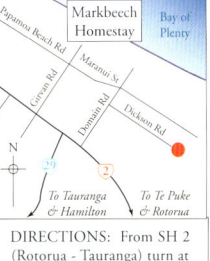

DIRECTIONS: From SH 2 (Rotorua - Tauranga) turn at Wilsons Garden Centre, Domain Rd - signposted 'Papamoa' - Dickson Rd, 5th turn right.

Bedrooms	Qty
Double	1
Twin	1
Single	1

Bed Size	Qty
King	
Queen	1
Single	3

Bathrooms	Qty
Ensuite	
Private	
Guest Share	1
Family Share	

Papamoa - Tauranga

YOUR HOSTS: Verlie and Barry Yeager Ph: (07) 542 3459

SANDTOFT
83 Simpson Road, Papamoa Beach, Tauranga
Ph (07) 542 3459, Fax (07) 542 3459
e-mail: *sandtoft@exite.com*

Features & Attractions
- Short walk to ocean beach
- Off-street parking
- Pitch and drive golf nearby
- Complimentary fruit basket
- Dinner/packed lunches by arrangement

Homestay / Beachstay

Double	$80
Single	$50
Child	$20

Bedrooms	Qty
Double	3
Twin	2
Single	1

Bed Size	Qty
King/Single	2
Queen/Double	3
Single	3

Bathrooms	Qty
Ensuite	
Private	
Guest Share	1
Family Share	

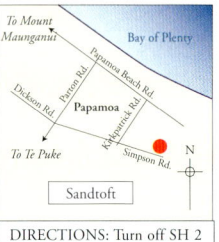

DIRECTIONS: Turn off SH 2 at 'Wilson's Garden Centre' follow Domain Rd to roundabout turn right onto Beach Rd. Proceed to Kirkpatrick right, then left into Simpson.

Sandtoft is a comfortable home, just 2 minutes walk from the beautiful Pacific Ocean. Enjoy a stroll along the sandy beach, sunbathe, swim, surfcast. Sample our local restaurants. We offer two spacious bedrooms with double, queen and single beds. These rooms each have their own wash basin, coffee table, and comfy chairs, plus a north facing balcony. Also available is a smaller double/single bedroom at a lower rate. Bath, shower, toilet facilities are each separate. A guest fridge, TV, tea/coffee are at your disposal. Continental only and/or cooked breakfast is offered. We are a semi-retired couple who enjoy travelling and meeting people. To meet you would be a pleasure.

Bay of Plenty

YOUR HOSTS: Genyth Harwood Ph: (07) 542 0279

PAPAMOA HOMESTAY
8 Taylor Road, Papamoa
Tauranga, Bay of Plenty
Ph (07) 542 0279, Mobile 021-215 1523

Features & Attractions
- Beautiful views of islands
- Dinner by arrangement
- Peaceful and relaxing
- Only 50m from the beach
- Safe swimming beaches
- Deep-sea fishing nearby

Homestay / Bed & Breakfast

Double	$70
Single	$40
Child	half price

Bedrooms	Qty
Double	1
Twin	2
Single	

Bed Size	Qty
King	
Queen	
Single	4

Bathrooms	Qty
Ensuite	1
Private	
Guest Share	1
Family Share	1

DIRECTIONS: Turn off State Highway 2 – Tauranga to Rotorua – at "Wilson's Garden Centre", proceed approx 2km to roundabout at Papamoa Domain, take right turn then about 4km to Motiti Road on the left then left again into Taylor Road.

My beachfront home is situated about 50 metres from the waves of the Pacific Ocean, with beautiful views of Mayor and Motiti Islands and at times extending from Coromandel to East Cape. Enjoy sunbathing and swimming on a safe swimming beach or go for a relaxing beach walk. Pursue your hobby and go surf casting or deep-sea fishing. Visit the vintage car museum in Te Puke or play golf – only 10 min. drive away.

In the morning choose between continental or scrumptious cooked breakfast. Home-cooked dinner is available by prior arrangement. You also have the choice of restaurants nearby. My two-storey home with guest accommodation on the lower level is situated in a peaceful, quiet area. Come and enjoy pure nature in a tranquil and relaxed environment. A warm welcome awaits you!

YOUR HOSTS: Susanne and Jörg Prinz   Ph: (07) 322 2182   **Matata - Whakatane**

POHUTUKAWA FARMHOUSE B&B

693 State Highway 2, RD 4 Whakatane, Pikowai
Ph (07) 322 2182, Fax (07) 322 2182
e-mail: bab@prinztours.co.nz
www.prinztours.co.nz

Tariff : N.Z. Dollars	
Double	$90
Single	$60-70
Child	

Bedrooms	Qty
Double	1
Twin	2
Single	

Bed Size	Qty
Super King	
King	
Queen	1
Single	4

Bathrooms	Qty
Ensuite	2
Private	1
Guest Share	
Family Share	

Bed & Breakfast Country Stay

Features & Attractions

- *Views to White Island*
- *Organic farm*
- *Sauna*
- *100 metres to the beach*
- *Outdoor swimming pool*
- *Dinner on request*
- *Guided tours arranged*
- *We speak German*

Pohutukawa Farmhouse is set in a picturesque location on the Pacific Coast Highway offering outstanding ocean views. Glance up from the breakfast table and see active volcano White Island. Sometimes dolphins and even whales pass by.

Pohutukawa Farmhouse is the base of our tour company "Prinz Tours". We are specialists for guided tours and offer day tours in the area and personalised itineraries for New Zealand wide holidays.

We encourage visitors to stay several days (discounts available). There is so much to see and do in the Bay of Plenty region. Or simply relax in our garden, by the pool at the beach or have a 'talk' to our many farm-animals.

Dinners with ingredients from our organic farm on request. We also speak German and are looking forward to meeting you.

DIRECTIONS:
Directly on State Highway 2, 8 km west of Matata, 34 km east of Te Puke.

73

Opotiki - Bay of Plenty YOUR HOSTS: Maryke and Mike Stuart   Ph: (07) 315 5540

TIROHANGA FARMSTAY

42 Tirohanga Road, Opotiki, Bay of Plenty
Ph (07) 315 5540, Fax (07) 315 5540
e-mail: Tirohangafarm@xtra.co.nz

Tariff : N.Z. Dollars	
Double	$80-100
Single	$60
Child	neg.

Bedrooms	Qty
Double	2
Twin	1
Single	

Bed Size	Qty
Super King	
King	
Queen/Double	2
King/Single	2

Bathrooms	Qty
Ensuite	
Private	
Guest Share	
Family Share	1

Farm - Countrystay Bed & Breakfast

Features & Attractions

- Farmers' meals
- Experience 400 cow dairy farm
- Cottage gardens and huge trees
- Safe and beautiful beaches
- Sea fishing
- Horse trekking
- Dinner from organically grown produce, $20 pp.

Mike and Maryke welcome visitors to enjoy the beautiful sandy beach, which bounds our dairy farm. Enjoy and experience life on a fully operational dairy farm. Ever wanted to try your hand at milking cows? We also breed sports horses – young horses love to be scratched and petted. Enjoy a variety of other farm animals.

Stay in a charming 80-year-old kauri farm homestead with large verandahs. You will enjoy superb views of White Island, an active volcano set in the blue Pacific Ocean, on the East Coast. Stroll along endless sandy beaches at the farm's edge, where you can enjoy good fishing and safe swimming. Or relax in the peaceful and quiet environment of the homestead's cottage gardens, listening to the many native birds that visit the huge specimen trees.

Tirohanga is rich in early Maori history with old Maori Pa and fort sites and a beautifully restored Marae which can be visited. Fishing both sea and freshwater can be enjoyed, plus bush walks, horse trekking and a golf course nearby. We welcome you to relax with us and enjoy our wonderful farmstay.

DIRECTIONS:
From Rotorua to Opotiki 1.5hrs drive. Take State Highway 35 coast road to Tirohanga as signposted, 8 km.

YOUR HOSTS: **George and Sheryll Beveridge**   Ph: (07) 3624497   **Rotorua**

BUSH HAVEN COTTAGE
146 Okere Rd, Okere Falls, RD4
Ph (07) 362 4497. Fax (07) 362 4417
Mobile 021- 396709, e-mail: *georgesheryll@xtra.co.nz*

Features & Attractions
- *Quiet, peaceful surroundings*
- *Ferns, native bush & native birds*
- *Across the lane to the lake - with boat mooring*
- *Swimming & trout fishing*
- *Okere Falls & bush walks*
- *Kayaking & white water rafting on the Kaituna River*

Lake at the end of our Lane

Bed & Breakfast
Self- contained Accommodation

DIRECTIONS:
Please phone for easy directions

As the name suggests, our property is a restful, peaceful retreat surrounded by ferns, native bush and native birds. Awake to the sounds of the Tuis and have breakfast delivered to the door of our cosy, private, fully self-contained two bedroom cottage. We also have a separate studio with ensuite bathroom and cooking facilities. It has its own private deck overlooking the beautiful native bush. Laundry facilities and gas barbecue available. We have travelled extensively and enjoy meeting new people. George is available to assist in planning your itinerary and Oscar, the Persian cat, will keep you entertained. The lake and Okere Falls are within short walking distance. Rotorua, the leading tourist destination in the North Island, is only 15 min. drive away.

Double	$95
Single	$50
Child	neg.

Bedrooms	Qty
Double	2
Twin	
Single	1
Bed Size	Qty
King	
Queen	2
Single	2
Bathrooms	Qty
Ensuite	1
Private	1
Guest Share	
Family Share	

YOUR HOSTS: **Bill Unwin and Laurice Smith**   Ph: (07) 362 4288   **Rotorua**

LAKESIDE BED & BREAKFAST
155G Okere Road, Okere Falls, RD 4,
Lake Rotoiti, Rotorua
Ph (07) 362 4288, Fax (07) 362 4288
Mobile 025-521 483
e-mail: tengae.physio@xtra.co.nz

Features & Attractions
- *Spacious and comfortable*
- *Friendly hospitality*
- *Scenic walks*
- *Laundry facilities*
- *Barbecue and mooring*
- *Handy location*

Bed & Breakfast
Homestay

Our lakeside Bed & Breakfast is just 1 kilometre off the Taupo-**Rotorua**-**Tauranga**-Coromandel Highway. The house is centrally heated and each room has its own ensuite, TV, refrigerator and tea/coffee making facilities. You have the choice of either enjoying your own space or joining us in our living areas. Our homestay bedroom has a private bathroom and all bedrooms have a view of the lake and surrounding countryside. Within walking distance are the Okere Falls, trout pools, kayaking and white water rafting. Lake Rotoiti is renowned for trout fishing, sailing, hot pools and boating activities. Gardens, a 9 hole golf course, thermal attraction and airport are within 10 minutes drive from the house.

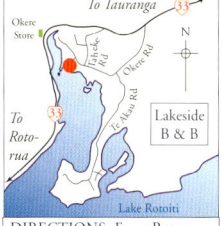

DIRECTIONS: From Rotorua - follow SH 33, after Okere Falls Store, 1st right, Taheke Rd., then right Okere Rd., 155 is on left. From Tauranga - turn left Okere or Taheke Rd., - proceed to 155

Double	$100
Single	$60
Child	$10-22

Bedrooms	Qty
Double	3
Twin	
Single	
Bed Size	Qty
Super King	1
Queen	2
King/Single	2
Bathrooms	Qty
Ensuite	2
Private	1
Guest Share	
Family Share	

Rotorua — YOUR HOSTS: Shirley and Neville Mann — Ph: (07) 332 2921

WOODBERY B & B COUNTRYSTAY
10 Atkins Lane, Hamurana, RD 2, Rotorua
Ph (07) 332 2921. Fax (07) 357 5701
Mobile 025-790 238
e-mail: the_manns@xtra.co.nz
http://home.clear.net.nz/pages/the.manns

Tariff : N.Z. Dollars	
Double	$120-150
Single	$100
Child	neg.

Bedrooms	Qty
Double	2
Twin	
Single	

Bed Size	Qty
Super King	
King	
Queen	2
Single	1

Bathrooms	Qty
Ensuite	2
Private	
Guest Share	
Family Share	

Countrystay Bed & Breakfast

Features & Attractions

- *New natural timber home*
- *Exquisite Lake views*
- *Close tourist attractions*
- *Comfortable homely atmosphere*
- *Country-style breakfast*
- *Expansive landscaped gardens*
- *Trout lake and stream close by*

A warm welcome awaits you at **Woodbery**. In a rural setting with lovely gardens our home was built with guests in mind. You can relax with tea and cookies on the decks in the summer or by the fire in winter, watched over by our pedigree tibetan terriers Jack and Megan. Our guest rooms with lovely views have flowers and chocolates to greet you. There is a TV in each room. Ensuites contain of heated towel rails, hair dryers, robes and toiletries. The guest wing with its own entry has tea and coffee, microwave and fridge. Cot, highchair and laundry are available. Phone, fax and e-mail may be used.

Try and plan several days in Rotorua as we have many and varied attractions. Rotorua is New Zealand's only Spa City and centre of Maori culture. From **Woodbery** we can help plan your time, tramping, fishing, boating, the Agrodome, Paradise and Rainbow Springs and the "Thermal Wonderland". Dinner is available with alfresco dining in summer. We have travelled and look forward to sharing our world with you.

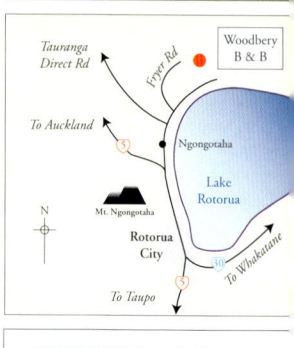

DIRECTIONS: Fryers Rd. is approx. 7km along Ngongotaha Rd. north of village on left opp.lake front reserve. Atkins Lane is at top end of Road.

YOUR HOSTS: Lyn and Lloyd Ferris   Ph: (07) 332 2366   **Rotorua**

Clover Downs Estate
175 Jackson Road, RD 2, Kaharoa, Rotorua
Ph (07) 332 2366, Fax (07) 332 2367
Mobile 025-712 866
e-mail: *reservations@cloverdowns.co.nz*
http://www.cloverdowns.co.nz

Bedrooms	Qty
Double	4
Twin	
Single	
Bed Size	**Qty**
Super King	3
King	1
Queen/Double	
King/Single	
Bathrooms	**Qty**
Ensuite	4
Private	
Guest Share	
Family Share	

**Luxury Accommodation
Bed & Breakfast Countrystay**

Tariff : N.Z. Dollars	
Double	$165-210
Single	$150-195
Child	neg.

Features & Attractions

- *Secluded, peaceful rural retreat*
- *We offer peace and tranquility*
- *Spacious and relaxing décor*
- *Laundry facilities available*
- *Tourist attractions nearby*
- *Trout fishing guide available*
- *4 golf courses in Rotorua*
- *Deer and ostrich farm tour*

"The Perfect Choice."

Clover Downs Estate situated on a 35 acre Deer and Ostrich farm is an ideal setting for the discerning traveller looking for a place to unwind and rediscover the simple pleasures in life. We offer luxury accommodation with a choice of the Governor's Suite, or three beautifully appointed king-size guestrooms with tea and coffee making facilities, refrigerator, TV and video. All four bedrooms have ensuite bathrooms complete with toiletries, hairdryer and bathrobes.

After a sumptuous breakfast take a farm tour with Lloyd and the dogs, maybe try a game of petanque, or just relax and enjoy the rural vistas from your private outdoor deck.

Major tourist attractions, golf and horse riding just 3 to 20 minutes drive away. We can arrange tours and make suggestions for sightseeing...there are so many activities and attractions to experience while staying in Rotorua.

"A Unique Place to Stay"

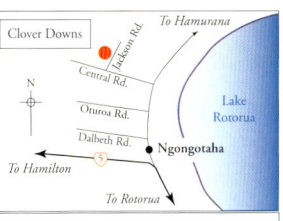

DIRECTIONS: Take SH 5 to round about. Travel north around lake, through Ngongotaha on Hamurana Rd. Take 3rd left into Central Rd, then turn right into Jackson Rd. travel 1.75km to **Clover Downs** on left.

Rotorua — YOUR HOSTS: **Betty and John Insch** — Ph: (07) 332 3458

DEER PINE LODGE

255 Jackson Road, Ngongotaha
Postal: P.O. Box 22, Ngongotaha
Rotorua, Bay of Plenty
e-mail: *deerpine@xtra.co.nz*
Ph/Fax (07) 332 3458. Mobile 025-261 9965

Tariff : N.Z. Dollars	
Double	$85-100
Single	$70-85
Child	neg.

Bedrooms	Qty
Double	4
Twin	1
Single	

Bed Size	Qty
Super King	
King	3
Queen	1
Single	2

Bathrooms	Qty
Ensuite	5
Private	
Guest Share	
Family Share	

Farmstay Bed & Breakfast
Self-contained Accommodation

Features & Attractions
- Quiet, peaceful surroundings
- Beach 30 minutes away
- Architect. designed units
- Beautiful views of lake
- Accredited deer farm
- Farm tours
- Horse riding close by
- No sulphur smells

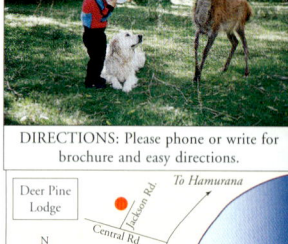

DIRECTIONS: Please phone or write for brochure and easy directions.

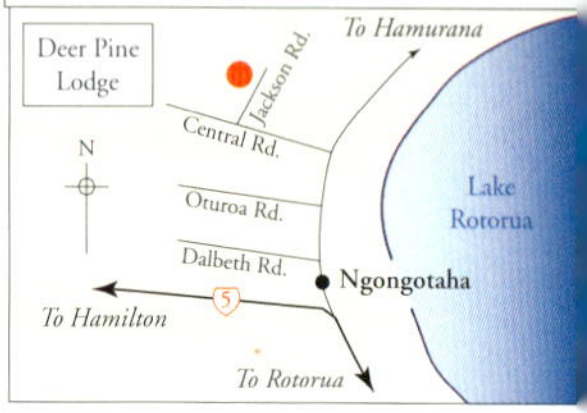

Welcome to **Deer Pine Lodge**. Enjoy the panoramic views of Lake Rotorua, Mt. Tarawera and Mokoia Island. We farm 260 deer on our accredited deer farm. Our property is surrounded with trees, planted by New Zealand Forest Research. We have a cat and a Golden Retriever (Josh), who is very gentle. The nearby city of Rotorua is fast becoming New Zealand's most popular tourist destination. Our lunch/breakfast units are private with own bathroom, T.V., radio, fridge, microwave, heaters, electric blankets on all beds and tea/coffee making facilities. There are heaters and hair dryers in bathrooms. Our two-bedroom fully self-contained units, designed by prominent Rotorua architect Gerald Stock, each have a private balcony, carport, sundeck, ensuite, spacious lounge, kitchen, also laundry facilities, T.V., radio, heaters etc. (cot/highchair available). Smoke detectors fitted in all bedrooms and lounges, fire extinguishers installed in all kitchens. We hold the N.Z. Certificate in Food Hygiene, which ensures high standards of food preparation and service. Please inform us on arrival if you are interested in a free conducted farm tour after breakfast. Observe the different species of deer and get first hand knowledge of all aspects of deer farming. An evening meal with pre-dinner drinks is available by prior arrangement. Hosts John and Betty, originally from Scotland, have travelled extensively overseas and have many years experience in hosting. We look forward to your stay with us. Budget accom. available.

YOUR HOSTS: Raema and Alf   Free Ph: 0800 RAEMAS   **Rotorua**

ALRAES LAKEVIEW HOMESTAY

124 Leonard Road, Ngongotaha, Rotorua
Ph (07) 357 4913, Fax (07) 357 4513
e-mail: *alraes@xtra.co.nz*

Tariff : N.Z. Dollars	
Double	$95-120
Single	$70-90
Child	

Bedrooms	Qty
Double	3
Twin	
Single	

Bed Size	Qty
Super King	
King	1
Queen	1
Single	2

Bathrooms	Qty
Ensuite	1
Private	1
Guest Share	1
Family Share	

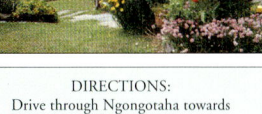

Homestay Bed & Breakfast

Features & Attractions

- A Million Dollar View
- Handy major tourist attractions
- Dinner prior notice
- Ideal Homestay for relaxing
- Quiet, peaceful atmosphere
- Trout stream and lake close by
- Laundry facilities available
- Transport available

DIRECTIONS:
Drive through Ngongotaha towards Hamurana over railway line, turn 2nd right into Waiteti Rd. 1st left into Leonard Rd. ALRAES sign 180m on left.

Welcome to our HOMESTAY WITH THE MILLION DOLLAR VIEW and our two acre lifestyle block, with black sheep and friendly atmosphere. Your comfort is our priority. Just 10min. from Rotorua City, handy to Skyline Skyrides, Agrodrome, Rainbow Springs, Hangi and Maori Concerts, walking distance to Lake Rotorua and Waiteti Stream where you can flyfish then smoke your catch in our smoker. Breakfast on scrumptious home-made food in the conservatory while you enjoy the stunning 200°+ views of Lake Rotorua, Mounts Ngongotaha and Tarawera. Enjoy our company or the privacy of the guest lounge with its peaceful lake and garden views or listen to the bird life on the terrace. You will have the choice of king/twin ensuite with spa bath or queen bed with private bathroom. Tea/coffee, cookies and laundry are available.

We have travelled extensively and after hosting for twelve years our sense of humour and enthusiasm is still as strong as ever. OUR HOME IS YOUR HOME. Reduce your stress and relax. We hope to meet you soon.

Rotorua

YOUR HOSTS: **Ann and Gordon** Ph: (07) 357 4020

NGONGOTAHA LAKESIDE LODGE
41 Operiana Street, Ngongotaha, Rotorua
Ph (07) 357 4020, Fax (07) 357 4020
Mobile (025) 200 7539
e-mail: lake.edge@xtra.co.nz

Features & Attractions
- Trout fishing in lake & stream
- Bird watching
- Good restaurants 9-10 km away
- Volcanic sites to visit
- Separate guest lounge
- Rods, canoe, golf clubs to use

Bed & Breakfast Boutique Accomodation

Double	$95-140
Single	$85-110
Child	neg.

Bedrooms	Qty
Double	2
or Twin	1/3
Single	

Bed Size	Qty
King	1
Queen	1
Single	2

Bathrooms	Qty
Ensuite	3
Private	
Guest Share	
Family Share	

DIRECTIONS: Take SH 5 to Ngongotaha. Drive through village, take 1st right after railway line into Wikaraka Street, left onto Okana Cresc., left onto Operiana St. We are on the right.

Our Lodge on the shores of **Lake Rotorua** commands **panoramic** views of the lake and surrounding mountains. From our **conservatory** you can sit and watch local fishermen try their luck for fighting rainbow and wily brown trout at the mouth of the Waiteti Stream. The upper level of this two-storey home is **exclusive** for guests. We offer friendly service and excellent accommodation at affordable prices. The **guest kitchen has** tea and coffee facilities and a fridge. We will help you plan your day using our complimentary map and knowledge of the area. Gordon is an experienced fisherman and will happily share his knowledge with you so you can try your luck for fighting trout just metres from the Lodge. **Free** use of the Lodge's canoes, fishing rods and golf clubs.

Lake Okareka & Lake Tarawera, Rotorua.

YOUR HOSTS: Yvonne and David Medlicott   Ph: (07) 332 5662

Rotorua

KAHILANI FARM

691 Dansey Road, RD 2,
Rotorua, Bay of Plenty
Ph/Fax (07) 332 5662, Mobile 025-990 690
e-mail: *kahilani@wave.co.nz*

Tariff : N.Z. Dollars

Double	$135-150
Single	$102-110
Child	half price

Bedrooms

Bedrooms	Qty
Double	2
Twin	1
Single	1

Bed Size

Bed Size	Qty
Super King	
King/Twin	1
Queen	2
Single	1

Bathrooms

Bathrooms	Qty
Ensuite	1
Private	2
Guest Share	
Family Share	

Farmstay Luxury Accommodation

Features & Attractions

- 100 ha Red Deer Farm
- Extensive gardens
- Tranquil surroundings
- Labrador breeding kennels
- Light or country cooked breakfasts
- Dinners by arrangement
- Farm tours & farm experiences
- Assistance with local sightseeing

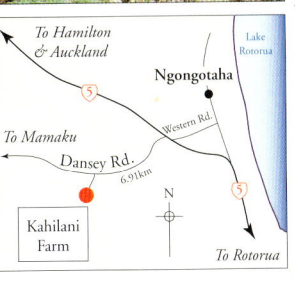

DIRECTIONS: Dansey Rd is off State Highway 5 on the north west side of Rotorua, 8km from city.

A fine accommodation, cuisine and real New Zealand country experience awaits you at **Kahilani.**
The modern country house, built largely of native Kauri timber is set in the midst of a commercial **Red Deer and SheepFarm** - the peace and quiet of its setting is a feature of the homestead, an ambience of rural, forest and lake views can be enjoyed with a feeling of safe seclusion, far away from city hustle and bustle, yet only minutes from the thermal wonderland, Maori culture and many other world-famous attractions of Rotorua.

Upstairs guest accommodation, separate from hosts ensures complete privacy and comfort. Centrally heated in winter, cool in summer, the facilities provide all the amenities discerning guests may expect.

Classy comfort food is the house speciality! **Superb Breakfasts** can be as light or as hearty as desired, while the choice of pre-booked dinners can be either family meals of fresh, seasonal produce at $25 pp, or the famous **Kahilani Silver-Service 4-course Banquet**, featuring farm raised cervena (venison) and slected new Zealand wines $55 pp. Kiwi-Host Yvonne has been an airline flight attendant, motelier and together with David has travelled extensively in New Zealand and overseas, making both well-versed in the needs of travellers.

Rotorua

YOUR HOSTS: David and Marilyn Howes Ph: (07) 348 7530

EMANDEE FARM
566 Paradise Valley Road,
RD 2, Rotorua
Ph (07) 348 7530, Fax (07) 348 7501

Features & Attractions
- Merino sheep, beef cattle
- Trout stream
- Peaceful, rural, private
- Horse-riding nearby
- Handy to attractions & City
- Join in farm activities

Farm stay / Self-contained Accomodation

Double	$80
Single	$50
Child	Half price

Bedrooms	Qty
Double	1
Twin	1
Single	

Bed Size	Qty
King	
Queen/Double	1
Single	2

Bathrooms	Qty
Ensuite	
Private	1
Guest Share	
Family Share	

DIRECTIONS:
From SH 5 north, right into Paradise Valley Rd, after 8 km #566 on left. From city take Sunset or Clayton Rd west, right into Paradise Valley Rd, 1 km past Paradise Valley Springs # 566 on right.

Emandee Farm is 25 acres in beautiful Paradise Valley, 12 km from Rotorua city. A warm welcome awaits and you will experience the farm life with seasonal activities including feeding hay, bottle-feeding orphan lambs, checking and moving stock, and walks over the rolling hills. Our separate facilities for guests comprise of two bedrooms, bathroom, kitchenette, dining and lounge area with pool table, television and a laundry. We have 3 (outside) dogs, (2 are David's hunting dogs), and a cat. A generous breakfast is served with style and we can assist you with local knowledge. Our interests include farm and family, boating and fishing, hunting, touring on our motorbike, walking and tramping. **Emandee Farm** - for wonderful memories.

Rotorua

YOUR HOSTS: Leonie and Paul Kibblewhite Ph: (07) 345 6303

LYNMORE HOMESTAY
2 Hilton Road, Lynmore, Rotorua
Ph (07) 345 6303, Fax (07) 345 6353
e-mail: kibble@xtra.co.nz

Features & Attractions
- Central - 4 km to city
- Beauty, comfort, space
- Yummy breakfast (full)
- Leonie parle francais
- Spacious guest lounge
- Knowledgeable hosts

Bed & Breakfast Homestay

Double	$90
Single	$60
Child	

Bedrooms	Qty
Double	2
Twin	
Single	

Bed Size	Qty
King	
Queen/Double	2
Single	

Bathrooms	Qty
Ensuite	1
Private	1
Guest Share	
Family Share	

Welcome! Discover real character and warmth in lovely Lynmore; easily found, just five minutes drive from the city centre and attractions. Enjoy the beautiful garden with its native collection and birdlife; stroll in the magnificent forest nearby; yet be centrally placed to visit the great variety of thermal, cultural and adventure activities Rotorua offers. Your hosts, Leonie, ex-teacher, and Paul, scientist, delight in being New Zealanders - use their enthusiasm and in-depth knowledge of this remarkable area of lake, forest, volcano, where every feature has its story. And meet Paul's guide dog, Toby, a character in himself. Sleep comfortably in well-appointed rooms: quality linen, electric blankets, robes, fruit, flowers. Relax in the guest lounge, patio, verandah, or garden - there is a choice of sunny and attractive spaces both indoors and out.... Great coffee, a generous and delicious breakfast: fresh fruit and juice, home delights, a choice of cooked course - this couple enjoys food! Smoke-free inside; laundry included.

DIRECTIONS: Route 30 east 2.5 km (towards airport). Turn right at roundabout onto Tarawera/ Blue Lake Rd., 3rd street left Lynmore Avenue, 2nd right Hilton Rd, opposite corner store. No 2 is on left.

YOUR HOSTS: Margaret and Noel Marson   Ph: (07) 377 6451   **Oruanui - Taupo**

"BRACKENHURST"
801 Oruanui Road, RD 1, Taupo
Ph (07) 377 6451, Fax (07) 377 6451

Features & Attractions
- Close to Taupo attractions
- Pitch and putt practice
- Dinner by arrangement
- Extensive gardens
- Lifestyle farming
- Peaceful and tranquil

Farmstay Bed & Breakfast

Double	$100
Single	$60
Child	$30

DIRECTIONS: Turn off SH 1 approx. 9km north of Wairakei- "Challenge" fertilizer-bins on Oruanui Rd. corner- 1/2 km on right. Please phone first.

Brackenhurst, set among flower gardens on a hillside overlooking picturesque farmland, offers a warm welcome, wonderful food, peace and tranquility. Enjoy the sounds of tuis and bellbirds. Practise your pitch and putt on the hillside green. A private guest wing in the house or a separate annex offer the ultimate in away from home comfort – fresh flowers and special touches. Breakfast to suit, healthy, indulgent or a little of both. Let us spoil you with fine food, freshly brewed coffee and selection of teas. Guests are welcome to relax by the fire, on the verandah or wander over the farm, viewing the animals. We have a house cat and small poodle. Come and enjoy **Brackenhurst** and share in our warm hospitality. Located close to the many 'wonders' of the Taupo area.

Bedrooms	Qty
Double	2
Twin	
Single	1
Bed Size	Qty
King	
Queen/Double	2
Single	2
Bathrooms	Qty
Ensuite	1
Private	1
Guest Share	
Family Share	

YOUR HOSTS: Barbara and Dermot Grainger   Ph: (07) 378 1931   **Oruanui - Taupo**

"MINARAPA"
620 Oruanui Road, RD 1, Taupo,
P.O. Box 1310, Taupo
Ph (07) 378 1931, Fax (07) 378 1932
Mobile 025-272 2367
e-mail: minarapa@voyager.co.nz
http://www.voyager.co.nz/~minarapa

Features & Attractions
- Tree-lined drive
- Picturesque grounds
- Tennis and billiards
- Tourist attractions nearby
- Dinner by arrangement
- German spoken

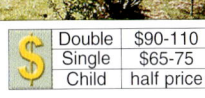

Countrystay Bed & Breakfast

Double	$90-110
Single	$65-75
Child	half price

DIRECTIONS: Please phone for easy directions.

Wend your way along a tree-lined drive to enter the peace and tranquility of our 11-acre country retreat 12 minutes from Taupo and only 45 minutes to Rotorua. Our home offers a games room with full-sized billiard table, or you may prefer to relax before the feature fireplace in the lounge. The spacious guest rooms, two with well appointed ensuite and balcony, have comfortable beds and individual character. They overlook picturesque grounds where you may relax among mature trees and colourful gardens, play tennis, practise golf or cross the pond and stream to visit our friendly farm animals. In addition to continental or cooked breakfast, a three-course evening dinner with wine is available. We enjoy travel, gardening, golf and bridge. Barbara spricht fliessend Deutsch.

Bedrooms	Qty
Double	2
Twin	2
Single	
Bed Size	Qty
King/Twin	1
Queen	2
Single	2
Bathrooms	Qty
Ensuite	2
Private	1
Guest Share	
Family Share	

Kinloch - Taupo

YOUR HOSTS: Rosemary and Graeme

Ph: (07) 378 6332

KINLOCH LODGE

R & G Morrissey
3 Yasmin Lane, Kinloch, Taupo
Ph/Fax (07) 378 6332. Mobile 025-242 0499
e-mail: *kinloch.lodge@xtra.co.nz*

Tariff : N.Z. Dollars

Double	$95-120
Single	$75
Child	$15-25

Bedrooms	Qty
Double	2
Twin	1
Single	

Bed Size	Qty
Super King	
King	1
Queen	2
Single	1

Bathrooms	Qty
Ensuite	3
Private	
Guest Share	
Family Share	

Quality Homestay Bed & Breakfast

Features & Attractions

- *15 minutes from Taupo*
- *10 min. walk to lake edge*
- *Fishing charters available*
- *10 hole golf course*
- *Horse riding*
- *Bush walks around lake*
- *E-mail facilities*
- *Local restaurant*

DIRECTIONS: On entering Kinloch turn left into Kenrigg Road immediately after golf course, then left into Yasmin Lane.

"Get away from the crowds, but close enough to see it all."

Fifteen minutes from Taupo, **Kinloch Lodge** is nestled in the small picturesque village of Kinloch. The Lodge backs onto the public golf course, and is only a 10 minute walk to the lake's edge, marina and restaurant. Central to the North Island **Kinloch Lodge** is an ideal base to explore Rotorua 1 hour, the Central Plateau, Napier and the Waitomo Caves, all within 1 3/4 hours drive. Kinloch is 3 1/2 hours drive from Auckland and five hours to Wellington. Purpose built, each bedroom has its own ensuite. Relax in the guest lounge, which opens onto a large terrace overlooking the garden and golf course. Tea and coffee facilities provided with home baking. Continental and cooked breakfast provided. Experience genuine Kiwi hospitality with your hosts, Rosemary and Graeme. Evening meal available on request. $35.00 pp. BYO. Experience the Lemon Meringue pie. Take the time to catch up on your washing or e-mail home. Rosemary will also help you with your itinerary with other HOSTLINK members to ensure that your journey throughout New Zealand is a memorable one.

YOUR HOSTS: **Elizabeth and Paul Whitelock** Ph: (07) 378 2862

Kinloch-Taupo

TWYNHAM AT KINLOCH
84 Marina Terrace, Kinloch, PO Box 326, Lake Taupo
Ph (07) 378 2862, Fax(07) 378 2868
Mobile (025) 285 6001
e-mail: *twynham.bnb@xtra.co.nz*

Features & Attractions

- Five minutes stroll to Lake
- Short 15 min. drive to Taupo
- Coffee, cake and relaxation
- Delightful home & large garden
- Wholesome dinners by arrangemt.
- E-mail and fax facilities

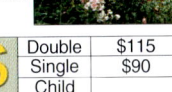

Country Village Accommodation

Double	$115
Single	$90
Child	

Nestled within large private gardens in the picturesque lakeside village of Kinloch - **Twynham** is a haven for fresh air, good coffee and relaxation and unequaled as a base for exploring the delights of the Taupo region, plus the more strenuous delights of golf (adjacent), fishing (5 min.), water sports, snow skiing, bush and mountain walks. Hearty breakfasts, wholesome dinners and warm welcomes assure guests of an enjoyable stay. Guest accommodation is a private wing with bedrooms, bathrooms and elegant lounge. Laundry available. Elizabeth has a wide knowledge of the volcanic and geothermal history of the region. Paul is a New Zealand Kennel Club Judge and golf, music, dog sports and travel are family interests. We are owned by two friendly dogs. Pets are welcome.

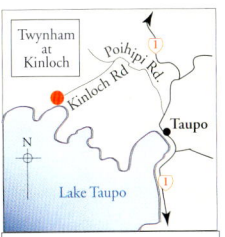

DIRECTIONS: Driving north out of Taupo on SH1 take the TeKuiti/Kinloch turn-off on left (Poihipi Road). Follow Kinloch signs to village.

Bedrooms	Qty
Double	1
Twin	1
Single	
Bed Size	**Qty**
King	
Queen	1
Single	2
Bathrooms	**Qty**
Ensuite	1
Private	1
Guest Share	
Family Share	

YOUR HOSTS: **Eric and Joan Leersnijder** Ph: (07) 378 3861

Acacia Bay - Taupo

PARIROA HOMESTAY
77A Wakeman Road, Acacia Bay, Taupo
Ph (07) 378 3861, Fax (07) 378 3866
Mobile 025-530 370
e-mail: *pariroa@xtra.co.nz*
www.mysite.xtra.co.nz/~Pariroa

Features & Attractions

- Magnificent views, very quiet
- Interesting walks, good beaches
- Restaurant nearby
- Close to lake
- 5 km from Taupo
- Breakfast of choice

Homestay

Double	$75
Single	$50
Child	$30

Views Views

Our home is Scandanavian style with a natural wooden interior, situated in a very quiet area of Acacia Bay and surrounded by native ferns and plants. We have magnificent, uninterrupted views of Lake Taupo, Mount Tauhara and the ranges, from the guest bedrooms, living room and sun deck. We are retired farmers, who have travelled extensively and enjoy meeting people. Eric, in his younger years, lived in several European countries and was a tea planter in Java before coming to New Zealand. We live 5 kilometres from Taupo and minutes from the beach. If you enjoy fishing, tramping, mountaineering, playing golf or relaxing in hot thermal pools, it is all in this area.

Bedrooms	Qty
Double	1
Twin	1
Single	
Bed Size	**Qty**
Queen	
Queen Single	1
Single	1
Bathrooms	**Qty**
Ensuite	
Private	
Guest Share	1
Family Share	

DIRECTIONS: Follow signs to Acacia Bay. Turn down between 95 & 99 Wakeman Rd. We are the last house on this short road.

Acacia Bay - Taupo YOUR HOSTS: Robin and John   Ph: (07) 378 8025

KOORINGA
32 Ewing Grove, Acacia Bay, Taupo
Ph (07) 378 8025, Fax (07) 378 6085
Mobile 025-272 6343
e-mail: *kooringa@xtra.co.nz*
http://www.kooringa.co.nz

Tariff : N.Z. Dollars	
Double	$110
Single	$60
Child	

Bedrooms	Qty
Double	2
Twin	
Single	

Bed Size	Qty
Super King	
Double	1
Queen	1
Single	1

Bathrooms	Qty
Ensuite	
Private	1
Guest Share	
Family Share	

Homestay Bed & Breakfast

Features & Attractions

- All activities easily arranged
- Close to all major attractions
- Wake to Tui & Bellbird song
- Watch the fantastic sunrise
- Magnificent views
- Generous breakfasts
- Quiet and relaxing
- 2 min.to lake edge

Kooringa is situated in sheltered Acacia Bay (2min. walk to the lake), surrounded by native bush and gardens with magnificent views of Lake Taupo and Mount Tauhara. The guest suite is tastefully furnished with the two bedrooms, comfortable lounge with Sky TV, tea & coffee making facilities and private deck area. We are a retired professional couple, have travelled extensively with our two sons, lived overseas and now enjoy a relaxed life-style in this beautiful area. We are within easy distance of fascinating geothermal activity, famous Huka Falls, bush walks, golf courses, restaurants and numerous other attractions. Our interests include gardening, sport, travel and hospitality. A generous breakfast with plenty of variety is served in the conservatory overlooking the lake. We assure you of a warm welcome and comfortable stay. Please phone, fax or e-mail for bookings.

DIRECTIONS: Follow the signs to Acacia Bay. Drive to the end of Wakeman Road, turn left into Ewing Grove, **Kooringa** is at the end of the grove.

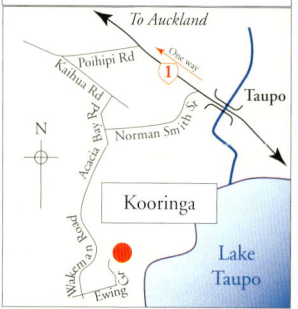

YOUR HOSTS: Barbara and John   Ph: (07) 378 8449   **Acacia Bay - Taupo**

PAEROA LAKESIDE HOMESTAY
21 Te Kopua Street, Acacia Bay, Taupo
Ph (07) 378 8449, Fax (07) 378 8446
Mobile 025-818 829
e-mail: *bibby@reap.org.nz*
http://www.taupohomestay.com

Tariff : N.Z. Dollars	
Double	$150-175
Single	$120-150
Child	$75

Bedrooms	Qty
Double	2
Twin	2
Single	1
Bed Size	**Qty**
Super King	
King	1
Queen	1
Single	2
Bathrooms	**Qty**
Ensuite	3
Private	1
Guest Share	
Family Share	

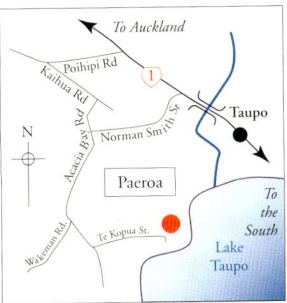

Absolute Lakefront Luxury Accommodation

Features & Attractions

- *Comfortable beds*
- *Private beach & jetty*
- *Generous breakfasts*
- *Quiet and relaxing*
- *Uninterrupted panoramic views*
- *Boat fishing, sightseeing trips*
- *Close to all major attractions*
- *Hot pool and golf nearby*

Paeroa Lakeside Homestay set on the lake edge with private beach, native bush and gardens, in sheltered Acacia Bay, with panoramic views of Lake Taupo and beyond. A warm, welcoming environment waits – comfort, private facilities, spacious lounge areas and outdoor living. Guest areas and beds are warm, comfortable and tastefully decorated. TV in rooms and tea and coffee facilities and e-mail service available.

We are both 5th generation New Zealanders. Retired sheep farmers, we enjoy living in our peaceful, private home beside the beach next to a bushwalk, just minutes from the town centre. 3 golf courses, thermal areas, restaurants, boating, fishing and all major attractions and within easy driving distance from mountains, National Park, extended thermal areas and wineries. Amongst our interests are travel, golf, gardening, fishing, hospitality, having travelled and fished extensively overseas. Guided fishing and sightseeing experiences available from John's new 30 foot cruiser. The catch can be smoked or may be cooked for breakfast. A welcome tea or coffee on arrival.

We assure you of a memorable stay. Please e-mail, fax or phone for bookings.

Acacia Bay - Taupo

YOUR HOSTS: Jay (Jennefer) and Bruce   Free Ph: 0800-663 642

TE MOENGA FARMSTAY
Reeves Road, Acacia Bay, Taupo
Ph (07) 378 7901, Fax (07) 378 7901
Mobile 025-457 729
e-mail: *temoenga@reap.org.nz*
http://www.temoenga.co.nz

Tariff : N.Z. Dollars	
Double	$140-230
Single	$100-180
Child	$50

Bedrooms	Qty
Double	5
Twin	1
Single	

Bed Size	Qty
Super King	
King	3
Queen/Double	1
Single	4

Bathrooms	Qty
Ensuite	5
Private	1
Guest Share	
Family Share	

Luxury Farmstay– Bed & Breakfast

Features & Attractions

- *Magnificent panoramic views*
- *Closest farmstay to Taupo*
- *Trout fishing arranged*
- *Farm walks*
- *Sheep dog demonstrations*
- *TV, tea and coffee in suites*
- *Luxury private Chalets*
- *Classic Jaguar sports cars*

Te Moenga Farmstay supremely located on a sheep, deer and cattle farm overlooking Lake Taupo presents guests with a unique opportunity to enjoy the New Zealand rural lifestyle still within close proximity to all the scenic, recreational and sporting attractions of the Lake Taupo Region. Guests can readily participate in leisurely farm activities including watching Bruce's sheepdogs working deer, cattle and sheep while spending the rest of the day tramping in the Tongariro National Park, playing golf at the Wairakei International Golf Course or catching that elusive Rainbow Trout from the crystal clear waters of Lake Taupo.

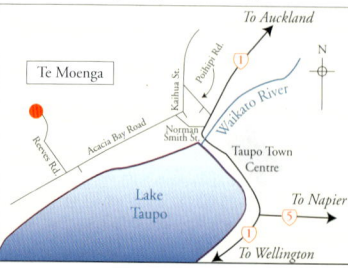

Te Moenga's rooms are tastefully decorated and extremely comfortable. All having private bathrooms, television, coffee and tea. From the Red and Sika Studio Suites with their lovely garden views to the luxurious Rusa and Elk Chalets with their spa baths, private decks and panoramic lake views.

Your stay at **Te Moenga** will rank amongst the most memorable of your visit to New Zealand.

DIRECTIONS: Please follow directions to Acacia Bay. Take first street to right, Reeves Rd and continue on to Te Moenga private road to the very end.

YOUR HOSTS: Bev and Tom Catley Ph: (07) 378 1403

Taupo

Catley's Homestay
55 Grace Crescent, Taupo
Central North Island
Ph (07) 378 1403, Fax (07) 378 1402
e-mail: *taupo@actrix.gen.nz*

Features & Attractions
- Quiet, peaceful area
- Close to lake
- Colourful garden
- Spacious home
- Stunning views
- Great fishing

Homestay Bed & Breakfast

Double	$90
Single	$60
Child	$20

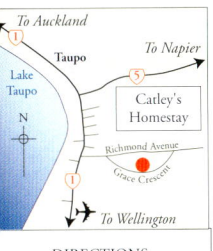

If you are wanting a quiet Homestay with panoramic views of lake and mountains, breakfasts to remember and warm hospitality, this is the place for you.

Upstairs guest rooms open onto a sheltered sundeck with extensive views of the lake and snow capped volcanoes. We also have a comfortable self-contained unit with its own garden entrance, bathroom and lounge with TV, microwave and tea making facilities. You are welcome to use our laundry.

All Taupo's famous attractions are nearby including Huka Falls and hot thermal pools. With prior notice we can offer an evening meal.

We know you will enjoy your stay in this lovely town.

Bedrooms	Qty
Double	2
Twin	1
Single	
Bed Size	**Qty**
King	
Queen	2
Single	2
Bathrooms	**Qty**
Ensuite	
Private	1
Guest Share	
Family Share	1

DIRECTIONS:
Approx. 5km south of town centre turn into Richmond Ave. Grace Crescent is first right.

YOUR HOSTS: Brenda and David Watson Ph: (07) 377 0773

Taupo

Fairviews
8 Fairview Terrace, Taupo
Ph (07) 377 0773
e-mail: *fairviews@reap.org.nz*
http://www.reap.org.nz/~fairviews

Features & Attractions
- Tranquil surroundings
- Generous breakfast
- Tea/coffee making facilities.
- Private entrance/patio
- Courtesy pick-up airport
- Golf, fishing and hunting

Bed & Breakfast Homestay

Double	$85-110
Single	$60-80
Child	

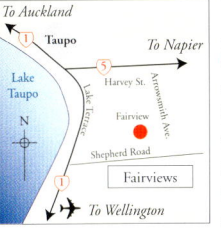

Brenda and David invite you to stay at **Fairviews** and look forward to offering you Kiwi hospitality. **Fairviews**, a new home with beautiful gardens and views of Lake Taupo and surrounding area, is situated 4.5 km from Taupo township and 4km from the airport. A couple who are well travelled with various interests including antiques and collectables (for sale on premises), theatre, gardening, skiing, cycling. We are *au fait* with the area and what it has to offer. Within walking distance of bistro dining, 5 minutes to the lake, botanical gardens and Taupo Hot Springs. Tongariro National Park and ski fields are 1 hour drive south. The Hawkes Bay vineyards 2 hours east and Rotorua thermal wonderland 1 hour away. Escape from the hustle and bustle of city life and rest a while with us.

Bedrooms	Qty
Double	1
Twin	1
Single	
Bed Size	**Qty**
King	
Queen	1
Single	2
Bathrooms	**Qty**
Ensuite	1
Private	
Guest Share	1
Family Share	

DIRECTIONS: From SH 1, turn onto SH 5 take 1st right then 2nd right FAIRVIEWS is on the left.

Taupo

YOUR HOSTS: Pat and Russell Jensen Ph: (07) 378 1888

JENSEN'S HOMESTAY
5 Te Hepera Street, Taupo
Ph/Fax (07) 378 1888, Mobile 025-836 888
e-mail: *scandic@xtra.co.nz*
www.mysite.xtra.co.nz/~scandic/

Features & Attractions
- Quality accommodation in private and tranquil setting
- Hot mineral pool
- Panoramic lake, town and mountain views
- Ample off-street parking

Homestay Boutique Accommodation

Double	$110
Single	$80
Child	$30

Bedrooms	Qty
Double	1
Twin	
Single	

Bed Size	Qty
King	
Queen	1
Single	

Bathrooms	Qty
Ensuite	
Private	1
Guest Share	
Family Share	

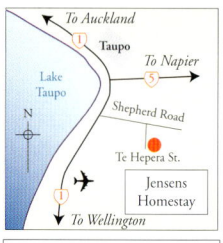

DIRECTIONS: Travelling south on SH1 take the 2nd turn left after the Napier SH 5 turnoff, onto Shepherd Rd, then 1st right into Te Hepera St.

Experience the warm hospitality and relaxed atmosphere in our sunny modern home, situated in a quiet cul-de-sac, stroll away from the lake and restaurants. Upstairs is exclusive to guests, featuring a large bathroom (shower and bath), sunny bedroom and lounge, both opening onto a private balcony. The lounge offers cable TV, tea/coffee making facilities, and well stocked bookcase. Relax on your balcony and view Taupo's magnificent sunsets and nightlight reflections, or soak in our hot mineral pool in its private garden setting. A sumptuous countrystyle breakfast is served at a time to suit you. Our launch is available for fishing and watersports on request. We are well travelled, retired farmers, now enjoying the lifestyle Taupo offers. Our guests are guaranteed to enjoy it too. Contact us anytime.

Taupo

YOUR HOSTS: Gae and Ray Thompson Ph: (07) 377 0241

LOCHINVER
33 Tamatea Road, Taupo
Ph (07) 377 0241, Mobile-025-278 1422
e-mail: *gabrielle.thom@xtra.co.nz*
http://www.mysite.xtra.co.nz/~taupothoms/

Features & Attractions
- Off-street parking
- Private guest lounge
- Priv. bathroom/sep. shower
- Home-baking & preserves
- Pleasant garden setting
- Restaurants/attractions close

Bed & Breakfast Homestay

Double	$85
Single	$60
Child	

DIRECTIONS: Heading south continue along Lake Tce. past main shopping area. At fire station turn left onto Rifle Range Rd. Tamatea Rd. is the 9th street on your right.

Bedrooms	Qty
Double	1
Twin	
Single	

Bed Size	Qty
King	
Queen	1
Single	

Bathrooms	Qty
Ensuite	
Private	1
Guest Share	
Family Share	

We aim to provide warm hospitality and a restful stop for friends and visitors. Being our only guests you are the centre of our attention! Or you may choose to enjoy the privacy of your own sun-filled lounge with television, VCR, well stocked bookshelf, tea/coffee making facilities, and complimentary homebaked biscuits. Cooked or continental breakfast is provided, with home-made preserves a 'specialty of the house'. In fine weather you may prefer to enjoy coffee on the deck overlooking the tree-fringed private garden. Our home is well situated for visiting the area's many attractions. Golf courses and restaurants are also within easy driving distance. The garden and house reflect Gae's interest in old roses, and floral art. Ray is ex RNZNVR, and now enjoying active semi retirement. We are well-travelled and are delighted to meet people from all walks of life. Our aim is to be welcoming hosts but at the same time respect our guests' privacy.

YOUR HOSTS: Raewyn and Neil Alexander   Ph: (07) 378 5481   **Taupo**

Pataka House

8 Pataka Road, Taupo
Ph: (07) 378 5481, Fax:(07) 378 5461
Mobile (025) 547 3881

Features & Attractions

- Quality hospitality
- Large colourful garden
- Quality restaurants nearby
- Private garden room/ensuite
- Spacious home in quiet area
- Central to Taupo's attractions

Double	$90-100
Single	$60
Child	$30

Homestay and Self-contained Cottage

Bedrooms	Qty
Double	2
Twin	2
Single	
Bed Size	Qty
King	
Queen	2
Single	4
Bathrooms	Qty
Ensuite	1
Private	1
Guest Share	1
Family Share	

Raewyn and Neil extend a warm welcome from **Pataka House** and enjoy meeting new people and making new friends. You will find us very easily, just 100 metres from Lake Taupo, and very close to restaurants and shops. Our home is off a quiet road, up a tree-lined driveway and most privately situated. You are provided with a beautiful environment where you are welcome to wander about the garden. **Pataka House** is spacious and has a private guest wing of three attractively furnished double bedrooms. We also offer a cosy honeymoon garden suite with a tastefully decorated ensuite. We are proud of our homestay business which offers all guests - hospitality, use of lounge, laundry facilities, swimming pool, barbecue and roomy carpark. We also prepare a hearty breakfast whether it be continental or cooked and use homemade preserves and home-baked bread. We aim to be welcoming in sharing our home and hospitality with you.

DIRECTIONS:
We are 100 metres off the Lake Taupo lakefront drive. Please phone or fax for bookings or directions.

YOUR HOSTS: Colleen and Bob Yeoman   Ph: (07) 377 0283   **Taupo**

Yeoman's Lakeview Homestay

23 Rokino Road, Taupo
Ph (07) 377 0283, Fax (07) 377 4683

Features & Attractions

- Beautiful views
- Warm, friendly hospitality
- Dinners a speciality
- Spacious, comfortable home
- Close to local attractions
- Vegetarians catered for

Double	$90
Single	$45
Child	$22

Homestay Bed & Breakfast Lake & Mountain Views

Bedrooms	Qty
Double	1
Twin	1
Single	1
Bed Size	Qty
King	
Queen	1
Single	3
Bathrooms	Qty
Ensuite	
Private	1
Guest Share	1
Family Share	

DIRECTIONS: Turn into Huia St. from lake front, take fourth turn on right into Rokino Road.

Our lake and mountain view homestay is handy to all of Taupo's local attractions and golf courses, only 2 minutes drive to shops and restaurants and a short walk to the lake. One hour drive to Rotorua thermal area, 1° hours to Ruapehu ski fields.

A very warm welcome awaits all who are looking for a relaxing homestay. Guest bedrooms are comfortable and tastefully furnished. Our spacious lounge and sun-deck are yours to enjoy, especially the beautiful sunsets (and log fires in winter). Washing and ironing facilities are available and ample off-street parking. Our interests since retiring from farming are travelling both home and abroad, golfing, handwork, traditional New Zealand meals and home hospitality.

Taupo

YOUR HOST: **Ngaire**

Mobile 025-294 0492

KOTIRI LODGE

P.O.Box 270, Taupo
Mobile 025-294 0492
e-mail: *kotirilodge@yahoo.com*

Tariff : N.Z. Dollars		
	Double	$195
	Extra	Adult $30
	Child	

Bedrooms	Qty
Double	2
Twin	1
Single	1
Bed Size	**Qty**
Super King	1
King	
Queen	2
King Single	3
Bathrooms	**Qty**
Ensuite	1
Private	
Guest Share	1
Family Share	

Self-contained Boutique Accommodation

Features & Attractions

- *1920's character villa*
- *Olde worlde gardens*
- *Outdoor spa pool*
- *World class golfing*
- *Views of lake & mountains*
- *Central location*
- *Totally independent*
- *Superb fishing*

Welcome to **Kotiri Lodge**, one of Taupo's best kept secrets. Located just 1 km from Taupo's wonderful shops and restaurants **Kotiri** captures the ambience and romance of a bygone era.

The four bedroom, two bathroom villa becomes your home away from home. All beds have electric blankets and feather down duvets. **Kotiri** is centrally heated along with two fireplaces for winter comfort.

In the upstairs garden room relax and view stunning sunsets across Lake Taupo to the Central Plateau Mountains. Nestled under the fig tree is the outdoor spa, a temptation not to be missed or alternately enjoy the luxury of the ensuite spa bath.

DIRECTIONS:
Please phone for bookings and directions.

Provisions for breakfast at your leisure include a fresh supply of eggs from the hen house. **Kotiri** is yours exclusively, with any booking for either 1 or up to 7 guests. The ideal retreat for friends or family. Come and share the pleasure of Taupo and the privacy of **Kotiri Lodge**, your enquiries are welcome.

OUR HOSTS: Lyn and Richard James   Ph: (07) 378 8023   **Taupo**

"RICHLYN"

1 Mark Wynd, Bonshaw Park, Taupo
Ph (07) 378 8023, Fax (07) 378 8023
Mobile 025-908 647
e-mail: richlyn.james.taupo@extra.co.nz
http://www.richlyn.co.nz

Tariff : N.Z. Dollars

Double	$120-140
Single	$80-90
Child	neg.

Bedrooms	Qty
Double	3
Twin	1
Single	

Bed Size	Qty
Super King	1
King	
Queen	2
Single	2

Bathrooms	Qty
Ensuite	1
Private	
Guest Share	1
Family Share	

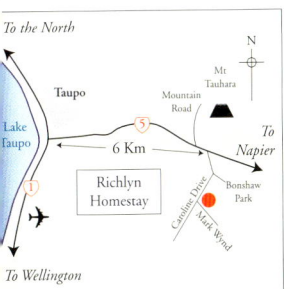

**Country Homestay
Boutique Accommodation**

Features & Attractions

- Friendly, peaceful, very comfortable
- Quality bedding and furnishings
- Tourist centre of New Zealand
- Complimentary laundry
- Eight minutes to Taupo
- Spa pool and gym
- Panoramic views & peaceful surroundings

It's hard to praise your own place, but I will try. Our large house is at the end of a long tree lined drive in a peaceful 8 acre park, It gets all day sun and panoramic views of the beautiful Lake Taupo area. We have made our home friendly and comfortable, quiet no smoking rooms, thick curtains, wonderful beds, friendship, privacy, secure car parking and breakfasts to remember - things that we have often looked for when travelling. There is a spa pool hidden in the extensive informal garden that surrounds the house. Our four big guestrooms allow us to cater for up to 4 couples. We offer group, off peak, firefighter and multiple night discounts.

Our 2 toy poodles, 2 black cats and lovebird are always happy to welcome guests and provide some entertainment. Richard is a Fire Officer and Lyn a part time Bank Officer Our interests are travel, reading, gardening, each other and lots of other things. Bookings are essential, inquiries welcome.

DIRECTIONS: From Taupo up Napier Rd 6km, right into Caroline Drive (Bonshaw Park) 2km to Mark Wynd on left, first drive on left is "RICHLYN".

Taupo

YOUR HOSTS: **Ruth and John Boddy**

Free Ph: 0800 200 983

"THE PILLARS"

7 Deborah Rise, Bonshaw Park, Taupo
Ph (07) 378 1512, Fax (07) 378 1511
Mobile 025-246 0777
e-mail: *enquiries@pillarshomestay.co.nz*
http://www.pillarshomestay.co.nz

Tariff : N.Z. Dollars	
Double	$250-450
Single	
Child	13 yrs.+

Bedrooms	Qty
Double	4
Twin	
Single	

Bed Size	Qty
Super King/Twin	1
King/Twin	1
Californian King Twin	2

Bathrooms	Qty
Ensuite	4
Private	
Guest Share	
Family Share	

Luxury Homestay Retreat

Features & Attractions

- Offers privacy and tranquility
- Five acre park-like rural grounds
- Lake and mountain views
- Tennis court & swimming pool
- World famous trout fishing
- Golf courses nearby
- Ski fields only 1 hour away
- Hot pools nearby

DIRECTIONS: 5.7 km from the lake edge up SH 5 towards Napier. Turn into Caroline Drive. Deborah Rise is the first on your left.

Welcome to Taupo's exclusive Homestay Retreat offering privacy and tranquility amidst five acres of park-like rural grounds with views of lake and mountains. At Lake Taupo, – New Zealand's largest lake, covering 616 square kilometres, – you will be amazed about how much there is to do in both summer and winter. **The Pillars**, built in Mediterranean style, is set in landscaped gardens, featuring a pond gazebo, swimming pool and tennis court (racquets and balls provided).

All rooms have underfloor heating, complimentary toiletries and quality furnishings, including TV, radio-clock, fridge with bottled water, selection of teas and coffee, fresh fruit and complimentary bottle of wine. Fresh flowers, home-cooked biscuits, bathrobes and hair dryers will add to the enjoyment of your stay with us.

The room rate with multiple night discounts and winter rates includes a continental breakfast. With prior notice we will provide a three-course evening meal with aperitifs, nibbles and a night cap for $55 per person.

If you wish to visit Taupo's many bars and restaurants, we will provide complimentary transport. Brochure available on request.

OUR HOSTS: **Jean, Ben and Kate**   Ph: (07) 378 0563

Taupo

FIVE MILE BAY HOMESTAY
60 Mahuta Road, Five Mile Bay, RD 2, Taupo
Ph/Fax (07) 378 0563,
Mobile (025) 217 1415
e-mail: *hughes.jbk@xtra.co.nz*
www.go.to/5milebay

Features & Attractions

- Absolute lake edge
- Panoramic views
- E-mail, fax, laundry
- Close to major attractions
- Inhouse babysitting
- Guided sightseeing trips

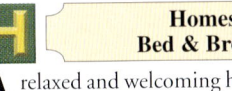

Homestay
Bed & Breakfast

	$
Double	$80-110
Single	$50-60
Child	neg.

A relaxed and welcoming home away from home. A wood lined lodge set amidst a quarter of an acre of gardens bordering the beautiful shores of Lake Taupo, two minutes from the fishing pools of the Waitahanui Stream, ten minutes south from Taupo township and an hour away from the ski fields of Whakapapa. Our modern ground floor unit is fully self-contained; kitchenette, TV, double spa bath, lake views, private access to the beachfront. Experience the sounds of lapping water from our Edwardian guest bedroom, furnished from a bygone era, yet retaining all of today's comforts. Whether relaxing by the cosy log fire, sunbathing on our extensive decks, reading the morning newspaper over breakfast in the sun drenched conservatory, we would like to share with you the tranquility of our lakeside living.

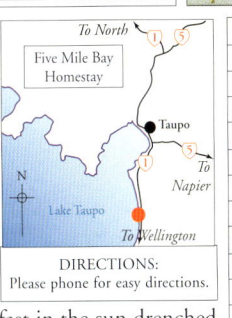

DIRECTIONS:
Please phone for easy directions.

Bedrooms	Qty
Double	2
Twin	1
Single	
Bed Size	**Qty**
King	
Queen/Double	2
Single	2
Bathrooms	**Qty**
Ensuite	1
Private	1
Guest Share	
Family Share	

YOUR HOST: **Louise Schick**   Ph: (06) 837 5898

Mahia Peninsula

REOMOANA
Mahanga Road, RD 8, Nuhaka, Hawkes Bay
Ph (06) 837 5898, Fax (06) 837 5990
e-mail: *louiseschick@hotmail.com*

Features & Attractions

- Panoramic ocean view
- Morere Hot Springs
- Mahia Scenic Reserve
- Safe, white sandy beaches
- Fishing Charters arranged
- Sunset Point Restaurant 6 km

	$
Double	$100
Single	$60
Child	$20

Coastal Bed & Breakfast
Self-contained unit

Bedrooms	Qty
Double	2
Twin	
Single	1
Bed Size	**Qty**
King	
Queen/Double	2
Single	1
Bathrooms	**Qty**
Ensuite	1
Private	1
Guest Share	
Family Share	

Welcome to **Reomoana** – the voice of the sea. Pacific Ocean front farm at beautiful Mahanga Beach on the Mahia Peninsula, the spacious, rustic home with Hungarian and NZ creativity makes this a home of character, with cathedral ceilings and hand-carved furniture.

Breath taking views to the Pacific. Come and relax and bring your paints - the area is a painter's paradise. Enjoy the miles of white sandy beaches. Go swimming, surfing, fishing or discover the unique rocky reefs of Mahia. Lake Waikaremoana in the Urewera National Park can be enjoyed for a day trip - or visit Mahia's Scenic Reserve. "Sunset Point Restaurant" is 6 km away or else dinner may be served by prior arrangement.

Reomoana is one hour south of Gisborne or 2¼ hours north of Napier.

DIRECTIONS:
Please phone for easy directions.

New Plymouth — YOUR HOSTS: **Ann and John Butler** — Free Ph: 0800 306 449

BIRDHAVEN
26 Pararewa Drive,
New Plymouth, Taranaki
Ph (06) 751 0432, Fax (06) 751 3475

Tariff : N.Z. Dollars	
Double	$72-80
Single	$50-60
Child	neg.

Bedrooms	Qty
Double	1
Twin	1
Single	

Bed Size	Qty
Super King	
King	
Queen	1
Single	2

Bathrooms	Qty
Ensuite	
Private	
Guest Share	1
Family Share	

Homestay Bed & Breakfast

DIRECTIONS:
From clock tower (opposite Queen St.) on Devon St. West, travel west 3.4 km to Spotswood College (LHS). Turn left 800m later into Barrett Road. We are the fifth street on the right.

Features & Attractions

- *Beautiful, peaceful country setting*
- *Native bush with abundant bird life*
- *Restful, friendly atmosphere*
- *Delicious complimentary homebaking*
- *Spectacular mountain view*
- *Free airport transfer*
- *Special candlelit dinner*
- *5 min. from city or port*

We have lived in England, South Africa and New Zealand and love to travel. We really enjoy welcoming guests to **Birdhaven** and endeavouring to exceed your expectations. Ensuring your comfort and pleasure is most important to us. This is reflected in the quality furnishings in the inviting guest rooms and throughout the house, the complimentary refreshments and the special breakfast of fresh seasonal and home-made temptations. Come and share the tranquillity and space of our comfortable, tastefully refurbished home. Relax in the secluded gardens, in the sun room or on one of the patios overlooking the flight paths of numerous birds as they flit amongst the trees. Stroll down to the duck pond and delight in the native bush, marsh and woodlands within our three acre farmlet. We want you to feel at home, relax and enjoy being at **Birdhaven**, sharing our appreciation of beautiful Taranaki and our spectacular view of Mt Egmont. "True hospitality at its very best – absolutely perfect, don't change a thing!", wrote one guest. Our visitors' book also includes: "Wonderful hospitality. The picnic hamper was superb. The attention to detail in all aspects of our stay has been memorable. We will be back." and "Found a gem! Superb meals. Shall be back!"

YOUR HOSTS: Vivien and Trevor Lewis   Ph: (06) 757 8866   **New Plymouth**

BALCONIES BED & BREAKFAST
161 Powderham Street,
New Plymouth, Taranaki
Ph (06) 757 8866, Fax (06) 757 8262
Mobile 025-423 789

Features & Attractions
- *110 year old character home*
- *Warm, relaxing atmosphere*
- *Attractive garden setting*
- *Central location*
- *Walking distance to park*
- *Close to many attractions*

Central Character Style Home

Double	$75
Single	$55
Child	

DIRECTIONS:
500m west of city centre on Powderham Street

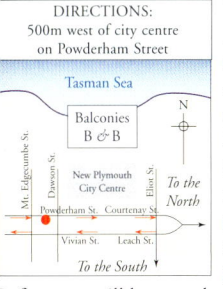

Balconies is nestled amongst mature trees and lovely gardens in the heart of the city, just 5 min. walk to New Plymouth's shopping centre. Our warm, comfortable 110-year old character-style home offers three tastefully decorated guest rooms, large guest bathroom with claw-foot bath, separate toilet facilities and spacious guest lounge with tea and coffee making facilities. Heated guest rooms are downstairs, beds are queen size and have electric blankets. Laundry facilities, courtesy transport and off-street parking available. Within walking distance are the art gallery, library, museum, Heritage Walks, indoor pool complex and beautiful Pukekura and Brooklands Parks. Before you will be served a generous fully cooked or continental breakfast, unwind in the peaceful surroundings of **Balconies**, we will ensure you have a comfortable night's rest.

Bedrooms	Qty
Double	1
Twin	2
Single	
Bed Size	Qty
King	
Queen	3
Single	2
Bathrooms	Qty
Ensuite	
Private	
Guest Share	1
Family Share	

YOUR HOSTS: Pat and Bruce Robinson   Ph: (06) 758 6555   **New Plymouth**

93 BY THE SEA
93 Buller Street, New Plymouth
Ph (06) 758 6555, Mobile 025-230 3887
e-mail: *pabron@xtra.co.nz*
http://mysite.xtra.co.nz/~93bythesea

Features & Attractions
- *Central yet peaceful*
- *Exclusive - 1 party only*
- *Off-street parking*
- *City, sand, surf, walkways*
- *National Park nearby*
- *Dinner by prior arrangement*

Double	$85
Single	$60
Child	

Boutique Bed & Breakfast

Bedrooms	Qty
Double	1
Twin	1
Single	
Bed Size	Qty
King	
Queen/Double	1
King/Twin	1
Bathrooms	Qty
Ensuite	
Private	1
Guest Share	
Family Share	

Convenient: An idyllic spot, combining tranquillity of a quiet cul-de-sac with closeness of the sea, riverside parks, restaurants and City Centre. **Comfortable:** Have exclusive use of **private lounge** (TV, fridge, tea/coffee, homemade goodies). **Spa bath**, shower, laundry. Breakfast served in lounge or shared with hosts while enjoying the sights, sounds and feel of gardens and ocean. **Commendable:** From the Visitors Book: "Fantastic breakfast, beautiful bed, great shower, lovely hosts, we couldn't have found a better place."

*"The sound of waves upon the shore,
The smell of roses by the door,
A spa to ease the muscles sore,
Who could ask for anything more?"*
   Dale Cameron, Auckland

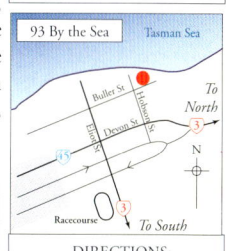

DIRECTIONS:
Please phone for easy directions.

Stratford - Taranaki

YOUR HOSTS: Berta and Keith Anderson Free Ph: 0800 668 682

ANDERSON'S ALPINE RESIDENCE
922 Pembroke Road, Stratford, Taranaki
Ph (06) 765 6620, Fax (06) 765 6100
Mobile 025-412 372
e-mail: *mountainhouse@xtra.co.nz*
http://www.mountainhouse.co.nz

Features & Attractions
- Native bush and garden
- Panoramic alpine views
- Egmont National Park
- Absolute peace and quiet
- Pet sheep, pigs, ducks, etc.
- International restaurant nearby

Double	$95-130
Single	$95-130
Child	

Farmstay Alpine Chalet

Bedrooms	Qty
Double	1
Twin	
Single	

Bed Size	Qty
King	1
Queen/Double	1
King Single	1

Bathrooms	Qty
Ensuite	3
Private	
Guest Share	
Family Share	

Our Swiss Chalet rests in five acres of native bush with views of Mount Egmont/Taranaki on our doorstep. The Egmont National Park starts opposite our front gate. We are five kilometres from the Mountain House and its interationally famed restaurant and a further 3km to the Stratford Plateau and skifields. The National Park offers family tramps, round the mountain trek, summit climbs (guides available) and snow skiing. Trout stream, gardens, museums and scenic drives nearby. Private helicopter for summit scenic flights. We have pet sheep, pig, ducks etc. Kiwi Keith and Swiss Berta Anderson owned mountain lodges for 25 years and won many tourist and hospitality awards. Keith is a noted Taranaki artist, specialising in landscapes and mountain scenes.

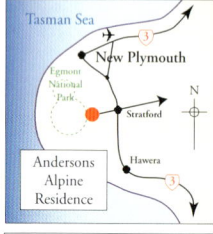

DIRECTIONS: Head west from Stratford 9km up Pembroke Road to Egmont National Park

---

King Country

YOUR HOSTS: Allan Soon and Julie Fletcher Ph: (07) 895 4669

AL & JULIE'S GARDEN & GALLERY
Otapouri Road, RD 1,
Rural # 157, Owhango
Ph (07) 895 4669

Features & Attractions
- Extensive bush & house gardens
- Breakfast essentials included
- Dinner: Asian/European on request
- Close to ski fields
- Hot baths in bush setting
- Wood turning gallery

DIRECTIONS: 18km south of Taumarunui, 20km north of Tongariro National Park.

Countrystay Self-contained Accom.

Double	$75
Single	$60
Child	$15

Bedrooms	Qty
Double	2
Twin	
Single	

Bed Size	Qty
King	
Queen	2
Single	1

Bathrooms	Qty
Ensuite	
Private	
Guest Share	1
Family Share	

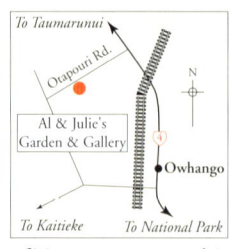

We welcome you to our rural 10 acre property, landscaped into gardens, bush walks and water gardens. Our home is set amongst rolling hills with pathways to explore at your leisure. Visit Allan's workshop, he is a professional wood turner, watch him at work and visit the gallery. Our self-contained unit, adjoining our home, is a fully restored jail from the 1860's and features fittings of solid New Zealand timbers. The unit has stunning views over farmland to Tongariro State Forest and beyond the volcanoes of Tongariro National Park. We provide generous breakfast essentials. Evening meals are available by arrangement, and as Allan is Malaysian Chinese, Asian foods are a speciality. However, we are equally happy to provide hearty NZ fare. We look forward to meeting you and sharing local knowledge to make your stay here memorable.

YOUR HOSTS: **Don and Phyl Cameron**   Free Ph: (0800) 385 413   **Ohakune**

HOROPITO LODGE

Matapune Road, off SH 4, National Park Road, Horopito
Ph (06) 385 4144, Fax (06) 385 4143
Mobile 025-241 5096
e-mail: *donphyl.cam@xtra.co.nz*
http://www.horopitolodge.com

Tariff : N.Z. Dollars	
Double	$200
Single	$100
Child	$25

Bedrooms	Qty
Double	2
Twin	3
Single	

Bed Size	Qty
Super King	
King	
Queen	2
Single	8

Bathrooms	Qty
Ensuite	
Private	
Guest Share	2
Family Share	

Accessible Isolation

Features & Attractions

- *Great views of Mt.Ruapehu*
- *Innovative architecture*
- *State of the art kitchen*
- *Winter/summer wonderland*
- *Exclusive use of Lodge*
- *20 min. to both skifields*
- *Single party bookings*
- *Bush and farm tours*

Horopito Lodge is a self-contained, multi storey retreat that encourages relaxation. Situated midway between Turoa and Whakapaka Skifields in the Central North Island and surrounded by the World Heritage Tongariro National Park. **Horopito** is an ideal venue for corporate meetings, family reunions or just a weekend away from the hustle of city life. Sleeping 12 very comfortably, the Lodge is self-catering...all you need is your food and a sense of adventure. Activities on site include trout fishing, farm tours and bush walks. Any of these can be arranged by your hosts as well as the long list of adventures in the district such as Kiwi viewing, hunting, four wheel drive adventures and so the list goes on. More details are available on your arrival. Restaurants abound in nearby Ohakune and you can enjoy the atmosphere of apres ski in one of these during the winter months if you wish to leave the comfort of your Lodge. Let us pamper you...check our flexible rates for groups and feel the luxury and adventure in 'accessible isolation' at **Horopito Lodge.**

DIRECTIONS:
20 km south on SH 4 from Tongariro National Park. Turn left over railway line - 2 km on Matapuna Rd. 13 km north from Ohakune or Raetihi.

Eskdale - Napier — YOUR HOSTS: **Joss and Kees** — Ph: (06) 836 6508

CORNUCOPIA LODGE
Joss Lamers & Kees Peters
361-363 State Highway 5, Eskdale, Napier, Hawkes Bay
Ph (06) 836 6508, Fax (06) 836 6518
e-mail: *info@cornucopia-lodge.com*
http://www.cornucopia-lodge.com

Tariff : N.Z. Dollars	
Double	$165-250
Single	$150
Child	

Bedrooms	Qty
Double	2
Twin	
Single	

Bed Size	Qty
Super King	
King	
Queen	2
Single	

Bathrooms	Qty
Ensuite	2
Private	
Guest Share	
Family Share	

Boutique Accommodation
Self-contained Cottage

Features & Attractions

- *Kiwi hospitality with European smiles*
- *Gourmet dinner by arrangement*
- *Great variety of fruit & nut trees*
- *Sumptious breakfasts*
- *Swimming pool*
- *Established gardens*
- *Grass tennis court*
- *Overlooking vineyards*

Situated on a 3 acre block with various fruit and nut trees the lodge is privately located with views over gardens and grapevines. The lodge with woodpanelling and open fire is pleasantly furnished and includes TV, video & stereo. The 'state-of-the-art' kitchen (dishwasher, fridge/freezer, microwave and turbo oven) allows you to cook yourself or you can have a 3-course gourmet dinner (including local wines to match each course) served in your dining room. The property has lots to offer for relaxation, be it indoors or outside with verandah & deckings, swimming pool, tennis court and barbecue area. Napier is only 15 minutes away and in close proximity there are the well known Hawkes Bay wineries, beaches, rivers and forests. If it is for 1 or 4 guests, with any booking the lodge is exclusively yours! **Cornucopia Lodge**: *where relaxation starts and hospitality is never ending.*

DIRECTIONS: 15km north/west from Napier on SH 5 (Napier - Taupo) Next to Linden Estate Winery.

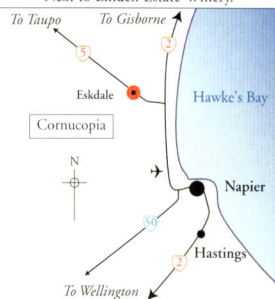

YOUR HOSTS: Brendon and Janet Parker   Ph: (06) 836 7190   **Bayview - Napier**

ESKVIEW HEIGHTS

261 Hill Road, Napier, P.O.Box 83, Bayview, Hawkes Bay
Ph (06) 836 7190, Fax (06) 836 7390
Mobile 025-939 004
e-mail: *eskviewheights@hotmail.com*

Tariff : N.Z. Dollars	
Double	$90
Single	$50
Child	$15

Bedrooms	Qty
Double	2
Twin	
Single	

Bed Size	Qty
Super King	
King	
Queen	3
Single	2

Bathrooms	Qty
Ensuite	
Private	1
Guest Share	
Family Share	

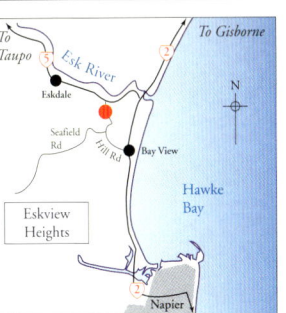

**Semi rural
Self-contained Accommodation**

Features & Attractions

- *Panoramic views of Napier*
- *Close to Eskdale River*
- *Spacious living area, log fire and full kitchen facilities*
- *Private deck with barbecue*
- *Relax in pool or spa*
- *Private squash court*
- *Wineries nearby*

Eskview Heights is located just north of Napier. We offer self-contained semi-rural accommodation with panoramic views of the Esk Valley and Napier.

Features include spacious living area with full kitchen, log fire and private deck with barbecue. The separate bedroom has a queen-size bed, two single bunk beds and a double bed settee. An extra cabin with a double bed is also available.

Guests will enjoy relaxing by the pool or in the spa, or may feel like releasing some tension on the private squash court or in home gym. There is a trampoline, table tennis, petanque and croquet set for use.

Linden Estate, Esk Valley Estate and Crab Farm Wineries are all very close and Napier is only 12 minutes away. The combined attractions of the Hawke's Bay area are all within a half hour drive.

Long term rates are available.

DIRECTIONS: <u>From Napier</u> - drive north on S H 2. At Bayview turn left towards Eskdale. Hill Rd. is 4th road on left after BP Service Station. Go through intersection and wind to top of Hill Rd.
<u>From Taupo</u> - After Eskdale Church take 1st road right, then to top of Hill Rd. <u>From Gisborne</u> - right at Napier/Taupo turn-off. Take 2nd left and go to top of Hill Rd.

Napier - Hawke's Bay

YOUR HOSTS: **Helen and Robert McGregor**   Ph: (06) 835 7434

A Room With A View
9 Milton Terrace, Napier,
Hawke's Bay
Ph (06) 835 7434, Fax (06) 835 1912
e-mail: *artdeco@hb.co.nz*

Tariff : N.Z. Dollars		
	Double	$80
	Single	$50
	Child	n/a

Bedrooms	Qty
Double	1
Twin	
Single	
Bed Size	**Qty**
Super King	
King	
Double	1
Single	
Bathrooms	**Qty**
Ensuite	
Private	1
Guest Share	
Family Share	

Homestay Bed & Breakfast

Features & Attractions
- Large garden
- Knowledge of local history
- Interesting walks
- Excellent restaurants nearby
- Centrally located
- Sea views
- Private bathroom
- Laundry facilities

When visiting Napier you are welcome to stay in our modern two-storeyed home on the sunny northern side of Napier's beautiful hill. The garden is over 100 years old, and the views are over Ahuriri, Westshore, Hawke's Bay and the Ruahine Mountains. The guest room with private bathroom is fully appointed and has a northern sea view. We are a 15-minute walk from town or from historic Port Ahuriri, both of which have excellent restaurants. We will be happy to collect you from your arrival point. We provide either cooked or continental breakfast. Laundry facilities available at a small charge and major credit cards are accepted. As we only have one guest room, we're unable to accommodate children over 12 months. We enjoy entertaining, conversation and laughter, and having experienced home-hosting overseas, we are firm believers in its advantages. Our interests are travel, gardening, the arts, and local history, and we are both involved in the preservation of Napier's Art Deco architecture.

Please telephone or write beforehand.

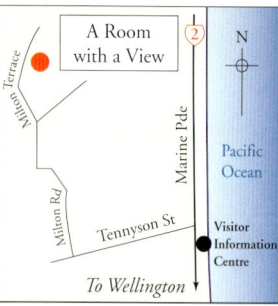

DIRECTIONS: From Tennyson St. in City Centre go up and over Milton Rd., watch for Milton Terrace on the left.

YOUR HOSTS: Soe Schofield   Ph: (06) 844 9319   **Taradale - Napier**

"TWINPEAK"

100 Puketapu Road, Taradale, Napier
Ph (06) 844 9319, Fax (06) 844 9219
Mobile 025-840 450
e-mail: *soe.twinpeak@xtra.co.nz*

Tariff : N.Z. Dollars

	Double	$80
	Single	$60
	Child	neg.

Bedrooms	Qty
Double	1
Twin	1
Single	1

Bed Size	Qty
Super King	
King	
Double	2
Single	2

Bathrooms	Qty
Ensuite	1
Private	
Guest Share	
Family Share	1

Homestay Bed & Breakfast

Features & Attractions

- *Spacious and private*
- *Nestled in extensive gardens overlooking Taradale and Napier*
- *Close to wineries and shops*
- *Midway between Napier and Hastings*
- *PC/printer – no charge*

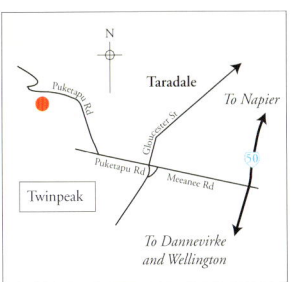

DIRECTIONS:
Please telephone for easy directions.

Twinpeak is situated in a tranquil setting away from the hustle and bustle of urban life, yet only minutes away from all the action. Wine trails, art deco walks, trout fishing, craft shops, sports grounds and the choice of four excellent shopping options. Taradale is five minutes away. Napier to the north – 9km. Hastings south – 10 km and Havelock North to the east – 12kms. **Twinpeak**, nestled in the hills overlooking the Bay, ensures a warm welcome from your host, Soe Schofield.

If weary after your journey or if arriving late, or if you want to be pampered, a meal can be pre-arranged at a reasonable additional cost. Two course $12.00 each, three course $15.00 each. Extra special silver service special occasion $25.00.

For the executive a PC and printer as needed – at no extra charge.

Napier-Hastings

YOUR HOSTS: **Sally and Gavin Ashcroft**   Ph: (06) 844 9446

JERVOIS ROAD BED & BREAKFAST
51 Jervois Road, Taradale, Napier
Ph (06) 844 9446, Fax (06) 844 9446
Mobile 025-415 740
e-mail: *croft@paradise.net.nz*
http://www.geocities.com/ashcroft_homestay

Tariff : N.Z. Dollars	
Double	$80
Single	$55
Child	

Bedrooms	Qty
Double	2
Twin	
Single	
Bed Size	**Qty**
Super King	
King	
Queen	2
Single	
Bathrooms	**Qty**
Ensuite	1
Private	1
Guest Share	
Family Share	

**Homestay
Bed & Breakfast**

Features & Attractions

- *Semi rural*
- *Halfway Napier - Hasting*
- *Restaurants, golf courses nearby*
- *Minutes from wineries & shops*
- *Friendly atmosphere*
- *Large swimming pool*
- *10 minutes from beach*
- *Peaceful garden setting*

Our home is semi-rural, situated halfway between Napier and Hastings.
We have a large sunny bedroom - living area, suitable for a family, with queen and two single beds and ensuite and tea and coffee making facilities. It opens onto a sundeck and garden.
Also available is a double room with bathroom and toilet next door.
Relax by the pool or under the trees in summer or visit wineries, orchards and vineyards of Hawkes Bay.
Breakfasts specialise in Hawkes Bay cuisine.
We enjoy people, having worked in garden centres and we specialise in tropical plants.
A home away from home.
Nearby are many restaurants, golf courses and parks.

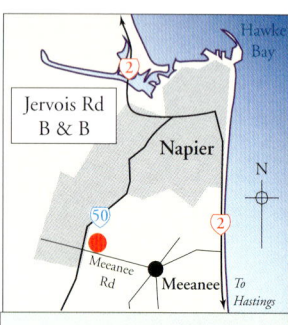

DIRECTIONS:
From motorway turn into Meeanee Road, then first left into Jervois Road.

YOUR HOSTS: **Annabelle and David**   Ph: (06) 857 8093   **Waipukurau**

MYNTHURST FARMSTAY
912 Lindsay Road, RD 3,
Waipukurau, Hawkes Bay
Ph: (06) 857 8093, Fax:(06) 857 8093
Mobile (025) 232 2458
e-mail: *mynthurst@xtra.co.nz*

Features & Attractions
- Excellent working farm
- Trout fishing
- Children welcome
- Swimming pool - trampoline
- Dinner by arrangement
- Farm tours complimentary

**Genuine Farmstay
Excellent Accomodation**

Double	$150
Single	$85
Child	$25

Mynthurst is a genuine working sheep and cattle farm covering 560 hectares. Guests from New Zealand and around the world have been welcomed and entertained for over 16 years. The homestead is large, warm and comfortable, in idyllic surroundings, with unspoilt views of the Ruahine Ranges. Feel free to observe the farm activities. Farm tour complimentary. Relax beside the pool, trampoline, tennis. Trout fishing available in local streams. 3 golf courses nearby. Visit local vineyards. Enjoy the many attractions of Hawkes Bay. Dinner available on request, we use only the finest locally grown produce. Children of all ages welcome. If you are looking for a short break in the heart of beautiful Hawkes Bay, you'll find Mynthurst the perfect retreat. Booking avoids disappointment.

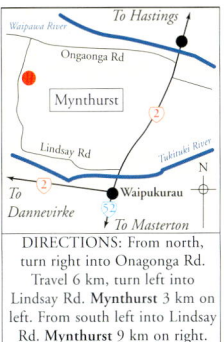

DIRECTIONS: From north, turn right into Onagonga Rd. Travel 6 km, turn left into Lindsay Rd. **Mynthurst** 3 km on left. From south left into Lindsay Rd. **Mynthurst** 9 km on right.

Bedrooms	Qty
Double	1
Twin	1
Single	1
Bed Size	**Qty**
Super King	1
Cot	
Single	3
Bathrooms	**Qty**
Ensuite	1
Private	1
Guest Share	
Family Share	

YOUR HOSTS: **Helen and Wayne Hermansen**   Ph: (06) 374 0735   **Norsewood - Dannevirke**

THE HERMYTAGE
158 Arthur Road, RD 11
Norsewood, Southern Hawkes Bay
Ph (06) 374 0735 Fax (06) 374 0735
Mobile 025-847 418
e-mail: *hermy@ihug.co.nz*

Features & Attractions
- Quiet, peaceful area
- Scandinavian settlement
- Historic village museum
- Dinner by arrangement
- Tea and coffee facilities
- Laundry available

**Farmstay
Bed & Breakfast**

Double	$80
Single	$65
Child	

DIRECTIONS
From Upper Norsewood go over the overhead bridge over the highway. Turn left - 100m - then right into Arthur Road. We are 1.5km on the right.

Guests will be warmly welcomed to our spacious home, where you can relax and enjoy the peace of the country, or be included in the farm activities.
We live on a dairy heifer grazing block and have a town-supply dairy farm. Our district is steeped in Scandinavian history with a very interesting museum. We have a golf course just around the corner, and you can do a day tramp in the Ruahine Ranges.
The men run a hay contracting business and you are welcome to watch the harvesting if you wish.
Waken from a refreshing night's sleep to the aroma of home-made bread and a nourishing breakfast. Then Wayne will take you for a tour of the dairy farm and points of interest in the district.
We enjoy people, love entertaining and a good game of cards, especially 500.

Bedrooms	Qty
Double	1
Twin	
Single	
Bed Size	**Qty**
King	
Queen/Double	1
Single	1
Bathrooms	**Qty**
Ensuite	1
Private	
Guest Share	
Family Share	

Hunterville YOUR HOSTS: Pauline and Ted Wilce   Ph: (06) 322 8215

PLAISTED PARK HOMESTAY

11 Feltham Street,
Hunterville,
Rangitikei
Ph (06) 322 8215, Fax (06) 322 8215

Tariff : N.Z. Dollars	
Double	$75-120
Single	$45-60
Child	

Bedrooms	Qty
Double	1
Twin	2
Single	

Bed Size	Qty
Super King	
King	
Queen	1
Single	4

Bathrooms	Qty
Ensuite	2
Private	1
Guest Share	
Family Share	

Homestay Bed & Breakfast

Features & Attractions

- *Tranquil setting*
- *5 acres of park*
- *Lovely bush walks*
- *Garden tours*
- *Golf - unique course*
- *Excellent fishing*
- *Antique shops & cafés*
- *Dinner by arrangement*

Plaisted Park offers you tranquility, privacy and our house is just two minutes from State Highway One and five minutes walk from Hunterville township.

Our warm and spacious home is secluded in five acres of park with many native trees and bush walks including sixty-year-old rhododendrons, a giant redwood tree and a variety of native birds. The house, built for the local solicitor in 1927, is ideal for entertaining friends and guests. Our bedrooms are comfortable with garden views, there is a family room and a spacious lounge. Local attractions are fishing, jet boating, rafting, and garden walks, 'Rathmoy' and 'The Ridges' are but two of the beautiful gardens to visit locally.

The Rangitira Golf Course is a must for golfers – it is unique with six holes on three levels, returning from the eighteenth by cable car. A three-course dinner is available by arrangement – $25 per person, and there are two local cafés.

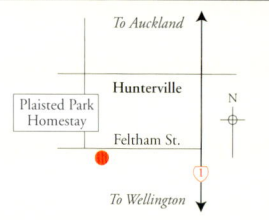

YOUR HOSTS: Margaret and Peter McAra   Ph: (06) 343 36557   **Wanganui**

ARLES
50 Riverbank Road, RD 3, Wanganui
Ph/Fax (06) 343 6557, Mobile (025) 507 295
e-mail: arles@xtra.co.nz

Features & Attractions
- Historic 19th century homestead
- 2 acres of gardens & trees
- Alongside Whanganui River
- Kauri and rimu staircase
- Indoor grape vine
- 5 min. to city/restaurants

Bed & Breakfast
Self-contained accomodation

We would like to share our lovely, late 19th century home with 2 acres of native trees, including New Zealand's most southern Queensland kauri, rhododendron, maples, oaks, camellias. We are situated on State Highway 4 on the road to National Park alongside the Wanganui River and only 5 min. from Wanganui City. Guests are welcome to share the lounge, large library and table tennis. Laundry and kitchen facilities are available. Our new lodge offers spacious, self contained, fully furnished, 2 bedroomed accommodation. Outside facilities include a swimming pool, barbecue and children's play area. We are close to Mount Ruapehu snowfields, mountain and bushwalks and the historic paddle steamer on the Wanganui River. Margaret is a nurse and enjoys flower arranging, needlework, cake decoration and gardening. Peter is a Lion's Club Member and enjoys tramping, photography, and family history.

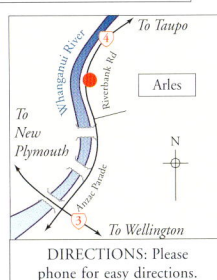

DIRECTIONS: Please phone for easy directions.

	Price
Double	$90-125
Single	$80-95
Child	Neg.

Bedrooms	Qty
Double	4
Twin	2
Single	
Bed Size	Qty
King	1
Queen/Double	2/1
Single	4
Bathrooms	Qty
Ensuite	2
Private	3
Guest Share	
Family Share	

YOUR HOSTS: Trissa and Peter McIntyre   Ph: (06) 342 8159   **Wanganui - Area**

OPERIKI
River Road 3302, RD 6
Wanganui
Ph (06) 342 8159,

Features & Attractions
- Working farm
- Hill country walks
- Dinner Bed and Breakfast
- Overlook Whanganui River
- Macadamia orchard
- Canoeing, jet boat rides

Double	$70
Single	$35
Child	Half price

Farmstay
Dinner, Bed & Breakfast

We have a working sheep and cattle farm, with a few deer and a macadamia orchard - overlooking the Whanganui River en route to the Bridge to Nowhere.
Enjoy a country walk and picnic or other farm activities - according to season.
Links to other river attractions can be arranged: Canoeing, jet boat rides, horse riding, mountain bike riding.
Explore the Whanganui River history from Operiki.
Dinner is available by arrangement, $20 per person, ½ price for children, lunch included where necessary.

Bedrooms	Qty
Double	1
Twin	1
Single	
Bed Size	Qty
King	
Queen/Double	1
Single	2
Bathrooms	Qty
Ensuite	
Private	
Guest Share	
Family Share	1

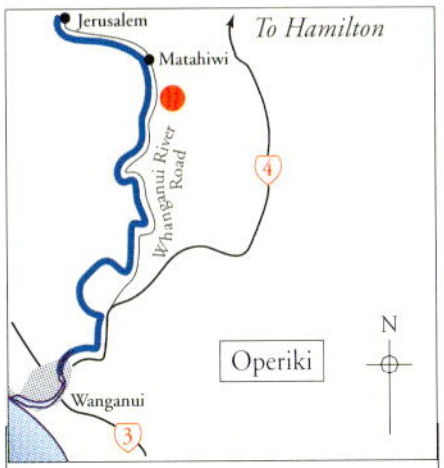

DIRECTIONS: Turn off SH 4 into Whanganui River Road. **Operiki** is 33 km from turn off. Approximately 1 hour drive from Wanganui (45 km).

Palmerston North — YOUR HOSTS: **Lyndall and John Whitelock** — Ph: (06) 353 3749

LARKHALL

42 The Strand, Palmerston North
Ph (06) 353 3749, Fax (06) 353 3748
Mobile 025-416 890

Tariff : N.Z. Dollars	
Double	$130
Single	$100
Child	

Bedrooms	Qty
Double	1
Twin	1
Single	

Bed Size	Qty
Super King	
King	1
Queen	
King Single	2

Bathrooms	Qty
Ensuite	2
Private	
Guest Share	
Family Share	

**Luxury Accommodation
Homestay Bed & Breakfast**

Features & Attractions

- *First class accommodation*
- *Quiet, peaceful location*
- *Great rural visits*
- *Indoor heated pool*
- *Private luxury facilities*
- *Outstanding views*
- *Close to City and University*
- *Within City boundary*

A stunning, newly created up-market home with picturesque views of Palmerston North City and the Manawatu Region. Your hosts, John and Lyndall, have a wealth of local knowledge and international experience. They can assist and direct you to a wide selection of sights and activities. Palmerston North, apart from local attractions, is on the central pathway leading to Wellington (New Zealand capital and Harbour City), Kapiti Coast and West Coast beaches, Lake Taupo (trout-fishing and unique scenery), Mount Ruapehu (skiing in winter months) and the Hawkes Bay (Art Deco and world-class vineyards of New Zealand). An added attraction is that Palmerston North is a centre of major agricultural, educational (Massey University and International Pacific College), business and sporting (Adidas Rugby Academy and museum) activities and interests. Palmerston North Airport offers domestic and international services.

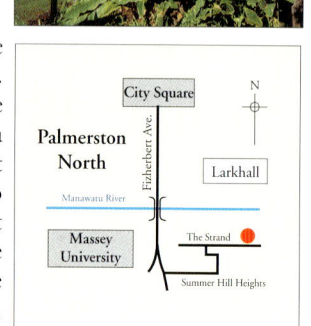

John and Lyndall invite you to enjoy the scenery and native dell as you take in the views from the patio. A warm welcome awaits you.

YOUR HOSTS: **Alice and Ron Tubman**   Ph: (06) 357 6551   **Palmerston North**

Ro Nali
11 Mountain View Road,
Palmerston North
Ph/Fax (06) 357 6551, Mobile 025-477 456

Features & Attractions

- *Quiet, comfortable home*
- *Panoramic views*
- *Warm hospitality*
- *Close to city and restaurants*
- *Walking tracks & golf courses*
- *Contin. & cooked breakfast*

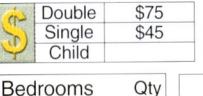

Homestay Bed & Breakfast

Double	$75	
Single	$45	
Child		

Bedrooms	Qty
Double	1
Twin	
Single	

Bed Size	Qty
King	
Queen/Double	1
Single	

Bathrooms	Qty
Ensuite	
Private	1
Guest Share	
Family Share	

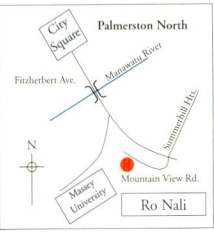

Relax and enjoy rooms with a view in our spacious, comfortable home overlooking Palmerston North city and mountains. Close proximity to Massey University, International Pacific College, the beautiful esplanade gardens and the Lido swimming complex, golf courses and many interesting walking tracks. Feel free to wander around our garden too and listen to the tuis and bellbirds in season. We are ex farmers and enjoy meeting tourists. Our interests are gardening, walking, travel, and Ron plays golf.

Our home is smoke free inside, and we have off-street parking for your vehicle. Please phone for reservations if this sounds right for you.

Bed & Breakfast
in
New Zealand
on the internet – visit
www.travelwise.co.nz

Levin

YOUR HOSTS: **Heather and Peter** Ph: (06) 368 9011

THE FANTAILS

Heather Watson & Peter Simpson
40 MacArthur Street, Levin, Horowhenua
Ph (06) 368 9011, Ph/Fax (06) 368 9279
Mobile 021-469 606
e-mail: *fantails@xtra.co.nz*, www.fantails.co.nz

Tariff : N.Z. Dollars	
Double	$90-100
Single	$60-80
Child	neg.

Bedrooms	Qty
Double	2
Twin	1
Single	4
Bed Size	**Qty**
Super King	
King/Single	1
Queen/Double	2
King/Single	4
Bathrooms	**Qty**
Ensuite	3
Private	1
Guest Share	1
Family Share	

DIRECTIONS: Please Phone for easy directions

Bed & Breakfast Homestay & Self-contained Cottages

Features & Attractions

* Quiet, peaceful surrounding
* Cafés, antique shops
* River rafting, horse riding
* Gardens, vintage cars, museums
* Guided bush walks, tramping
* Golf courses, mountain biking

Organic food a speciality.

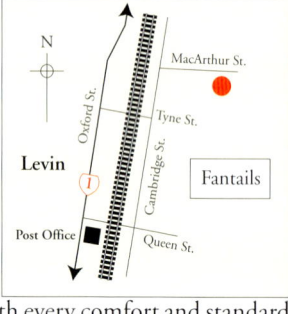

As you enter the **Fantails** you will feel the tranquility and marvel at the lovely surroundings with its English trees, native bush and bird life. Enjoy the English style home with your hosts Heather and Peter, who will provide you with every comfort and standard you require. All bedrooms have a delightful outlook plus TV and video. Enjoy a **Fantail's** special breakfast and the view. We can offer an evening meal with organic food and N.Z.-wines at $35 pp. Levin is situated 1½ hours from Wellington ferry and ½ hour from Palmerston North. Levin with its excellent climate and tourist attractions is a great place to spend those extra days. We can provide a scrumptuous picnic basket and assist with planning your stay and onward travel. We also offer self-contained retreat cottages in our one acre of garden. 'Tui Cottage' sleeps two ($100) and 'Times Past' sleeps four (from $45 per person). (Ideal for romantic hideaway or anniversaries, which are Heather's speciality). Meals can be provided. Our cottages are wheelchair-friendly and smoke free. Feel free to browse in our gifts and souvenirs gallery.

YOUR HOSTS: Leonie and Bill Stevens   Ph: (06) 364 8440

Otaki

"Naumai" Otaki Gracious Lady

112 Waerenga Road, Otaki, Kapiti Coast
Ph (06) 364 8440
e-mail: *naumai-kapiti@xtra.co.nz*
http://www.travelwise.co.nz

Features & Attractions

- *Warm hospitality*
- *Quiet peaceful garden*
- *Inter-Island Ferry 1 hour*
- *Off-street parking*
- *Historic Otaki*
- *Wheelchair friendly*

Double	$80	
Single	$55	
Child		

Historical Boutique Accomodation

Bedrooms	Qty
Double	1
Twin	2
Single	
Bed Size	**Qty**
King	
Queen/Double	1
Single	4
Bathrooms	**Qty**
Ensuite	
Private	
Guest Share	1
Family Share	

Enjoy a stay in our restored 1911 Edwardian Villa. "Naumai" is an historic home built in rimu, matai and kauri timbers, with original high ceilings, wide doors and stained glass windows. "Naumai" is set in an old world garden with magnolias, kowhai holly ewe and three lovely walnut trees. It has an orchard of citrus, crab apple and plum trees. Otaki is rich in native Maori history and culture with the Te Wananga O Raukawa, the Maori University: Pukekaraka Maori mission, with the historical St Mary Catholic Church. We can arrange for you to visit Kapiti Island and experience its rare endangered native bird life. "Naumai" is a good base to visit Wellington and Te Papa, the National Museum or travel on the inter-island ferries to the South Island.

DIRECTIONS:
Turn off SH 1. At New World Supermaket into Waerenga Road, travel 500 m to B&B sign.

YOUR HOST: Mary Bacon   Ph: (04) 904 0700

Waikanae

Kapiti Vistas

17 Kereru Street, Waikanae
Kapiti Coast, north of Wellington
Ph (04) 904 0700,

Features & Attractions

- *45 minutes to ferry*
- *Native bush reserve*
- *2 minutes off SH 1*
- *Oasis of tranquillity*
- *Beaches, rivers, hills*
- *Variety of restaurants*

Quality Homestay Bed & Breakfast

Bedrooms	Qty
Double	1
Twin	1
Single	
Bed Size	**Qty**
King	
Queen	1
Single	2
Bathrooms	**Qty**
Ensuite	
Private	2
Guest Share	
Family Share	

Just 45 minutes north of Wellington Interislander ferry terminal, this oasis of tranquility offers you peace and serenity. Nestled below native bush clad hills **Kapiti Vistas** has an outlook towards Kapiti Island and the Tasman Sea. Be welcomed with complimentary refreshments or supper when you arrive, and start the new day with a continental style breakfast served at a time that suits you best. Nearby you will find a variety of restaurants, native bush walks, beaches, bird sanctuary, river rafting, sea kayaking, cheese and ice cream factory, vintage car museum, butterfly garden, scenic flights, golf, and tour of Kapiti Island. Ideal if you are entering or departing the capital.
"Happy trails to you."

Double	$85	
Single	$55	
Child	n/a	

DIRECTIONS: Turn off SH 1 at Waikanae traffic lights. Crossing the railway line. Take the third street on the left (Winara Avenue), then Kereru Street, which is second on the right, No.17.

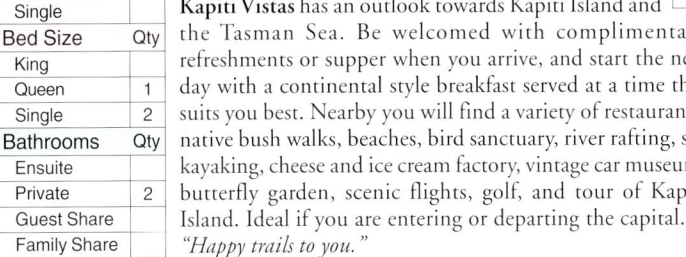

Waikanae

YOUR HOSTS: **Brian and Sue Wilson**

Ph: (04) 293 5165

COUNTRY PATCH

18 Kea Street, Waikanae
Ph (04) 293 5165, Fax:(04) 293 5164
Mobile 025- 578 421
e-mail: *wilbri@freemail.co.nz*

Tariff : N.Z. Dollars

$	Double	$85-150
	Single	$60-120
	Child	

Bedrooms	Qty
Double	3
Twin	3
Single	

Bed Size	Qty
Super King	4
King	
Queen	1
Single	6

Bathrooms	Qty
Ensuite	3
Private	
Guest Share	
Family Share	

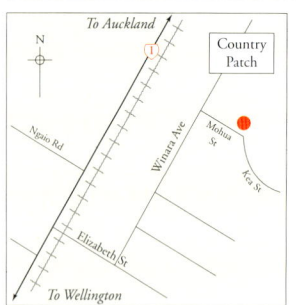

Self-contained Bed & Breakfast

VISA MasterCard

Features & Attractions

- *Delightful country style*
- *Magnificent views*
- *Cosy and comfortable*
- *Hearty meals available*
- *2 minutes drive from SH 1*
- *7 min. to Wellington commuter train*
- *Cottage has large verandah and wheelchair access*

It's the little extras.....that keep guests staying an extra night. Our visitor's book glows with appreciative accolades. 2 delightful self-contained accommodation sites....**Country Patch** studio with its own entrance and deck, has a queen bed with ensuite and twin beds on the mezzanine floor of the kitchen-lounge. **Country Patch** cottage (due for completion by the end of 2000) has an open fire and large verandah with magic views. It is wheelchair accessible and the two bedrooms (ech with ensuite) have superking beds that can unzip to make twins. Set on 2$^1/_2$ acres in the Waikanae foothills with breathtaking views over the Kapiti Coast and historic Kapiti Island, the property is handy to Wellington and the Manawatu. Bush walks can be enjoyed from over the back fence. Hosts Brian (homemaker) and Sue (country GP) with their children Kate and Simon, and labrador Holly, display an infectious hospitality. Try breakfast of fresh eggs from the house chooks! Superb restaurants are close by, or arrange a hearty meal with Grandma and Grandpa next door.
  A treat you can't beat!

YOUR HOSTS: Mary and Robert Burnard   Ph: (04) 293 3371   **Waikanae - Wellington**

BURNARD GARDENS
236 Reikorangi Road, RD, Waikanae
Ph/Fax (04) 293 3371, Mobile 025 222 5675
e-mail: *burnard@kapiti.co.nz*
www.burnardgardens.co.nz

Tariff : N.Z. Dollars	
Double	$80 -100
Single	$60-80
Child	$10

Bedrooms	Qty
Double	
Twin	1
Triple	

Bed Size	Qty
Super King/twin	
King	
Queen	1
Single	1

Bathrooms	Qty
Ensuite	
Private	1
Spa Bath	
Guest Share	

Countrystay Self-contained Bed & Breakfast

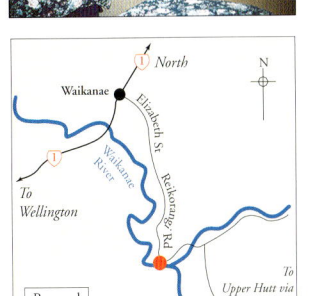

Features & Attractions

- Beautiful well-known garden
- Private, safe swimming hole
- Restaurants & shops nearby
- Spacious self-contained accom.
- Quiet, peaceful surroundings
- Tennis court
- Dutch, French and German understood

The house and attached self-contained guest accommodation, built in 1986, is located in the picturesque Reikorangi Valley on twenty acres, ten of which have been developed into a landscaped English-style garden with herbaceous borders, a rose garden, woodland garden and a vegetable garden, all set against a natural native bush backdrop and bounded by the Waikanae River.

The garden is open to the public on Sundays from mid-September - 31 January. The accommodation unit is available throughout the year. It is very spacious and occupies the attic area of a 3-car garage directly behind the house. There is a kitchenette with dining facilities and a lounge area (with TV, radio and telephone) as well as a double and a single bed in the same room. A private bathroom with shub/shower is downstairs. We are now semi-retired. Robert is a lawyer and Mary a garden writer and landscape designer.

We have travelled extensively in NZ and overseas and lived in the USA, England, Holland and Switzerland. (Mary understands and speaks conversational Dutch, German and French).

DIRECTIONS: Travelling north from Wellington on SH1 turn right at Waikanae traffic lights and drive towards Reikorangi for 3km.

New Zealand Association of Farm & Home Hosts

This logo represents the leading organisation of Farm and Home Accommodation in New Zealand, namely Homestay, Bed & Breakfast, Farmstay and Countrystay. It assures you of a warm welcome in a private home where guests are treated as friends of the family and given personal care and time by the hosts, with meals available. Members' homes are inspected on a regular basis.

Carterton Golf Course – Wairarapa.

YOUR HOSTS: **Kaye and Ron Keene** Ph: (06) 379 5583   **Carterton - Wairarapa**

TERRACOTTA LODGE LTD
6 Rutland Road, Carterton
Ph (06) 379 5583, Fax (06) 379 5593
Mobile 025-732 962
e-mail: *ronaldvkeene@xtra.co.nz*
http://www.wairarapa.co.nz/terracottalodge

Tariff : N.Z. Dollars

	Double	$160
	Single	$120
	Child	

Bedrooms	Qty
Double	2
Twin	1
Single	

Bed Size	Qty
Super King	
King	
Queen	2
Single	2

Bathrooms	Qty
Ensuite	3
Private	
Guest Share	
Family Share	

AMERICAN EXPRESS · MasterCard · VISA

Luxury Homestay

Features & Attractions

- *Scenic country setting*
- *Home with historic connections*
- *Dine with your hosts*
- *Tours and activities arranged*
- *Extensive gardens*
- *Craft studio*
- *Hot spa pool*
- *Petanque court*

Nestled in five acres with large established gardens and developing orchard, **Terracotta Lodge** is an idyllic home away from home with all the amenities of a luxury lodge. While away your time with a book from the library, play petanque, take a relaxing hot spa, visit the doll and gift studio or just wander the garden and take in the warm Wairarapa sunshine. You will enjoy the individual attention given by your hosts, Kaye and Ron Keene, and the delicious breakfasts included in the room rates. Bush walks in the nearby Tararua Park, hot air ballooning, river or sea fishing, golf at one of the four local golf courses, craft and wine trails are some of the many leisure activities close by.

Your hosts will help you plan relaxing days before your return to the Lodge for dinner by arrangement. Both Ron and Kaye are excellent chefs and innovative four-course dinners, at $50 per person including wine, using the fresh produce of the Wairarapa, are an additional delight to conclude a day of enjoyment of the Wairarapa.

Greytown - Wairarapa

YOUR HOST: Donna Evans
Ph: (06) 304 9070

FROGGY COTTAGE
4 Wood Street, Greytown, Wairarapa
Postal: Froggy Farm, Morison's Bush, Greytown
Ph/Fax (06) 304 9070, Mobile 025-458 404
e-mail: *froggy@winz.co.nz*

Features & Attractions

- 1½ hour to Wellington
- 1 hour to rugged coast lines
- Stone's throw to cafés
- ½ hour to famous wine regions
- 25 min. to Masterton
- 60m off State Highway 2

Self-contained Boutique Accommodation

Double	$120
Extra	Adult $30
Child	free

Bedrooms	Qty
Double	2
Twin	
Single	

Bed Size	Qty
Double	2
Queen	
Single	

Bathrooms	Qty
Ensuite	
Private	
Guest Share	1
Family Share	

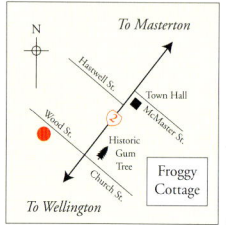

For the weary traveller **Froggy Cottage** offers that olde worlde charm: *welcoming open fire, clawfooted bath, cottage gardens*; the luxuries of modern-day living: *TV, fridge, microwave, electric blankets...*; the fun things: *gas-bbq, sun-drenched verandahs, the outdoor table and chairs, the wine glasses and corkscrew.* In fact, it's a delightfully restored 1800's cottage that has become one of Greytown's most popular self-contained stopovers. You're a stone's throw away from everything Greytown has to offer. Better still, you're only 1.25 hours from Wellington Airport and ferry terminal. You'll be welcomed by Terry, the resident cat (who shouldn't be resident!). He was adopted by my English guests Helen and (you guessed it!) Terry earlier this year and has now made himself king of the cottage. You'll be pleased you made the choice!

Greytown - Wairarapa

YOUR HOSTS: Gavin and Raewyn Southey
Ph: (06) 304 9367

SOUTHEY MANOR
182 West Street
Greytown
Ph (06) 304 9367 Fax (06) 304 9789
Mobile 025-424 035

Features & Attractions

- Spacious, relaxed atmosphere
- Cafes, restaurants nearby
- Walk to village shops
- Only ten minutes to golf course and vineyard
- Swimming pool & barbecue

Bed & Breakfast

Double	$80-90
Single	$45-80
Child	

Bedrooms	Qty
Double	2
Twin	1
Single	

Bed Size	Qty
King	
Queen	2
Single	2

Bathrooms	Qty
Ensuite	1
Private	
Guest Share	1
Family Share	

Our home offers a spacious relaxed atmosphere. We enjoy guests' company, but respect their desire for privacy if they need to just relax.

We are situated within walking distance from Greytown's cafés, restaurants and village shops. Ten minutes drive to Martinborough's vineyard and golf course. Facilities include a queen bedroom with ensuite, twin bedroom and queen bedroom with shared bathroom, lounge andsatellite TV.

Outdoor areas with pool and barbecue. Tariff includes continental breakfast at your leisure.

We look forward to your company.

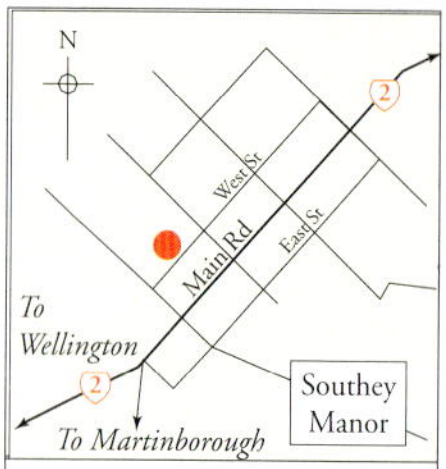

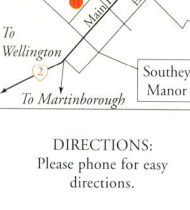

DIRECTIONS:
Please phone for easy directions.

YOUR HOSTS: **Marilla and Steve Davis**   Ph: (06) 304 8588   **Greytown - Wairarapa**

THE AMBERS

78 Kuratawhiti Street, Greytown, Wairarapa
Postal: PO Box 11723, Wellington
Ph (06) 304 8588. Fax (06) 304 8590
Mobile 025-994 394
e-mail: *ambershomestay@xtra.co.nz*

Features & Attractions

- *Glorious garden setting*
- *Close to wineries*
- *Beautiful breakfast*
- *Cafés and antique shops*
- *Quiet, peaceful surrounds*
- *Cosy open fire*

$	Double	$80-100
	Single	$65
	Child	$20

**Boutique Accommodation
Bed & Breakfast**

Bedrooms	Qty
Double	3
Twin	
Single	
Bed Size	**Qty**
King	1
Queen/Double	2
King/Single	
Bathrooms	**Qty**
Ensuite	1
Private	
Guest Share	1
Family Share	

DIRECTIONS: North through Greytown to old post office, turn left, past cricket grounds to 78 Kuratawhiti Street.

From the moment you come down **The Ambers'** treelined driveway you begin to experience the "olde worlde" charm of our gracious home. Built in the late 1800s by Mr Hawkins, one of Greytown's first carpenters, as his family home, the original totara façade and many interior features are still intact. We have two acres of garden with many beautiful old trees for you to wander and soak up the country atmosphere. Sit in our gazebo and watch the birds bathe in the fountain or enjoy refreshments on your verandah. For anyone wanting to relax, enjoy life and experience historic Greytown, you are minutes from cafés, restaurants, antique shops, ten minutes from Martinborough's vineyards and golf course. We offer guests luxurious bedrooms, one with ensuite bathroom and king bed, one with queen bed, one with double bed, guest bathroom, elegant lounge with open fire, spa pool and a delicious breakfast of muesli, fresh fruit and home-made muffins.

Gardens – Greytown, Wairarapa.

Upper Hutt - Wellington YOUR HOSTS: **Ruth and Graham** Ph: (04) 526 7785

WHISPERING PINES

207 Colletts Road, RD 1, Mangaroa, Upper Hutt
Ph (04) 526 7785, Fax (04) 526 7785
Mobile: 025 233 0999
e-mail: *whisperingpines@xtra.co.nz*

Tariff : N.Z. Dollars	
Double	$100
Single	$60
Child	neg.

Bedrooms	Qty
Double	1
Twin	1
Single	1
Bed Size	**Qty**
Super King	
Queen/Double	1
King/Single	2
Single	1
Bathrooms	**Qty**
Ensuite	1
Private	
Guest Share	1
Family Share	

Farmstay Bed & Breakfast

Features & Attractions

- *Spacious and comfortable*
- *Ideal stopover (ferry/airport)*
- *Dinner by arrangement*
- *Beautiful Mangaroa Valley*
- *A country welcome*
- *Enchanting views*
- *Peaceful location*
- *67 acres of farmland*

A country welcome awaits you at **Whispering Pines**, where the air is fresh and clean.

Our spacious Swiss Chalet style home has a Douglas Fir theme, and is set at the end of Colletts Road on 67 acres of elevated farmland. A quiet location, with enchanting views, overlooking the north end of the Mangaroa Valley. We breed pedigree Hereford cattle, and also keep coloured sheep, goats, poultry, bees, two collie dogs and one cat. It is an ideal out of town stopover, when you travel to or from the Wellington Ferry, or just want to get away for a change.

Our travels have taken us to many countries, and now we are semi retired and particularly enjoy meeting people from around the world. The farm, garden, and handcrafts along with our local Church keep us active. Further to Bed & Breakfast, perhaps you may wish to join us for a three course evening meal, which usually consists of produce from our farm, garden or orchard. Please contact us for reservations at earliest convenience.

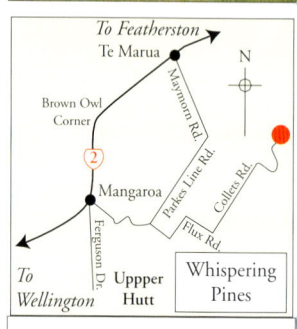

DIRECTIONS:
Please phone for bookings and easy directions. We are only 6km from State Highway 2.

YOUR HOSTS: Jenny and Randall Shaw   Free Ph: 0800 369 311   **Pauatahanui - Wellington**

BRAEBYRE

Flightys Road, Pauatahanui, Wellington
Postal: Flightys Road, RD 1, Porirua
Ph (04) 235 9311, Fax (04) 235 9345
e-mail: *braebyre@paradise.net.nz*

Tariff : N.Z. Dollars	
Double	$100-160
Single	$90-150
Child	half price

Bedrooms	Qty
Double	4
Twin	1
Single	

Bed Size	Qty
Super King	1
King	1
Queen	2
Single	2

Bathrooms	Qty
Ensuite	3
Private	
Guest Share	1
Family Share	

Countrystay Bed & Breakfast

Features & Attractions

- 2 studio suites
- Large landscaped gardens
- Close to Picton Ferry
- Dinner by arrangement
- Mohair goats and jerseys
- Golf courses nearby
- **Hostlink** member
- Accommodation for disabled

DIRECTIONS:
Blue Bed & Breakfast sign on State Highway 58. 2km east of Pauatahanui.

Are you looking for something special and restful away from city noise yet easily accessible on major highways? Stay close but not in the city, at **Braebyre**, one of Wellington's fine country homes, nestled in a beautiful rural environment on a small mohair goat farm with four acres of landscaped gardens. You will love the peace and tranquillity and the opportunity to experience seasonal activities with a tour of the garden and the goats.

Jenny and Randall (Rotarian) have been hosting for many years and enjoy the experience.

Two new spacious studio suites in the garden are self-contained with wheelchair access. The private guest wing in the house includes a lounge, table tennis and an indoor spa pool.

Evening dinner featuring homegrown produce is available on request. Home baking and preserves are a speciality.

We are a vital link in the active HOSTLINK network of quality homestays throughout New Zealand and are happy to assist with forward bookings.

Lower Hutt - Wellington YOUR HOST: Sue Perry   Ph: (04) 586 6466

BLACK FIR LODGE

236 Stratton Street, Normandale
Lower Hutt, Wellington
Ph (04) 586 6466, Mobile 025-397 614
e-mail: *i.perry@xtra.co.nz*

Features & Attractions

- *Peaceful rural surroundings*
- *Guest lounge with log fire*
- *Very friendly house pets*
- *Hearty breakfast*
- *20 min. from ferries*
- *Next to Regional Park*

DIRECTIONS: Take Maungaraki turnoff from SH 2. Turn left into Stratton St at big sign St Aidans on the Hill church.

Countrystay Bed & Breakfast

Double	$80
Single	$50
Child	

Bedrooms	Qty
Double	1
Twin	1
Single	

Bed Size	Qty
King	
Queen	1
Single	2

Bathrooms	Qty
Ensuite	
Private	
Guest Share	1
Family Share	

Although only 20-30 minutes drive away, our modern home is a tranquil haven from the bustle of Wellington. On our 12-hectare property we have sheep and we share our home with two dogs (Woodstock and Lucy) and Splotch the cat. Our home is ideal for quiet relaxation. You are welcome to curl up in an armchair with a good book. We have a variety of jigsaws and board games to enjoy. The guest bathroom has a separate bath and shower, and for serious unwinding what could be better than a luxurious soak in the bath.

The neighbouring Belmont Regional Park is popular for walking, mountain biking and horse-riding. We are handy to the many cafés, museums (including the must-see Te Papa), and other attractions of Wellington. Our daily lives tend to revolve around our dogs, but we also love to travel. Other interests include natural history, family history and practising our basic French, German and Korean.

Fair day in Jackson Street, Petone.

Photo. Ross de Rouffignac

YOUR HOSTS: Jennifer and Brian Timmings   Ph: (04) 479 5325   **Ngaio - Wellington**

HOMESTAY WELLINGTON

56 Fox Street, Ngaio, Wellington
Ph (04) 479 5325, Fax (04) 479 4325
e-mail: *jennifer.timmings@clear.net.nz*

Tariff : N.Z. Dollars	
Double	$95-115
Single	$65
Child	neg.

Bedrooms	Qty
Double	2
Twin	1
Single	1
Bed Size	**Qty**
Super King	
King	
Queen/Double	2
Single	3
Bathrooms	**Qty**
Ensuite	3
Private	1
Guest Share	
Family Share	

Homestay
Self-contained Accommodation

Features & Attractions

- *Family home atmosphere*
- *Safe, quiet surroundings*
- *Off-street parking*
- *Extensive views*
- *2 min. walk to local train station*
- *Ferry 5min., city 10min. by car*
- *Booking assistance - tours/ferry*
- *Music salon*

Welcome to Wellington! Capital City of New Zealand, spectacular scenery, beautiful harbour, dramatic skies, the seat of government, home of "Te Papa" National Museum, Westpac Sports Stadium, theatres, art galleries, churches, exciting restaurants and cafés, botanic gardens – it's all happening in Wellington and we love it! Share your Wellington experience with us and enjoy personalised hospitality. We have an unconventional open-plan family home in the suburb of Ngaio. Guests have their own area with french doors opening onto a deck and private garden. Tea/coffee facilities in room. Two single rooms adjacent to ensuite room allow a family to be together yet separate. The two fully furnished apartments are separate from the house, giving guests their own space and independence. Each unit has one double bedroom, bath, shower, laundry, equipped kitchen, couch in lounge converts to additional double bed, cable TV, phone, linen, all newly appointed. Our interests are people, music, arts, outdoors. Jennifer is a pianist and Brian formerly an accountant. Breakfast is continental. Evening meals optional, $20 pp. Discounts offered for longer stays. Disabled persons may enquire.

DIRECTIONS: From ferry take north exit, left at first traffic lights – Ngaio Gorge Rd., at roundabout take Ottawa Rd. fork, at shops turn left Awarua St. – Fox St. is second on right. Use driveway at No. 56.

121

Khandallah - Wellington

YOUR HOSTS: Judy and Bernie Robinson Ph: (04) 479 1776

SHALIMARES

9 Shalimar Crescent, Khandallah, Wellington
Ph (04) 479 1776, Fax (04) 479 1786
Mobile 021-895 996
e-mail: *sales@shalimares*
http://www.shalimares.co.nz

Features & Attractions

- Stunning sea & city views
- Ferry terminal 5min.
- 5 min. to Westpac Stadium
- 5 km to city
- Spacious accom.
- Office available

Double	$225-280
Single	
Child	

Bed & Breakfast Luxury Accommodation

Bedrooms	Qty
Double	2
Twin	1
Single	
Bed Size	**Qty**
King	1
Queen	1
Single	2
Bathrooms	**Qty**
Ensuite	1
Private	1
Guest Share	
Family Share	

Judy and Bernie would like to welcome you to Shalimares in the exclusive Wellington suburb of Khandallah. Five kilometres to the "Beehive", 5 minutes to the Inter Island Terminal, Westpac Trust Stadium and 20 minutes to the airport. Shalimares offers spectacular panoramic and city views from all rooms with spacious living and entertaining areas, all centrally heated. Our luxury guest wing has two spacious bed rooms with balconies and private lounge with Sky TV. Jerningham Suite has a queen bed, dressing room, bidet, spa bath and shower. Halswell Room has a private bath room. Bathrobes, electric blankets, phones, TV and extra jack points for modem connections in each room. Toiletries and hairdryers are supplied. Self service tea and coffee. Laundry and same day dry-cleaning service. Taxis can be arranged for pick-up from the airport or ferry terminal. An office is available with comprehensive facilities with privacy and confidentiality assured. Our interests include golf, horse racing and watching sports on TV.

Hataitai - Wellington

YOUR HOSTS: Dennis and Cathryn Riley Ph: (04) 386 2718

TOP O' T'ILL

2 Waitoa Road, Hataitai, Wellington
Ph (04) 386 2718, Fax (04) 386 2719
Mobile 025-495 410
e-mail: *top.o.hill@xtra.co.nz*

Features & Attractions

- Friendly and helpful hosts
- Attractive warm rooms
- Popular suburb near city
- Continental/cooked breakfast
- Excellent local restaurants
- Self-contained, serviced studio

Double	$85-120
Single	$55-110
Child	neg.

Homestay / Bed & Breakfast Self-contained

Bedrooms	Qty
Double	2
Twin	1
Single	1
Bed Size	**Qty**
King	
Queen	2
Single	3
Bathrooms	**Qty**
Ensuite	2
Private	1
Guest Share	1
Family Share	

Hataitai ('breath of the ocean') is situated in the eastern suburbs of Wellington, midway between Airport and City. A homely atmosphere is provided for guests in our comfortable 1919 two storey home, which has been in our family over 60 years. From the bedrooms there are views of Evans Bay, Hataitai Village and Mount Victoria. The lovely new studio (Áit Siocháin - Peaceful Place), has a fully appointed kitchenette ensuite, cable TV, phone line, private entrance and patio. We enjoy the beauty of our vibrant harbour city, including its cultural life and range of superb restaurants. Distance to the CBD, airport, ferry, Te Papa National Museum and sports venues, is 5-10 minutes by bus or car. We have travelled widely overseas and in New Zealand, and share interests in music, the arts, historic places and meeting people. We will be glad to help you make the most of your visit to Wellington. Our home is smokefree inside and not suitable for young children.

DIRECTIONS: Please phone, write or fax.

YOUR HOSTS: Raema and Rex Collins   Ph: (04) 934 6985   **Hataitai - Wellington**

MATAI HOUSE
41 Matai Road, Hataitai, Wellington
Ph (04) 934 6985. Fax (04) 934 6987
Mobile 025-240 4477
e-mail: *matai@paradise.net.nz*
http://www.travelwise.co.nz

Tariff : N.Z. Dollars	
Double	$150
Single	$150
Child	

Bedrooms	Qty
Double	2
Twin	
Single	

Bed Size	Qty
Super King	
King	2
Queen	
Single	

Bathrooms	Qty
Ensuite	2
Private	
Guest Share	
Family Share	

**Superior Bed & Breakfast
Beautiful Water Views**

Features & Attractions

- *Quiet residential area*
- *Extensive sea views*
- *City 3 km, airport 4 km*
- *Suites adjoin guest lounge*
- *Delicious full breakfast*
- *Espresso coffee*
- *27 channel cable TV*
- *NZ Travel Booking Service*

Matai House takes its name from its surroundings. Matai, translated from Maori, means "gaze out to sea".
Built in 1913, this fine two storey villa is conveniently located in the eastern suburb of Hataitai, between the airport and city. A quiet residential area with great sea views and a small garden of New Zealand native plants. City bus is just a 300 m walk. Off-street car park available.

The guest suites are refurbished in harmony with the era of the home and have folding doors onto decking overlooking the garden and sea views and access a lounge with private entrance. Each room is tastefully decorated, heavenly king-size beds, with a thick pillow-top mattress, crisp linen, goose down covers and plump pillows. Ensuites feature hair dryer, toiletries, bathrobes and heated towel rail. Tea and coffee making facilities, fridge and ironing facilities. Fresh flowers.

Breakfast includes espresso coffee, homemade muesli, fruit and cooked options at a time to suit. Enjoy an open fire on winter evenings.

Guests are most welcome to join their hosts or retain their privacy.

DIRECTIONS:
On State Highway1 follow airport signs until exiting Mt. Victoria tunnel, drive ahead into Hataitai, left and then right into Waitoa Rd. Drive up Waitoa Rd. and 2nd left into Matai Rd. From airport turn right at lights into Evans Bay Pde, 2nd left into Rata Rd., left and left again into Matai Rd.

Seatoun - Wellington

YOUR HOSTS: **Margo and Len Frost** Ph: (04) 388 6829

SEAVIEW HOMESTAY
44 Fortification Road,
Seatoun Heights, Wellington
Ph/Fax (04) 388 6829, Mobile 025-242 9827
e-mail: *seaview@paradise.net.nz*

Features & Attractions
- *Stunning sea views*
- *Delicious breakfasts*
- *Beautiful garden*
- *Track down to Karaka Bay*
- *Leafy peaceful surroundings*
- *Romantic rooms*

Double	$90
Single	$65
Child	

Boutique Accommodation Bed & Breakfast

Bedrooms	Qty
Double	2
Twin	
Single	

Bed Size	Qty
King	
Queen	2
Single	

Bathrooms	Qty
Ensuite	1
Private	1
Guest Share	
Family Share	

DIRECTIONS: Please phone for easy diections.

Our home with off-street parking is situated in a beautiful garden above Scorching Bay, with views over the harbour and out to the harbour entrance. We are 7 minutes to the airport and 15 minutes to the city, yet in a romantic, peaceful setting.

Our aim is to make your stay with us as enjoyable and relaxing as possible. Whether you want privacy or to be more sociable, we'll respect your wishes.

Both rooms are beautiful. The self-contained room with own ensuite is very private; you can lie in bed and watch the boats go by and the ever changing play of light and colour on the harbour. The double room in the house with its own bathroom is bright and spacious, with a door to the deck and the same fabulous views. There is a television set in both rooms.

A delicious breakfast is served as light or as hearty as desired at a time to suit you. Track to the sea from the bottom of the garden.

.....you're never far from water!

YOUR HOST: Frances Drewell   Ph: (04) 388 6719   **Seatoun - Wellington**

FRANCESCA'S HOMESTAY
10 Monro Street, Seatoun, Wellington
Ph (04) 388 6719, Fax (04) 388 6719
Mobile 025-241 4089

Tariff : N.Z. Dollars	
Double	$80
Single	$50
Child	$25

Bedrooms	Qty
Double	1
Twin	1
Single	

Bed Size	Qty
Super King	
King	
Queen	1
Single	2

Bathrooms	Qty
Ensuite	
Private	
Guest Share	1
Family Share	

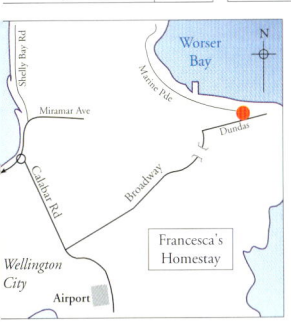

Homestay Bed & Breakfast

Features & Attractions

- *Quiet seaside village*
- *Personalised service*
- *Cooked breakfast included*
- *Home away from home*
- *Handy to Wellington Airport*
- *Excellent bus service*
- *Good restaurants nearby*
- *Laundry facilities available*

Handy to Wellington Airport (only 3 km away) our modern home is located in a quiet seaside village. A unique 'Fairy Shop' is a must to visit.

Enjoy a NZ-style dinner or dine at the local Village Inn or at one of the many nearby restaurants. A warm welcome awaits those who want a home away from home.

I have varied interests but mainly in sport, craft and travel. I play golf regularly at the Links close by.

Laundry facilities are available to those who have been travelling.

Seeing Wellington by bus:
From our home walk one minute to the bus stop, then travel around Wellington 'The City of a Thousand Views' on a **Day Tripper Ticket**. Discover New Zealand history by visiting 'Te Papa', Wellington's unique new museum.

DIRECTIONS:
Entering Wellington from the north or off the Interisland Ferry follow signs to the airport, then using the left lane follow the signs to Seatoun. Monro Street. is the 2nd on the left after the shops. From the airport take the 1st turn right then as above.

Seatoun - Wellington — YOUR HOSTS: **Stella and Colin Lovering** — Ph: (04) 388 4446

EDGEWATER

459 Karaka Bay Rd., Karaka Bay, Seatoun, Wellington
Ph (04) 388 4446, Fax (04) 388 4649
Mobile 021-613 357
e-mail: *edgewaterwellington@xtra.co.nz*
http://www.EDGEWATERWELLINGTON.co.nz

Tariff : N.Z. Dollars	
Double	$100-140
Single	$80-120
Child	

Bedrooms	Qty
Double	3
Twin	1
Single	

Bed Size	Qty
Super King	
King	1
Queen	2
Single	1

Bathrooms	Qty
Ensuite	2
Private	
Guest Share	1
Family Share	

Boutique Accommodation Bed & Breakfast

Features & Attractions

- *Gourmet dinners available*
- *Comprehensive wines selection*
- *Guest balcony*
- *Expansive seaside views*
- *Sea shore strolls*
- *Historic seaside village*
- *Fishing, swimming, snorkeling*
- *Te Papa Museum*

Seatoun is a historic seaside village where waterfront houses were originally built as convalescent and holiday homes. Located on a historic Maori site at the water's edge in Karaka Bay, this Mediterranean-style home was built to an award-winning design by David Lauder in 1976.

Featuring expansive ocean views, **Edge Water** offers four airy guest bedrooms with peaked cedar ceilings beneath separate roofs.

Stella serves fresh fruits, home-made breads, pancakes and egg dishes for breakfast in the dining room or alfresco in the inner courtyard or on the guest balcony in the morning sun. Dinner is also offered, specialising in premium quality meats, seafood and game. As ex-owner/chef of an award-winning Wellington restaurant, Stella's motto is "fresh is best".

DIRECTIONS:
From City, follow signs towards Airport and Seatoun. Turn left into Broadway Road. Travel through tunnel to Seatoun. Continue to waterfront and follow shoreline, till **Edgewater** on the left.

YOUR HOSTS: Marianne and Robin Hercock   Ph: (04) 383 5357   **Island Bay - Wellington**

SALTAIRE

318 The Esplanade, Island Bay, Wellington
Ph (04) 383 5357, Fax (04) 383 5396
Mobile 025- 247 7955
e-mail: saltaire@xtra.co.nz

Tariff : N.Z. Dollars	
Double	$110-120
Single	$70
Child	n/a

Bedrooms	Qty
Double	2
Twin	
Single	

Bed Size	Qty
Super King	
King	1
Double	1
Single	

Bathrooms	Qty
Ensuite	2
Private	
Guest Share	
Family Share	

**Boutique Accommodation
Bed & Breakfast**

Features & Attractions

- Magnificent sea views
- Easy access to city centre
- Walk to public transport
- Restaurants nearby
- Coastal walks
- Central heating

You will find "**Saltaire**" tucked into the rocky cliff right on the beach front at Island Bay. Magnificent sea views can be enjoyed from every room. There is always something to watch while enjoying your "Saltaire" breakfast. You may see surfcasters on the beach, divers and snorkelers in the bay, the inter island ferries sailing in and out of Wellington Harbour and/or the legendary Island Bay fishing boats returning with their early morning catch. Our bedrooms have a fresh but romantic decor. Both have ensuite and tea and coffee making facilities. There are popular restaurants nearby and the Wellington city centre or airport are easily accessible in less than 10 minutes. If you don't wish to drive in the city, you can take a short walk to the bus stop and purchase a $7 Day Tripper ticket. We are from a farming background, enjoy overseas travel and the diversity of cultural and sporting activities Wellington has to offer. We look forward to making you welcome in our home.

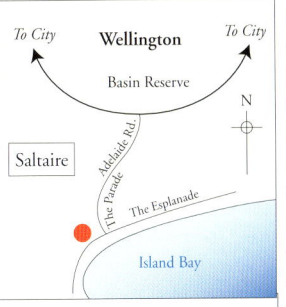

DIRECTIONS: From Basin Reserve travel down Adelaide Road through Island Bay to the sea. Turn right then along Esplanade ½ kilometre.

127

South Island

SOUTH ISLAND HOSTS

GOLDEN BAY – NELSON – MARLBOROUGH

- 132 — Twin Waters Lodge, *Collingwood*
- 133 — Oban, *Takaka*
- 133 — Glendale, *Takaka*
- 134 — Patons Rock Homestay, *Takaka*
- 135 — Doone Cottage, *Motueka Valley*
- 136 — Mahana Country Homestay, *Upper Moutere*
- 136 — Estuary Bed & Breakfast, *Mapua*
- 137 — Hartridge House, *Mapua*
- 138 — Kimeret Place, *Mapua*
- 138 — Chester Le House, *Richmond*
- 139 — Althorpe, *Richmond*
- 140 — Bay View Bed & Breakfast, *Richmond*
- 141 — Mapledurham, *Richmond*
- 142 — Almond Cottage, *Stoke*
- 143 — Arapiki, *Stoke*
- 143 — Tarata Homestay, *Stoke*
- 144 — Riversong, *Nelson*
- 145 — Roevyn Homestay, *Nelson*
- 145 — Atawhai Homestay, *Atawhai*
- 146 — Drumduan, *Atawhai*
- 147 — Stornoway Lodge, *Havelock South*
- 148 — House of Glenora, *Picton*
- 148 — Whatamonga Homestay, *Picton*
- 149 — Karaka Point Lodge, *Picton*
- 150 — Charmwood, *Blenheim*
- 150 — Rhododendron Lodge, *Blenheim*
- 151 — Tamar Vineyard, *Blenheim*

WEST COAST

- 152 — Beachfront Farmstay, *Karamea*
- 153 — Awapiriti, *Murchison*
- 154 — Havenlee Homestay, *Westport*
- 154 — River View Lodge, *Westport*
- 155 — The Rocks Homestay, *Punakaiki*
- 155 — Paroa Homestay, *Greymouth*
- 156 — Piners Homestay, *Greymouth*
- 157 — Craidenlie Lodge, *Hokitika*
- 158 — Rossendale, *Hokitika*
- 158 — Teichelmann's Bed & Breakfast, *Hokitika*
- 159 — Dahlia Cottage, *Ross*
- 159 — Carrickfergus, *Harihari*
- 160 — Wapiti Park Homestead, *Harihari*
- 161 — Matai Lodge, *Whataroa*
- 161 — Okuru Beach Bed & Breakfast, *Haast*

CANTERBURY – CHRISTCHURCH

- 162 — Albergo Hanmer, *Hanmer Springs*
- 163 — Ardara Lodge, *Kaikoura*
- 163 — Ballindalloch, *Culverden*
- 164 — Devondale House, *Belfast*
- 165 — Fairleigh Garden Guest House, *Harewood*
- 166 — Lavender Towers, *Avonhead*
- 166 — Greatstay, *Riccarton*
- 167 — Villa 121, *Merivale*
- 168 — Croydon House, *Central Christchurch*
- 169 — The Grange, *Central Christchurch*
- 169 — Hulverstone Lodge, *Avondale*
- 170 — Willow Lodge, *Richmond*
- 171 — Kleynbos & The Grand Cottage, *St. Martins*

SOUTH ISLAND HOSTS

PAGE

- 172 Locarno Gardens Apartment, *St. Martins*
- 172 Southshore Homestay, *Southshore*
- 173 Bloomfields Bed & Breakfast, *Spreydon*
- 174 Panorama Homestay, *Sumner*
- 175 Cavendish House, *Lyttelton*
- 176 Menteith Country Homestay, *Lincoln*
- 177 Blythcliffe, *Akaroa*
- 178 Meychelle Manor, *Kirwee*
- 179 Garden Vineyard Homestay, *West Melton*
- 180 Green Gables Deer Farm, *Methven*
- 181 Tyrone Deer Farm, *Methven*
- 182 The Brae Farmstay, *Geraldine*
- 183 Rivendell Lodge, *Fairlie*
- 184 Pleasant Point Bed & Breakfast, *Pleasant Point*
- 184 Cedarwood Lodge, *Timaru*
- 185 Ethridge Gardens, *Timaru*

SOUTHERN LAKES DISTRICT

- 186 Bellbird Cottage, *Lake Hawea*
- 187 Larchwood Lodge, *Wanaka*
- 188 Monterey Lodge, *Hawea Flat*
- 188 Hunt's Homestay, *Wanaka*
- 189 Aspiring Images Homestay, *Wanaka*
- 190 Lake Wanaka Home Hosting, *Wanaka*
- 191 Oakridge Lake Wanaka, *Wanaka*
- 192 Parklands Lodge, *Wanaka*
- 193 Squires Bed & Breakfast, *Wanaka*
- 194 Te Wanaka Lodge, *Wanaka*
- 195 Temasek House, *Wanaka*
- 196 Wanaka Springs Lodge, *Wanaka*
- 197 Villa Amo, *Cromwell*
- 197 Hiburn Farmstay, *Cromwell*
- 198 Quartz Reef Creek, *Cromwell*
- 199 Walnut Grove, *Cromwell*
- 200 Willowbrook, *Arrowtown*
- 201 Villa Sorgenfrei, *Queenstown*
- 202 The Inn at 670, *Queenstown*
- 203 Bridesdale, *Queenstown*
- 204 The Old' Ferry Hotel, *Queenstown*
- 205 Bush Creek Health Retreat, *Queenstown*
- 206 Campbells B & B, *Queenstown*
- 206 The Historic Stone House, *Queenstown*
- 207 Queenstown House, *Queenstown*
- 208 Larch Hill Homestay, *Queenstown*
- 209 Trelawn Place, *Queenstown*
- 210 Windsor Heights, *Queenstown*
- 211 Driftwood, *Queenstown*
- 212 Mataura Valley Station, *Garston*
- 213 Kowhai Lodge, *Mossburn*
- 214 Tapua, *Te Anau*
- 214 Cosy Kiwi Bed & Breakfast, *Te Anau*
- 215 Little Blue House, *Te Anau*
- 215 Shakespeare House, *Te Anau*
- 216 Perenuka Farm, *Te Anau*

SOUTHERN SOUTH ISLAND

- 217 Tokarahi Homestead, *Tokarahi*
- 218 Glen Haven Bed & Breakfast, *Oamaru*

SOUTH ISLAND HOSTS

PAGE

- 218 Glen Foulis, *Waianakarua*
- 219 Atanui, *Port Chalmers*
- 220 Alloway, *Dunedin*
- 221 Castlewood, *Dunedin*
- 222 Cill Chainnigh, *Dunedin*
- 223 Deacons Court, *Dunedin*
- 223 Heriot House B&B, *Dunedin*
- 224 Gowrie House, *Dunedin*
- 225 Hulmes Court, *Dunedin*
- 226 Pine Heights Retreat, *Dunedin*
- 227 The Station Master's Cottage, *Dunedin*
- 228 Stranalyth Gables, *Mosgiel-Dunedin*
- 229 Balcairn Farmstay, *Balclutha*
- 230 Argyll Farmstay, *Clydevale*
- 231 Blackhills Farmstay, *Waikaka*
- 231 McRae's Homestay, *Gore*
- 232 Smith's Farmstay, *Wyndham*
- 233 Southern Home Hospitality, *Invercargill*
- 233 93 Towack Homestay B & B, *Riverton*

THE CATLINS

- 234 Barrs Falls, *Owaka*
- 234 Kepplestone, *Owaka*
- 235 Gorge Stream Cottage, *Tahakopa*
- 236 Alsted Farmstay, *Tokanui*

STEWART ISLAND

- 236 Port of Call, *Leask Bay*

Lake Hayes – Central Otago

Collingwood

YOUR HOSTS: Laurel and Clemens

Ph: (03) 524 8014

TWIN WATERS LODGE

Totara Avenue, PO Box 33,
Collingwood
Ph/Fax (03) 524 8014, Mobile (025) 956 766
e-mail: *twinwaters@xtra.co.nz*

Tariff : N.Z. Dollars	
Double	$110-140
Single	$85-110
Child	neg.

Bedrooms	Qty
Double	3
Twin	1
Single	
Bed Size	**Qty**
Super King/Twin	1
King	
Queen/Double	2
Single	
Bathrooms	**Qty**
Ensuite	2
Private	
Guest Share	
Family Share	1

Boutique Accommodation Bed & Breakfast

Features & Attractions
- Bookings and pick-up point for Farewell Spit Tours
- 50 metres to Sand Beach
- Peaceful setting
- Abundant birdlife
- Comfortable beds
- Guest lounge w. woodburner
- Meals prepared by Chef

Nestled harmoniously beside a tidal estuary, **Twin Waters Lodge** features curved timber ceilings, floor to ceiling windows and multi level decks. The ensuite rooms open onto private decks, and the cosy guest lounge has pleasant views of the estuary and forested hills. **Twin Waters Lodg**e is a great base to explore the Golden Bay region. Wander along the wild West Coast beaches, take a tour of Farewell Spit, a bird sanctuary of world renown, visit Kahurangi and Abel Tasman National Parks, try your hand at gold panning, horse trekking or sea kayaking. Indulge your passion for walking, swimming, tennis or golf, or join Clemens and Laurel for a game of petanque. Visit local artists and find out what it is about Golden Bay that inspires them. Waking to the sound of tuis, breakfasting in the sun, or savouring a delicious dinner, there's sure to be a special moment to remember your stay. Laurel and Clemens have been in the hospitality industry for many years, and take pride in creating a relaxing atmosphere for you. They also have a passion for travelling and love meeting fellow travellers and sharing their experiences. "Chef's Dinner" by prior arrangement $35 pp. Light evening meals on short notice $20 pp.

DIRECTIONS: 9km north of Collingwood towards Farewell Spit.

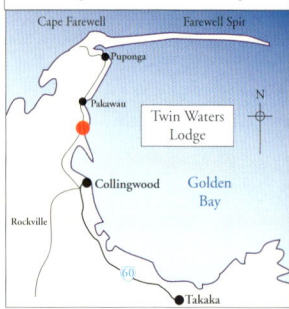

YOUR HOSTS: Bev and Don Gay   Ph: (03) 525 9904   **Takaka - Golden Bay**

OBAN

Charlett Point Road, Rangihaeata, RD 2, Takaka
Ph (03) 525 9904, Fax (03) 525 9910
e-mail: *oban@voyager.co.nz*

Features & Attractions

- Quality accommodation
- Centrally located
- Cafe style refreshments
- Your party are our only guests
- Restful coastal setting
- Local courtesy pick up

Boutique Accommodation Bed & Breakfast

Double	$80
Single	$55
Child	

We are centrally located – 10 minutes north of Takaka Township. You are welcomed with complimentary café style refreshments as soon as you arrive in the Bay. Oban was built in the 1920's. Our restored home features twin and double guest rooms with private facilities. There is a separate guest lounge. You may also share our family facilities.

Oban is adjacent to Charlett Point Beach. You can swim at high tide, meander along the beach or explore the rock pools at low tide. The walk around Rangihaeata Heads features "pancake" rock formations, fossils and wildlife.

Early retirement has allowed us to travel and enjoy our interests which include patch work and quilting, bridge, gardening, fishing and making country wines. We accept only one booking at a time. A full cooked breakfast is provided. You are welcome to share the evening meal which features local produce. The cost is $25 per person and includes complimentary country wines.

Bedrooms	Qty
Double	1
Twin	2
Single	
Bed Size	Qty
King	
Queen/Double	1
Single	4
Bathrooms	Qty
Ensuite	
Private	1
Guest Share	
Family Share	

YOUR HOSTS: Jean and Philip   Ph: (03) 525 9593   **Takaka - Golden Bay**

GLENDALE

Golden Bay Homestays, Dodson Road,
Takaka, Golden Bay
Postal: *RD 1, Takaka 7172*
Ph (03) 525 9593

Features & Attractions

- Warm hospitality
- Excellent cuisine
- Peaceful countryside
- Gateway to Farewell Spit
- Two National Parks nearby
- Beautiful beaches abound

Homestay Bed & Breakfast

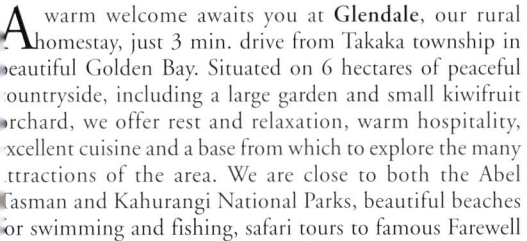

Double	$80
Single	$50
Child	half price

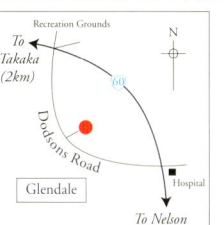

A warm welcome awaits you at **Glendale**, our rural homestay, just 3 min. drive from Takaka township in beautiful Golden Bay. Situated on 6 hectares of peaceful countryside, including a large garden and small kiwifruit orchard, we offer rest and relaxation, warm hospitality, excellent cuisine and a base from which to explore the many attractions of the area. We are close to both the Abel Tasman and Kahurangi National Parks, beautiful beaches for swimming and fishing, safari tours to famous Farewell Spit, tramping, horse trekking or farm visits. We provide tastefully furnished double or twin rooms with private facilities, including own lounge area and welcome family groups. By arrangement we can provide a delicious evening meal and cater for any dietary requirement. We are Kiwihosts and look forward to meeting you.

Bedrooms	Qty
Double	1
Twin	2
Single	1
Bed Size	Qty
King	
Queen	1
Single	5
Bathrooms	Qty
Ensuite	
Private	1
Guest Share	1
Family Share	

Takaka - Golden Bay YOUR HOST: Wout (Wally) Kalis   Ph: (03) 525 7230

PATONS ROCK SEAVIEW HOMESTAY

Patons Rock, RD 2,
Takaka, Golden Bay
Ph (03) 525 7230, Fax (03) 525 7231

Tariff : N.Z. Dollars	
Double	$70-75
Single	$30-35
Child	

Bedrooms	Qty
Double	1
Twin	2
Single	

Bed Size	Qty
Super King	
King	1
Queen	
Single	5/6

Bathrooms	Qty
Ensuite	
Private	
Guest Share	2
Family Share	

Homestay Bed & Breakfast & Self-contained Accommodation

Features & Attractions

- View over whole of Golden Bay
- Private lounge/kitchen/balcony
- Separate shower and bathroom
- Safe, clean beach 2min.
- Good log burner
- Very comfortable & cosy

Our separate upper floor gives a beautiful view over the Bay from Farewell Spit to Separation Point. We are only two minutes from a safe, clean, good walking beach. You will enjoy our big lounge with log burner and TV. Bathroom, toilet and shower are separate. A balcony on three sides gives ample room to sit and enjoy the views. Patons Rock area has about 100 houses and no shops.

In Takaka or Collingwood you find facilities like restaurants, pubs and shops , only 12km away. Golden Bay has plenty to offer with its variable scenery and good walkways. We can pick you up from the end of Tasman or Heaphy Track, at Browns Hut or in Takaka or drop you off at Collingwood for a Farewell Spit Safari. Canoe and windsurfer available.

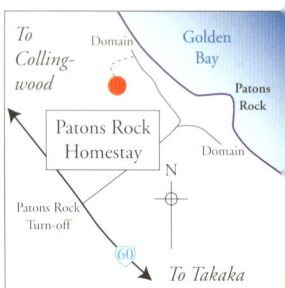

DIRECTIONS: From Takaka Post Shop drive 10km towards Collingwood, take Patons Rock turn-off. At end of Road take private track "Byders Terrace" We are last house on left.

Self-contained option:

Our downstairs self-contained flat comprises of an open-plan kitchen/ living area and has on bedroom with queen-size bed and one bedroom with 3 single beds. Divan in lounge. Tariffs pe night: $45 for double and $25 for single, extra person $10. Breakfast is available ($5 p.p.)

YOUR HOSTS: Glen and Stan Davenport Ph: (03) 526 8740 **Motueka-Nelson**

"Doone Cottage"

Motueka Valley, RD 1, Motueka, Nelson Region
Ph (03) 526 8740, Fax (03) 526 8740
e-mail: *doone-cottage@xtra.co.nz*

Tariff : N.Z. Dollars

	Double	$120-145
	Single	$80-95
	Child	

Bedrooms	Qty
Double	2
Twin	1
Single	

Bed Size	Qty
Super King	
King/Twin	2
Queen	1
Single	1

Bathrooms	Qty
Ensuite	3
Private	
Guest Share	
Family Share	

Country Homestay

Features & Attractions

- 100 year old homestead
- Dinner by arrangement
- Trout fishing
- Three National Parks
- Cottage gardens
- Weaving & wool craft studio
- Art, craft and wine trails
- Mountain scenery

DIRECTIONS: From Motueka: Turn off SH 60 at Clocktower (Caltex Service Station) onto Motueka Valley H'way. **Doone Cottage** 28km. From South: Turn off SH6 at Motupiko (Kohatu Hotel). **Doone Cottage** 26km

Homely hospitality, peace and tranquility, fishing, beautiful garden, native birds, house pets, sheep, chickens, ducks and donkeys, all abound at **Doone Cottage**, which we have enjoyed sharing with guests for many years. A lovely country home, comfortably furnished cottage style, set in a secluded 4 acre setting of native trees and flower gardens overlooking the Motueka Valley and the Mt Arthur range in Kahaurangi National Park. Guest rooms - 2 inhouse plus **Garden Chalet**, all full ensuite. Countrystyle meals, homemade breads, preserves, homegrown produce, free range eggs etc. Activities within 45 minutes include: access to 3 National Parks, (Abel Tasman, Kahaurangi, and Nelson Lakes); Beaches (kayaking, boat trips), Mountains (horse trekking, walking), Golf Courses. The Motueka River is at the gate with several other trout streams closeby, offering excellent brown trout fishing. (Licences & guiding available) This is one of NZ's main fruit producing regions where the sun shines over 2,400 hours annually.

Hosts will gladly assist with bookings for activities/ongoing accommodation. We are members of the **Hostlink Network**.

Motueka-Nelson

YOUR HOSTS: Lavona and Graeme Sands **Ph:** (03) 543 2626

Mahana Country Homestay

338 Old Coach Road, Upper Moutere
Ph (03) 543 2626, Fax (03) 543 2626
Mobile 025-483 903

Features & Attractions

- *Quiet, peaceful garden*
- *Wonderful views*
- *Warm hospitality*
- *Abel Tasman National Park*
- *Beaches and sea kayaking*
- *Crafts and wine trails*

Countrystay Bed & Breakfast

Double	$85
Single	$50
Child	half price

DIRECTIONS: On SH 60 to Motueka, 16km from Richmond turn Dominion Rd. 2km, turn right, 3rd house on right.

Bedrooms	Qty
Double	1
Twin	1
Single	1
Bed Size	**Qty**
King	
Queen/Double	2
King/Single	3
Bathrooms	**Qty**
Ensuite	
Private	1
Guest Share	1
Family Share	

A warm welcome awaits you at our comfortable home surrounded by lovely gardens and apple orchard. Enjoy our outdoors with the bird life and breathtaking view over Tasman Bay and Nelson in a quiet, relaxed atmosphere. Our spacious guest rooms are comfortable, heated and supplied with electric blankets. (Twin share includes private bathroom facilities.) We welcome you to share our family area. In the morning enjoy an appetizing continental or cooked breakfast including a selection of home-made jams and other delicious food in our sunny dining room. A delectable three-course traditional New Zealand dinner and wine shared with hosts is available by prior arrangement ($20pp). We are halfway between Richmond and Motueka – the gateway to the Abel Tasman National Park, Kaiteriteri and Golden Bay. A great place to stay, with everything you need close by, 10–30 minutes to beaches, golf course, pottery, wine trails and many other outdoor activities like sea kayaking. We look forward to meeting you soon.

Mapua-Nelson

YOUR HOST: Elenore Searle **Ph:** (03) 540 2458

Estuary Bed & Breakfast

6a Moreland Place, Mapua Village
Ph (03) 540 2458, Fax (03) 540 2458
e-mail: *estuarybnb@paradise.net.nz*
http://homepages.paradise.net.nz/estuarybnb

Features & Attractions

- *Centrally located*
- *Quiet waterfront site*
- *Beautiful beach walks*
- *Continent./cooked breakfast*
- *Wir sprechen deutsch*
- *Excellent restaurants nearby*

Beach walk

Homestay Bed & Breakfast

Double	$75-85
Single	$50
Child	half price

Take a walk on the beach before breakfast after a superbly quiet good night's sleep. Relax over a continental breakfast and take advantage of your host's 25 years of local knowledge to plan your day. Our attractive, comfortable home, overlooking the estuary with its interesting bird life is centrally located for all Abel Tasman Park, Kahurangi National Park, Nelson and Motueka River attractions. We would be pleased to make your bookings for these activities. Come back to an airy, spotless home right by the water. A 10-minute walk will take you to one of three character restaurants. Treat yourself to manuka-smoked fish while watching the sea birds and the sunset over the estuary. Quiet, comfortable and clean, with reasonable rates. Be assured of a warm welcome.

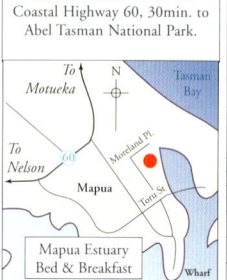

DIRECTIONS:
30min. west of Nelson via Coastal Highway 60, 30min. to Abel Tasman National Park.

Bedrooms	Qty
Double	1
Twin	1
Single	
Bed Size	**Qty**
King	
Queen	1
Single	2
Bathrooms	**Qty**
Ensuite	1
Private	1
Guest Share	
Family Share	

YOUR HOSTS: Sue and Dennis Brillard Ph: (03) 540 2079 **Mapua - Nelson**

HARTRIDGE

103 Aranui Road, Mapua, Nelson
Ph/Fax (03) 540 2079, Mobile 025-247 4854
e-mail: Hartridge@Mapua.gen.nz

Tariff : N.Z. Dollars

Double	$155
Single	$115
Child	N/A

Bedrooms	Qty
Double	2
Twin	
Single	

Bed Size	Qty
S.King or Twins	1
King	
Queen	1
Single	

Bathrooms	Qty
Ensuite	2
Private	
Guest Share	
Family Share	

Mapua Wharf

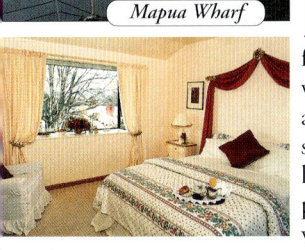

DIRECTIONS: Enter Aranui Road from SH 60 at Mapua Tavern. **Hartridge** is 400m on left.

Village Style Bed & Breakfast With a Coastal Flavour

Features & Attractions

- *Abel Tasman 40 min.*
- *Picton ferry 2 hours*
- *Nelson Airport 25 min.*
- *Walk to beach, cafés, wharf*
- *Nelson City 30 min.*
- *Near wineries & art*
- *Near golf & trout fishing*
- *Antiques and fine art works*

Blend the 1915 ambience and romance of **Hartridge**, the peace and quiet of its mature garden setting, with the courteous, friendly, unobtrusive hosting, and then add the fun of joining in with the many stimulating local experiences and activities. Here are all the ingredients for a truly memorable holiday, with the spirit restored. Listed with the Historic Places Trust, **Hartridge** is located in the delightful coastal village of Mapua. Relax in your private first floor guest accommodation, a later addition. Enjoy views over the countryside, and glimpse the sea from these sunny, spacious rooms. Complimentary port, sherry, fruit, home baking, tea and coffee. Indulge in your delicious gourmet breakfasts, which include sorbet, homemade granola, fresh fruit, and various cooked dishes using our own hens' eggs, plus choice of teas or specially blended local coffee. It is served using grandmother's silver and china, in the drawing room overlooking the rose garden, or on the sunny verandah amongst orchids and passionflower. A 3-course dinner is available, with candlelight, wine, music, open fire. $35.00 pp. Friendly dog, Jack, vintage Morgan, easy private parking, smokefree house.

Mapua - Nelson

YOUR HOSTS: Peter and Clare Jones Ph: (03) 540 2727

KIMERET PLACE

Bronte Road East, Nr. Mapua
R.D.1 Upper Moutere, Nelson
Ph (03) 540 2727. Fax (03) 540 2727
e-mail: *kimeretplace@xtra.co.nz*

Features & Attractions

- Stunning views
- Tranquil setting
- Jacuzzi/spa pool
- Heated swimming pool
- Beaches, fishing & golf
- Craft & wine trails

Coastal Bed & Breakfast

Double	$100-140
Single	$70-95
Child	

Set in 4 acres, **Kimeret Place** enjoys tranquillity, abundant bird-life and stunning views of the Waimea Inlet and Richmond Mountains. Our heated swimming pool and spa as well as numerous local wineries and fine restaurants are the perfect antidote for stress. For the more energetic, kayaking/tramping the Abel Tasman National Park is only a short drive away. The two bedrooms in the main house are tastefully furnished in country style, each with direct access to the verandah and gardens. A further 2 bedrooms in the cottage with ensuite bathrooms, shared lounge and kitchen/diner, as well as a separate garden, equipped for outdoor cooking and dining. With complimentary tea & coffee, TV, toiletries, hairdryers, laundry facilities and optional evening meals, we think we've thought of everything to make your stay enjoyable.

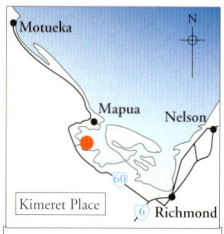

DIRECTIONS:
From Richmond on SH 60 turn right after 12km into Bronte Rd. East. We are 750m on right.
From Mapua: - 4km.

Bedrooms	Qty
Double	4
Twin	
Single	

Bed Size	Qty
King	
Queen/Double	4
Single	

Bathrooms	Qty
Ensuite	2
Private	
Guest Share	1
Family Share	

Richmond - Nelson

YOUR HOSTS: Noelene and Mike Ph: (03) 544 7279

CHESTER LE HOUSE

39 Washbourn Drive, Richmond, Nelson
Ph (03) 544 7279, Fax (03) 544 7279
e-mail: *n.smith@xtra.co.nz*

Features & Attractions

- Rural and sea views
- National parks and beaches
- Award winning restaurants
- Private, peaceful setting
- Wineries, arts & crafts nearby
- Courtesy car/covered parking

Double	$80-90
Single	$50
Child	

Bed & Breakfast & Self-contained Suite

Bedrooms	Qty
Double	1
Twin	2
Single	

Bed Size	Qty
King	
Queen	1
Single	4

Bathrooms	Qty
Ensuite	1
Private	
Guest Share	1
Family Share	1

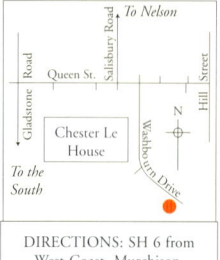

DIRECTIONS: SH 6 from West Coast, Murchison, Motueka or Nelson, Picton and Blenheim. Then please follow area map.

If you are looking for something special and restful away from city noise yet conveniently located to Nelson City and Abel Tasman National Park, then **Chester Le House** beckons. Our lovely modern home has rural and sea views with safe walkways for evening strolls just a few steps away. Evening dinner featuring fine New Zealand wines or a typical Kiwi barbecue is available on request. Our outdoor living area is relaxing and welcoming. Our guest rooms are spacious, combining charm with modern facilities, warmth and comfort. Locked garaging, laundry facilities and a dryer are available for your convenience. We love to share our home with both business and leisure travellers. A courtesy car for pick-ups is available. Why not spoil yourself, extend your stay to relax and explore our beautiful province.

YOUR HOSTS: Jenny and Bob Worley   Ph: (03) 544 8117   **Richmond - Nelson**

ALTHORPE

13 Dorset Street, Richmond, Nelson
Ph (03) 544 8117, Fax (03) 544 8117
e-mail: *rworley@voyager.co.nz*

Tariff : N.Z. Dollars	
Double	$110-120
Single	$90-100
Child	

Bedrooms	Qty
Double	1
Twin	1
Single	

Bed Size	Qty
Super King	
King	
Queen/Double	1
King/Single	2

Bathrooms	Qty
Ensuite	1
Private	1
Guest Share	
Family Share	

**Boutique Accommodation
Bed & Breakfast**

Features & Attractions

- *Special breakfast selection*
- *Large private gardens*
- *Swimming pool and spa*
- *Award winning restaurants*
- *Warm hospitality*
- *National parks & beaches*
- *Wineries, arts and crafts*
- *Trout fishing & kayaking*

Call us out of this world if you will. But with two intimate guest rooms **Althorpe** provides warm old fashioned fuss and care that defines the art of hospitality.

An ensuite serves our double bedroom while a private bathroom is provided for the twin/king suite. Guests are afforded the quiet luxury of two relaxing lounge rooms while outside spacious gardens with their own swimming pool and spa invite a casual stroll or dip in summer.

Among the services that have our guests reluctant to leave us, you'll find a delightful, tasty gourmet breakfast. By arrangement guests may also enjoy an evening meal complimented by a local wine ($40.00 per person).

All this comes within the walls and grounds that carry the echoes of bygone colonial years. At the end of the day's journey you deserve nothing but a little pampering, personal attention and all the comforts of home. Bob, Jenny and Tackles, our cat, look forward to making your stay a special highlight of your holiday.

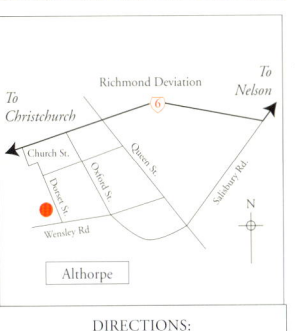

DIRECTIONS:
Please phone for easy directions

Richmond - Nelson

YOUR HOSTS: Janice and Ray O'Loughlin   Ph: (03) 544 6541

BAY VIEW BED & BREAKFAST

Bay View, 37 Kihilla Road, Richmond
Ph/Fax (03) 544 6541, Mobile 025-623 0252
e-mail: *bayview@ts.co.nz*

Tariff : N.Z. Dollars		
	Double	$80-100
	Single	$65
	Child	

Bedrooms	Qty
Double	3
Twin	
Single	

Bed Size	Qty
Super King	1
King	
Queen	2
Single	

Bathrooms	Qty
Ensuite	1
Private	1
Guest Share	1
Family Share	

Bed & Breakfast & Self-contained Suite

Features & Attractions

- *Spectacular views*
- *Quiet, peaceful setting*
- *Wine and craft trails*
- *Tasty, tempting breakfasts*
- *Award-winning restaurants nearby*
- *Close to great outdoor activities*

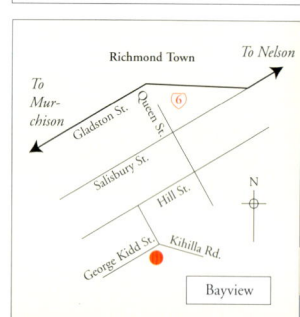

Bay View is a modern, spacious home, built on the hills above Richmond, with spectacular views of Tasman Bay and mountain ranges.

We offer rooms that are quiet, private and immaculately furnished with your complete comfort in mind. The large guest bathroom has shower and spa bath for two. To ensure your complete privacy we offer 'no share' accommodation if requested. The lounge opens onto a sheltered deck where you can relax, enjoy a drink or sit and chat. The self-contained suite with off-street parking, private entrance, kitchen, laundry/bathroom, lounge area and queen bed offers privacy and all home comforts.

We have two miniature schnauzer dogs, a variety of birds in a large aviary, tend our colourful garden and enjoy meeting people from New Zealand and overseas.

By car, **Bay View** is 15 min. from Nelson and 2 min. from Richmond. National parks, golden beaches, vineyards and many crafts are close by.

Be assured of warm, friendly hospitality and a happy stay in our smoke-free home.

YOUR HOSTS: Deborah and Giles Grigg   Ph: (03) 544 4210   **Richmond - Nelson**

MAPLEDURHAM

8 Edward Street, Richmond
Ph (03) 544 4210, Fax (03) 544 4210
Mobile 025-226 2908
e-mail: *mapledurham@ts.co.nz*

Tariff : N.Z. Dollars	
Double	$185-215
Single	$145-180
Child	

Bedrooms	Qty
Double	2
Twin	1
Single	
Bed Size	**Qty**
Super King	
King	
Queen	3
Single	1
Bathrooms	**Qty**
Ensuite	2
Private	1
Guest Share	
Family Share	

Boutique Accommodation and Bed & Breakfast

Features & Attractions

- Warm hospitality
- Central location
- Peaceful setting
- Gourmet breakfasts
- National Parks and beaches
- Arts, crafts and glassblowing
- Award winning restaurants
- Wineries and superb seafoods

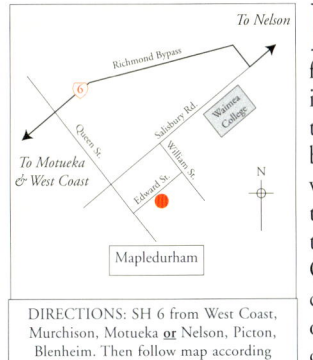

DIRECTIONS: SH 6 from West Coast, Murchison, Motueka **or** Nelson, Picton, Blenheim. Then follow map according to your direction.

In its peaceful setting, midway between the city and the wonders of Nelson Province, **Mapledurham** provides the perfect base from which to explore. It is a charming and elegant old home set in half an acre of tree-lined gardens and has a welcoming presence that enchants guests from the moment they arrive. Each guest bedroom has a style and character of its own; all are furnished with a greeting of fresh fruit and flowers and posture-sprung beds that are soft enough to offer the very best night's sleep, and for the morning, a tea-tray-with-everything plus home-made cookies. Once settled in, it's time for a welcoming drink, either in the comfortably furnished lounge with its varied art works and piano, or on one of the three verandahs. **Breakfast** is a real treat; eye-catching, healthy and satisfying, emphasising fresh, home-grown, home-made and gourmet. Deborah and Giles, being seasoned travellers with extensive local knowledge, will willingly help plan your Nelson itinerary. Those who wish simply to relax will find sanctuary in the vine-covered pergola with the scent garden nearby, or in winter a cosy log fire beckons in the lounge. Whatever has brought you to Nelson, your stay at **Mapledurham** will remain one of your treasured memories.

Stoke - Nelson

YOUR HOSTS: Tom and Janet Jones Ph: (03) 547 9486

ALMOND COTTAGE
3/60 Songer Street, Stoke, Nelson
Ph/Fax (03) 547 9486, Mobile 025-233 0996
e-mail: *almond.cottage@paradise.net.nz*
http://www.travelwise.co.nz

Features & Attractions
- *Breakfast in garden setting*
- *300 metres to sea walks*
- *10 minutes to City centre*
- *Agents for Abel Tasman Enterprises*
- *Olde English pub/restaurant nearby*
- *Warm, friendly cottage home*

Double	$80
Single	$55
Child	

Bedrooms	Qty
Double	1
Twin	1
Single	

Bed Size	Qty
King	
Queen	1
Single	2

Bathrooms	Qty
Ensuite	
Private	
Guest Share	1
Family Share	

Homestay Bed & Breakfast

Welcome to Nelson, New Zealand's sunshine province with sea, lakes, mountains, rivers and Abel Tasman Park, with one of New Zealand's most popular coastal walks. We are 1hr from "Rainbow Skifields", alpine St. Arnaud and the Nelson Lakes Park. There is an abundance of interesting places such as restaurants and local wineries in this beautiful fruit growing area of Tasman Bay. Nelson Airport is only 5 min away and we provide a complimentary airport pick-up. **Almond Cottage** is situated in the suburb of Stoke, only minutes from seaside walks and charming old English-style pub/restaurant "The Honest Lawyer". Our cottage, in a quiet, secluded situation, offers warm hospitality in a pleasant garden setting. Janet loves to serve your breakfast on our garden patio. It includes home-made bread, yoghurt and hot croissants or alternatively a cooked breakfast. We look forward to sharing our cottage home with you.

Sea Kayaking, Abel Tasman National Park.

Photo: Ian Trafford

YOUR HOSTS: **Kay and Geoff Gudsell**   Ph: (03) 547 3741

Stoke - Nelson

ARAPIKI
21 Arapiki Road, Stoke, Nelson
Ph (03) 547 3741. Fax (03) 547 3742
Mobile (025) 517131
e-mail: *arapiki@tasman.net*
http://www.ts.co.nz/brochures/arapiki

Features & Attractions

- Centrally located in Nelson area
- Fully self-contained units
- Continental breakfast option $5 pp
- Attractive garden setting
- Private deck or balcony
- Off-street parking

Self-contained Homestay Units in Attractive Garden Setting

Double	$65-$75	
Single	$55-$60	
Child		

Enjoy a relaxing holiday in the midst of your trip. The two self-contained smokefree units in our large home offer you comfort and privacy and are also very suitable for longer stays. These quality units in an attractive garden setting are centrally located in the Nelson area which has NZ's highest sunshine hours. Unit 1, which is larger, is in a pleasant and private garden setting. A ranchslider opens out to a deck with outdoor furniture for your use. It contains an Electric Stove, Microwave, TV, Auto Washing Machine and Phone.

Unit 2 has a balcony setting with seating to enjoy sea and mountain views. It contains a TV, Microwave and Phone.

At present our reasonable prices offer excellent value for money for the 'home away from home' accommodation provided.

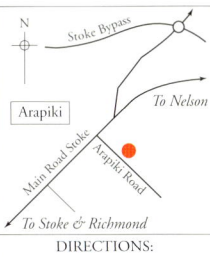

DIRECTIONS:
From the Stoke Shopping Centre Arapiki Rd is on the right approx. 1km north along the Main Rd Stoke. It is approx.6 km from Central Nelson.

Bedrooms	Qty
Double	2
Twin	
Single	
Bed Size	**Qty**
King	
Queen/Double	2
Single	1
Bathrooms	**Qty**
Ensuite	2
Private	
Guest Share	
Family Share	

YOUR HOSTS: **Mercia and John**   Free Ph: 0800-107 308

Stoke - Nelson

TARATA HOMESTAY
5 Tarata Street, Stoke, Nelson
Ph (03) 547 3426, Fax (03) 547 3640
e-mail: *hosts@taratahomestay.co.nz*
www.taratahomestay.co.nz

Features & Attractions

- Off-street parking
- Guest lounge
- Close to Isel Park
- Private facilities
- Very clean and quiet
- Generous breakfasts

Double	$75-80
Single	$57-60
Child	$20

Homestay Bed & Breakfast

Bedrooms	Qty
Double	1
Twin	1
Single	
Bed Size	**Qty**
King	
Queen	1
Single	2
Bathrooms	**Qty**
Ensuite	
Private	1
Guest Share	
Family Share	

Nelson is one of the most popular recreation areas of New Zealand! Many Kiwis come here to enjoy fine weather, warm seas, golden sands, delightful picnic spots, the Abel Tasman National Park, a wide range of craft activities and award winning wineries. In fact many of our guests wish they had allowed more time to stay with us! **Tarata Homestay** is located in Stoke in a quiet secluded street. There is ample off-street parking and guests have their own private entrance to the house which is surrounded by gardens and mature trees. We take only one group of guests at a time so that they have exclusive use of the private bathroom and a comfortable guest lounge with TV, video and complimentary tea and coffee. A comprehensive selection of local information is available to suit a wide variety of activities and interests. In the morning enjoy our sumptuous continental breakfast enhanced by the aroma of freshly ground coffee.

DIRECTIONS:
From Main Rd. Stoke turn into Maitland Ave. Take 3rd turn right then next left. Our sign is out front.

Nelson

YOUR HOSTS: Debbie Knapp and Mike Murphy Ph: (03) 546 7297

RIVERSONG

369 Hardy Street, Nelson
Ph (03) 546 7297, Fax (03) 546 7297
e-mail: *riversong@xtra.co.nz*

Tariff : N.Z. Dollars	
Double	$95
Single	$70
Child	n/a

Bedrooms	Qty
Double	2
Twin	
Single	1
Bed Size	**Qty**
Super King	
King	
Queen	2
Single	1
Bathrooms	**Qty**
Ensuite	
Private	
Guest Share	1
Family Share	

Bed & Breakfast

Features & Attractions

- *Park-like setting*
- *Lovely riverside views*
- *Delicious breakfasts*
- *5 min. walk to town*
- *Complimentary port/chocolate*
- *Exclusive upstairs guest area*
- *Guest bicycles and helmets*
- *Rainbow Ski-Field 1½ hours*

DIRECTIONS: Hardy St. crosses Nelson's main street, Trafalgar St., one block below the cathedral. **Riversong** is three blocks east – the last house on the left, beside the river.

Riversong is a charming, historic two-storey home beside Nelson's Maitai River, close to town yet peaceful and quiet. The house was built in the 1890's and has been beautifully restored, featuring New Zealand native rimu timber, stained glass windows and the open spaciousness of that era. There are lovely bush and river trails within easy walking distance, as well as Nelson's fine shops, cafés and galleries. We offer two queen and one single bedroom with a maximum of four guests. All rooms are warm and sunny with stylish, comfortable furnishings. One queen and the single room both have french doors opening out onto a private verandah overlooking the river. The other queen bedroom is more secluded with views out over the tree tops. The cozy guest sitting room has a large sun-deck and is fully equipped with tv, fridge, tea/coffee facilities. Breakfast is just as you like it, using organic local produce as available. Deb (born in San Francisco) and Mike (NZ) welcome you to the wonderful Nelson Region with its fabulous scenery, exciting vineyards, unique art and crafts, Abel Tasman National Park and great weather all year round.

YOUR HOSTS: Rose and Merv Hosie   Free Ph: 0800 763 896   **Nelson**

Roevyn Homestay

32 Atawhai Drive, Nelson
Ph (03) 548 8756, Fax (03) 548 8756
Mobile (025) 302 700
e-mail: *rhosie@xtra.co.nz*

Features & Attractions

- *Friendly helpful hosts*
- *Centrally located*
- *Close to all attractions*
- *Spacious accommodation*
- *Spa pool on deck*
- *Private guest access*

Homestay Bed & Breakfast

Double	$85-120	
Single	$75-90	
Child		

Our home is modern and spacious with a warm, friendly, relaxed atmosphere. We are only 2 minutes from the Central City, an excellent base for exploring the Nelson Region, with its arts and crafts, wineries, national parks and golden beaches. We love meeting people and making new friends and would welcome you to enjoy our home as your own. You can lounge around on our huge deck overlooking Nelson to the mountain ranges, have a relax in our **Spa** or be as independent as you wish. We will happily provide information and make arrangements as required. Our spacious ensuite room has private access, car port, TV, table, tea/coffee facilities. Laundry/fax/e-mail/business rates available. We look forward to enjoying your company in our patch of paradise.

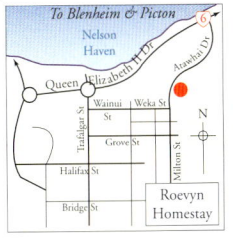

Bedrooms	Qty
Double	2
Twin	
Single	
Bed Size	**Qty**
King	
Queen/Double	2
Single	1
Bathrooms	**Qty**
Ensuite	1
Private	
Guest Share	
Family Share	1

YOUR HOSTS: Mike Cooper & Lennane Kent   Ph: (03) 545 1671   **Atawhai - Nelson**

Atawhai Homestay Mike's B&B

4 Seaton Street,
Atawhai, Nelson
Ph (03) 545 1671, Fax (03) 545 1671
e-mail: *cooperkent@actrix.gen.nz*

Features & Attractions

- *Safe, quiet, comfortable*
- *Close to sea*
- *Panoramic views*
- *En route to West Coast*
- *Gateway to National Parks*
- *1½ hours to ferry*

Homestay Bed & Breakfast

Double	$65	
Single	$40	
Child	neg.	

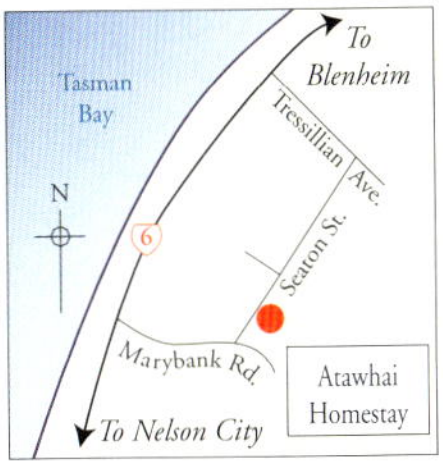

Only five minutes from Nelson City Centre we offer you quiet, comfortable, safe accommodation. Widely travelled ourselves, we know the importance of a hot shower, a clean, comfortable bed and helpful service.

Our guest accommodation is virtually self-contained on the ground floor of our two level home. The bedrooms each have ensuite facilities. The small guest lounge houses part of our large collection of books among which you are welcome to browse. Tea and coffee making facilities, a microwave oven and a washing machine are available for your use. Our interests include education, sea fishing and boating, veterans class running and canine obedience with our beautiful schnauzer dog. Breakfast is served in the conservatory, giving you superb views across Tasman Bay to the mountains beyond.

Bedrooms	Qty
Double	1
Twin	1
Single	
Bed Size	**Qty**
King	
Double	1
Single	2
Bathrooms	**Qty**
Ensuite	2
Private	
Guest Share	
Family Share	

Nelson

YOUR HOSTS: Helen and George Dixon Ph: (03) 545 0090

Drumduan
148 The Glen Road, RD 1, Nelson
Ph (03) 545 0090, Fax (03) 545 0090
Mobile 021-545 009

Features & Attractions
- *11 km from nelson City*
- *Safe, peaceful location*
- *Spa in garden setting*
- *19th century farm homestead*
- *Sea and mountain views*
- *Dinner by arrangement*

Bed & Breakfast Countrystay

Double	$90
Single	$30-40
Child	

Bedrooms	Qty
Double	1
Twin	
Single	2

Bed Size	Qty
King	
Queen/Double	1
Single	2

Bathrooms	Qty
Ensuite	1
Private	
Guest Share	
Family Share	1

Drive 10 minutes north of Nelson to the start of the spectacular Boulder Bank and enjoy the peaceful views of farmland, Tasman Bay and the mountains beyond – all at **Drumduan's** doorstep. Experienced travellers ourselves, we also appreciate the value of peaceful, quiet and warm surroundings. With our friendly dog Tip we invite you to share this wealth with us during your stay in Nelson. Helen has a keen interest in gardening and there is a spa pool under the trees. Observe farm life first hand, wander along the Boulder Bank or take the Cable Bay Walkway. While dinner is by prior arrangement, Nelson boasts many fine cafés and restaurants, with local seafood a speciality. We are also equipped and happy to provide information on other acitivities in the Nelson Region.

Magic beaches – endless and unspoiled.

YOUR HOSTS: Neville and Philippa McCallum   Ph: (03) 579 8020

Marlborough Sounds

"STORNOWAY LODGE"

Four Fathom Bay, Private Bag, Marlborough
Ph (03) 579 8020, Fax (03) 579 8021
Mobile 025-372 631
e-mail: n.p.mccallum@xtra.co.nz
stornoway.co.nz

Tariff : N.Z. Dollars	
Double	$118-129
Single	$85
Child	$65

Bedrooms	Qty
Double	2
Twin	1
Single	
Bed Size	**Qty**
Super King	
King	1
Double	1
Single	3
Bathrooms	**Qty**
Ensuite	
Private	1
Guest Share	
Family Share	1

Private Wilderness Retreat

Features & Attractions

- Quiet, idyllic, private.
- Fish, hunt, swim, walk, relax
- Pure native bush drinking water
- Water taxi $199 per group return
- Piano, pool table, farm deer
- Single party bookings only
- Walks - bush, bluffs, ridgetops
- Complimentary dinghy and fishing gear

Unique, idyllic touch of paradise, only 30 minutes from State Highway. Older style farm homestead set amongst large trees, native and exotic forest, 2 acres of lawns, native birds, wild animals, on waters edge and floating jetty.

Barbecue meals or formal dining with open fire and mounted trophy heads. Fish from jetty, snapper close by or the deep holes around the outer Marlborough Sounds in our fast vessel, with heated cabin and toilet.

Hunt deer, pigs, goats around our Lodge with your host of 20 years guiding experience and view hunting videos of New Zealand game. Twelve km of easy/medium walking roads, through exotic and native forests, high bluffs and breathtaking ridge tops at 600 m. Guided 4X4 transport available.

Water taxi includes cruising 60 km of beautiful coastline. Visit Marine Farm and return to Havelock after farmstay. Your enjoyment is our pleasure. Season discounts apply. We supply all meals (extra charge for lunch and evening meal).

DIRECTIONS:
Four Fathom Bay is situated in the Pelorous Sound, just 35 minutes boat travel from Havelock. Havelock is on the main highway between Blenheim and Nelson in the South Island.

Picton - Marlborough

YOUR HOST: Birgite Armstrong Ph: (03) 573 6966

HOUSE OF GLENORA
22 Broadway cnr Wellington Street, Picton,
Ph (03) 573 6966, Fax (03) 573 7735
Mobile 025-224 0594
e-mail: *glenora.house@clear.net.nz*
www.glenora.co.nz

Features & Attractions

- Art, craft & wine trails
- Weaving workshops
- Great outdoor activities
- Courtesy car
- Laundry facilities
- Off-street parking

Double	$85-120
Single	$55-85
Child	n/a

Boutique Accom. Bed & Breakfast

Bedrooms	Qty
Double	3
Twin	2
Single	1

Bed Size	Qty
Super King	1
King	1
Queen	1
Single	5

Bathrooms	Qty
Ensuite	2
Private	1
Guest Share	1

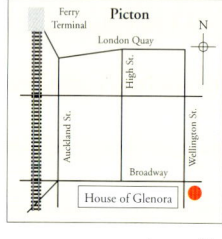

Welcome to **House of Glenora**, one of Marlborough Sounds' historical homes. Built in 1860 and surrounded by a sprawling garden, it is situated in the heart of Picton, yet very secluded and peaceful. Scandinavian creativity and NZ hospitality is blended into a colourful and vibrant home with a difference. As Birgite is a Masterweaver, **House of Glenora** incorporates the International Weaving School, studio and gallery. The bedrooms, living areas, large verandahs and patios are decorated with a stunning mixture of antiques and contemporary pieces. Enjoy magnificent views and the delightful garden. The Swedish style "smorgassbord" breakfast together with the warm and vivacious feeling of **House of Glenora** and the beauty of Marlborough Sounds will surely make your stay here a memorable experience. Winners of Marlborough Awards 1993 and 1997.

Picton-Marlborough

YOUR HOSTS: Alex and Colette Wilson Ph: (03) 573 7192

WHATAMONGA HOME STAY
425 Port Underwood Road, Picton
Ph (03) 473 7192, Fax (03) 573 7193
Mobile 025-430 834
e-mail: *info@whsl.co.nz*
www.whsl.co.nz

Features & Attractions

- Magnificent views
- Set in native bush
- Direct access to water
- Self-contained seclusion
- Brand new luxury fit out
- Dinner by arrangement

Luxury Self-Ccontained Accommodation

Units	$75-112
Tariff	$60-95
Child	

Your hosts at **Whatamonga Home Stay** are Alex and Colette Wilson. The homestay offers accommodation in 2 brand new free standing secluded units, or in 2 separate bedrooms with own bathroom and deck under the main house. The home stay has been specifically designed by one of Marlborough's leading designers to face north for best sun and to allow guests to enjoy the view and their seclusion, or enjoy the interaction with the sea offered by accommodation with direct access to the water. Evening meals are served in the main house as are cooked breakfasts. Continental breakfasts can be delivered to the units or downstairs bedrooms by prior arrangement. Bookings are essential, especially during the summer months of October to May.

Bedrooms	Qty
Units	2
Double	2
Single	

Bed Size	Qty
Super King	2
King	1
Single	2

Bathrooms	Qty
Ensuite	2
Private	2
Guest Share	
Family Share	

DIRECTIONS: From Picton take Waikawa Rd. From Waikawa shop take Port Underwood Rd. past Karaka Point. After 2 km **Whatamonga Homestay** sign is on left.

YOUR HOSTS: **Juliet and Brian Kirke**   Ph: (03) 573 7700   **Picton**

KARAKA POINT LODGE

Private Road,
312 Karaka Point, PO Box 586, Picton
Ph/Fax (03) 573 7700, Mobile (025) 614 3878
e-mail: *KarakaPointLodge@paradise.net.nz*

Tariff : N.Z. Dollars

Double	$250-300
Single	$175
Child	

Bedrooms	Qty
Double	2
Twin	
Single	
Bed Size	**Qty**
Super King	
King	1
Queen	1
Single	
Bathrooms	**Qty**
Ensuite	1
Private	1
Guest Share	
Family Share	

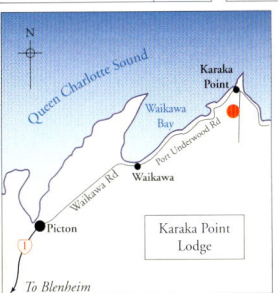

**Boutique Accommodation
Bed & Breakfast**

Features & Attractions

- Stunning views from all rooms
- Ferry terminal 15 minutes
- Spacious decks for relaxing
- Superior comfort beds
- Warm friendly hospitality
- Gourmet province
- Cooked or continental breakfast
- Dinner by arrangement ($55pp)

This is a rare gem in a gourmet paradise. Enjoy our genuine friendly hospitality at our exclusive home in the fabulous Marlborough Sounds. Every room has a stunning panoramic view. The bedrooms have french doors leading onto the spacious decks - a perfect place for breakfast or for you to unwind and recharge your batteries, before sampling the delights of the area. Comfortable beds and good wholesome food are assured. Our rooms are fitted out with all the necessities such as TVs, electric blankets, heaters, hair dryers and tea making facilities. Should you prefer total privacy, that is fine with us. Karaka Point is 8 km drive from the Ferry Terminal. **Karaka Point Lodge** faces north, getting maximum all day sunshine. In an elevated position, the views of the Sounds (sea flooded river valleys) are superb. All photos are taken from our house, a peaceful haven of tranquility. Restaurants, cafés and numerous attractions and activities are close by at Waikawa Bay and Picton. Blenheim, with all its marvellous wineries, is only 30 minutes away.

Blenheim

YOUR HOSTS: Linda and Peter Gibson   Ph: (03) 570 5409

CHARMWOOD
158 Murrays Road, RD 3, Blenheim
Ph (03) 570 5409, Fax (03) 570 5110
Mobile 025-847 403
e-mail: *Charmwood@xtra.co.nz*
www.charmwood.co.nz

Features & Attractions

- Wine trails
- Queen Charlotte Walk
- Mussel farm tours
- Garden visits
- Craft trails
- Fishing

Rural Retreat Bed & Breakfast

	Price
Double	$95-110
Single	$60
Child	

Bedrooms	Qty
Double	2
Twin	1
Single	
Bed Size	**Qty**
King	
Queen	2
Single	2
Bathrooms	**Qty**
Ensuite	1
Private	2
Guest Share	
Family Share	

Peter and Linda welcome you to **Charmwood** for a retreat in the countryside of Marlborough. Start your day with a country fare cooked breakfast while we would love to help you plan your itinerary, then stroll around our garden with Murdoch the cat, perhaps play some tennis, then cool off in the swimming pool. In the colder months curl up in front of the open fire or bubble away in the spa pool. Ask if our yacht 'Sunshine' is available - Peter may be able to take you sailing in the Queen Charlotte Sound. Linda's background is fashion and she enjoys handcrafts, gardening, music and sailing. Peter's background is construction. He is a keen yachtsman and also interested in olive growing and travel.

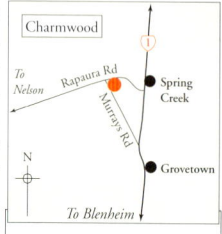

DIRECTIONS:
Turn off SH 1 at Spring Creek into Rapaura Rd. Murrays Road corner 700 m on left.

Blenheim

YOUR HOSTS: Audrey and Charlie Chambers   Ph: (03) 578 1145

RHODODENDRON LODGE
SH 1, St Andrews, RD 4,
Blenheim
Ph (03) 578 1145, Fax (03) 578 1145

Features & Attractions

- Large swimming pool
- Wine trails
- Purified water
- Fresh farm breakfast
- Local art and crafts
- Laundry available

Homestay Bed & Breakfast

	Price
Double	$70-90
Single	$50
Child	Half price

Bedrooms	Qty
Double	2
Twin	1
Single	
Bed Size	**Qty**
King	
Queen/Double	2
Single	2
Bathrooms	**Qty**
Ensuite	1
Private	1
Guest Share	
Family Share	

Welcome to our guests.

We have retired to an attractive small farm in Blenheim, where we provide quality accommodation in our spacious home. You will find excellent beds with woolrest underlays and electric blankets. Our Executive Suite has a "Bechstein" piano in it. If you like a full breakfast, we recommend delicious bacon, eggs and tomatoes produced on our farm. Outside a private courtyard with tree ferns and gardens surrounds a large swimming pool. Our house is set within extensive lawns and gardens with rhododendrons, roses and trees.

We are close to gourmet restaurants and have a selection of their menus. Marlborough has beautiful parks, wine trails, scenic sounds and walkways. Visitors travelling by train or bus will be met in Blenheim. We offer a courtesy phone call for your next homestay - "Happy Holidays!".

DIRECTIONS:
1.5 km south from town on SH 1. Large sign at gate. Twenty-five minutes from Picton Ferry.

YOUR HOSTS: **Clive and Yvonne Dasler** Free Ph: 0800-429 922

Rapaura - Blenheim

TAMAR VINEYARD
67 Rapaura Road, RD 3
Rapaura, Blenheim Region
Ph (03) 572 8408, Fax (03) 572 8405
e-mail: *tamar.vineyard@xtra.co.nz*
www.tamarvineyard.co.nz

Features & Attractions

- A romantic retreat
- Four poster bed
- Sumptuous breakfast
- Heart of the wine trail
- 15 minutes to Blenheim
- 30 minutes to Picton

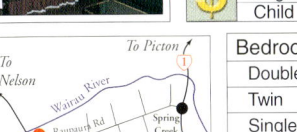

Self-contained Vineyard Cottage

Double	$120
Single	$100
Child	$30

Situated in the heart of the wine region, **Tamar** is one of Marlborough's oldest vineyards. Your newly-built cottage is a secluded, warm, romantic retreat with an ornately carved four-poster bed, featherdown duvet and classic leather couch. From the wide verandah you have breathtaking views through the vines to the Richmond Ranges. Our sumptuous three-course breakfasts feature homegrown produce and preserves. As we are an easy stroll from several wineries and restaurants you may choose to lunch or dine out, or cater for yourself in your full-equipped kitchenette. Clive and Yvonne enjoy showing you round the vineyard and we can help arrange winery tours or trips to the Marlborough Sounds (30 minutes drive) and Rainbow Skifield (1 hour's drive). We look forward to welcoming you for a memorable stay.

Bedrooms	Qty
Double	1
Twin	
Single	
Bed Size	**Qty**
King	
Queen	1
Single	1
Bathrooms	**Qty**
Ensuite	
Private	1
Guest Share	
Family Share	

New Zealand has an abundance of bird life.

Karamea - West Coast   YOUR HOSTS: **Dianne and Russell Anderson**   Ph: (03) 782 6762

BEACHFRONT FARMSTAY
Karamea, RD 1, Westport
Ph (03) 782 6762, Fax (03) 782 6762
Mobile 025-222 1755
e-mail: *farmstay@xtra.co.nz*
http://www.travelwise.co.nz

Tariff : N.Z. Dollars

Double	$100
Single	$65
Child	neg

Bedrooms	Qty
Double	2
Twin	
Single	1
Bed Size	**Qty**
Super King	
King	
Queen	2
Single	1
Bathrooms	**Qty**
Ensuite	1
Private	
Guest Share	
Family Share	2

Farmstay Bed & Breakfast

MasterCard   VISA

Features & Attractions

- 2 min. walk to beach
- Peaceful surroundings
- Wonderful views
- Native forest walks
- Close to famous **Heaphy Track**
- Generous cooked breakfast
- We offer horse trekking, hunting and fishing

Karamea Beachfront Farmstay is 2 minutes walk from a deserted sandy beach. Come as far north as you can on the West Coast and relax for a few days. The only noise you will hear is the sound of the sea breaking on the shore.
We have a dairy farm with 320 milking cows.
I enjoy cooking. Breakfasts are generous with fresh baked bread and pan-fried fish straight from the sea (if the tide is right). Dinners include farm-grown meat and vegetables and delicious desserts.

DIRECTIONS:
Karamea Beachfront Farmstay is 84 km north of Westport and 3 km north of Little Wanganui.

New Zeland wine is complimentary.
For the more adventurous we can offer horse trekking, hunting, fishing and forest walks. Long stay rates are available.
In Karamea you can see the spectacular Limestone Arch and Honeycomb Caves, Kahurangi National Park and wonderful scenery.
The famous **Heaphy Track** starts just north of Karamea.

152

YOUR HOSTS: Irene and David Free　　Ph: (03) 523 9466　　**Murchison**

Awapiriti
Highway 65, Murchison
Nelson Region
Ph (03) 523 9466, Fax (03) 523 9777
e-mail: *free@paradise.net.nz*

Tariff : N.Z. Dollars	
Double	$105
Single	$85
Child	n/a

Bedrooms	Qty
Double	2
Twin	1
Single	
Bed Size	**Qty**
Super King	
Queen	1
Double	1
Single	2
Bathrooms	**Qty**
Ensuite	2
Private	1
Guest Share	
Family Share	

Farmstay - Bed & Breakfast

Features & Attractions

- *Breathtaking scenery*
- *Unique setting*
- *Bush and farm walks*
- *River boundary*
- *Cottage gardens*
- *Glow worms*
- *Tame ducks*
- *Fishing*

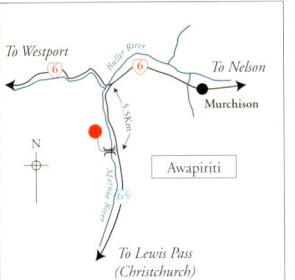

DIRECTIONS: From north: 5.5km past SH 65 turn-off, turn right over bridge. From south: 5km from Maruia Falls turn left over bridge. **Awapiriti** signposted.

Awapiriti is nestled in the beautiful Maruia Valley and occupies its own unique position accessed by a large bridge. Here we farm elk, deer, cattle, sheep and a friendly bison family along with a few other farm pets. The comfortable Homestead is complemented by extensive lawns, gardens and pond. We have a special interest in our native birds and enjoy sharing this with our visitors. Guests are welcome to take a casual bush or farm walk or perhaps just relax in the garden. The Maruia River, which bounds the farm, offers trout fishing and swimming. The guests' bedrooms are sunny and attractively decorated in colonial style with ensuites for your comfort. Dinner is by arrangement. We provide healthy country style meals that mostly consist of home-grown produce. Breakfast is full or continental with seasonal fresh fruit and home-made bread. **Awapiriti** is a haven for adults, unsuitable for children. Please phone or fax for a reservation.

Westport YOUR HOSTS: Jan and Ian Stevenson   Free Ph: (0800) 673 619

HAVENLEE HOMESTAY
76 Queen Street, Westport
Ph (03) 789 8543, Fax (03) 789 8502
Mobile 025-627 2702

Features & Attractions

- Great hospitality
- Lovely garden setting
- Generous breakfast
- Tranquil central location
- Nearby scenic attracions
- Two national parks nearby

Double	$80
Single	$50
Child	neg.

Rural Town Homestay

DIRECTIONS:
Along Palmerston St, right at Wakefield St, left at Queen St, 1st house on left.

Bedrooms	Qty
Double	2
Twin	1
Single	
Bed Size	Qty
King	
Queen/Double	2
Single	2
Bathrooms	Qty
Ensuite	
Private	
Guest Share	1
Family Share	

Peace in Paradise - this is **Havenlee**, the perfect spot for those seeking tranquil, central location. We are both born and bred West Coasters - hospitality is part of our heritage. We welcome and invite you to share our modern, spacious home set amongst native and exotic trees and shrubs just 300 metres from the town centre. Breathtaking scenery is in abundance in the northern West Coast. Westport is sited between the Kahurangi and Paparoa National Parks - home to the magnificent towering rain forests with rare bird and plant life. In close proximity is the Tauranga Bay seal colony, Punakaiki Pancake Rocks and the scenic Charming Creek Walkway. As our guests, you will enjoy a continental - plus breakfast, warm, comfortable beds, a well appointed bathroom with a large bath tub and separate shower room, full laundry facilities, restaurants within walking distance, lots of local knowledge in a friendly, relaxed smokefree environment. One cat residing.

Westport YOUR HOST: Noeline Biddulph   Free Ph: (0800) 184 656

RIVER VIEW LODGE
SH 6 Lower Buller Gorge,
PO Box 229, Westport
Ph/Fax (03) 789 6037, Mobile 025-249 1286
e-mail: rivervie@voyager.co.nz

Features & Attractions

- *Rooms with views*
- *Quiet & peaceful*
- *Close to Westport*
- *Full breakfast included*
- *One of NZ's "gardens to visit"*
- *Evening meal by arrangement*

Double	$130-145
Single	$97-106
Child	Half price

Boutique Accommodation Bed & Breakfast

Bedrooms	Qty
Double	3
Twin	1
Single	
Bed Size	Qty
King	
Queen/Double	3
Single	2
Bathrooms	Qty
Ensuite	4
Private	
Guest Share	
Family Share	

Sited above the Buller River. Rural accommodation was purpose-built in 1994 as a Bed and Breakfast. The rooms are spacious and open onto a large deck overlooking the garden. Facilities in the rooms include toiletries, hair dryers, heated towel rails, tea and coffee making facilities, TV, fresh flowers, clock radios. Wardrobe and seating area in each room.
Separate dining room lounge. Laundry available.
We are close to the seal colony and white water rafting, trout fishing, golf and underworld rafting.

YOUR HOSTS: Peg and Kevin Piper   Free Ph: 0800-272164   **Punakaiki-West Coast**

THE ROCKS HOMESTAY
Hartmount Place, PO Box 16, Punakaiki
Ph (03) 731 1141, Fax (03) 731 1142
Mobile 025-204 9833
e-mail: *therocks@minidata.co.nz*
www.minidata.co.nz/therocks/

Features & Attractions

- *Pancake Rocks, Blowholes*
- *Wilderness location*
- *Eco tours available*
- *Spectacular panoramas*
- *Quality hospitality*
- *Dinner by arrangement*

Double	$100-130
Single	$70-85
Child	$40-50

Homestay Bed & Breakfast

Bedrooms	Qty
Double	2
Twin	1
Single	
Bed Size	Qty
King	
Queen/Double	2
Single	2
Bathrooms	Qty
Ensuite	2
Private	1
Guest Share	
Family Share	

We welcome you to share the recently built **The Rocks Homestay** in its unique wilderness setting at Punakaiki (midway between Greymouth and Wesport) within view of the famous Blowholes and Pancake Rocks. Enjoy exclusive panoramas of the Tasman Sea coast, the limestone cliffs, rainforest of the Paparoa National Park, and magnificent sunsets. Heated towel rails, laundry service, hair dryers, e-mail and an extensive library of New Zealand books enhance your stay. Breakfast includes cereals, muesli, fresh yoghurt, fresh-baked muffins, toast and spreads. We provide home-cooked evening meals and wine by prior arrangement. Our associated Green Kiwi Nature and Heritage Tours can organise eco-tours of the rainforest and dramatic landscapes of the West Coast. Come share our interests in photography and the outdoors.

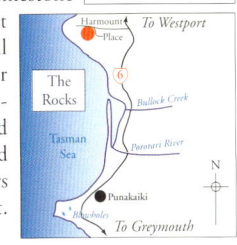

YOUR HOST: Pam Sutherland   Ph: (03) 762 6769   **West Coast**

PAROA HOMESTAY
345 Main South Road, Greymouth
Ph (03) 762 6769, Fax (03) 762 6765
Mobile 025-208 7293

Features & Attractions

- *Ensuite & private facilities*
- *Luxurious guest's lounge*
- *Special continental breakfast*
- *2 min. walk to beach*
- *Brilliant sunsets*
- *Bush walks, fishing*

Double	$95-99
Single	$75-79
Child	$30 u/12

Homestay Bed & Breakfast

Bedrooms	Qty
Double	1
Twin	
Single	
Bed Size	Qty
Super King	1
King	1
Single	
Bathrooms	Qty
Ensuite	1
Private	1
Guest Share	1
Family Share	

"Home away from Home" - Ensuite and private facilities. Super-king size beds, double bed in single room. Wonderful West Coast hospitality awaits you in spacious contemporary home overlooking Tasman Sea. Take a walk to beach (2 minutes) and experience beautiful sunsets from twin terraces. Awake to aroma of freshly baked bread, fresh fruit salad, muffins and yoghurt. Meeting travellers and sharing experiences and laughter around the cosy open fire. My hobbies are antiques, collecting china, baking and bush walking. Excellent eating establishments nearby. Being West Coast born my local knowledge and contacts are an asset in assisting with itinerary suggestions. Smoking outside please. Established shrubs and towering Pohutukawa trees attract birdlife (tuis, bellbirds and fantails).) TV, bathrobes, hairdryers, ironing boards and irons in bedrooms. Everyone is so welcome. (Courtesy pickup from Trans Alpine or bus)

Greymouth - West Coast

YOUR HOSTS: **Bev and Graham Piner**

Ph: (03) 768 5397

PINERS HOMESTAY

75 Main South Road, Karoro, Greymouth
Ph (03) 768 5397, Fax (03) 768 5396

Tariff : N.Z. Dollars	
Double	$80-85
Single	$55-60
Child	$20

Bedrooms	Qty
Double	1
Twin	1
Single	
Bed Size	**Qty**
Super King	
King/Single	
Queen	1
Single	1
Bathrooms	**Qty**
Ensuite	
Private	
Guest Share	1
Family Share	

Homestay Bed & Breakfast

Features & Attractions

- Wonderful West Coast hospitality
- Amazing mountain views
- Delicious food
- Off-street parking
- 5 minutes walk to seaside
- Very comfortable beds
- Special diets no problem
- Budget price rental cars arranged

How would you like a legendary West Coast experience? West Coasters are famous world wide for their hospitality. Bev and Graham, born and bred Coasters, offer you an experience that you will long remember. We offer luxury at an affordable price. Enjoy amazing mountain views and watch the sun go down over the sea. We are nestled in the bush and plenty of bird life abounds. Graham, a goldminer until recently, has a wealth of knowledge about goldmining and enjoys fishing. Bev enjoys reading the many books in their home and is a real "foodie", so cooking great meals is no problem. Interior decorating and antiques are other interests and of course, we both love meeting people. We have two very spoiled "children" (our cats) sharing our home. Guests are welcome to smoke out on our terrace. Special diets are no problem - vegetarian, diabetic etc. We have courtesy pick-up from buses or Tranz Alpine. There is an extra toilet and hand basin adjacent to bedrooms. We take pleasure in helping arrange tours and things to do while in our lovely district.

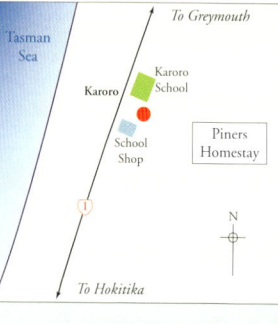

DIRECTIONS:
Approximately 5 minutes from Greymouth Centre heading south.

YOUR HOSTS: Bruce and Jenny Smith Free Ph: 0800-361 361

Hokitika

CRAIDENLIE LODGE

Blue Spur, PO Box 182, Hokitika
Ph (03) 755 5063, Fax (03) 755 8647
e-mail: *bruce@craidenlielodge.co.nz*
www.craidenlielodge.co.nz

Tariff : N.Z. Dollars	
Double	$140
Single	$100
Child	

Bedrooms	Qty
Double	6
Twin	2
Single	

Bed Size	Qty
Super King	
King	
Queen	6
Single	4

Bathrooms	Qty
Ensuite	3
Private	
Guest Share	2
Family Share	

**Bed & Breakfast
Tour included in Tariff**

Features & Attractions

- *Quiet private surroundings*
- *Sheep - deer - cattle - goat - dogs*
- *Rate includes minimum of one tour*
- *Lake Kaniere - Hokitika Gorge*
- *Farm setting*
- *Wonderful gardens*
- *Glow worm dell*
- *Gold mine*

DIRECTIONS:
From Main St. into Hokitika turn east into Hampden St. Proceed straight for approximately 2km until sign on right.

Our visitors book has some interesting entries: John and Jane Adamson from the UK - *"Thank you for the best B&B and guided tour we ever had"*. Roy and Mary Watts from the UK - *"Outstanding in all respects, great conducted tours"*.

Jenny and Bruce converted their 6500 square foot family home into a lodge in 1999. Located on a 40 acre section their home allows guests complete privacy. The native Kahikatea Trees that surround the lodge are unique. Rain forests, views of snow-capped mountains and Mt Cook make this property unique.

Bruce is a tennis nut, a born and bred 4th generation Coaster and entrepreneur. He will delight you with his local knowledge and loves to take guests on guided tours. Bruce has had involvement with gold mining since 1984, so taking guests to an operating gold mine is a must. What about trying one of Hokitika's fabulous restaurants and a tour to the glow worm dell? For those that stay longer, a picnic lunch at the Hokitika Gorge is great. How about taking our 4 wheel drive bike and trailer for up to 15 km south down the beach for a picnic lunch and fishing or just sightseeing. Would you like to try a microlight flight or a scenic flight around Mt Cook?

Hokitika - West Coast

YOUR HOSTS: Violet and Arthur Haworth Ph: (03) 755 6620

ROSSENDALE

234 Gibson Quay, Hokitika, Westland
Ph (03) 755 6620. Fax (03) 755 6620
e-mail: *rossendale.homestay@xtra.co.nz*

Features & Attractions

- Quiet location
- Off-street parking
- Good golfing nearby
- Warm hospitality
- 10 min. walk to town
- 15 minutes to beach

Homestay Bed & Breakfast

Double	$80
Single	$50
Child	

Warm hospitality awaits you at **Rossendale!**
We are a semi-retired couple with a grown up married family, who enjoy travelling and meeting people from both overseas and New Zealand. Our hobbies include gardening, fishing, bush walks and gold panning. We offer hospitality in a spacious home, situated 1 km from the centre of town on the banks of the Hokitika River and with panoramic views of the Southern Alps. We have two guest bedrooms, one queen with H&C and one twin. All our beds have electric blankets and woolrest underlays. Guests have their own bathroom. We offer continental or cooked breakfast, whichever you prefer. Dinner is by prior arrangement.
Hokitika is within easy reach of all "West Coast" main attractions, from the beaches to the Alps, together with pleasant bush walks and scenic drives. We can meet your plane or bus and we can assist you in your sightseeing arrangements. We would be happy to show you, free of charge, the fascinating Hokitika glow worm grotto.

Bedrooms	Qty
Double	1
Twin	1
Single	
Bed Size	**Qty**
King	
Queen	1
Single	2
Bathrooms	**Qty**
Ensuite	
Private	
Guest Share	1
Family Share	

Hokitika

YOUR HOSTS: Lorraine and Norm Free Ph: 0800-743 742

TEICHELMANNS BED AND BREAKFAST

20 Hamilton Street, PO Box 156, Hokitika
Ph (03) 755 8232, Fax (03) 755 8239
e-mail: *teichel@xtra.co.nz*
www.teichelmanns.co.nz

Features & Attractions

- Quiet, central location
- Walk to beach and shops
- Close to restaurants
- Warm friendly service
- Craft and heritage trails
- Walks, golf and fishing

Bed & Breakfast

Double	$100-130
Single	$70-100
Child	n/a

DIRECTIONS: Turn left at Town Clock, then first right.

New Zealand born hosts Lorraine and Norm pride themselves in offering friendly, informal hospitality with the comforts of a warm character home, and the opportunity to relax after an eventful day. Teichelmann's is a large home giving our guests the freedom to come and go as they please. Our comfortable guest lounge enables you to interact with others if desired. Teichelmann's has been recently refurbished including new beds, quality furnishings and modern bathroom facilities. Centrally heated in winter. Moments away by foot from our central, yet quiet location, is a comprehensive range of services, shopping, museum, excellent restaurants, beach and river. Hokitika is the craft Mecca of the West Coast. We will be pleased to assist you in getting the most from your stay, including local attractions, excellent day trips to National Parks including the Glaciers, Punakaiki Pancake Rocks, and the dramatic Arthurs Pass. We have a non-smoking environment and are suitable for children 10 years old and over.

Bedrooms	Qty
Double	5
Twin	2
Single	
Bed Size	**Qty**
King	3
Queen/Double	2
Single	4
Bathrooms	**Qty**
Ensuite	5
Private	
Guest Share	1
Family Share	

YOUR HOSTS: Dianne and Bill Johnston   Ph: (03) 755 4160   **Ross - West Coast**

Dahlia Cottage

47 Aylmer Street, Ross, West Coast
Ph (03) 755 4160, Fax (03) 755 4160
Mobile 025-29 65934

Features & Attractions

- Great stopover to Glacier
- Hearty cooked breakfast
- Delicious evening meal
- Private and peaceful cottage
- Glow worms, gold panning
- Fishing, hunting, bush walks

Countrystay Self-contained Accom.

Double	$70
Single	$40
Child	$20

Bedrooms	Qty
Double	1
Twin	1
Single	1
Bed Size	**Qty**
King	
Queen	1
Single	3
Bathrooms	**Qty**
Ensuite	
Private	
Guest Share	1
Family Share	

Dianne and Bill welcome you to **Dahlia Cottage**. We are a 20 minute drive south from Hokitika and 1½ hours scenic drive from the Glaciers, which makes our place an ideal stopover. In summer our home is surrounded by beautiful dahlias. Enjoy total privacy in the cosy, peaceful self-contained cottage next to our home with private parking. In the morning you have the choice of continental or full cooked breakfast. A delicious evening meal – served with "pavlova" can be arranged. We have a 16-year-old son, Danny. We enjoy our country music, farming, fishing, hunting, cooking, crafts and our dahlia garden. Country people at heart we enjoy our guests' company. We offer drives around the lakes and fishing-trips to our peaceful rivers. By arrangement you can enjoy, at your leisure, gold panning or bush walks and guided walks to the glow worms. We look forward to meeting you and will make your stay a memorable one. DIRECTIONS: **Dahlia Cottage** is situated on the main north-south highway, travelling from the north, we are the second house on your right.

YOUR HOSTS: Catherine and Lindsay   Ph: (03) 753 3124   **Harihari - South Westland**

Carrickfergus

Robertson Road, Harihari
Ph (03) 753 3124, Fax (03) 753 3124
e-mail: *carrickfergus@actrix.co.nz*

Features & Attractions

- Fishing and hunting
- Bushwalks / hot springs
- Suite with accessible facilities
- Mountain and rural views
- Peace and tranquility
- Dinner by arrangement

Lifestyle Farm Homestay & Self-contained Suites

Double	$100
Single	$65
Child	

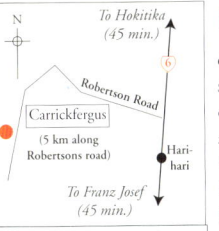

Bedrooms	Qty
Double	3
Twin	1
Single	
Bed Size	**Qty**
King	
Queen/Double	3
Single	2
Bathrooms	**Qty**
Ensuite	2
Private	1
Guest Share	
Family Share	

To Hokitika (45 min.)
Carrickfergus (5 km along Robertsons road)
To Franz Josef (45 min.)
Hari-hari

DIRECTIONS: Turn into Robertson Rd. Blue signpost on SH 6. 1.5km north of Harihari - follow map.

Our home is north facing, set in landscaped grounds, which adjoin a 32 acre sheep and Highland cattle farmlet with extensive mountain and rural views. Have breakfast at your self-contained suite which has private facilities or join us in our home for continental breakfast. We endeavor to make your stay comfortable. Stroll in our gardens or browse our West Coast book collection. Allow time to explore the Harihari Coastal Walkway, "a delight from start to finish, a two to three hour feast for the senses", or visit our natural hot springs and glowworms, or pit your skills against brown trout in local spring-fed streams. Leave time for a visit to the glaciers and the White Heron Colony. **Carrickfergus** – a comfortable midway rest between Christchurch/Wanaka or Nelson/Queenstown.

Harihari - South Westland   YOUR HOSTS: **Beverleigh and Grant Muir**   Free Ph: 0800 WAPITI

WAPITI PARK HOMESTEAD

State Highway 6, Hari Hari, South Westland
Ph/Fax (03) 753 3074
e-mail: *wapitipark@xtra.co.nz*
www.countrylodge.co.nz

Tariff : N.Z. Dollars	
Double	$125-195
Single	$100-150
Child	n/a

Bedrooms	Qty
Double	4
Twin	2
Single	

Bed Size	Qty
Super King	
King	2
Queen/Double	2
King/Single	3

Bathrooms	Qty
Ensuite	3
Private	2
Guest Share	
Family Share	

Country Lodge

Features & Attractions

- *Quiet, peaceful surroundings*
- *Superior comfort beds*
- *Dinner by arrangement*
- *Evening glow worm tour*
- *Large, spacious rooms & lounges*
- *Traditional hospitality*
- *Farm tour to feed Wapiti*
- *Guided hunting/fishing available*

Hosts Grant and Beverleigh invite you to discover the unique experience of staying at **Wapiti Park Homestead**, South Westland's premier hosted establishment for the discerning traveller. Enjoy a special combination of elegance and warm hospitality. Relax in complete comfort and affordable luxury. Set

DIRECTIONS: On the west side of SH 6 at southern approach to Hari Hari. Look for the sign.

in tranquil surroundings, the modern colonial-style lodge overlooks its own small farm which specialises in breeding Wapiti (Rocky Mountain Elk). The 6pm farm tour enables one to learn about and hand-feed the Wapiti. Enjoy the spacious living areas with two lounges and trophy/games room, large, airy bedrooms with either ensuite or private facilities and superior comfort beds. Bountiful meals feature traditional country fare. Wander in the gardens, relax on the deck or stroll to the ornamental lake and settle in peace with a good book and a cool drink – the choice is yours. Located on SH6 ,the Lodge is the ideal stopover between the Picton/Nelson/Christchurch and Wanaka/Queenstown areas. An increasing number of guests stay several nights, so they can explore this scenic wonderland of glaciers, national parks, rain forests and walkways at their leisure. Superb guided fishing for brown trout and salmon, and hunting for all New Zealand species is available. A warm welcome awaits you at **Wapiti Park**. Not suitable for young children. Advance booking recommended to avoid disappointment.

YOUR HOSTS: Glenice and Jim Purcell   Ph: (03) 753 4156   **Whataroa - South Westland**

Matai Lodge

Whataroa, South Westland, South Island
Ph (03) 753 4156, Fax (03) 753 4156
e-mail: *jpurcell@xtra.co.nz*

Features & Attractions

- Glacier flights
- Forest & glacier walks
- 3-course dinner $30 pp
- Fishing - salmon and trout
- **White heron** bird sanctuary
- Golf, kayaking, horse riding

Farmstay Bed & Breakfast

Double	$120
Single	$75
Child	half price

DIRECTIONS: Whataroa – 20min. north of Franz Josef Glacier. 3km west of SH 6: Blue B & B sign.

If you are coming to see the **Glaciers**, walk in the **World Heritage Park**, the coastal track at Okarito or visit the **White Heron Bird Sanctuary** in **Whataroa**, you are warmly welcomed to share with us our tranquil, rural retreat in our modern, spacious home on a 400 acre farm of sheep, cows and a farm dog. Upstairs is a suite of two bedrooms, conservatory and private bathroom and downstairs a king size ensuite. You are welcome to join us for a home-cooked dinner with NZ wine.
Our motto is: "A stranger is a friend we have yet to meet". Glenice speaks Japanese and has taught felting, spinning and weaving in Japan. We both play tennis and golf.

Bedrooms	Qty
Double	2
Twin	1
Single	
Bed Size	Qty
King	
Queen/Double	2
King/Single	2
Bathrooms	Qty
Ensuite	1
Private	1
Guest Share	
Family Share	

YOUR HOSTS: Marian and Derek Beynon   Ph: (03) 750 0719   **Okuru - Haast**

Okuru Beach

Okuru, Haast, South Westland
Ph (03) 750 0719, Fax (03) 750 0722
e-mail: *okurubeach@xtra.co.nz*
www.minidata.co.nz/maryglen/okuru.htm

Features & Attractions

- Walking distance to beach
- Fiordland Crested Penguins
- Enjoyable forest walks
- Good trout fishing
- Craft shop for guests
- Friendly and relaxed

Double	$65-70
Single	$35
Child	$20

DIRECTIONS: From SH 6 turn into Jackson's Bay Rd. Drive 14km south and right into Okuru - look for sign.

Homestay Bed & Breakfast

Bedrooms	Qty
Double	2
Twin	1
Single	
Bed Size	Qty
King	
Double	2
Single	2
Bathrooms	Qty
Ensuite	1
Private	
Guest Share	1
Family Share	

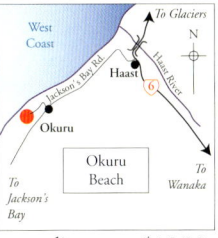

Okuru Beach gives you the opportunity to stay in a unique part of our country, where time moves slowly. Enjoy the coastal beaches with interesting driftwood and shells. On a walk in the rainforest a variety of native birds can be viewed. In the season, Fiordland Crested Penguins can be seen, within walking distance along a rocky beach, near Jackson's Bay, a 30-minute drive away. We and our friendly labrador dog enjoy sharing our comfortable home and local knowledge of the area. With prior notice we can serve dinner at $15.00 per person, BYO, vegetarian is available. Our interests are handcrafts, photography, fishing, shooting and tramping. We enjoy the chance to meet new people from New Zealand and overseas. Complimentary tea or coffee on arrival. Laundry facilities available (minimal charge).

Hanmer Springs

YOUR HOSTS: **Bascha and Beat Blattner** Free Ph: 0800 342 313

ALBERGO HANMER

88 Rippingale Road, Hanmer Springs,
P.O. Box 79, North Canterbury
Ph (03) 315 7428 Fax (03) 315 7428
e-mail: *albergohanmer@hotmail.com*
http://www.albergohanmer.com

Tariff : N.Z. Dollars	
Double	$110-160
Single	$95
Child	on request

Bedrooms	Qty
Double	3
Twin	
Single	
Bed Size	**Qty**
Super King/twin	2
King	1
Queen	
Single	
Bathrooms	**Qty**
Ensuite + Spa	2
Ensuite	1
Guest Share	
Family Share	

Fine Accommodation

Features & Attractions

- All day sun, majestic mountain views
- Underfloor heating, double glazing
- 2 min. drive to Thermal Pools/Centre
- Across from 18 hole golf course
- 3-course gourmet breakfast (10 choices)
- Dinners by prior arrangement
- Excellent service - attention to detail
- Large ensuites with private spa bath

'True hospitality without compromise!'

Albergo Hanmer is set on 2 acres of sweeping lawns and alpine grasses with surrounding fields of grazing cattle and sheep, yet only 10 min. walk to pools. The interior styling is modern European, creating a fresh, light and comfortable feel. The guest wing features spacious rooms with majestic mountain views from all windows. Unwind under a wonderful hot shower (high pressure) or in the spa bath, then relax in the private guest lounge. **Albergo's** unique 3-course gourmet breakfast menue, served in the sunny conservatory, presents you with 10 different choices to start your day - from scrumptious Eggs Benedict on fresh Hollandaise Sauce, to a full English Breakfast. All dishes served with homemade Swiss bread, fresh fruit platter or traditional Swiss Bircher Muesli. Dedicated hosts, Bascha and Beat Blattner, are a young couple (NZ and Swiss origin) with 14 years experience in the hospitality and tourism industry. Languages spoken: English, Swiss German and German, Italian and Spanish. Experience '**Cuisine du Marché**' dinners (3-6 courses from $40.00-$60.00) at **Albergo Hanmer,** served in private dining room: Prime fillet beef, racks of baby lamb, fresh ocean salmon, tempting Swiss desserts, prepared by Beat and beautifully food-styled by Bascha, using the freshest produce (Check for dinner availability).

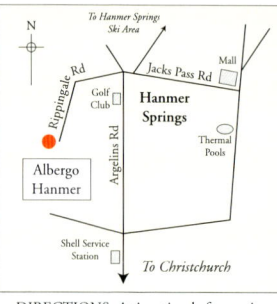

DIRECTIONS: At junction before main village, 300m past Shell Garage, take **Argelins Road**. (Centre Branch), go past Hanmer Golf Club, take first road on left **Rippingale Road**. (no exit). **Albergo Hanmer** is 900 m down at the very end of this country lane.

YOUR HOSTS: Ian and Alison Free Ph: 0800 226 164 **Kaikoura**

Ardara Lodge
233 Schoolhouse Road, Kaikoura
Ph (03) 319 5736. Fax (03) 319 5732
e-mail: *aemboyd@xtra.co.nz*
www.ardaralodge.com

Features & Attractions

- *Spectacular mountain views*
- *Whalewatch/Dolphins 5 min.*
- *Quiet & tranquil – lovely gardens*
- *Bush and coastal walks*
- *Walk to 'Donegal House', Irish restaurant and bar*

Double	$90-$110
Single	$60
Cottage	$110

Countrystay Self-contained Acc.

Bedrooms	Qty
Double	5
Twin	1
Single	
Bed Size	Qty
King	
Queen	5
Single	3
Bathrooms	Qty
Ensuite	3
Private	1
Guest Share	
Family Share	

We welcome you to our modern home and cottage on eleven acres of farmland, which Ian's Great Great Uncle bought in 1882 after emigrating from Ardara, Ireland in 1876. You can experience the magic of the beautiful Kaikoura Mountains from our viewing decks. Walk over to 'Donegal House', Ian's brother's Irish Restaurant, and have a meal of locally caught fish or crayfish (lobster) and a glass of Guinness. We are five minutes from Whalewatch, Dolphins, Seal Swimming, horse riding, bush and coastal walks.
Our timber cottage is popular with groups, families and honeymoon couples. All ensuite rooms have tv, fridge, hair dryer and coffee/tea making facilities.
We look forward to meeting you and sharing our local knowledge of Kaikoura with you.

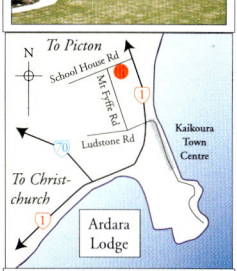

DIRECTIONS: Driving north from Kaikoura on SH.1 (Atheney Rd.), turn left into **Schoolhouse Rd.** drive 1.5 km to **Ardara Lodge**.

YOUR HOSTS: Diane and Dougal Norrie Ph: (03) 315 8220 **Culverden - Canterbury**

Ballindalloch
95 Long Plantation Road, Culverden, RD 2
North Canterbury
Ph/Fax (03) 315 8220, Mobile 025-373 184

Features & Attractions

- *Quiet, peaceful surroundings*
- *Complimentary farm tour*
- *Excellent trout/salmon fishing*
- *Magnificent mountain views*
- *Dinner by arrangement, $30pp*
- *30 min. to Hanmer Springs*

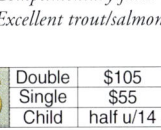

Double	$105
Single	$55
Child	half u/14

Farmstay Bed & Breakfast

Bedrooms	Qty
Double	1
Twin	1
Single	
Bed Size	Qty
King	
Queen	1
Single	2
Bathrooms	Qty
Ensuite	
Private	
Guest Share	1
Family Share	

Welcome to **Ballindalloch**, a 2000 acre fully irrigated dairy and sheep property, 3 kilometres south of Culverden. We milk 1100 cows in two floating rotary dairy sheds (parlours), a concept unique to New Zealand. We farm 3000 Corriedale sheep as well as a Corriedale stud. Our German daughter-in-law has just introduced emus to our farming scene. Our newly refurbished ranch-style home is set amongst lawns and garden with a swimming pool. Panoramic views of the hills and mountains surround us. The house is centrally heated in winter and has a log fire. Culverden is situated between two excellent fishing rivers. There is a golf course in Hanmer Springs and skifields at Mt Lyford. We are 100 kilometres from Christchurch, $1/2$ hour to Hanmer Springs thermal pools and $1 1/2$ hours to the Kaikoura Whale Watch. We have travelled extensively and appreciate relaxing in a homely atmosphere and extend this to all our guests. Complimentary farm tour. Please ring or fax for reservations. We are a non smoking household and have one cat.

Christchurch — YOUR HOSTS: **Sue and Stuart Fox** — Free Ph: 0800-167 735

DEVONDALE HOUSE

66 Johns Road, Belfast, Christchurch
Ph (03) 323 6616, Fax (03) 323 8723
Mobile 025-200 7236
e-mail: *sfox@xtra.co.nz*

Tariff : N.Z. Dollars	
Double	$145-165
Single	$110
Child	

Bedrooms	Qty
Double	2
Twin	
Single	

Bed Size	Qty
Super King	
King	1
Queen	1
King/Single	

Bathrooms	Qty
Ensuite	2
Private	
Guest Share	
Family Share	

Bed & Breakfast Boutique Accommodation

Features & Attractions

- Peace, tranquillity & views
- Personal, friendly hospitality
- Large garden with tennis
- Security gate
- The ultimate B & B experience
- Farm & wildlife reserve walk
- Pre dinner drinks with hosts
- Cavalier King Charles Spaniel

Devondale House is a lovely rural retreat, only minutes from the airport and city, yet quiet behind security gates with a relaxing walkway through adjacent farmland. This tranquil haven, set in expansive gardens, with tennis court and country walks, offers guests warm hospitality in elegant surroundings. An unbeatable location from which to explore the Canterbury area, from Hanmer to Kaikoura and the whale watch. Take an evening stroll through the adjacent farm to the beautiful Groynes, an area with fish-filled waterways and abundant bird life. Close by, enjoy an evening meal at the **Willowbank** restaurant, followed by a tour to see the **Kiwis**. The Antarctic Centre takes you on a snow and ice experience to the South Pole. At **Devondale House** you will be treated to a memorable stay with comfortable, gracious rooms, and warm friendly hospitality. Two especially large elegant bedrooms with ensuites and rural mountain views featuring writing desks, quality linen, fresh flowers, and tea & coffee making facilities. A traditional English breakfast is served in the sunny breakfast room or al fresco on the terrace.

DIRECTIONS: Johns Rd. is the main road between Airport and Main Rd. North, 15 min. from City Centre. Look for statue at gate.

YOUR HOSTS: **Valerie and Allan Carleton** Free Ph: 0800-611 411   **Christchurch**

FAIRLEIGH GARDEN GUEST HOUSE
411 Sawyers Arms Road, Harewood, Christchurch
Ph (03) 359 3538, Fax (03) 359 3548
Mobile 025-224 3746
e-mail: *fairleighgardenbb@xtra.co.nz*
http://www.fairleighgarden.co.nz

Tariff : N.Z. Dollars	
Double	$130-150
Single	$90-110
Child	$45

Bedrooms	Qty
Double/Triple	2
Twin	1
Single	

Bed Size	Qty
Super King	1
King/Single	2
Queen	2
Single	1

Bathrooms	Qty
Ensuite	3
Private	
Guest Share	
Family Share	

Bed & Breakfast Homestay

Features & Attractions

- *Airport 4 min./city 10 min.*
- *Dinner by arrangement*
- *Large cottage garden*
- *Laundry available*
- *Fresh home baking & great coffee*
- *Courtesy car to organic restaurant 'Untouched World'*
- *Ample onsite parking*

The tranquil environment of country living - so close to the airport and the city - is loved by all who visit. There is a wonderful atmosphere of complete relaxation at **Fairleigh Garden Guest House**.

Our country-style cedarwood guest house has native heart rimu throughout, quality furnishings and native timber antique dressers.

Relax in our comfortable lounge or conservatories and enjoy music, chess, reading or playing the piano. Great coffee and fresh homebaking are always there for you.

Delicious flexitime breakfasts are specially prepared for you, using the finest homegrown and local produce.

The honeymoon suite with double spa bath/shower, outdoor garden entrance, fresh flowers and luxurious sheepskin rugs give you that special feeling of being pampered.

We are **Hostlink Hosts** and we welcome you.

DIRECTIONS:
Turn off State Highway 1 at the Sawyers Arms Road/Casebrook Roundabout. You will find **Fairleigh Garden** on the right - 800 m along Sawyers Arms Rd.

Christchurch

YOUR HOSTS: Sandy and Chris McClelland Ph: (03) 358 4387

LAVENDER TOWERS
11 Kedleston Drive, Avonhead, Christchurch
Ph (03) 358 4387,
e-mail: *sandy@inet.net.nz*

Features & Attractions
- Friendly family home
- Beautiful cottage garden
- Continental breakfast
- Dinner by arrangement ($25 pp)
- Free pickup
- Close transport to city

Double	$95
Single	$65
Child	

Homestay Bed & Breakfast

Bedrooms	Qty
Double	1
Twin	
Single	1
Bed Size	**Qty**
King	
Queen/Double	1
Single	1
Bathrooms	**Qty**
Ensuite	
Private	
Guest Share	
Family Share	1

DIRECTIONS: Travelling south on Riccarton Rd. turn right into Yaldhurst Road. After 2 km turn right into Cutts Rd/Apsley Drive. Then 3rd. street on left.

Welcome to New Zealand's Garden City. We would like to make your holiday as comfortable and memorable as possible while staying with us. We are situated on the north-west side of the City in a quiet, safe suburb with off-street parking. 7 km to city - 2 km to airport. A short walking distance to shopping mall and two beautiful parks. Interests include boating, gardening, doll-making, sport and travel. We have travelled extensively throughout New Zealand and are happy to help you with your sightseeing and garden tours. Continental breakfast includes yoghurt, homemade muffins and jam. Relax in our barbecue area in summer and by the warm fire in winter. Guest lounge available for quiet times. Free tea, coffee and cookies. Laundry and e-mail facilities at small cost. Two of our three children are at home and we all look forward to meeting guests. We would not be a complete family without our pets - 2 samoyed dogs and one cat. A very warm **Kiwi** welcome awaits you.

Christchurch

YOUR HOSTS: Lesley and John Ruske Ph: (03) 343 1377

Greatstay Bed & Breakfast
43b Kilmarnock Street, Riccarton, Christchurch
Ph/Fax: (03) 343 1377, Mobile 025 - 622 0788
e-mail: *ruske.greatstay@xtra.co.nz*
www.greatstay.co.nz

Features & Attractions
- Courtesy pickup
- Off-street parking
- Quiet, restful environment
- Close large shopping complex
- Vicinity to Westpac Centre
- Close to city centre

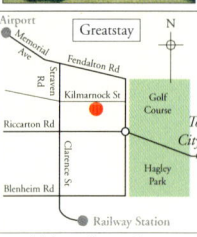

Bed & Breakfast Homestay

Double	$100
Single	$70
Child	

Our four-year-old Mediterranean home offers spacious and comfortable accommodation. We have sought to create a friendly atmosphere with the accent on comfort and luxury. "Home away from home." Our house is back from the road and is quiet and restful. Off-street parking. Breakfast can be as healthy or wicked as you wish. **Greatstay** is 25min. walk to the city centre through Hagley Park, Botanic Gardens, Art Centre and Museum. Beautiful walks, golf course and shopping complex only minutes away. We are close to the Public Hospital, University, Airport, Railway Station and restaurants. City bus at gate. We have courtesy pickup for your convenience. We are 50+ with three grown children and now grandchildren. We would be pleased to assist planning your holiday. "Come as a guest. Leave as a friend."

Bedrooms	Qty
Double	1
Twin	1
Single	
Bed Size	**Qty**
King	
Queen	1
Single	2
Bathrooms	**Qty**
Ensuite	1
Private	1
Guest Share	
Family Share	

YOUR HOSTS: **Trish Grace and Barry Greig**   Ph: (03) 355 8128

Christchurch

Villa 121

121 Winchester Street
Merivale, Christchurch
Ph (03) 355 8128, Fax (03) 355 8126

Tariff : N.Z. Dollars	
Double	$95
Single	$80
Child	$20

Bedrooms	Qty
Double	2
Twin	
Single	

Bed Size	Qty
Super King	
King	1
Queen	1
Single	

Bathrooms	Qty
Ensuite	
Private	
Guest Share	1
Family Share	1

DIRECTIONS:
From Papanui Road turn into Office Road. Winchester Street is the first street on your left. **Villa 121** is on the corner.

**Homestay
Bed & Breakfast**

Features & Attractions

- *Friendly hosts*
- *Centrally located*
- *Delicious breakfast*
- *Merivale Mall 2 min.*
- *Golf course nearby*
- *Dinner by arrangement*
- *Old-world garden*
- *Tennis court 3 min.*

We are well travelled, fun loving and really enjoy meeting people. We provide a relaxing atmosphere and look forward to making your stay a happy and memorable one.

Villa 121 is a tastefully and stylishly restored villa set in a lovely old-world garden - only 2 minutes walk to Merivale Mall - 4 minutes by car to the central city (or a 20 - 25 minute walk). Delicious continental and/or cooked breakfast is available at a time to suit you and complimentary tea & coffee and homebaking is available at any time.

Your hosts are Trish (school teacher), Barry (consultant surveyor) and Melanie (fine arts student). We are very keen sports people and love especially tennis, golf and skiing. We are happy to help you organise your sporting activities. Closest golf course and tennis courts are only 3 minutes away.

Relax in the sun on the wisteria and vine clad verandah in summer and enjoy the open fire in the winter.

Christchurch YOUR HOSTS: **Nita and Siegfried Herbst** Free Ph: 0800-276 936

CROYDON HOUSE BED & BREAKFAST HOTEL

63 Armagh Street, Christchurch
Ph (03) 366 5111, Fax (03) 377 6110
Free Ph (0800) 276 936
e-mail: *welcome@croydon.co.nz*
http://www.croydon.co.nz

Tariff : N.Z. Dollars	
Double	$95-120
Single	$70-90
Child	$10

Bedrooms	Qty
Double	6
Twin	4
Single	2
Bed Size	**Qty**
Super King	1
King	
Queen/Double	5
King/Single	12
Bathrooms	**Qty**
Ensuite	5
Private	1
Guest Share	3
Family Share	

Bed & Breakfast - Guest House

Features & Attractions

- *Charming accommodation*
- *Delightful garden*
- *On historic tram route*
- *Personal service*
- *Five minutes walk to City Centre*
- *Booking inf. & travel bureau*
- *Gateway to the South Island*
- *German, Japanese, English spoken*

Croydon House is a charming hotel offering fine accommodation in the heart of New Zealand's Garden City. Deluxe rooms are with private ensuite facilities, Standard rooms have share bathroom facilities. Garden Rooms in our tranquil adjoining cottage include an ensuite bathroom.

Start your day with our scrumptious breakfast buffet and indulge yourself in a deliciously cooked breakfast prepared especially for **you**.

Explore the city – perhaps a ride on the tram that passes by **Croydon House's** front door, or a punt on the nearby Avon River.

Major attractions for the more ambitious: great restaurants, conference venues, Art Centre and the famous Botanical Gardens are within easy walking distance.

For more information, visit our Home Page on the Internet.

YOUR HOSTS: **Paul and Marie Simpson**   Ph: (03) 366 2850   **Christchurch**

THE GRANGE GUEST HOUSE
56 Armagh Street, Christchurch
Ph (03) 366 2850, Fax (03) 374 2470
Mobile 021-366 608
e-mail: *reservations@thegrange.co.nz*
http://www.thegrange.co.nz

Features & Attractions

- City Centre 5 min. walk
- On tourist tram route
- Art Centre & gardens close
- Full cooked breakfast
- On-site car park
- Friendly service

Bed & Breakfast Guest House

Double	$98-115
Single	$85-95
Child	$15-25

The Grange Guesthouse – a gracious Victorian mansion – is situated in walking distance from most of Christchurch's favourite spots, including Cathedral Square, the Art's Centre, Art Gallery and Museum, also the Botanic Gardens, Hagley Park and Mona Vale. Built before the turn of the century, and now tastefully refurbished **The Grange Guesthouse** offers a high standard of accommodation. You can relax in the guest lounge or in the garden. During your stay you will be treated to superior accommodation, complimentary tea and coffee, multi-channel TV, off-street parking, laundry service. Sightseeing tours and onward travel can be arranged. Non-smoking is encouraged. Banks, shops, restaurants, night clubs and cafés are all in easy walking distance.
Paul and Marie Simpson are a mother and son team whose hospitality will ensure your stay is a pleasurable and pleasant one. All our tariffs include GST and full cooked breakfast. Please enquire about our winter rates, 1st June through 1st October.

Bedrooms	Qty
Double	6
Twin	2
Single	3
Bed Size	**Qty**
King	3
Queen/Double	5
King/Single	4
Bathrooms	**Qty**
Ensuite	6
Private	
Guest Share	1
Family Share	

YOUR HOSTS: **Diane and Ian Ross**   Ph: (03) 388 6505   **Christchurch**

HULVERSTONE LODGE

18 Hulverstone Drive, Avondale, Christchurch
Ph (03) 388 6505, Fax (03) 388 6025
Mobile 025-433 830
e-mail: hulverstone@caverock.net.nz

Features & Attractions

- Complimentary pick-up
- Discount from third night
- Diane spricht deutsch
- Visa/Mastercard accepted
- Fax facilities
- Diane parle francais

Bed & Breakfast Accommodation

Double	$80-110
Single	$60-80
Child	

Bedrooms	Qty
Double	3
Twin	2
Single	1
Bed Size	**Qty**
Super King/	1
King/Twin	1
Queen	1
Single	1
Bathrooms	**Qty**
Ensuite	1
Private	1
Guest Share	1
Family Share	

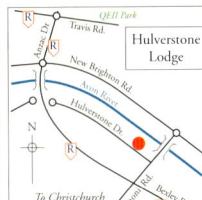

DIRECTIONS:
Follow the Ring Road, marked with an **R** on the big blue road signs, until it crosses the Avon River.

Gracing the bank of the Avon River in a quiet suburb, yet only 10 minutes from the city, stands picturesque **Hulverstone Lodge**. Watch the sun rise over the river, or catch glimpses of the Southern Alps and Port Hills from our charming guest rooms. Delightful walks pass the door. There are golf courses and other recreational facilities nearby, while frequent buses provide convenient access to the city. A stroll along the riverbank leads to New Brighton's restaurants, sandy Pacific Ocean beach and pier. An ideal base for a year-round holiday, **Hulverstone Lodge** is within a couple of hours' drive of Akaroa, Hanmer Hot Springs, skifields and Kaikoura, each with its own attractions. We guarantee you warm hospitality, quality accommodation and delicious breakfasts. Come and experience the ambience of Hulverstone Lodge!

Christchurch — YOUR HOST: Grania McKenzie — Ph: (03) 389 9395

Willow Lodge

71 River Road, Richmond, Christchurch
Ph (03) 389 9395, Fax (03) 381 5395
e-mail: *willow@inet.net.nz*

Tariff : N.Z. Dollars		
	Double	$95-120
	Single	$70
	Child	$25

Bedrooms	Qty
Double	2
Twin	1
Single	1
Bed Size	**Qty**
Super King	1
King	
Queen	1
King/Single	3
Bathrooms	**Qty**
Ensuite	1
Private	2
Guest Share	
Family Share	

Homestay - Bed & Breakfast

Features & Attractions

- 1928 Art Deco style home
- Spacious bedrooms
- Family room
- Friendly atmosphere
- Beautiful river setting
- Central City - 20min. walk
- Central City - 5min. by car
- Fresh and generous breakfast

"And you really live by the river? What a jolly life...." - 'Wind in the Willows'.

Yes! We have a superb location; quiet, wonderful views overlooking the river, plus close to the city centre. The house was built in 1928, Art Deco influence in style and furnishings, with contemporary art and books. Spacious bedrooms with river views - leadlight windows and native timber (rimu) doors and robes.

Breakfast is fresh and generous - organic breads, cereals, fresh fruit, bacon and eggs, good coffee and teas.

It is a 20 minute riverside walk to Christchurch's cafés, historic areas, galleries and public gardens. Excellent food and wine choices available. Also interesting walks and day trips around Canterbury. Sam is our elderly black Labrador dog. Mountain bike, laundry facility and off-street parking available.

Taxi or shuttle service available to gate from Airport, Railway Station or coach terminus.

DIRECTIONS:
Drive to eastern end of Bealey Avenue (City), right into Fitzgerald Avenue, then fourth left into River Road.

YOUR HOSTS: Gerda and Hans   Ph: (03) 332 2896   **Christchurch**

KLEYNBOS & THE GRAND COTTAGE

59 Ngaio Street, St. Martins, Christchurch
Ph (03) 332 2896, Fax (03) 332 2896
e-mail: *bandb@voyager.co.nz*

Tariff : N.Z. Dollars

	Double	$70-85
	Single	$45-70
	Child	neg.

Bedrooms	Qty
Double	2
Twin	1
Single	
Bed Size	**Qty**
Super King	
King	
Queen/Double	2
King/Single	
Bathrooms	**Qty**
Ensuite	2
Private	
Guest Share	1
Family Share	

Homestay & Self-contained Accommodation

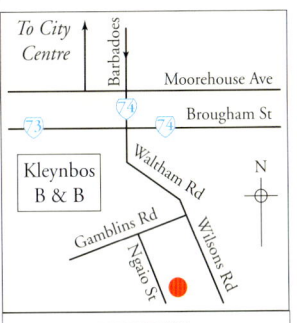

DIRECTIONS:
Please phone for easy directions

Features & Attractions

- *Tranquil quiet treelined street*
- *Art, oil paintings, native wood*
- *City centre nearby*
- *Discounts for self-catering*

KLEYNBOS **B&B** HOMESTAY – Away from the 'hustle and bustle', close to the city centre, in an easy to find street. That's us! As travelling is rather wearing on your body and mind, your room is generous in size, has an ensuite (or guest share) bathroom and - very important - a comfortable bed. We have enjoyed the privilege to live in New Zealand for almost 15 years and having guests is a little like family who have come to stay.
Hans and Gerda look forward to meeting you.

THE GRAND COTTAGE: This lovely, spacious, free-standing and totally private 1920 character quality holiday home has 2 living areas, 2 toilets, 3 double bedrooms and a garden. It is fully equipped. Situated next to Kleynbos B&B, 4km from the city centre. Close to parks, hills and walkways.
Self catering $ 85.00 per nights for 2.
Extra person $ 10.00 per night.
Breakfast $ 10.00 per person per night.
Sleeps 6 comfortably.

Christchurch

YOUR HOSTS: Aileen and David Davies Ph: (03) 332 9987

LOCARNO GARDENS APARTMENT

25 Locarno Street, St. Martins, Christchurch
Ph/Fax (03) 332 9987, Mobile 025-399 747
e-mail: *locarno@xtra.co.nz*

Features & Attractions

- *5 min. drive to city centre*
- *Quality furnishings and décore*
- *Fish and watergarden, laundry facilities*
- *Breakfast optional extra*
- *Off-street parking*
- *Shops, Lyttelton, Gondola, Jade Stadium close*

Two self-catering Apartments

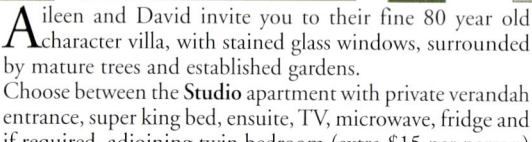

Double	$85-95
Single	$85-95
extra person	$15

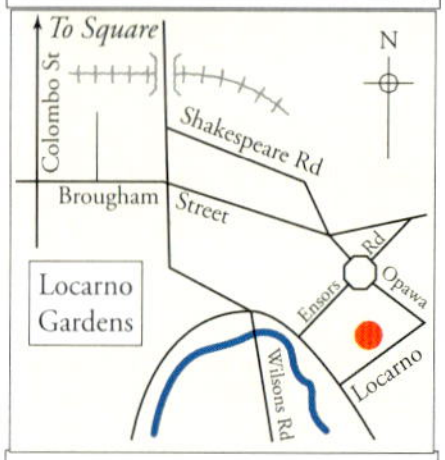

Aileen and David invite you to their fine 80 year old character villa, with stained glass windows, surrounded by mature trees and established gardens.
Choose between the **Studio** apartment with private verandah entrance, super king bed, ensuite, TV, microwave, fridge and if required, adjoining twin bedroom (extra $15 per person) or the **Stand-alone** architecturally designed Apartment with separate lounge, queen bed, ensuite, bed-settee, TV microwave and fridge.
Relax in the picturesque garden courtyard by the goldfish pond. River walks and a tennis court close by.
Aileen's knowledge of restaurants is extensive and David enjoys diving, deer hunting and outdoor activities.
3 minutes walk to bus.

Bedrooms	Qty
Double	2
Twin	1
Single	
Bed Size	**Qty**
Super King	1
Queen	1
Single	2
Bathrooms	**Qty**
Ensuite	2
Private	
Guest Share	
Family Share	

DIRECTIONS: Locarno Street is opposite St Marks Anglican church near 99 Opawa Road.

Christchurch

YOUR HOSTS: Jan and Graham Pluck Ph: (03) 388 4067

SOUTHSHORE HOMESTAY

71A Rockinghorse Road,
Southshore, Christchurch
Ph (03) 388 4067
e-mail: posmerch@posmerch.co.nz

Features & Attractions

- *Direct beach access*
- *Private and peaceful*
- *Varied bird-life on estuary*
- *Miles of sandy beach nearby*
- *Lovely views from both rooms*
- *Only 20 minutes from City*

Homestay Bed & Breakfast

Bedrooms	Qty
Double	1
Twin	1
Single	
Bed Size	**Qty**
King	
Queen	1
Single	2
Bathrooms	**Qty**
Ensuite	1
Private	
Guest Share	
Family Share	1

Double	$75-90
Single	$60-75
Child	n/a

DIRECTIONS: Please phone for easy directions. City and airport pick-up if required.

Share with us an environment unique to Christchurch - Southshore. Only 20 minutes from the city, Southshore is situated between the ocean and the estuary of the Avon River. This seaside enclave offers walkways to enjoy the open water views of the estuary and its varied bird-life, or miles of sandy beach for strolling or swimming. Our house is situated down a private driveway with access to the beach.
A large double room with ensuite and a smaller twin room are available to guests. Both rooms are warm and welcoming and overlook the dunes wilderness. We are in our sixties and together enjoy gardening, music and collecting antiques. Jan is a keen embroiderer and Graham a member of the Vintage Car Club.
We are non-smokers - including Jaffa the cat. Dinner by arrangement, $25pp, includes wine. Please phone for reservations.

YOUR HOSTS: Bev and Kerry Bloomfield   Ph: (03) 332 5360   **Christchurch**

BLOOMFIELDS BED & BREAKFAST
105 Lyttelton Street, Hoon Hay - Spreydon
Christchurch
e-mail: bloomfield@clear.net.nz
Ph (03) 332 5360, Fax (03) 332 5362

Tariff : N.Z. Dollars

Double	$75
Single	
Child	$10

Bedrooms	Qty
Double	1
Twin	1
Single	

Bed Size	Qty
Super King	
King	
Queen	1
Single	2

Bathrooms	Qty
Ensuite	
Private	1
Guest Share	
Family Share	

Bed & Breakfast
Self-contained Accommodation

Features & Attractions

- *Quiet, peaceful surroundings*
- *Continental breakfast*
- *Raceway Addington close by*
- *Close to large shopping mall*
- *Close to indoor swimming pool*
- *Westpac Trust Centre*
- *Close to railway station*
- *Off-street parking*

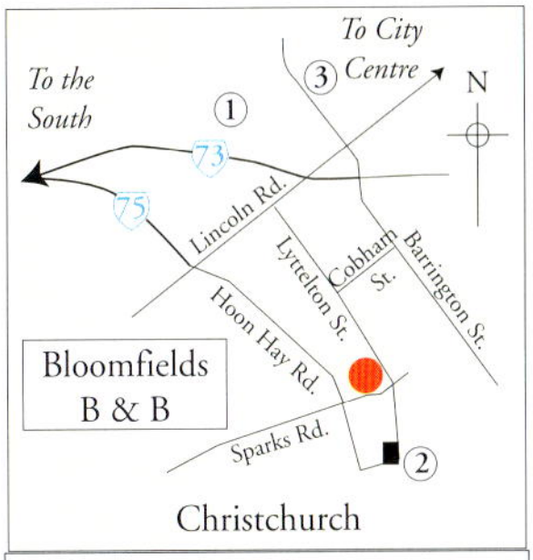

DIRECTIONS:
Between Addington Raceway and Centennial Park.

1. Addington Raceway
2. Centennial Park
3. Railway Station

If you would like peace and quiet in our lovely city, our two-bedroom apartment is ideal. Our apartment, adjoining our home, has a large lounge and fully self-contained kitchen, washing facilities, phone and TV. For your privacy and enjoyment you have your own front lawn to sit and relax on. If we can be of any assistance to make your holiday more enjoyable, we are only too pleased to help. Children are welcome and there is a cot and highchair available if needed.

We provide a comprehensive style continental breakfast. This is prepared and placed in your apartment, so you can breakfast at your leisure. If you prefer, you may do your own catering (discount tariff).

Bev and Kery wish you a safe journey!

Sumner - Christchurch YOUR HOSTS: **Jo and Derek** Ph: (03) 326 5755

"PANORAMA" HOMESTAY

Panorama Road, Clifton Hill, Sumner, Christchurch
Ph (03) 326 5755, Fax (03) 326 5701
e-mail: *PANORAMAhomestay@xtra.co.nz*

Tariff : N.Z. Dollars	
Double	$85
Single	$60
Child	

Bedrooms	Qty
Double	1
Twin	
Single	

Bed Size	Qty
Super King	
King	
Queen	1
Single	

Bathrooms	Qty
Ensuite	
Private	1
Guest Share	
Family Share	

Homestay - Bed & Breakfast

Features & Attractions

- *Peaceful surroundings*
- *Guest lounge available*
- *Superb views from all rooms*
- *Twenty min. to city centre*
- *3 min. drive to beach*
- *Fine local restaurants*
- *Relaxed, friendly hosts*
- *Large terraced garden*

When you stay with us, you will be our only guests. Your bedroom and lounge have, like all rooms in the house, superb views of the ocean, the estuary, the city and across the plains to the mountains. Photographs cannot really do it justice.

The three decks and terraced garden make the most of the all day sun, and you can take a quiet country walk on the Port Hills within minutes of the house. We are about 20 minutes drive from Christchurch city centre and three minutes drive from our local Sumner Village and its popular beach, cafés and restaurants.

There are just two of us at home now and our interests centre around the outdoors, gardening, sport, music and art. We are well travelled both within New Zealand and abroad and are always delighted to meet the many interesting people who choose to stay with us, but if you want some private time, there is a comfortable lounge with TV and stereo and a separate deck for your use. For breakfast we serve a selection of cereals and toast with fresh fruit and a range of teas and coffees. We are always happy to share our knowledge of Christchurch and the South Island with our guests.

YOUR HOSTS: Graham and Jenny Sorell   Ph: (03) 328 9505   **Lyttelton - Christchurch**

CAVENDISH HOUSE
10 Ross Terrace, Lyttelton
Ph (03) 328 9505, Fax (03) 328 9502
Mobile 025-616 0266
e-mail: *gsorell@xtra.co.nz*

Tariff : N.Z. Dollars	
Double	$130-150
Single	$110
Child	Neg.

Bedrooms	Qty
Double	1
Double/Twin	1
Single	
Bed Size	**Qty**
Super King	
King	
Queen	1
King/Single	1
Bathrooms	**Qty**
Ensuite/Spa	1
Ensuite/Shower	1
Guest Share	
Family Share	

**Bed & Breakfast
Boutique Accommodation**

Features & Attractions

- *Dramatic scenery of ships and the sea*
- *Charming old world garden*
- *Spacious areas for relaxation*
- *Discount Airport transfer arranged*
- *Luxury spa bath*
- *Generous breakfast*
- *Fabulous walks*
- *History galore*

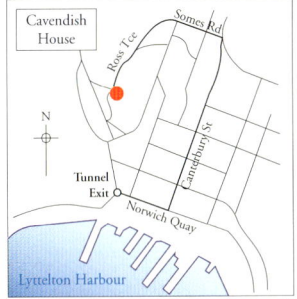

The bustling Port of Lyttelton, the original settlement of Canterbury, has retained that special romantic charm of ships and the sea. Explore its history in the Maritime Museum, visit the Time-Ball, walk in the footsteps of the pioneers up the Bridle Path, or take advantage of the commanding view from our gracious Edwardian villa and watch the ballet of ships and boats as they go about their business. Each elegantly furnished guest-room offers spacious accommodation and privacy, whilst both of the modern ensuite bathrooms are luxuriously appointed; the Venice Suite with double spa bath.

You are welcome to relax in the former Ball-Room, whose huge bay window looks over the beautiful terraced garden to the steep hillsides of Lyttelton township, where the houses are reminiscent of a Mediterranean fishing village.

Fine teas, coffee and other refreshments are freely available in the Chart Room with its spectacular harbour views. As evening approaches, complimentary drinks are served on the adjoining verandah. Venture down the quaint laneways to the cafés and restaurants, then call us to save you the walk home.

Christchurch

YOUR HOSTS: Fay and Stephen Graham   Ph: (03) 325 2395

MENTEITH COUNTRY HOMESTAY
Springs Road, RD 6, Christchurch
between Prebbleton & Lincoln
Ph (03) 325 2395, Fax (03) 325 2469
e-mail: *menteith@clear.net.nz*

Tariff : N.Z. Dollars	
Double	$85-95
Single	$60
Child	

Bedrooms	Qty
Double	2
Twin	1
Single	

Bed Size	Qty
Super King	1
King	1
Queen	
Single	1

Bathrooms	Qty
Ensuite	1
Private	1
Guest Share	
Family Share	

Quality Country Homestay

Features & Attractions

- Indoor swimming/spa pool
- Easy city/airport access
- Peaceful rural setting
- 3 km to golfcourse
- 3 km Lincoln University
- Two friendly cats
- Try your hand at spinning!
- Email facilities

Our tranquil 10 acre farmlet nestles among mature trees with spectacular mountain views and easy 15 minute city/airport access. It supports a lucerne crop, a small flock of sheep (to provide specialist fleeces for Fay's spinning - you're welcome to try your hand!) and two beehives (to maintain Stephen's interest and expertise in this fascinating industry).

Menteith, so named after an ancient Graham clan in Scotland, is an alpine-style home built from local riverbed stone, complemented in the interior with a collection of imported timbers and brick, offering a warm atmosphere. Relax in our warm indoor spa/swimming pool conservatory (robes provided) before your busy day of sightseeing. Spacious rooms offering cosy firm beds, TV, tea/coffee facilities and cookies, electric blankets, heating and hairdryer. Laundry facilities available. Hearty breakfasts served from home-grown produce - the time is your choice.

Delightful reasonably priced restaurants nearby or dinner by arrangement $30 pp. Lincoln golf course and university 3 km. Our retirement interests include golf, Rotary, skiing, genealogy and travel. Smoking welcome outside.

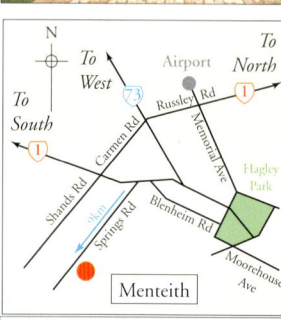

DIRECTIONS:
9 km from SH 1 at Wigram/Hornby.

176

YOUR HOSTS: **Rose & Jan Shuttleworth** Free Ph: 0800-393 877   **Akaroa - Banks Peninsula**

BLYTHCLIFFE

37 Rue Balguerie, Akaroa, Canterbury
Ph/Fax: (03) 304 7003
e-mail: blythcliffe@xtra.co.nz
www.blythcliffe.co.nz

Tariff : N.Z. Dollars	
Double	$125-150
Single	$100-150
Child	

Bedrooms	Qty
Double	3
Twin	
Single	

Bed Size	Qty
Super King	
King	
Queen	3
Single	

Bathrooms	Qty
Ensuite	2
Private	1
Guest Share	
Family Share	

Old World Ambience

Bed & Breakfast
Luxury self-contained Cottage

Features & Attractions

- 200m from town centre
- Internet and e-mail facilities
- 5th generation local knowledge
- Vast range of NZ native trees
- Croquet, pétanque, full size billiard table
- Help with interests & activities freely given
- Cat.1 listing, NZ Historic Places Trust
- Restful & quiet garden environment

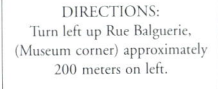

ANYONE FOR CROQUET?

DIRECTIONS:
Turn left up Rue Balguerie,
(Museum corner) approximately
200 meters on left.

Just 200 m from the centre of Akaroa village, the walled street frontage of Blythcliffe belies what awaits you beyond the gate. The house was built in 1858 and has a category 1 listing with the New Zealand Historic Places Trust. A shelled path leads around the edge of the lawn to a shady pavillion that provides guests with the perfect place to enjoy special continental breakfast outdoors. Croquet mallets and pétanque boules are housed here just in case you feel like a little light recreation. Or cross a bridge over the stream bordering this garden and stroll through an acre stand of native bush.

Two quaint double guest rooms overlooking different portions of the garden are freshly decorated in blue, yellow and greens. Both have private bathrooms, one ensuite. A small upstairs guest lounge opens onto the upper balcony and provides guests with tea and coffe making facilities and a television.

Beyond, a modern self-contained cottage providing accommodation for two, sits in its own private garden and has its own streamside BBQ area. Inside is spa bath, fully featured kitchen, TV, Video and CD-player. The privacy and understated elegance of this charming bed and breakfast is waiting for you. Just lift the latch and wander into the secret garden.

Darfield - Christchurch YOUR HOSTS: **Brian and Michelle** Free Ph: 0800-181 144

MEYCHELLE MANOR

Main West Coast Road, SH 73, PO Box 162
'S' Bends, Kirwee, Canterbury
Ph (03) 318 1144, Fax (03) 318 1965
e-mail: *meychelle.m@inet.net.nz*
www.meychellemanor.inet.net.nz

Tariff : N.Z. Dollars

Double	$170
Single	$110
Child	neg.

Bedrooms	Qty
Double/Twin	2
Twin	
Single	

Bed Size	Qty
Super King/Twin	2
King	
Queen	
Single	

Bathrooms	Qty
Ensuite	2
Private	
Guest Share	
Family Share	

Luxury Farmstay Bed & Breakfast

Features & Attractions

- Easy to find on SH 73
- Shopping, restaurants, train 3 min.
- Skiing, golf courses, wineries very close
- Astronom. telescope, DVD home theatre
- Delicious breakfast
- Private beautiful rooms
- E-mail, fax, laundry avail.
- Exotic & farmyard animals

We warmly welcome you to our family home, **Meychelle Manor**, a deer farm 25 minutes from Christchurch International Airport, 35 minutes from the city, right on SH 73. You can enjoy a seat beside our lake and feed the ducks and fish or putt on our golf green, play pentonque or swim in our indoor heated pool. Our private luxiourious ensuite rooms offer comfortable super-king/twin beds, central heating, hair dryers, clock radios and balconies. For breakfast we offer a delicious continental and/or cooked kiwi-style selection. An evening meal can be enjoyed at a variety of local restaurants/cafés or by arrangement with us. After dinner you may want to enjoy our digital home surround sound theatre, listen to music or play puzzles in our entertainment room, have a night swim in our softly lit pool room or star-gaze through our 8" Newtonian telescope. Next day you could connect to the Tranz Alpine train excursion (one of the top train rides in the world) or by appointment we can arrange hunting and fishing trips and more.

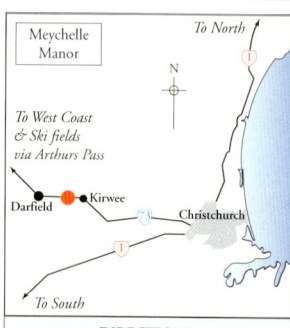

DIRECTIONS:
From **Christchurch**: On SH 73 on the left after S-Bends after Kirwee.
From **Darfield**: 3 min. from township on SH 73 on right, just before 'S' bends at Kirwee.

YOUR HOSTS: Ann and Drew Garden   Ph: (03) 347 7556   **Christchurch/West Melton**

Garden Vineyard Homestay

Torlesse Road, West Melton, RD 1, Christchurch
Ph (03) 347 7556, Fax (03) 347 7558
e-mail: *drewann@ihug.co.nz*
www.gardenvineyard.co.nz

Features & Attractions
- *Superb independent unit*
- *Christchurch Airport 15 min.*
- *Golf - 10 courses nearby*
- *Special long stay rates*
- *Wine tasting*
- *Relaxing garden setting*

Self-contained Country Vineyard Stay

	Double	$80-125
	Single	$60-110
	Child	Half price

If you want to do "your own thing" but still experience a "Kiwi" homestay holiday in the countryside, a stay on our vineyard is for you. Our comfortable self-catering unit is in a peaceful garden setting, surrounded by trees, amidst 5 acres of grapevines. We are situated 15 minutes from Christchurch Airport and 25 minutes from the city centre.

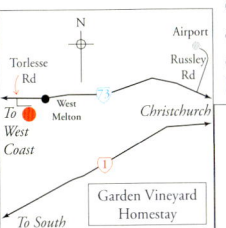

Our unit is particularly suited to one or two couples, or a family of up to 4 members. Being keen golfers we can advise clients on the 10 courses nearby. All linen is supplied and a continental breakfast is provided daily.

Complimentary tea and coffee. If you do not wish to cook, there are several local restaurants nearby, or a meal can be provided by arrangement from your hosts.

DIRECTIONS: From airport, turn right Russley Rd. At next roundabout. Turn right SH 73. 13 km to West Melton. Torlesse Rd. 3 km on left past West Melton Hotel. We are approx. 1 km on the right.

Bedrooms	Qty
Double	1
Twin	1
Single	
Bed Size	**Qty**
King	
Queen	1
Single	2
Bathrooms	**Qty**
Ensuite	
Private	1
Guest Share	
Family Share	

Methven - Mt. Hutt — YOUR HOSTS: **Colleen & Roger Mehrtens** — Free Ph: 0800-466 093

GREEN GABLES DEER FARM

Waimarama Road, Methven
Ph (03) 302 8308, Fax (03) 302 8309
e-mail: *greengables@xtra.co.nz*
www.travelwise.co.nz

Tariff : N.Z. Dollars	
Double	$110-130
Single	$95-100
Child	half price

Bedrooms	Qty
Double	2
Twin	1
Single	
Bed Size	**Qty**
Super King	2
King	
Queen	
SuperKing Single	2
Bathrooms	**Qty**
Ensuite	2
Private	1
Guest Share	
Family Share	

Farmstay - Bed & Breakfast

Features & Attractions

- *Fishing, golf, hot air ballooning*
- *Country cuisine - dinner $30 pp*
- *Skiing Mt Hutt, horse riding*
- *5 hours from Queenstown*
- *1 hour to Christchurch - International Airport*
- *Scenic bush walks - open gardens*
- *Restaurants nearby*

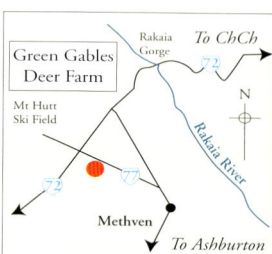

A warm welcome awaits you at **Green Gables,** which is minutes from Methven - Mount Hutt, a beautiful, picturesque village, which has to offer an impressive range of summer and winter activities. This is an area of freshness, adventure and enjoyment, situated one hour from Christchurch, the garden city of New Zealand and its international airport. Relax in our peaceful farmhouse, which is the closest accommodation to Mt Hutt Skifield. The tastefully appointed guest wing is complete with ensuite facilities, super king beds, wool underlays, electric blankets, heaters, hair dryers and clock radios. French doors opening from all bedrooms provide private access. **Green Gables** presents magnificent views of Mount Hutt and the surrounding mountains. Hand-feed pet deer "Lucy" and her lovely fawn in a tranquil setting with white doves, Royal Danish White Deer, "Max" the golden labrador and "Harry" the silver-grey cat. Dine in the evening with delicious New Zealand country cuisine and wine. Relax by the open fire with TV in our comfortable sitting room. We delight in sharing our knowledge of this fascinating area, its history and its wide range of all season activities.

YOUR HOSTS: Pam and Roger Callaghan   Free Ph: 0800 428 438

Methven - Mt.Hutt

TYRONE DEER FARM

Methven/Rakaia Gorge Alternative Route
No.12 RD, Rakaia,
Mid Canterbury
Ph (03) 302 8096. Fax (03) 302 8099

Tariff : N.Z. Dollars	
Double	$95-100
Single	$70
Child	

Bedrooms	Qty
Double	2
Twin	1
Single	
Bed Size	
Super King	
King	
Queen	2
Single	2
Bathrooms	**Qty**
Ensuite	2
Private	1
Guest Share	
Family Share	

Countrystay Bed & Breakfast

Features & Attractions

- Centre of South Island
- Evening meal $25 p.p.
- Skiing MtHutt & heli-skiing
- Jet boating/hot air ballooning
- 1hour Christchurch Airport
- Tramping alpine & bush walks
- Fishing, hunting guides avail.
- Golf 18-hole courses, club hire

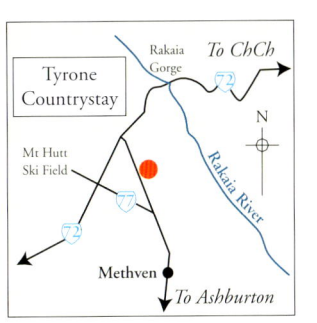

Welcome to **Tyrone Deer Farm**, centrally situated in the Mt Hutt Methven Rakaia Gorge area in the middle of the South Island, 5 km from the Inland Tourist Route (Highway 72) and one hour from Christchurch International Airport making **Tyrone** an ideal stopover if heading south to Queenstown etc, north to Picton/Nelson or Highway 73 to the West Coast. Positioned on the farm our home has views of the mountains (Mount Hutt) which also builds the back-drop of grazing deer a few metres away.

As our family have left home, we have plenty of room for guests with electric blanket, and duvets on beds, heaters and hair dryers in the bedrooms, a lounge with open fire, TV, tea/coffee facilities and guest fridge. Come and meet Guz, our pet deer, her daughter $$ and 10.30, our cat. Laze in the garden or swim in our pool. Dinner by arrangement is a three-course evening meal with pre-dinner drinks and New Zealand wine. We are able to arrange professional guides for fishing salmon and trout, and for hunting: especially Tahr, Red Deer and Chamois.

Geraldine YOUR HOSTS: **Valery and John Parish** Ph: (03) 697 4809

THE BRAE

156 Patrick Road, Gapes Valley, RD 21
Geraldine, South Canterbury Region
Ph (03) 697 4809, Fax (03) 697 4809
e-mail: john.val@xtra.co.nz

Tariff : N.Z. Dollars	
Double	$90
Single	$50
Child	neg.

Bedrooms	Qty
Double	1
Twin	2
Single	
Bed Size	**Qty**
Super King	
King	
Queen	1
Single	4
Bathrooms	**Qty**
Ensuite	
Private	1
Guest Share	
Family Share	1

Farmstay Bed & Breakfast

Features & Attractions

- Panoramic views
- Country cuisine
- Laundry facilities
- Phone, fax, e-mail
- 2 hrs Christchurch/Mount Cook
- Geraldine's 'Barkers'
- Peel Forest Reserve
- Rangitata Rafting

Val and John, farm hosts since 1987, warmly invite you to stay at 'The Brae', our 205 hectare accredited deer, cattle and lamb fattening property. Travel 14 km (15 minutes) from the well known picturesque village of Geraldine to Gapes Valley. **The Brae** is centrally positioned 1.5 km west of State Highway 79, halfway between Christchurch and Mount Cook - Queenstown. Our home has an inviting atmosphere, delightful pool, BBQ area set in an attractive garden. Guest rooms have a superb outlook, restful décor, beds with duvets, electric blankets, hair dryers and toiletries for your comfort. John has resided all his life in the area, interests are farm related, gardening and all sports. Val enjoys golf, all crafts and cooking. Her experience as a resthome/hospital cook ensures guests of very high standards in food preparation and hygiene (NZQA Certificates). A three course meal using fresh, locally grown produce is available by prior arrangement – wine included, $25pp. Be assured of warm and friendly hospitality at **The Brae.**

DIRECTIONS: 14 km from Geraldine. 1.5 km from SH 79 towards Fairlie, to Stalker Road on your right, just before Gapes Valley Hall. Then right on Patrick Road for 1.5 km. From Fairlie turn left off SH 79 onto Patrick Road at Gapes Valley Hall, follow above directions.

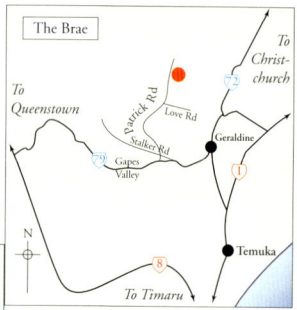

YOUR HOST: Joan Gill   Ph: (03) 685 8833   **Fairlie - South Canterbury**

RIVENDELL LODGE
Stanton Road, Kimbell, RD 17, Fairlie
Ph (03) 685 8833. Fax (03) 685 8825
Mobile 025-819 189
e-mail: *rivendell.lodge@xtra.co.nz*
http://fairlie.co.nz/rivendell

Tariff : N.Z. Dollars
Double	$90
Single	$50
Child	neg.

Bedrooms	Qty
Double	2
Twin	
Triple	1

Bed Size	Qty
Super King	
King	
Queen/Double	2
Single	1

Bathrooms	Qty
Ensuite	
Private	2
Guest Share	
Family Share	1

Country Homestay

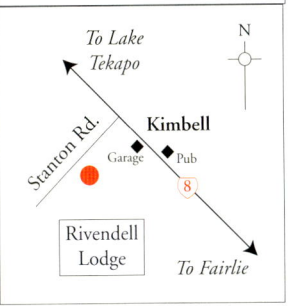

Features & Attractions

- *Peaceful rural retreat*
- *Great home cooking*
- *Skifield 5 km*
- *Spa bath available*
- *Magnificent alpine scenery*
- *Guided walking & tramping*
- *Families welcome*
- *Internet/ e-mail access*

DIRECTIONS: 100m up Stanton Rd. at Kimbell on SH 8, 8km west of Fairlie.

"They stayed long in Rivendell and found it hard to leave. The house was perfect whether you liked sleep, or work, or storytelling, or singing, or just sitting and thinking best, or a pleasant mixture of them all. Everyone grew refreshed and strong in a few days there. Merely to be there was a cure for weariness, fear and sadness." - Tolkien.

Welcome to my one acre paradise; a haven of peace and tranquility offering quality country comfort and hospitality. I am a well travelled writer with a passion for mountains, literature and good conversation. I enjoy cooking and gardening and use home grown produce wherever possible. Evening meals, with local wines, are available by arrangement. Take time out from the Christchurch-Queenstown route and enjoy our magnificent country-side. Fishing, skiing, walking, golf and water sports nearby. Relax in our beautiful garden, complete with stream and cat, or come with us to some of our favourite places.

Complimentary refreshments on arrival. Laundry facilities available.

Pleasant Point

YOUR HOSTS: Murray and Shirley Beynon Ph: (03) 614 7221

PLEASANT POINT BED & BREAKFAST

21 Ameer Street, Pleasant Point
South Canterbury
Ph (03) 614 7221, Fax (03) 614 7231

Features & Attractions

- *On road to Mount Cook, & the Southern Lakes*
- *18 hole golf course*
- *Steam train*
- *"Richard Pearse First Flight Memorial"*

Homestay & Self-contained Accomm.

Double	$70
Single	$50
Child	$5

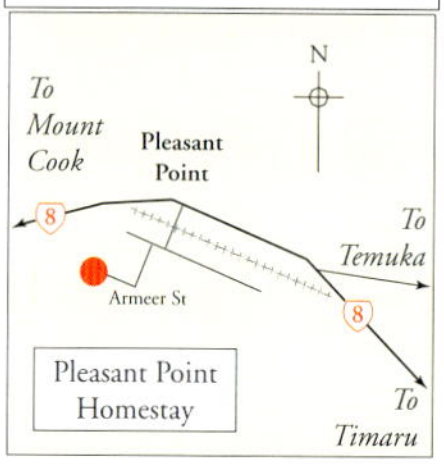

Bedrooms	Qty
Double	1
Twin	1
Single	

Bed Size	Qty
King	
Queen/Double	1
Single	2

Bathrooms	Qty
Ensuite	1
Private	1
Guest Share	
Family Share	

Pleasant Point is located 20 km south of Timaru on State Highway 8 - one of the main roads to Mount Cook, the Southern Lakes and the Hydro Electric Dams. An excellently maintained steam train operates through the township regularly. Another nostalgic trip can be made at the "Richard Pearse First Flight Memorial". We have a top class 18 hole golf course and only 8 km towards the historical landmark of Hanging Rock, you can wine and dine at the new Opihi Vineyard and Café. Shirley and Murray extend a warm welcome and look forward to your custom. We have a fully self contained, modern unit with complete bathroom/kitchen/laundry facilities and lock-up garage. Alternatively you can join us in a comfortable homestay and enjoy the spectacular mountain views from your upstairs bedroom/ensuite, family lounges and outside decking.

Timaru

YOUR HOSTS: Jack and Nona Johnston Ph: (03) 684 7748

CEDARWOOD LODGE

18 Braemar Place, Timaru,
South Canterbury
Ph (03) 684 7748

Features & Attractions

- *Caroline Bay*
- *Pleasant surroundings*
- *Warm welcome*
- *Aorangi Park*
- *Adjacent golf course*
- *Off-street parking*

Homestay Bed & Breakfast

Double	$70
Single	$50
Child	half price

Bedrooms	Qty
Double	
Twin	1
Single	1

Bed Size	Qty
King	
Queen	
Single	3

Bathrooms	Qty
Ensuite	
Private	
Guest Share	1
Family Share	

Nona and Jack invite you to stay at **Cedarwood Lodge**, situated in a quiet suburb of the City with off-street parking. Enjoy fine views of Mt Cook to the west and the City overlooking the Highfield Golf Course (10m from the fairway). Aorangi Park with all its sporting facilities is within walking distance. Our architecturally designed home is very comfortable, there are electric blankets in the guest rooms. You are most welcome to share our family area if you so desire. We are retired and enjoy music (classical, opera, jazz), travel, photography, the garden and flower arranging. Having travelled extensively ourselves, we love hosting overseas guests. If you are in doubt about finding our home, just telephone us on your arrival in the City and we will escort you home.

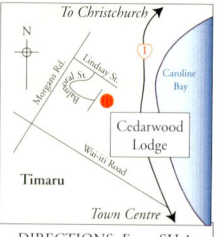

DIRECTIONS: From SH 1 turn into Wai-iti Rd, through roundabout to Morgans Rd. Turn right into Lindsay St., right again into Balmoral St., then into Braemar Place.

YOUR HOSTS: Nan and Wynne Raymond   Ph: (03) 684 4910   Timaru

ETHRIDGE GARDENS

10 Sealy Street, Timaru
Ph (03) 684 4910, Fax (03) 684 4910
Mobile 025-365 365

Tariff : N.Z. Dollars	
Double	$120
Single	$90
Child	$30

Bedrooms	Qty
Double	1
Twin	1
Single	1
Bed Size	**Qty**
Super King	
King	
Queen	1
Single	1
Bathrooms	**Qty**
Ensuite	
Private	1
Guest Share	
Family Share	

Bed & Breakfast Homestay

Features & Attractions

- Charter flights over Mt Cook & Alps
- Private gardens to visit
- Excellent fishing rivers
- 5 ski fields within easy distance
- Bush walks
- Golf course nearby
- Christchurch 2 hours
- Queenstown 4 hours

Ethridge Gardens is a beautiful character house built in 1911 and set in romantic English-style gardens. Iron gates and rose-covered archways lead through to exciting vistas. High brick walls divide the garden into rooms, each one differing in style, colour and design.
To stay here is to enjoy the very best in old-fashioned hospitality. Guests are welcome to relax in a large gracious sitting-room which opens onto the terrace and courtyard with its fountain and pond.
Afternoon tea on arrival can be served indoors or in a rose-clad gazebo overlooking a delightful rose garden and heated swimming pool.
Tea, coffee, chocolates, robes and fresh flowers in the bedrooms. TV in the main bedroom.
Delicious breakfasts, continental and traditional, available.
Excellent restaurants nearby. Wine and aperitifs with your hosts early evening if desired.
Nan is a renowned New Zealand gardener and Wynne is Mayor of Timaru with a wide knowledge of the region.

DIRECTIONS: Just north of Timaru township on SH 1, turn west into Wai-iti Rd. Travel 2km, then turn right into Sealy St. **Ethridge Gardens** is on left.

Lake Hawea - Wanaka YOUR HOSTS: **Marjorie, Sheila and Brian** Ph: (03) 443 7056

BELLBIRD COTTAGE

121-125 Noema Terrace, Lake Hawea, Ctrl. Otago
Ph (03) 443 7056, Fax (03) 443 1807
or Ph (03) 443 8678
e-mail: *marge@xtra.co.nz*
www.mysite.xtra.co.nz/~marge/

Tariff : N.Z. Dollars

	Double	$100
	Single	$100
	Child	n/a

Bedrooms	Qty
Double/Twin	1
Twin	
Single	1

Bed Size	Qty
Super King	
King	
Queen/Double	1
Single	1

Bathrooms	Qty
Ensuite	1
Private	
Guest Share	
Family Share	

Self-contained Luxury Accommodation

Features & Attractions

- Seven-day-dining close by
- Microwave & dishwasher
- Two television sets
- Fully equipped kitchen
- Full private laundry
- Log fire, stereo, video
- Central to activities
- Co-operative hosts

Our modern, self-contained cottage is situated in beautiful Lake Hawea village, surrounded by majestic mountains, We are just 12 kilometres from Lake Wanaka in the centre of the Lakes District of Central Otago. With Queenstown just an hour away,

DIRECTIONS:
Please telephone for easy directions.
Advance booking is recommended.

less than 2 hours to Mount Cook, you are close to all attractions. We are located about 30 minutes from two major ski fields – Treble Cone and Cadrona. Lake Hawea is renowned for fishing with guides available. Horse riding, nature walks, adventure trips, canoeing, paragliding are just some of the local attractions. The cottage construction is timber and rammed earth. The bedroom has a double and single bed and there is a double sofa sleeper in the lounge. If required we have a double self-contained bedroom adjacent complete with ensuite. A typical comment from our guest book is: "This is an outstanding cottage, cosy, tastefully decorated and thoughtfully well equipped. Together with warm hospitality this has perfected our holiday in New Zealand." Hosts are Majorie Goodger, who has had a career in hotel management, and her sister Sheila McCaughan from a farming background. Should you wish, your log fire will be burning on your return from skiing. Dinner by arrangement hosted by Majorie, Sheila and Brian McCaughan. Easy to find – Noema Terrace leads off the main road, Capell Avenue, where you are welcome at 121 & 125.

YOUR HOSTS: Carol and Dan Orbell | Free Ph: 0800-325 914 | **Dublin Bay - Wanaka**

LARCHWOOD LODGE

Dublin Bay, 2 RD, Wanaka
Ph (03) 443 7914. Fax (03) 443 7910
Mobile 025-239 6123
e-mail: *larchwood@xtra.co.nz*
www.larchwood.co.nz

Tariff : N.Z. Dollars

Double	$125-150
Single	$110
Child	$30

Bedrooms	Qty
Double or Twin	5/4
Twin	
Single	

Bed Size	Qty
Super King	
King	3
Queen/Double	1
King/Single	2

Bathrooms	Qty
Ensuite	5
Private	
Guest Share	
Family Share	

Homestay - Bed & Breakfast

Features & Attractions

- *Tranquil rural atmosphere*
- *3 minute walk to lake*
- *Extensive private gardens*
- *Fishing at your door-step*
- *Full-size tennis court*
- *Kayaks & mountain bikes avail.*
- *Disabled/elderly facilities avail.*
- *Pure spring water on tap!*

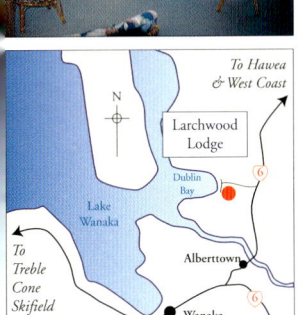

DIRECTIONS:
7km north of Wanaka on SH 6.
turn left into Dublin Bay Road -
3km to **Larchwood** sign
on the left.

Why stay with us… unless our secret hideaway, meandering down to the shores of Lake Wanaka, to walk, kayak, swim, fish or relax by, sounds like **you**. Explore our tranquil gardens, trees framing the majestic mountains, or use the tennis court and mountain bikes, to expend any energy, left over from skiing, golfing, tramping or enjoying a good book. Maybe the 'olde-worlde' rustic charm of the Lodge, wide doors opening to summer's heat, or crackling fires on cold winter nights, has appeal. To others, a room to dry clothing and sportsgear may be of interest, or where the good fishing spots might be found! A choice of five bedrooms, with king sized zip-to-single beds, all overlook Lake Wanaka and the mountains and open onto outdoor balconies. TVs are banished to bedrooms, leaving the lounge for soft music, exchanging good yarns and sharing our life in Central Otago with you. Our kids have left the nest, so our golden retriever 'Mac' helps form the 'Welcoming Committee', (the cat's more elusive). Dan's a professional fishing guide.

Hawea Flat - Wanaka

YOUR HOSTS: Vicki and John Billingham   Ph: (03) 443 1983

MONTEREY LODGE

173 Camphill Road, Hawea Flat, RD 2, Wanaka
Ph (03) 443 1983, Mobile 025-522 211
e-mail: *john.bill@xtra.co.nz*

Features & Attractions

- Swimming pool
- Baby sitting service
- On-site trout fishing
- Total seclusion
- Set in 120 acres
- Magnificent scenery

Luxury Family Bed & Breakfast Accom.

Double	$140-200
Single	$90-135
Child	$50

Bedrooms	Qty
Double	3
Twin	
Single	
Bed Size	**Qty**
King Single	1
Queen/Double	1
Single	3
Bathrooms	**Qty**
Ensuite	3
Private	
Guest Share	
Family Share	

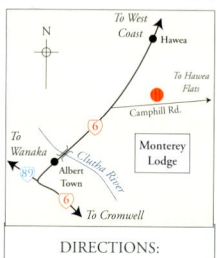

DIRECTIONS: Camphill Rd. turns off SH 6 midway between Wanaka and Hawea. **Monterey Lodge** is 1.8km on left.

Our homestay lodge is set in the centre of 120 acres of rolling countryside only 10 minutes from the beautiful township of Wanaka. Its ski fields and multitude of activities, make it an ideal year round retreat. Stunning mountain views and total seclusion provides our guests with an unforgettable stay in Wanaka. Horse riding, trout fishing, wonderful walks, solar heated swimming pool and a great deck to relax on whilst absorbing the amazing vista, are all available on site. **Monterey Lodge** is a great place for children with tree swings, trampoline, huge grounds to explore and a baby sitting service. Our three luxury guest rooms all have ensuite facilities and superb views. Combine this with our unique location and friendly, relaxed atmosphere - our guests just don't want to leave!

Wanaka

YOUR HOSTS: Ruth and Bill Hunt   Ph: (03) 443 1053

HUNT'S HOMESTAY

56 Manuka Crescent, Wanaka
Ph (03) 443 1053, Fax (03) 443 1355
Mobile 025-265 0114
e-mail: *hunts.homestay@xtra.co.nz*

Features & Attractions

- New house in large garden
- Access to many activities
- Free laundry facilities
- Safe off-street parking
- Farm visits available
- Complimentary tea/coffee

Homestay Bed & Breakfast

Double	$90
Single	$55
Child	$30

Bedrooms	Qty
Double	1
Twin	1
Single	
Bed Size	**Qty**
King	
Queen	1
Single	2
Bathrooms	**Qty**
Ensuite	
Private	
Guest Share	1
Family Share	

DIRECTIONS: From town take Lakeside Rd. to Beacon Point Rd., right to Manuka Crescent. We are opposite Manuka Cresent Motels.

Once settled in our roomy ground floor bedroom and lounge, our guests remark on the beauty of the lake and mountain views and how they change throughout the day. It was this aspect that drew us to this peaceful °-acre section, when we left farming near Wanaka four years ago. Our architectually designed house has four spacious bedrooms and 360° views of lake and mountains. By chance we became involved in homestay activities and have greatly enjoyed the experience. We realised we had a great wealth of information about the area that we could pass on to our guests, as Bill has lived here all his life and is a volunteer at the Information Centre and can keep up with all the activities in and around Wanaka. Whatever you want to do, we are happy to organise it.
We look forward to enjoying your company in our beautiful area.

YOUR HOSTS: **Betty and George Russell** Ph: (03) 443 8358

Wanaka

ASPIRING IMAGES HOMESTAY

26 Norman Terrace, Wanaka
Ph (03) 443 8358, Fax (03) 443 8327
e-mail: *grussell@xtra.co.nz*

Tariff : N.Z. Dollars

	Double	$85-95
	Single	$50-65
	Child	$25

Bedrooms	Qty
Double	2
Twin	
Single	

Bed Size	Qty
Super King	
King/Twin	1
Double	1
Single	

Bathrooms	Qty
Ensuite	1
Private	1
Guest Share	1
Family Share	

Homestay - Bed & Breakfast

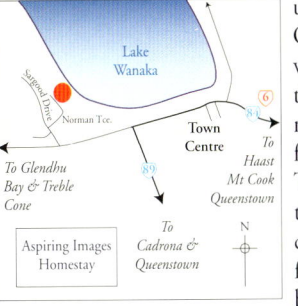

Features & Attractions

- *Stunning views*
- *Close to the lake*
- *Adjacent to large park*
- *4WD eco & photo tours*
- *Two mountain bikes*
- *Wide range of activities*
- *Help with travel plans*
- *e-mail & internet facilities*

"We'll be back!"

Wanaka, with its dramatic lake and mountain scenery, is a magical, unforgettable place which draws people back again and again. Our architect designed home has captivating lake and mountain views, a sunny aspect and a peaceful parkside setting. Secure within the natural stone exterior, guest rooms enjoy the warmth and rich restfulness of heart Rimu timber, sunny sheltered patios, quality furnishings and really comfortable beds.

There is a wealth of activities and attractions offered here, using the lakes and rivers, the glacier-planed countryside and the sharply clear air above. Perhaps you'd like to settle down with a book from our library or browse through our collection of New Zealand books and maps while you consider your next move. We're qualified to help if you wish.

We've travelled widely ourselves, been involved in education, played and coached many sports and sung in a lifetime of choirs. We came under Wanaka's spell many years ago, and enjoy sharing with our guests **"Life the way it should be!"**

Wanaka YOUR HOSTS: **Joyce and Lex Turnbull**   Ph: (03) 443 9060

LAKE WANAKA HOME HOSTING

19 Bill's Way, Rippon Lea
Wanaka, Central Otago
Ph (03) 443 9060, Fax (03) 443 1626
Mobile 025-228 9160

Tariff : N.Z. Dollars	
Double	$100-125
Single	$65
Child	$25

Bedrooms	Qty
Double	2
Twin	1
Single	

Bed Size	Qty
Super King	1
King	
Queen	1
Single	2

Bathrooms	Qty
Ensuite	
Private	2
Guest Share	
Family Share	

Homestay - Bed & Breakfast

Features & Attractions

- *Spacious, relaxing decor*
- *Mountain and lake views*
- *15-20 min. walk to shops*
- *A little luxury*
- *Peaceful lake walks*
- *Close to Rippon Vineyard*
- *Meals on request*
- *Lovely patio garden*

We welcome visitors to Lake Wanaka and enjoy sharing our natural surroundings with others. We have a large, peaceful home where our guests can experience not only the austerity of the lake and mountains around, but also experience the ambience of Wanaka itself. The picturesque 20–30 minute walk to Wanaka Town is very worth while.

Our guest room upstairs has the super king size bed with an adjoining lounge with tea and coffee making facilities, fridge and T.V. and a private bathroom. Our double guestroom also has a private bathroom. We have smoke alarms, central heating and electric blankets in all beds. Good laundry facilities. We have no children living at home and no pets. Our interests are sport, gardening, boating, farming and good cuisine. Lex and I enjoy your company.

OUR HOSTS: **Nora, Beth and Robyn**   Free Ph: 0800-869 26252

Wanaka

OAKRIDGE LAKE WANAKA

Cnr Cardrona Valley Rd. / Studholme Rd.
Postal: PO Box 220, Wanaka, Central Otago
Ph (03) 443 7707. Fax (03) 443 7750
e-mail: *info@oakridge.co.nz*
www.oakridge.co.nz

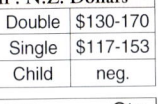

Tariff : N.Z. Dollars	
Double	$130-170
Single	$117-153
Child	neg.

Bedrooms	Qty
Double	12
Twin or	12
Single or	12

Bed Size	Qty
Super King	12
Queen	
King/Single	2
Single	26

Bathrooms	Qty
Ensuite	12
Private	
Guest Share	
Family Share	

Luxury Bed & Breakfast

Features & Attractions

- Quiet, peaceful, rural surroundings
- Superb golf, fishing and hunting
- Tennis court, swimming pool & spa
- Horse trekking and parapenting
- Jet boats, rafting, kayaking
- Bush and mountain walks
- Downhill and nordic skiing
- Spa baths ensuite

Located only 2 minutes drive from the centre of Wanaka Township, the careful blending of the old and the new create at **Oakridge** a holiday experience unique in terms of comfort, design, location and ambience. Central to the development is a purpose-built hunting, fishing and skiing lodge completed in the 1980's in traditional New Zealand rural style. The old lodge has been extensively remodelled and redecorated, and new east and west wings have been added to provide a range of accommodation designed to meet the needs of the most judicious traveller. Set against a backdrop of the majestic mountain peaks of the Soutern Alps amongst sweeping lawns, gardens and open woodland, **Oakridge** offers sumptuous hosted accommodation in a rural setting within a stone's throw of the restaurants, shops and galleries of Lake Wanaka. We offer fly fishing, skiing, golf and mixed activity packages and can arrange wine tasting tours, scenic flights to Milford Sound, Mt Cook and Mt Aspiring, horse trekking, canyoning, kayaking, mountain biking, paragliding, jet boating, white water sledging, and 4X4 motorbike adventures. A shuttle bus service is available to and from Queenstown Airport and Central Wanaka. "**Oakridge Lake Wanaka**, life the way it should be."

DIRECTIONS: Arriving from Queenstown via SH 89 (Cardrona Valley), you will see **Oakridge** on the left just before entering Wanaka. Arriving in Wanaka from any other direction, proceed along Ardmore St. along the lake front, turn into Mac Dougall St. and as you breast the hill at Wanaka Golf Course, leaving Wanaka, you look directly at the red roofs of **Oakridge**.

Wanaka

YOUR HOSTS: **Lawrence & Margaret Mikkelsen** Ph: (03) 443 7305

PARKLANDS LODGE
Ballantyne Road, RD 2, Wanaka
Ph (03) 443 7305, Fax (03) 443 7345
Mobile (025) 955 160
e-mail: *parklandslodge@xtra.co.nz*
http://www.parklandswanaka.co.nz

American Express, Visa, MasterCard

Tariff : N.Z. Dollars	
Double	$135-165
Single	
Child	$20

Bedrooms	Qty
Double	4/2
or Twin	2
Single	

Bed Size	Qty
Super King	2
King	
Queen	2
Single	

Bathrooms	Qty
Ensuite	4
Private	
Guest Share	
Family Share	

Bed & Breakfast Luxury Accommodation

Features & Attractions

- *Spectacular mountain views*
- *Relaxing rural environment*
- *Swimming pool & barbecue area*
- *Ski fields nearby, Airport 2 km*
- *Continental/cooked breakfast inclusive*
- *Spa pool and guest lounge*
- *Dine with hosts an option*

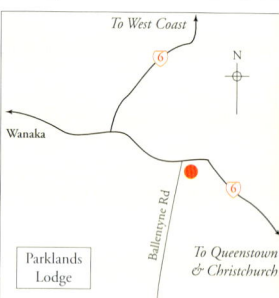

Parklands Lodge has been created to give our guests a tranquil, relaxing experience. Your hosts Margaret and Lawrence offer warm, friendly hospitality, a place of refuge from the hustle and bustle of urban life.

The guest rooms have private ensuites, and an added attraction is the swimming pool and barbecue area. What better way to start the day than with a superb breakfast including freshly brewed coffee, home-made bread and jams and a selection of fresh fruits and cereals, followed by a cooked breakfast. **Parklands Lodge**, with spectacular mountain views is nestled on 10 acres of rural farmland, 6 kilometres south of Wanaka Lake and alpine resort. Just one hour's drive to Queenstown, two hours to Mt Cook and an hour (by air) from Milford Sound.

Wanaka Airport is just 2 kilometres south of Parklands Lodge.

YOUR HOSTS: **Jol and Sandie Squires**   Ph: (03) 443 6633   **Wanaka**

SQUIRES BED & BREAKFAST

68 Totara Terrace, Wanaka
Ph (03) 443 6633, Fax (03) 443 6634
Mobile (025) 602 7669
e-mail: *squires@paradise.net.nz*

Tariff : N.Z. Dollars

Double	$90
Single	$60
Child	$20

Bedrooms	Qty
Double	1
Twin	1
Single	

Bed Size	Qty
Super King	
King	
Queen	1
Single	2

Bathrooms	Qty
Ensuite	
Private	1
Guest Share	
Family Share	

Self-contained Bed & Breakfast & Pottery Studio

Features & Attractions

- *Continental breakfast*
- *Close to town/lake*
- *Only one booking at a time*
- *Pottery studio on site*
- *Privacy plus hospitality*
- *Lovely tree-clad section*
- *Plenty to see and do*
- *Off-street parking*

We welcome you to **Squires B & B** where our 1/3 of an acre property is comprised of our home, a two bedroom self contained annex and our pottery studio, all nestled into a lovely tree-clad garden setting. Our smoke-free guest unit is warm and comfortable with a queen-size bed-sitting room plus an extra twin bedroom should your party require it. TV, microwave, fridge, toaster plus complimentary tea and coffee are just a few of the items on hand.

It allows you the privacy of your own space and yet the opportunity to socialise with us as you wish to.

Feel free to wander around the gardens or visit our pottery studio to watch us at work - you may even feel inclined to have a try on the wheel yourself. We have been potting professionally together for over 20 years and enjoy socialising, music, wining, dining, reading and walking. Wanaka offers you New Zealand at its best and we are more than happy to tell you about the wonderful activities and restaurants in our area.

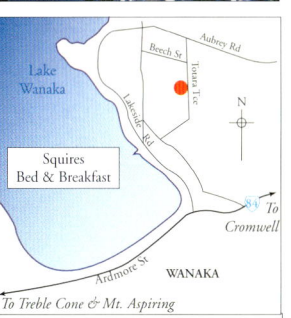

DIRECTIONS:
Along Lakeside, drive onto Beaconspoint Road, right into Beech Street, then right into Totara Terrace.

Wanaka

YOUR HOSTS: Graeme and Andy Oxley   Free Ph: 0800-926 252

TE WANAKA LODGE

23 Brownston Street, Wanaka
Ph (03) 443 9224. Fax (03) 443 9246
Mobile 025-345 065
e-mail: *tewanakalodge@xtra.co.nz*
www.tewanaka.co.nz

Bedrooms	Qty
Double	9
Twin	4
Single	
Bed Size	**Qty**
Super King	
King	
Queen/Double	9
Single	8
Bathrooms	**Qty**
Ensuite	13
Private	
Guest Share	
Family Share	

Deluxe Lodge Accommodation

Tariff : N.Z. Dollars	
Double	$135-165
Single	$125-145
Child	n/a

Features & Attractions

- *Garden hot tub*
- *Private court yard garden*
- *All rooms with ensuites/balconies*
- *Shops/restaurants in walking dist.*
- *Ski / drying room*
- *Gourmet buffet breakfast*
- *Gateway to Aspiring Nat.Park*
- *Golf course a minute away*

The unique design and use of local materials and craftsmanship, give **Te Wanaka Lodge** a contemporary yet warm and welcoming atmosphere.

Our two cosy guest lounges, private courtyard garden, tea kitchen and breakfast room are all there for you to enjoy.

Te Wanaka Lodge - an unforgettable place to relax!!

Nestling in the heart of Wanaka, the Lodge is located close to restaurants, shops, the beach and golf course. On a hot summer's day, relax under the walnut tree, enjoy the mountain views from your private balcony or stroll to the lake for a swim.

Shake off winter's chill by the log fire and after a hard day's skiing throw your gear in our drying room and relax those muscles in the garden hot tub.

If you enjoy adventure and the outdoor life or good food and wine in an unspoiled pristine environment take time **all year round** to enjoy our unique outdoors and the stimulating surroundings of **Te Wanaka Lodge.**

DIRECTIONS: Take SH 6 north of Cromwell towards Wanaka. Continue on SH 84 to Wanaka. At Caltex service station turn left into Brownston St. Continue 100m to **Te Wanaka Lodge** on right.

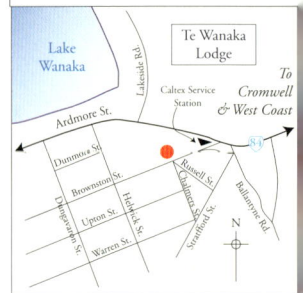

YOUR HOSTS: Poh Choo and David Turner   Ph: (03) 443 1288   **Wanaka**

TEMASEK HOUSE

7 Huchan Lane, Wanaka, Central Otago
Ph/Fax (03) 443 1288
Mobile 025-277 9594
e-mail: *temasek.house@xtra.co.nz*

Tariff : N.Z. Dollars	
Double	$90-105
Single	$55
Child	half price

Bedrooms	Qty
Double	2
Twin	
Single	1
Bed Size	**Qty**
Super King	
King	
Queen/Double	2
Single	2
Bathrooms	**Qty**
Ensuite	1
Private	
Guest Share	1
Family Share	

**Homestay - Bed & Breakfast
Self-contained Accommodation**

Features & Attractions

- *Private & spacious guest area*
- *Ample private parking*
- *All year round activities*
- *Laundry facilities*
- *Views of mountains and lake*
- *Suitable for children*
- *Close to town centre*

Temasek House offers its guests the luxury of their own separate upper floor area equipped with TV, log fire, coffee and tea making facilities, extensive reading collection, large sun-deck, small kitchenette and most importantly for travellers – a washing machine and dryer (small additional charge).

We survive downstairs with our two young children. They try to organise everything although if it gets overwhelming, we can lock them away with the cat!

We try to keep fit – you are welcome to join us for a run, make use of our bikes or even accompany us to the local gym.

Temasek House is a non-smoking home with smoke alarms, heaters and electric blankets in all rooms with ample off-street parking. We offer ample off-street private parking.

Our home contains many artefacts acquired from overseas travel with Asia a strong theme throughout.

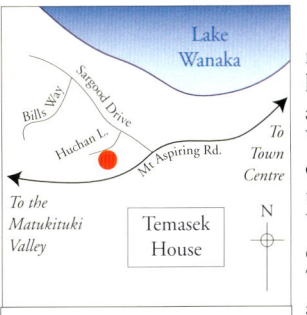

DIRECTIONS: From Wanaka town head towards Matukituki Valley along Mount Aspiring Rd. turn right into Sargood Drive then left into Huchan Lane. **Temasek House** driveway is on the left.

Wanaka | YOUR HOSTS: **Linzi and Brian** | Ph: (03) 443 8421

WANAKA SPRINGS LODGE

21 Warren Street, PO Box 25, Wanaka
Ph (03) 443 8421, Fax (03) 443 8429
Mobile 025-223 8959
e-mail: *info@wanakasprings.com*
www.wanakasprings.com

Tariff : N.Z. Dollars
Double	$140-210
Single	
Child	

Bedrooms	Qty
Double	5
Twin	3
Single	

Bed Size	Qty
Super King	
King	
Queen/Double	5
Single	6

Bathrooms	Qty
Ensuite	8
Private	
Guest Share	
Family Share	

Luxury Accommodation

Features & Attractions

- Landscaped gardens
- Peaceful in-town retreat
- 3-min stroll to shops
- Business facilities
- Breathtaking views
- Fine fabrics & furniture
- Special Honeymoon room
- Full activity service

Opened in 2000, **Wanaka Springs** is a purpose-built luxury lodge featuring local timbers and schist stone to reflect traditional Central Otago styles. The name refers to the natural springs that surface around the Lodge and which form the central and relaxing water features of the landscaped gardens. The Lodge exudes an air of understated elegance and is designed as an 'in-town retreat', with the high standards of hospitality and comfort expected by the discerning guest. The décor of each guest room is individually designed to reflect the superb views of Lake Wanaka and the surrounding mountains. Hidden behind the Lodge's stylish façade, the guest accommodation comprises 5 Queen and 3 Twin-size, tastefully appointed and spacious rooms each with private ensuites. Savour our special breakfast buffet and afternoon tea in the sunny dining room from your private deck/courtyard - all with stunning views. Or unwind with aperitifs in the cosy lounge with its blazing log fire, fascinating book collection and sumptuous furnishings. Wheather you choose to relax and be pampered or enjoy the countless activities Wanaka has to offer, we will ensure that your stay is just what you need. **Wanaka Springs** – a unique experience of informal sophistication for discerning travellers.

DIRECTIONS: Take SH 84 to Wanaka. At Caltex Service Station turn left into Brownston St. Take third left into Helwick St. and second left into Warren St. **Wanaka Springs** is at the end of the cul-de-sac on the left.

| YOUR HOSTS: Pam and Ken Scott | Ph: (03) 445 0788 | ☎ | **Cromwell** |

VILLA AMO

Shine Lane, Pisa Moorings, No 3 RD, Cromwell
Ph (03) 445 0788, Fax (03) 445 0711
e-mail: *VillaAmo@xtra.co.nz*

Features & Attractions

- *Situated on Lake Dunstan*
- *Rugged mountain scenery*
- *Skifields within an hour*
- *Historic walks*
- *Superb fishing summer/winter*
- *Vineyard and orchard tours*

Double	$110
Single	$95
Child	na

Homestay Bed & Breakfast

Bedrooms	Qty
Double	2
Twin	
Single	

Bed Size	Qty
King	
Queen/Double	2
Single	

Bathrooms	Qty
Ensuite	
Private	1
Guest Share	
Family Share	

Welcome to **Villa Amo** in its tranquil setting on the shore of Lake Dunstan. Built in late 1996 it is the ideal base from which to explore the delights of beautiful Central Otago. We have superb fishing and water sports at our doorstep and many other activities only a 10 minute drive away in Cromwell. Queenstown, Wanaka and Alexandra all within 45 minutes. Our two spacious guest rooms are private and quiet and the well appointed bathroom is private – single party booking only. To start the day enjoy a substantial breakfast, cooked or continental, at a time that is convenient to you. After a day exploring the many wonderful attractions of the region relax on our sunny patio or in the outdoor therapeutic spa pool.

DIRECTIONS: Please phone for easy directions.

| YOUR HOSTS: Claire and Jack Davis | Free Ph: 0800-205 104 | ☎ | **Cromwell** |

HIBURN FARMSTAY

Hiburn, RD 2, Cromwell
Ph (03) 445 1291, Fax (03) 445 1291
e-mail: *hiburn@xtra.co.nz*

Features & Attractions

- *Peaceful setting*
- *Outstanding views*
- *Hill walks*
- *A real farmstay*
- *Share farming activities*
- *Amazing sheepdogs*

Double	$80
Single	$50
Child	$30

Farmstay Bed & Breakfast

Bedrooms	Qty
Double	1
Twin	1
Single	

Bed Size	Qty
King	
Queen/Double	1
Single	2

Bathrooms	Qty
Ensuite	
Private	
Guest Share	1
Family Share	

Welcome to **Hiburn Farmstay**, ideally situated at Cromwell, the centre of beautiful Central Otago. Between main tourist attractions, yet off the beaten track. We are farming 400 hectares with Merino sheep and deer. Guests are welcome to join in.
Farm activities are always included and working sheepdogs are a speciality. We encourage our guests to come to dinner and enjoy time chatting over a meal. Dinner is available by arrangement. Home produce is used as much as possible. Our interests include sport, curling, sheepdog competitions, gardening and handcrafts. **Hiburn Farmstay** is an ideal place to explore this region, children are welcome. We treat our guests as friends and invite you to relax with us and enjoy our wonderful farmstay.

DIRECTIONS:
Hiburn is 10 km north from Cromwell off State Highway 6. Please phone for further directions.
Best time to catch us in is mealtimes or evenings.

Cromwell YOUR HOSTS: **June Boulton** Ph: (03) 445 0404

Quartz Reef Creek
Rapid 349, SH 8, RD 3 Northburn
Cromwell
Ph (03) 445 0404, Fax (03) 445 0404

Features & Attractions
- *Quiet, peaceful surroundings*
- *Lakeside setting*
- *Private deck & entrance*
- *Architecturally designed home*
- *Christchurch/Queenstown Highway*
- *Stunning lake & mountain scenery*

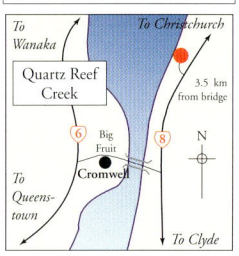

Homestay Bed & Breakfast

Double	$100
Single	$60
Child	

Quartz Reef Creek is situated in the mountains and lakes of Central Otago, a dry climate with high average sunshine hours, in a rapidly expanding wine-growing area. Your sunny room has a panoramic views of mountains and lake, and total privacy. Also tea making facilities, fridge, microwave and TV. Another room has twin beds and a private bathroom. Enjoy a walk along the lake front, a trip to local goldmining areas or visit local wineries. I have a pottery studio on site and supply local galleries. I also have a friendly black cat called Tom. My home is the first house north of the bridge on the lake front.

Bedrooms	Qty
Double	1
Twin	1
Single	

Bed Size	Qty
King	
Queen/Double	1
Single	3

Bathrooms	Qty
Ensuite	1
Private	1
Guest Share	
Family Share	

Bed & Breakfast
in
New Zealand
on the internet – visit
www.travelwise.co.nz

YOUR HOSTS: Olivia, Adrian and Hollie   Ph: (03) 445 1112   **Cromwell**

WALNUT GROVE

Adrian and Olivia Somerville
SH 6, Lowburn, RD 2, Cromwell
Ph (03) 445 1112, Fax (03) 445 1115
Mobile 025-774 695
e-mail: *walnut.grove@xtra.co.nz*

Tariff : N.Z. Dollars	
Double	$110
Single	$95
Child	

Bedrooms	Qty
Double	2
Twin	
Single	

Bed Size	Qty
Super King	1
King	
Queen/Double	1
Single	

Bathrooms	Qty
Ensuite	2
Private	
Guest Share	
Family Share	

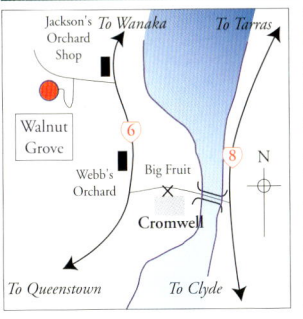

Countrystay - Bed & Breakfast

Features & Attractions

- *Historic gold mining area*
- *Beautiful scenery*
- *Queenstown/Wanaka 45 min.*
- *Close to Lake Dunstan*
- *Spacious home and garden*
- *Cromwell 4 min. drive*
- *Orchard on boundary*
- *Fishing, golf, sightseeing*

Relax and enjoy our world! A place for all seasons – with a dry climate, wonderful scenery, fine fishing in Lake Dunstan and rivers, excellent golf course, historic gold mining sites and towns, orchards, vineyards, wineries, the adventure activities of nearby Queenstown and Wanaka, it is unforgettable. The spring and autumn colours are magical. Comfortable non-smoking guest bedrooms have TV, clock radio, coffee/tea making facilities and ensuite bathrooms. (The super king is also available as two single beds.) We have a large lounge with wood burner fire for winter and separate dining room.

Breakfast is served when it suits you and we would be delighted to help plan your stay. A laundry is available. Our home is set in 4 acres with large garden and shady walnut trees in the grounds. With views of the valley and mountains and a working orchard beside us, it is a lovely setting. We have two siamese cats and a labrador dog. We have travelled extensively, just love meeting people and would like you to make our home your home when in Central Otago. Please ring for directions and reservations.

Arrowtown-Queenstown ☎ YOUR HOSTS: Roy and Tamaki Llewellyn   Ph: (03) 442 1773

WILLOWBROOK
Malaghan Road, RD 1, Queenstown
Ph (03) 442 1773, Fax (03) 442 1773
Mobile 025-516 739
e-mail: *wbrook@queenstown.co.nz*

Tariff : N.Z. Dollars	
Double	$105-125
Single	$90-110
Child	'POA'

Bedrooms	Qty
Double	2
Twin	1
Single	

Bed Size	Qty
Super King	1
King	
Queen	1
Single	2

Bathrooms	Qty
Ensuite	2
Private	1
Guest Share	
Family Share	

Guest House Bed & Breakfast

BB G JCB VISA MasterCard AMERICAN EXPRESS (Diners)

Features & Attractions
- *Peaceful rural location*
- *Guest lounge, 2 open fires*
- *Luxurious outdoor spa*
- *Large garden with tennis court*
- *Door to ski lift - 15 min.*
- *Millbrook Resort - 3 min.*
- *Beautiful scenic walks*
- *Japanese spoken*

Willowbrook is a 1914 farm house at the foot of Coronet Peak in the beautiful Wakatipu Basin. The setting is rural, historical and distinctly peaceful, and with the attractions of Queenstown only 15 minutes away, **Willowbrook** can truly claim to offer the best of both worlds. The old homestead has been beautifully renovated. While the character of the original house has been retained, it now boasts such modern comforts as central heating, Sky TV and a luxurious spa pool. Guest rooms contain a bed (or beds) more comfortable than you would find in most hotels and are ensuite or have a private bathroom. The front deck is an ideal spot to sit back and watch hanggliders drifting down from Coronet Peak. In the colder months, enjoying one of the open fires in the lounge, following an apres-ski spa, can be addictive. We have a tennis court and are within easy reach of four ski fields and three golf courses. An Anglo/Japanese couple with a wealth of cross cultural experiences, we are only too happy to help with local bookings and itineraries in general.

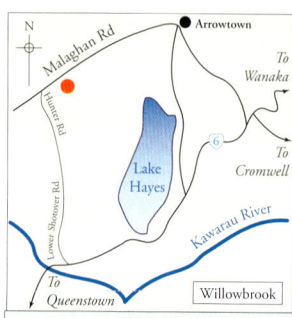

DIRECTIONS:
Willowbrook is on Malaghan Rd, the 'back road' between Queenstown and Arrowtown. Queenstown 15 min., Arrowtown 5 min., Millbrook Resort 3 min.

YOUR HOSTS: Micha and Klaus Lenk   Free Ph: 0800-271 128   **Lake Hayes - Queenstown**

VILLA SORGENFREI

11 Arrowtown/Lake Hayes Road, Queenstown
Ph (03) 442 1128. Fax (03) 442 1239
e-mail: *villa@xtra.co.nz*

Tariff : N.Z. Dollars	
Double	$195
Single	$165
Child	

Bedrooms	Qty
Double	2
Twin	
Single	
Bed Size	**Qty**
Super King	2
King	
Queen	
Single	
Bathrooms	**Qty**
Ensuite	1
Private	1
Guest Share	
Family Share	

**Boutique Accommodation
Bed & Breakfast**

Features & Attractions

- *Beautiful lake, fishing, swimming*
- *Country peace close to Queenstown*
- *Multitude of outdoor activities*
- *Golf courses nearby*
- *Stacked stone house*
- *German spoken*
- *4 ski fields within region, or just holiday relaxation*

Dear Friends –

Found this lovely place called **Villa Sorgenfrei** at Lake Hayes. Just fifteen minutes from Queenstown or five minutes from Arrowtown. Played golf yesterday (choice of four golf courses), then into Queenstown. What a choice of restaurants and bars. Sure was nice to come back here though, to this **so** relaxing stacked stone house – transported us to another world – humm –. Today we'll go to the winery for lunch to build up courage for a Bungi Jump! Might check out historic Arrowtown and its interesting museum **or** better still, go fishing in the lake for those trout that keep waving to me (can see them from the breakfast table!). My god, there's so much to do and see in this area. Shame we didn't allow more time for here. When you come, just phone Micha and Klaus.
Cheers.
(Wish you were here now.)

DIRECTIONS:
From Queenstown or Cromwell take SH 6 to Lake Hayes.
Turn onto the Arrowtown/Lake Hayes Road, take first turn left.

Lake Hayes - Queenstown

YOUR HOSTS: **Garry and Marie**   Ph: (03) 442 0730

"THE INN AT 670"

670 Lake Hayes - Arrow Junction, Lake Hayes,
RD 1, Queenstown
P (03) 442 0730, Fax(03) 442 0731
Mobile 025-336 304
e-mail: *opm@xtra.co.nz*

Features & Attractions

- 4 skifields within region
- Golf courses nearby
- Very quiet location
- Electric blankets, feather down duvets
- Beautiful lake - fish or swim
- Close to Queenstown and Arrowtown

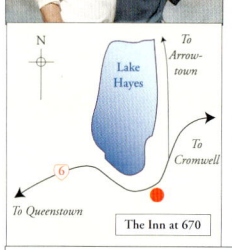

Bed & Breakfast Homestay

Double	$130-160
Single	$65-80
Child	Half price

Bedrooms	Qty
Double	1
Twin	1
Single	1

Bed Size	Qty
King	
Queen/Double	1
Single	3

Bathrooms	Qty
Ensuite	
Private	1
Guest Share	1
Family Share	

Garry and Marie invite you to stay with us at our home, **"The Inn at 670"**. –The whole of this majestic mountain area is a photographer's dream. Breathtaking magic views are continuously mirrored by Lake Hayes.

We provide privacy, with comfort and top quality beds, individual heating and double-glazed windows. Enjoy a sumptuous buffet breakfast with home-made jams, fresh fruit and yoghurt, cereals, breads, freshly brewed coffee, and special teas. Our home is 15 minutes from Queenstown and 5 minutes from Arrowtown. There is a choice of four golf courses, 4 skifields, fishing and so many other exciting things to do.

Long stayers most welcome.

DIRECTIONS: From Queenstown or Cromwell take SH 6 to Lake Hayes.

Old Stock Yards

YOUR HOSTS: **King and Fran Allen** Ph: (03) 442 0864   **Queenstown**

BRIDESDALE

Walnut Lane, Ladies Mile, Queenstown, Otago
Ph: (03) 442 0864, Fax:(03) 442 0860
Mobile (025) 360 403
e-mail: *bridesdale@xtra.co.nz*

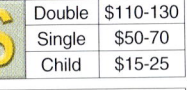

Tariff : N.Z. Dollars

Double	$110-130
Single	$50-70
Child	$15-25

Bedrooms	Qty
Double	1
Triple	1
Single	

Bed Size	Qty
Super King	
King	
Queen	1
Single	2

Bathrooms	Qty
Ensuite	
Private	1
Guest Share	
Family Share	

**Farmstay - Bed & Breakfast
Separate Self-contained Cottage**

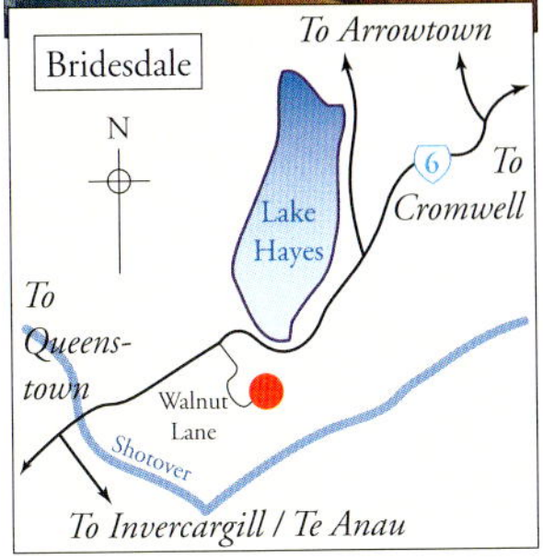

Features & Attractions

- *Cattle Farm*
- *Trout fishing*
- *Close to Skifields*
- *Mountain views*
- *Close to unlimited Queenstown Adventures and Attractions*
- *Peaceful and private*

Our farm is midway between Queenstown and Arrowtown, one kilometre off SH 6, 10 minutes to Queenstown and 8 minutes to Arrowtown.

The farm boundaries the Kawarau River and the Hayes Creek where there is excellent private fly fishing. We have beef cattle, a few sheep and a farm dog.

If you ski you can be on two out of three local ski fields in half an hour. The cottage is yours exclusively and is fully self-contained with kitchen, electric blankets, hair dryers, TV, stereo, BBQ, washing machine and your own private area with beautiful mountain views. If preferred you can join us for breakfast as we enjoy meeting people.

Our prices include a continental breakfast. We have a shy cat called "Fergus" and a friendly little Fox Terrier called "Trouble". No smoking inside please.

Queenstown

YOUR HOSTS: Glenys and Kevin Reynolds   Ph: (03) 442 2194

THE OLD' FERRY HOTEL GUESTHOUSE

Spence Road, Lower Shotover, Queenstown
Ph (03) 442 2194, Fax (03) 442 2190
e-mail: *info@ferry.co.nz*
www.ferry.co.nz

Tariff : N.Z. Dollars

Double	$155
Single	$100
Child	half price

Bedrooms	Qty
Double	2
Twin	1
Single	
Bed Size	**Qty**
Super King	
King	
Double	2
Single	2
Bathrooms	**Qty**
Ensuite	1
Private	
Guest Share	1
Family Share	

Bed & Breakfast Guest House

Features & Attractions

- Country kitchen for guests' use
- 10 min. to Queenstown & Arrowtown
- Fishing advice & guide
- Central to ski fields & local attractions
- Genuine historic building
- Peaceful & relaxing location
- Photo display of Hotel's history
- Huge wood-burning fire

Old World Elegance aptly describes this delightful Guest House – not just a place to stay but a feature of your holiday. Formerly a popular hotel for 100 years, the Guest House is a local landmark. Your hosts Kevin and Glenys have traced the hotel's history back to 1868 and in the process ascertained that they are the 25th owners of the Hotel. Kevin and Glenys, their daughter Clare and everyone's favourite, Chester the English springer spaniel, have separate accommodation which adjoins the Guest House, but are on hand at any time to help with tour bookings, advice and information. They are equally happy to sit and chat with guests who look for local information and companionship. Kevin can guide or advise you on all aspects of local fishing. Ferry Hotel Guest House has three bedrooms, one of them with an antique brass bed and character ensuite bathroom. There is a kitchen that Granny would have been proud of and a charming lounge-dining room, decked with historic photos, paintings and memorabilia, and kept warm by a roaring log wood-burner. Laundry facilities and a gas barbecue are available. Alfresco eating areas are situated in the English cottage garden. Kevin and Glenys enjoy helping you to make the most of your stay in Queenstown and look forward to meeting you.

DIRECTIONS:
From SH 6 turn into Lower Shotover Road – Blue Sign, follow left turn into Spence Road.

| YOUR HOST: Ileen Mutch | Ph: (03) 442 7260 | **Queenstown** |

BUSH CREEK HEALTH RETREAT

21 Bowen Street,
Queenstown
Ph (03) 442 7260, Fax (03) 442 7250

Tariff : N.Z. Dollars

Double	$110
Single	$60
Child	neg.

Bedrooms	Qty
Double	1
Twin	2
Single	

Bed Size	Qty
Super King	
King	
Queen	1
Single	4

Bathrooms	Qty
Ensuite	
Private	
Guest Share	2
Family Share	

DIRECTIONS: From Queenstown follow the road to Coronet Peak Ski field. **Bush Creek Health Retreat** is sign posted.(Approx. 1km)

Homestay - Bed & Breakfast
Specialized Health Retreat

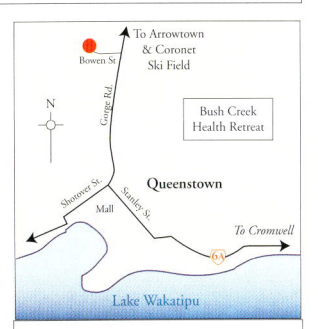

Features & Attractions

- 3 acres of natural paradise
- Organically grown food
- Internationally recognised Natural Healing Practitioner
- Renowned old-world garden
- Deep Tissue Massage Therapy
- Wholesome, nutritious meals
- Pure, natural spring water

Advance booking is recommended.

Bush Creek is one of the longest established Health Retreats in New Zealand. It is set in three acres of natural paradise only ten minutes walk from the centre of Queenstown, your base for the majestic splendour of the Southern Alps, lakes and Fiords. The rooms are fully appointed with all the extras that provide the ultimate in comfort. Enjoy nutritious, organically grown and prepared food and pure natural spring water.

Ileen Mutch, who owns and operates **Bush Creek Health Retreat**, is an internationally recognised natural healing practitioner, one of the longest practising in this part of the globe. Still your soul and revitalize your energies in harmony with her renowned old-world garden, listening to songs of native birds and the cascading waterfall.

There is also Deep Tissue Massage Therapy available to you.
Come and join the list of travellers that return again and again for their rejuvenating stay.

Queenstown

YOUR HOST: Ruth Campbell
Ph: (03) 442 9190

CAMPBELLS B&B
10 Wakatipu Heights, Queenstown
Ph (03) 442 9190, Fax(03) 442 4404
Mobile 021-116 8801
e-mail: *roosterretreat@xtra.co.nz*

Features & Attractions
- *Child friendly*
- *Tranquil garden setting*
- *Self-contained guest unit*
- *Panoramic views*
- *Generous breakfast*
- *Walk to town centre*

Double	$100-120
Single	$60
Child	

Bed & Breakfast and Self-contained Unit

Bedrooms	Qty
Double	2/3
or Twin	1
Single	

Bed Size	Qty
Super King	1
Queen	1
Double	1
Single	1

Bathrooms	Qty
Ensuite	
Private	1
Guest Share	1
Family Share	

Our 2 girls, 1 cat and 2 bantams welcome other children to share their playground with them. We have a tranquil home with off-street parking and a ½ acre garden to relax in. It has outstanding views of Lake Wakatipu, Queenstown and the surrounding mountains including the Remarkables.

Our fully self-contained cottage garden unit has proven immensely popular with guests – especially those with children! It includes a fully equipped kitchen and laundry. This allows you complete privacy or you can mix with us as you wish. A super king (or twin) room with private bathroom is in the house.

Complimentary tea, coffee and laundry facilities. There are no stairs as all guest facilities are on ground level. Enjoy a generous continental breakfast with fresh baked bread and real coffee at your leisure.

Guests say "Excellent value for money".

> DIRECTIONS: Turn off Frankton Rd. and up Suburb St. First right into Panorama Terrace, second on left into Wakatipu Heights. (1.5 km north-east of town centre or 20 min. walk to town and $5 taxi back home - uphill).

Queenstown

YOUR HOSTS: Steve and Jo Weir
Ph: (03) 442 9812

THE HISTORIC STONE HOUSE
47 Hallenstein Street
Ph (03) 442 9812, Fax (03) 441 8293
Mobile 025-573 903
e-mail: *stone.house@xtra.co.nz*
www.stonehouse.co.nz

Features & Attractions
- *Outdoor Jacuzzi*
- *Historic ambience*
- *Fire-side drinks*
- *4 min. from downtown*
- *Tour-booking service*
- *Lake views*

Boutique Bed & Breakfast Inn

Double	$220
Single	
Child	

Originally built of local Otago stone in 1874, **The Stone House** has been restored to provide charming accommodation for travellers. We are a short walk from the main village of Queenstown, and also provide car parking. Guestrooms feature hairdryers, bathrobes, radio alarm and telephone. Each room has private bathroom facilities and beds are made up with feather duvets and pillows and crisp cotton sheets. Choose between king or queen bed, lake or garden view, ensuite shower or private bathtub. Breakfast is served overlooking Lake Wakatipu, and includes cooked choices such as pancakes or Eggs Benedict, as well as a Continental selection accompanied by freshly brewed coffee and tea. Soak up the alpine ambience in the outdoor hot tub, then meet Baz the cat and your fellow guests over a fire-side aperitif. We will help you choose the best restaurant to suit your mood, and provide advice on how to spend the next day in Queenstown, New Zealand's Adventure Playground.

> DIRECTIONS: Coming from Frankton on SH 6A, after 7 km turn right into Dublin St., then left Hallenstein St. We are on your right.

Bedrooms	Qty
Double	4
Twin	
Single	

Bed Size	Qty
King	3
Queen/Double	1
Single	

Bathrooms	Qty
Ensuite	3
Private	1
Guest Share	
Family Share	

YOUR HOSTS: Louise Kiely and Staff Ph: (03) 442 9043

Queenstown

QUEENSTOWN HOUSE
69 Hallenstein Street
Queenstown
Ph (03) 442 9043, Fax (03) 442 8755
Mobile 025-324 146
e-mail: queenstown.house@xtra.co.nz

Tariff : N.Z. Dollars

	Double	$185-225
	Single	$185
	Child	

Bedrooms	Qty
Double	8(3)
or Twin	5
Single	

Bed Size	Qty
Super King	
King/Twin	5
Queen/Double	3
Single	

Bathrooms	Qty
Ensuite	8
Private	
Guest Share	
Family Share	

Superior Inn

Features & Attractions

- *4 minutes walk to town centre*
- *Small weddings a speciality*
- *High quality beds and pillows*
- *Tea and coffee provided*
- *Separate guest entrance*
- *Quiet location*

"The best small B&B hotel in which we have stayed" comment our returning guests. Our elevated position has wonderful views over the town centre, lake and mountains.

A delux breakfast menu served in our lakeview dining room is included, plus our very popular, complimentary cocktail hour each evening, hosted in either the fireside sitting room or rose-filled courtyard.

Guest laundry, bag storage, TV, hairdryers and supplied. Experience our unique style of hospitality, local knowledge and cheerful staff.

Owner Louise Kiely, an ex restauranter and world traveller.

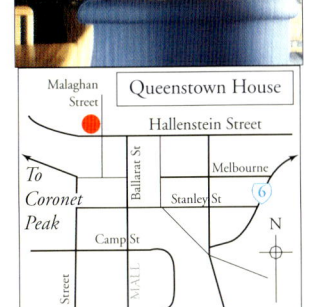

DIRECTIONS:
300 metres from Queenstown PO.
Take Ballarat St north to "T" intersection.
Turn left into Hallenstein St.
Queenstown House is on the right,
on the corner of Malaghan St.

Queenstown — YOUR HOSTS: **Maria and Chris Lamens** — Ph: (09) 442 4811

LARCH HILL HOMESTAY/B&B

16 Panners Way, Goldfields, Queenstown
Ph (03) 442 4811, Fax (03) 441 8882
e-mail: *information@larchhill.com*
www.larchhill.com

Tariff : N.Z. Dollars	
Double	$120-140
Single	$75-100
Child	neg.

Bedrooms	Qty
Double	3
Twin	1
Single	
Bed Size	**Qty**
Super King	1
King	1
Queen	1
King/Single	2
Bathrooms	**Qty**
Ensuite	2
Private	2
Guest Share	
Family Share	

**Homestay/Bed & breakfast
Superb Accommodation**

Features & Attractions

- *Magnificent scenery*
- *Tranquil setting*
- *Gourmet breakfast*
- *Italian & German spoken*
- *Dine with hosts option*
- *Golf courses & fishing nearby*
- *Adventure/itinerary planning*
- *Music, art and craft lovers*

Maria and Chris offer you a warm welcome to **Larch Hill** in beautiful Queenstown. **Larch Hill Homestay** is built on an elevated site overlooking the blue waters of Lake Wakatipu. It is surrounded by spectacular mountains which are snow-capped in winter. Larch Hill is only a 3 minute drive from the centre of Queenstown and in walking distance from the lake. Public transport passes the driveway.

All rooms and sundeck overlook the lake and surrounding mountains. This home provides a feeling of relaxation. A restful theme flows through the bedrooms into the dining room with its library, opening to a sunny courtyard surrounded by cottage gardens. On arrival you are welcomed with fresh coffee and home-made cake. In winter a roaring log fire awaits your return from a day's skiing or sightseeing. Having worked as a chef, Maria provides three-course dinners by prior arrangement. Breakfast: continental, home-made bread and yoghurt and fresh fruit salad. We have pleasure in organising any Queenstown experience. We provide: Complimentary pick-up from Queenstown Airport or Bus Station. Fax and e-mail communications facilities.

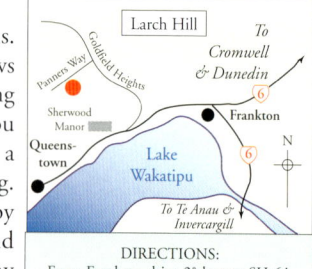

DIRECTIONS:
From Frankton drive 2" km on SH 6A
towards Queenstown.
At 'Sherwood Manor' turn right into
Goldfields Heigths. Panners Way is
2nd left, then 1st access on left.

YOUR HOSTS: **Nery Howard and Michael Clark** Ph: (03) 442 9160

Queenstown

TRELAWN PLACE
Gorge Road, Arthurs Point, Queenstown
Postal: PO Box 117, Queenstown
Ph/Fax (03) 442 9160, Mobile 025-224 2819
e-mail: *trelawn@ihug.co.nz*
www.trelawnb-b.co.nz

Tariff : N.Z. Dollars

	Double	$155-215
	Single	
	Child	

Bedrooms	Qty
Double	5
Twin	1
Single	

Bed Size	Qty
Super King	2
King	1
Queen/Double	2
Single	

Bathrooms	Qty
Ensuite	4
Private	1
Guest Share	
Family Share	

Bed & Breakfast and Self-contained Accom.

Features & Attractions

- *Unique location beside the Shotover River*
- *Fantastic views of surrounding mountains*
- *Large private garden*
- *Five minutes from centre of Queenstown*

Sited dramatically above the Shotover River with gardens and lawns sweeping to the cliff edge, **Trelawn Place** is a superior country lodge only four kilometres from busy Queenstown. We have four comfortably appointed ensuite rooms, furnished with country chintz and antiques. Our guest sitting room has an open fire and a well stocked library. Outdoors you will find quiet sitting areas and shady vine-covered verandahs. Generous cooked breakfast features home-made and grown produce. If you are missing your pets, a cat and friendly corgis will make you feel at home.
A forty eight hour cancellation policy applies.

DIRECTIONS: Take SH 6A into Queenstown, right at 2nd roundabout into Gorge Road, travel 4km towards Arthurs Point. **Trelawn Place** is sign posted beside gate on right.

Fly Fishing Guide. Michael guide is available for trout fishing trips in the area. We can also help with bookings for all other local activities.

Self-contained cottage. With its own fireside and roses framing the door, the two bedroom stone cottage is a honeymoon hideaway.

Queenstown

YOUR HOSTS: **Diane and Bill Forsyth**   Free Ph: 0800-271 617

WINDSOR HEIGHTS

5 Windsor Place, Queenstown
Ph (03) 442 5949, Fax (03) 441 8989
e-mail: *windsor.heights@queenstown-holiday.co.nz*
http://www.queenstown-holiday.co.nz

Tariff : N.Z. Dollars	
Double	$120
Single	$100
Child	

Bedrooms	Qty
Double	1
Twin	1
Single	
Bed Size	**Qty**
Super King	
King	
Queen	1
Single	2
Bathrooms	**Qty**
Ensuite	1
Private	1
Guest Share	
Family Share	

Homestay - Bed & Breakfast

Features & Attractions

- Surely the best views in town
- Very quiet location
- Multi-choice cooked breakfast
- Secluded courtyard with hot tub
- Use of our laundry facilities
- Walking tracks close by
- E-mail and internet access
- 4th generation local knowledge

DIRECTIONS:
Entering Queenstown on SH 6A, pass Quality Resort Terraces on right, then take 2nd street on right (Dublin St). Continue uphill into Edinburgh Drive, then left into Windsor Place – we are No. 5 on left.

Our modern home sits high above Queenstown, offering breathtaking views of mountains and lake. The sheltered courtyard provides a relaxed outdoor living style, complete with gas barbecue and large spa/hot tub. On summer evenings this area is a real favourite, before moving to the lounge and watching fabulous sunsets across the lake. We invite our guests to join us for refreshments in the evening before leaving for dinner in one of the many wonderful restaurants that Queenstown offers.

A courtesy car is available to meet guests. As authorised booking agents we will gladly offer advice and help arrange your Queenstown activities. If walking is your pleasure, we have the Queenstown Hill Track close by. We have one very shy cat named Zinny, who chooses to hide from our guests as a rule, but might be persuaded to say hello to cat lovers!

YOUR HOSTS: **Vicky and Eddie** Ph: (03) 442 7088 **Queenstown**

DRIFTWOOD
Kelvin Peninsula,
Postal Address: P.O.Box 2176, Wakatipu,
Ph (03) 442 7088, Fax(03) 442 7044
e-mail: *info@driftwood.net.nz*
www.driftwood.net.nz

Tariff : N.Z. Dollars	
Double	$150-175
Single	$100
Studio	$150

Bedrooms	Qty
Double	3/4
Twin	1
Single	
Bed Size	**Qty**
Super King	
King	1
Queen/Double	4
Single	2
Bathrooms	**Qty**
Ensuite	3
Private	2
Guest Share	
Family Share	

**Absolute Lakefront
Self-contained Accommodation**

Features & Attractions

- *Private access to Lake*
- *Large secluded garden*
- *Sauna, outside bath, laundry*
- *Golf course - 5 min. walk*
- *E-mail, fax, phone available*
- *Music, art. library, maps*
- *Homemade preserves, fresh coffee*
- *Kayaks, rowboat, swimming*

DIRECTIONS: Brochure with map available ... or phone for easy directions. Bookings essential

Nestled in native bush beneath "The Remarkables" on the "wild side" of Kelvin Peninsula, **Driftwood** offers a secluded retreat right on the edge of Lake Wakatipu. Wake to bellbirds and sunrise on the mountains. Wander down through the garden to the lake where the view is breathtaking, the water clear and the beach deserted. Both Studio Apartments are finished in natural timber have queen bed, ensuite, logfire, TV, stereo, kitchen stocked with basic ingredients. Abasket of seasonal fare gives Bed & Breakfast guests the option to eat in their apartment, on the deck, the beach or in the garden. (Weekly rate for studio $900)

The **Three Bedroom House**, elegant and comfortable with king double and twin rooms is also available for single party bookings - minimum 4-day-booking, minimum 4 nights, $300 night, $1800 week.

We are widely travelled outdoor enthusiasts, who have lived locally for 30 years – happy to help you plan and book your daily expeditions. We appreciate good food and wine and can advise on Queenstown's many wonderful restaurants. Above all we want you to feel at home in the relaxed, casual atmosphere at **Driftwood**.

Garston - Southern Lakes — YOUR HOSTS: **Robyn and David Parker** — Free Ph: 0800-265 192

MATAURA VALLEY STATION

850 Cainard Road (Rapid Number)
Garston, Southern Lakes
Postal: PO Box 2, Garston, Southland
Ph (03) 248 8552. Fax (03) 248 8552
e-mail: *matauravalley@xtra.co.nz*

Tariff : N.Z. Dollars	
Double	$110-150
Single	$80-100
Child	$10-55

Bedrooms	Qty
Double	3
Twin	1
Single	1

Bed Size	Qty
Super King	
King	2
Queen/Double	1
Single	3

Bathrooms	Qty
Ensuite	2
Private	
Guest Share	1
Family Share	1

High Country Farmstay Fishing Lodge

Features & Attractions

- Working high country station
- 19,000 acres
- 10,000 sheep, 300 cattle
- Trout fishing river
- Queenstown Airport 45 min.
- Glorious views & tranquility
- Day visitors welcome
- Aerial & 4-wheel-drive tours

Welcome to our 19,000 acre high country sheep and cattle station. On a sunny site, overlooking the Mataura River, famous for brown trout fishing, our comfortable, modern home has glorious views. Alpine tranquility only 45 min. scenic drive from Queenstown's airport. Join in farm activities, walk or mountain bike on marked trails, take a 4-wheel-drive tour into high mountain pastures, or relax and enjoy the views, the garden and the skylarks. Paradise ducks nest on the creek, hawks soar, a New Zealand falcon may rest on the roof top. Return to roaring log fires to toast marshmallows after a day at the ski fields. We feature delicious 3-course farm-style meals with fresh organically grown vegetables, homebaking and NZ wines. Morning and afternoon teas are complimentary. A great base from which to travel throughout Southland, to Queenstown or Milford Sound. Meet our pet lamb, two cats, the pig, six sheep dogs, 300 catttle and 10,000 sheep. Aerial and 4WD trips by arrangement. Take a break on your way between Queenstown and Te Anau. Day visitors welcome. Reservations essential. We aim to make your stay a special memory.

The view from our garden.

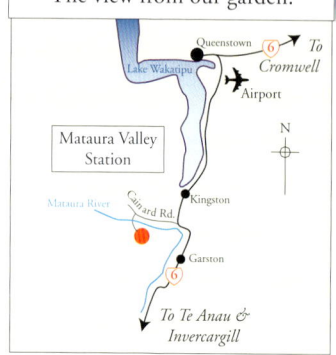

YOUR HOSTS: Ailsa, Johnny and Family   Ph: (03) 248 6137   **Mossburn**

Kowhai Lodge

5665 Highway 94, Post Office
Mossburn - Te Anau Highway
Ph (03) 248 6137, Fax(03) 248 6137

Features & Attractions

- Working sheep and deer farm
- Guiding available for hunting
- Mountain and rural views
- Central fishing location
- Close to amenities
- Horse riding available

**Farmstay Cottage
Fishing Lodge**

Double	$100-120
Single	$90-100
Child	$15

Come and enjoy a farm lifestyle with us and our family. Our rustic 2 bedroom lodge features a hand-built stone chimney and large open fire. Completely redecorated in 1999 with comfortable beds and cosy atmosphere. **Kowhai Lodge** is surrounded by red deer in their natural environment, including a pet hind to hand feed! Native landscaping blends with ancient kowhai trees rising steeply on the ridge behind the Lodge. Great for an evening stroll to view the surrounding area. Mossburn, the Deer Capital of NZ, is centrally located, half way between Fiordland, Queenstown, Invercargill or The Catlins. The Oreti River boundary's the property for top fishing. Let us help you plan your stay, help us on the farm, ride our horses or enjoy the garden. Flexibility is our byword. Totally self contained, the Lodge provides a central base to enjoy your break. We have two skifields within an hour's drive, return to a roaring fire and relax. **Kowhai Lodge** is 1 km west of the Mossburn township, on the left hand side of Highway 94 to Te Anau and Milford Sound. We look forward to meeting you and sharing our lifestyle.

Bedrooms	Qty
Double	1
Twin	1
Single	
Bed Size	**Qty**
King	
Queen/Double	1
King/Single	2
Bathrooms	**Qty**
Ensuite	
Private	
Guest Share	1
Family Share	

A fisherman's paradise.

Te Anau

YOUR HOSTS: Dorothy and Donald Cromb Ph: (03) 249 5805

"TAPUA"
66 Wilderness Road (Rapid No), 2 RD,
The Key, Te Anau
Ph (03) 249 5805, Fax (03) 249 5805
Mobile 025-201 9109
e-mail: *Tapua.Cromb@xtra.co.nz*

Features & Attractions
- *Working sheep farm*
- *Milford/Doubtful Sound trips*
- *3700 sheep - 100 cattle*
- *Wonderful scenery*
- *Trout fishing rivers*
- *Walking tracks, golf*

Farmstay Bed & Breakfast

Double	$110
Single	$70
Child	Half price

Bedrooms	Qty
Double	1
Twin	1
Single	
Bed Size	**Qty**
King	1
Queen/Double	
Single	2
Bathrooms	**Qty**
Ensuite	
Private	
Guest Share	1
Family Share	

You are surrounded by "Million Dollar" views while enjoying the comfort of our large modern family home. Electric blankets/wool underlays on all beds - heaters in bedrooms. Enjoy traditional farm-style meals, homemade preserves and jams. Evening meals by prior arrangement $25 pp. Children under 12, $1/2$ price.

We are situated in a very handy position close to the main road, only 15 minutes from Te Anau or Manapouri, an excellent base for your sightseeing trips to magnificent Milford and Doubtful Sounds. We recommend a two night stay so you can enjoy a relaxing trip to the Sounds, as well as look over our 348 ha (870 acre) farm with 3700 sheep and approximately 100 cattle. Some of New Zealand's best fishing rivers within a few minutes drive and the finest walking tracks in the world, golf course etc. We are happy helping plan your day trips. Personal attention and service assured. We have 2 cats. Smoke free home.

DIRECTIONS: Please phone for simple directions.

Te Anau - Fiordland

YOUR HOSTS: Virginia & Gerhard Hirner Free Ph: 0800-249 700

COSY KIWI BED & BREAKFAST
186 Milford Road, Te Anau
Ph (03) 249 7475. Fax (03) 249 8471
Postal: Po Box 172, Te Anau
e-mail: *cosykiwi@teanau.co.nz*

Features & Attractions
- *Wir sprechen deutsch*
- *Immaculately clean*
- *Sumptuous breakfast buffet*
- *Trip booking and pick-up*
- *3 minute walk to centre*
- *E-mail and fax facilities*

Bed & Breakfast Guest House

Double	$80-99
Single	$55-70
Child	$5-15

Bedrooms	Qty
Double	4
Twin	3
Single	
Bed Size	**Qty**
King	2
Queen	4
Single	6
Bathrooms	**Qty**
Ensuite	7
Private	
Guest Share	
Family Share	

"**Cosy**" truly describes how you will feel within our warm, architecturally designed, modern Bed & Breakfast House. We provide privacy with comfort. Our quiet bedrooms are spacious, ensuited with top quality beds, TV, individual heating and double glazed windows. Enjoy a sumptuous buffet breakfast of home-made breads, topped with home-made jams, marmalade, fresh fruit salad, yoghurt, home-bottled fruits, brewed coffee, special teas and our legendary pancakes with maple syrup. We have a modern laundry, good off-street parking and luggage storage for track walkers. Our warm guest lounge provides excellent space to relax, chat and a computer to access e-mails. Relax outside on our sun-terrace overlooking the ever changing moods of the Murchison Mountains or stroll into the town centre to highly recommended restaurants (3 min.) We can recommend and book any sightseeing trips around Fiordland.

YOUR HOSTS: **Dawn and Ross**   Ph: (03) 249 7739   **Te Anau - Fiordland**

LITTLE BLUE HOUSE
14 Lakefront Drive, PO Box 50
Te Anau
(03) 249 7739, Fax (03) 249 77 55

Features & Attractions
- *Local knowledge*
- *Friendly homely atmosphere*
- *Therapeutic massage service*
- *Trip bookings and pick-up*
- *Opposite Fiordland Park - Information Centre*

Homestay Bed & Breakfast

Double	$80
Single	$60
Child	

Bedrooms	Qty
Double	2
Twin	
Single	

Bed Size	Qty
King	
Queen/Double	2
Single	2

Bathrooms	Qty
Ensuite	1
Private	
Guest Share	
Family Share	1

Welcome to our home, peacefully situated on the Te Anau lakefront, 10 minutes walk to the town centre, "and opposite the National Park Information Centre". Dawn is from a farming background, having worked with organic husbandary and still has a keen interest in that area. Ross is a Senior Ranger with the National Park. He also does Port lecturing on some cruise ships visiting the Fiordland coastline.

Evening meals are available, $30 pp. Specialising in organic food and complimentary wines.

We have two rooms available.
Room 1: Has one queen bed and one single bed, with private toilet/bath ensuite.
Room 2: Has one queen bed and one single bed adjacent to a shared shower facility.
Off-street parking, laundry service, no credit card facilities.
Therapeutic massage available $40 an hour. Bookings essential please.

YOUR HOSTS: **Marg and Jeff Henderson**   Ph: (03) 249 7349   **Te Anau - Fiordland**

SHAKESPEARE HOUSE
10 Dusky Street, Te Anau
Postal: PO Box 32, Te Anau, Fiordland
Ph (03) 249 7349. Fax (03) 249 7629
Mobile 025-392 225
e-mail: *marg.shakespeare.house@xtra.co.nz*

Features & Attractions
- *World Heritage Park*
- *All ground-floor units*
- *Courtesy car*
- *Milford & Doubtful Sound tours*
- *Continental & cooked breakfast*
- *Walking track, golfing, fishing*

Double	$98-112
Single	$80
Child	5-15

Guest House & Self-contained Accom.

Bedrooms	Qty
Double	4
Twin/Triple	3
Quad	1

Bed Size	Qty
Super King	2
Queen/Double	4
King/Single	2

Bathrooms	Qty
Ensuite	8
Private	
Guest Share	
Family Share	

DIRECTIONS: Drive north on Lake Front Drive, carry on along Te Anau Tce. Dusky Street is the last right turn before the boat harbour.

Fiordland – the "Walking Capital" of the world – is right on your doorstep when you stay at **Shakespeare House**. Marg and Jeff extend a warm welcome to you and offer personal attention in a homely atmosphere. We are situated in a quiet residential area, yet are within walking distance of shops, lake, restaurants and attractions. Our units have their own private facilities, are warm and comfortable with tea/coffee, TV and have the choice of king, double or twin beds. They open onto a sunny, relaxing conservatory where you may share your holiday experiences with other guests. We also have a two bedroom self-contained unit, which is popular with families or two couples travelling together. Our dining room catches the morning sun and has a lovely view of the mountains. Enjoy a substantial breakfast – either cooked from the menu or buffet-style continental.
Good off-street parking, washing machine and dryers are available. We invite you to experience our hospitality and meet our cats 'Sleepy' and 'Brothersoul'.

Fiordland

YOUR HOSTS: Margaret and Les Simpson Ph: (03) 249 7841

PERENUKA FARM

2 Sinclair Road, No.1 RD, Te Anau
Ph (03) 249 7841, Fax (03)249 7841
e-mail: *perenuka@xtra.co.nz*

Tariff : N.Z. Dollars		
	Double	$95-105
	Single	
	Child	

Bedrooms	Qty
Double	2
Twin	
Single	
Bed Size	**Qty**
Super King	
King	
Queen	2
Single	1
Bathrooms	**Qty**
Ensuite	2
Private	
Guest Share	
Family Share	

Homestay Bed & Breakfast

Features & Attractions

- *Friendly hosts*
- *Tame sheep*
- *Farm walk*
- *Quiet and peaceful*
- *Magnificent views*
- *Privacy*
- *On road to Milford Sound*
- *Fiordland National Park*

Perenuka is a 750 acre working sheep and cattle farm. Our home and accommodation is high on a terrace which allows for fabulous panoramic views of the lake and mountains.

The spacious guest rooms are separate from the house, in a garden setting, for total privacy. Each room has high quality furnishings, firm beds with electric blankets, heaters, tea/coffee and other facilities to make your stay comfortable and warm.

We encourage guests to join us for breakfast and in the evenings for friendship.

Being situated on the edge of the beautiful Fiordland National Park provides a number of walking options, ranging from very short to 3 to 5 hours. If you want a spell from driving, we can highly recommend a private operator for a day trip to Milford Sound.

Te Anau (5 minutes drive) has many fine cafés and restaurants with a wide range of cuisine.

Perenuka is not suitable for children.

DIRECTIONS:
From Te Anau continue towards Milford Sound for 5 km. Turn right into Sinclair Road, then immediately right again into our driveway.

YOUR HOSTS: **Lyn and Mike Gray** Ph: (03) 431 2500   **North Otago**

Tokarahi Homestead

47 Dip Hill Road, Tokarahi, RD 12C, Oamaru
Ph (03) 431 2500. Fax (03) 431 2551
e-mail: tokarahi@xtra.co.nz
www.homestead.co.nz

Features & Attractions

- *Challenging golf course*
- *Gateway to Danseys Pass*
- *Fishing guides available*
- *Horse trekking available*
- *Maori rock drawings*
- *Centrally heated*
- *Heritage trails*
- *Wheel-chair access*

Tariff : N.Z. Dollars	
Double	$150-220
Single	$115-165
Child	neg

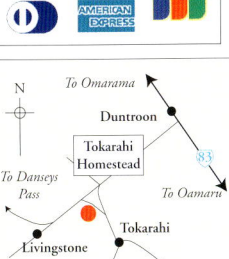

Bedrooms	Qty
Double	4
Twin	
Single	

Bed Size	Qty
Super King	1
King	
Queen	3
Single	

Bathrooms	Qty
Ensuite	4
Private	
Guest Share	
Family Share	

DIRECTIONS: South of Duntroon turn towards Danseys Pass, then turn left at Dip Hill Road.

**Historic Homestead
Luxury Accommodation**

Described as a 'hidden treasure' **Tokarahi Homestead** (1878) is an authentic, completely restored Victorian limestone homestead. Many original features have been retained, including the unique, embossed imitation leather wallpaper in the entrance hall. Using imported period wallpapers and fabrics, we have created an atmosphere of past opulence, but with all the luxury features of today.

Relax and enjoy open fires, and elegant period surroundings. Soak in an antique clawfoot bath. Enjoy delicious food and good wines 'silver service style' at the big kauri table. View the Southern stars in clear, dark, skies through our telescope. Nothing is overlooked in providing guests with exceptional personal hospitality and a memorable experience of colonial grandeur, in a superb country setting. Oamaru, with its Victorian limestone architecture and Blue Penguin colony is only 35 minutes away.

Christchurch – 3$^{1}/_{2}$ hours...........................Queenstown – 3 hours
Dunedin – 1$^{3}/_{4}$ hours...................Mount Cook – 2 hours

Oamaru

YOUR HOSTS: Betty and Brian Lloyd Ph: (03) 437 0211

GLEN HAVEN BED & BREAKFAST
5 Forth Street,
Oamaru
North Otago
Ph (03) 437 0211. Fax (03) 437 0201

Features & Attractions

- BBQ area in quiet, peaceful garden
- Interesting Matchbox car collection
- Pool table available in garage
- Delightful public gardens
- "Oamaru Stone" quarry
- Historic buildings

Double	$50-60
Single	$40-45
Child	half price

DIRECTIONS: From north – 1st Street on right past Meadow Bank Dairy. From south – 1st street on left past Orana Park

B & B Homestay & Separate Self-contained Unit

Bedrooms	Qty
Double	2
Twin	
Single	

Bed Size	Qty
King	
Queen	2
Single	1

Bathrooms	Qty
Ensuite	1
Private	
Guest Share	
Family Share	1

We offer a separate self-contained unit, as well as a bedroom in our home. Our location is north of the township, close to the main highway. The familiar blue B&B-sign makes finding us trouble free. A menu folder is available for a wide selection of local restaurants and eating establishments and we are within walking distance of dairies and takeaways. Having travelled extensively throughout New Zealand on our retirement in 1990, we are happy to provide budget accommodation for those wishing to enjoy the many pleasures our country provides. "Oamaru Stone" is unique to the area and a visit to the quarry is a must, followed by a tour of the town to admire the many grand buildings. The two penguin colonies are well worth looking at – nature at its best. After a walk in the Oamaru public gardens you will agree with us, that it is one of this country's most beautiful parks. Our motto for hospitality is "Your comfort – our pleasure".

North Otago

YOUR HOSTS: John and Margaret Munro Ph: (03) 439 5559

GLEN FOULIS
39 Middle Ridge Road, Waianakarua
ORD 9, Oamaru
Ph (03) 439 5559, Fax (03) 439 5220
Mobile 021-940 777
e-mail: hjm@clear.net.nz

Features & Attractions

- Biking, forest trails
- Country picnic trail
- Clear sparkling river
- Meals by arrangement
- Music and home theatre
- Yamaha Clavicord keyboard

Double	$80
Single	$50
Child	$20

Country Homestead

Bedrooms	Qty
Double	1
Twin	1
Single	

Bed Size	Qty
Super King	1
Queen/Double	
Single	2

Bathrooms	Qty
Ensuite	
Private	
Guest Share	1
Family Share	1

Our hidden valley - called Waianakarua - is just off the Main South Highway to Dunedin. Twenty minutes south of Oamaru with its renowned attractions of penguins and beautiful buildings.

Glen Foulis, a modern homestead, elegantly styled with Oamaru Stone, surrounded by acres of green lawns, tall beech, birch, weeping willows, maples. It has underfloor heating and two efficient open fireplaces. French doors open out to expansive views and sunny terraces lined with roses and covered in wisteria. Native birdsong close by. If you plan more than one night here, we can show you hidden treasures of North Otago from our tough but comfortable 4-wheel drive.

We both work at Energy Efficiency businesses at home. Our two Golden Retrievers, McDuff and Adam delight in greeting your car. Mishka the ginger pussycat follows on behind. Cooked breakfast included with fresh eggs from our hens.

YOUR HOSTS: Bob and Betty Melville   Ph: (03) 482 1107   **Port Chalmers - Dunedin**

ATANUI

Heywards Point Road, No 1 RD
Port Chalmers, Dunedin
Ph (03) 482 1107, Fax (03) 482 1107
e-mail: *atanui@actrix.gen.nz*

Tariff : N.Z. Dollars

Double	$100-120
Single	$80-100
Child	$40

Bedrooms	Qty
Double	1
Twin	1
Single	

Bed Size	Qty
Super King	
King	
Queen	1
Single	1

Bathrooms	Qty
Ensuite	1
Private	1
Guest Share	
Family Share	

Farmstay with a spectacular view

Features & Attractions

- *Walking tracks and beaches*
- *Pet animals and spa*
- *30 minutes from Dunedin*
- *Spa bath*
- *Spectacular views*
- *Quiet and relaxing*
- *Dinner by arrangement.*
  $25 per person

We welcome you to our spacious renovated stone house, in a peaceful rural setting only 30 minutes from Dunedin. From our home, which is heated throughout with radiators off the rayburn range, you can enjoy spectacular views looking out across the Otago Harbour.

Relax in the spa pool or feed our animals - emus, alpaccas, peacocks, pig and pet sheep. Walking tracks and beaches are close by.

Morning and afternoon teas with home baking are complimentary. Three course farm style meals are available by prior arrangement.

We invite you to experience our hospitality and meet our cats "Honey", "Penny" and "Meg".

DIRECTIONS: From north turn left at Waitati, follow sign to Port Chalmers till crossroads. Turn left (No Exit) on to next junction take Heywards Point Road (metal road) 4 k on right. From south down to Port Chalmers highway 88, follow sign up the hill to Long Beach till Heyward Point Road (metal road) 4 k on right.

219

Dunedin   YOUR HOSTS: **Lorraine and Stewart Harvey**   Ph: 0800-387 245

ALLOWAY

65 Every Street, Dunedin
Ph (03) 454 5384. Fax (03) 454 5364
e-mail: *alloway@xtra.co.nz*

Tariff : N.Z. Dollars

Double	$90-120
Single	$85-115
Child	

Bedrooms	Qty
Double	2
Twin	1
Single	

Bed Size	Qty
Super King	
King	
Queen/Double	2
Single	2

Bathrooms	Qty
Ensuite	
Private	
Guest Share	1
Family Share	

Homestay - Bed & Breakfast

Features & Attractions

- *Wildlife, Walking Tracks*
- *Taiaroa Head, Albatross Colony*
- *Disappearing Gun, Seal Colonies*
- *Rhododendrons*
- *Yellow-eyed Penguins*
- *Glenfalloch Gardens*
- *7 minutes to Dunedin City*
- *Great Architecture*

We are situated on the gateway to the Otago Peninsula, which features wildlife, walking tracks, Taiaroa Head, Albatross Colony, Disappearing Gun, Seal Colonies, Yellow-eyed Penguins, Glenfalloch Gardens and much more. We are 7 minutes from the town centre. Our home is a modern interpretation of a traditional Scottish house and set in one acre of gardens and lawns, with indoor/outdoor living. Awaken to the sound of abundant bird-life in a quiet and secure neighbourhood. We serve delicious, healthy breakfasts. One luxury bedroom complete with one queen and one single bed, plus one luxury bedroom with one double and one single bed. Both rooms have tea making facilities, TV, heaters, electric blankets. Separate facilities with modern guest bathroom.
Relax far from the madding crowd. Businesspeople welcome. All non smoking, no pets and not suitable for young children.

DIRECTIONS:
Please phone for easy directions.
Advance booking is recommended.

YOUR HOSTS: Donna and Peter Mitchell   Ph: (03) 477 0526   **Dunedin**

CASTLEWOOD

240 York Place, Dunedin, Otago
Ph (03) 477 0526. Fax (03) 477 0526
e-mail: *relax@castlewood.co.nz*
www.castlewood.co.nz

Tariff : N.Z. Dollars

Double	$95-125
Single	$65
Twin	$85

Bedrooms	Qty
Double	2
Twin	1
Single	1

Bed Size	Qty
Super King	
King	
Queen	2
Single	2

Bathrooms	Qty
Ensuite	1
Private	1
Guest Share	1
Family Share	

**Boutique Accommodation
Bed & Breakfast**

Features & Attractions

- Centrally located
- Gracious old-world charm
- Sumptuous continental breakfasts
- 800m from Octagon & Olveston
- Expansive city views,
- Sunny and peaceful
- Feather duvets
- Spa and sauna

Relax at **Castlewood** and experience the old-world charm of our graciously restored Tudor residence. Set on a hill above Dunedin, **Castlewood** offers expansive views and all-day sun, yet is only 800m (10 min. walk) from the best restaurants, live theatre, cafés, shops and attractions such as Olveston and the Dunedin Art Gallery. **Castlewood's** hospitality includes sumptuous continental breakfasts to make the start of your day a welcome experience. There is a sauna, spa bath and library for added relaxation. Both Peter and Donna are Dunedin-born and know New Zealand intimately. They provide useful and friendly advice on local attractions and having travelled internationally, appreciate the requirements of discerning travellers. Peter is an author and artist. His water-colour paintings are displayed throughout **Castlewood** for your enjoyment.

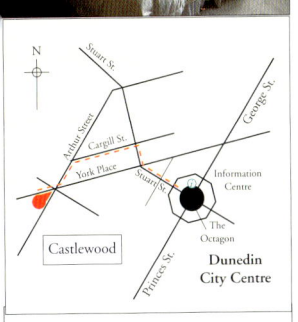

DIRECTIONS: From Octagon travel up Stewart St., turn left into Cargill St., then left into Arthur St. At the next traffic lights **Castlewood** is diagonally opposite.

Dunedin

YOUR HOSTS: **Eileen and Wallie Waudby**   Ph: (03) 477 4963

CILL CHAINNIGH

33 Littlebourne Road, Roslyn, Dunedin
Ph (03) 477 4963. Fax (03) 477 4965
Mobile 025-228 7840
e-mail: *wallie.waudby@xtra.co.nz*

Tariff : N.Z. Dollars		
	Double	$85
	Single	$50
	Child	

Bedrooms	Qty
Double	1
Twin	1
Single	

Bed Size	Qty
Super King	
King	
Queen	1
Single	2

Bathrooms	Qty
Ensuite	
Private	
Guest Share	1
Family Share	

Homestay - Bed & Breakfast

Features & Attractions

- *Quiet, peaceful surroundings*
- *1km from centre of Dunedin*
- *Close to historic "Olveston"*
- *Friendly reception*
- *Surrounded by bush*
- *Tasty home-baking*
- *Close to Moana Pool Swimming Complex*

CILL CHAINNIGH

Eileen and Wallie would like to welcome visitors to Dunedin to their smoke-free home, situated in a quiet street just off Stuart Street and opposite Roberts Park. We have travelled extensively ourselves and understand how visitors feel when they arrive in a new town. Our home is in short walking distance to Dunedin's stately home "Olveston", the Moana Swimming Complex and just over one kilometre to the town centre. The guest bedrooms, situated on the top floor for privacy and quietness, are warm and sunny and as a backup all beds have an electric blanket. Tea and coffee making facilities are available to you. You are sure of a warm welcome and comfortable stay at **Cill Chainnigh**.

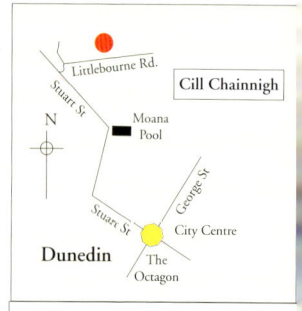

Advance booking is recommended.

YOUR HOSTS: **Karen & Dene MacKenzie**   Free Ph: 0800-268 252

Dunedin

DEACONS COURT

342 High Street, Dunedin
Ph: (03) 477 9053, Fax:(03) 477 9058
Mobile 025-518 664
e-mail: *deacons@es.co.nz*
www.deaconscourt.bizland.com

Features & Attractions

- *Spacious bedrooms*
- *Private facilities*
- *Generous cooked breakfast*
- *Close to city centre*
- *Large rose garden*
- *Historical home*

Bed & Breakfast Homestay

Double	$110-120
Single	$70
Child	

Bedrooms	Qty
Double	2
Twin	1
Single	1
Bed Size	**Qty**
King	1
Queen/Double	2
Single	3
Bathrooms	**Qty**
Ensuite	2
Private	1
Guest Share	
Family Share	

Enjoy that special feeling of being a guest in our comfortable private historical Victorian home, which is surrounded by trees and a sheltered rose garden. Pamper yourself while you are here. Karen has a diploma in massage and aromatherapy and has those facilities available for guests in our home. We are 1km to the city centre, the Dunedin Art Gallery, the visitors centre, the Octagon and a wide choice of restaurants.

Our Rose Room has a stunning view across the city to the harbour and the sea while our Garden Room overlooks the rose garden. We offer a wide range of breakfast options. Home baking available to guests.

We have a wide knowledge of Dunedin attractions and can help you with your sightseeing. Family groups welcome. We have a friendly cat. What our guests say: Lovely room and excellent massage - Kay, the UK. Excellent hospitality and excellent breakfast –Bryon, Australia. I felt most comfortable here - Junko, Japan.

YOUR HOST: **Louise Calvert**   Ph: (03) 477 7228

Dunedin

HERIOT HOUSE

26 Pitt Street, Dunedin
Ph (03) 477 7228, Mobile 025-274 4726
e-mail: *lcalvert@es.co.nz*

Features & Attractions

- *Centrally located*
- *3 minutes stroll to cafés, bars and restaurants*
- *Quaint cottage garden*
- *Gracious Edwardian home*
- *Friendly, helpful hostess*

Homestay Bed & Breakfast

Double	$100-120
Single	
Child	Neg.

Bedrooms	Qty
Double	3
Twin	
Single	
Bed Size	**Qty**
King	
Queen/Double	3
Single	
Bathrooms	**Qty**
Ensuite	1
Private	
Guest Share	1
Family Share	

Louise welcomes you to stay in her gracious old home situated right in the heart of Dunedin. Only a casual stroll to shops and the local restaurants, bars and cafés. The quaint cottage garden has a pleasant charm that will draw you out of doors to inspect the treasures hidden from view.

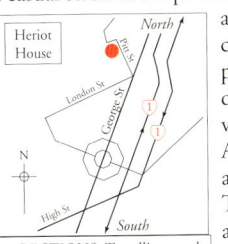

All guest rooms are on the second floor with an area set aside in each room for those who prefer to relax in private. There is also a separate television room and a sitting room available for those who want a coffee and to chat.

You are sure of a warm, friendly and comfortable stay at **Heriot House**.

DIRECTIONS: Travelling south on George St turn sharp right at Knox Church into Pitt St.

Dunedin YOUR HOSTS: **Vivienne and Rod Nye** Ph: (03) 477 2103

GOWRIE HOUSE
7 Gowry Place,
Roslyn, Dunedin
Ph (03) 477 2103. Fax (03) 471 9169

Tariff : N.Z. Dollars	
Double	$85
Single	$55
Child	

Bedrooms	Qty
Double	1
Twin	1
Single	

Bed Size	Qty
Super King	
King	
Queen	1
Single	2

Bathrooms	Qty
Ensuite	
Private	
Guest Share	1
Family Share	

Boutique Accommodation Bed & Breakfast

Features & Attractions

- 5 min. drive from city
- Paved patio off double room
- Tea and coffee-making facilities in double room
- Warm & sunny bedrooms
- Otago Peninsula nearby
- 20-min. walk from city
- Courtesy car available

Gowrie House is in a quiet suburb on a sunny west-facing site with lovely rural views. We are only a 20 minute walk from the city, close to bus routes. A courtesy car is provided within the city. Our garden has a cosy cottage atmosphere, with all available space occupied by perennial and biennial flowers – regularly picked for rooms.

The guests' bedrooms are warm and sunny. The bathroom is handily placed across the hall. All beds have electric blankets. The double room has access to the patio and cottage garden where one can enjoy the floral fragrances.

Otago Peninsula is easily accessible, as are bush walks and historic buildings.

We will happily provide information about popular attractions.

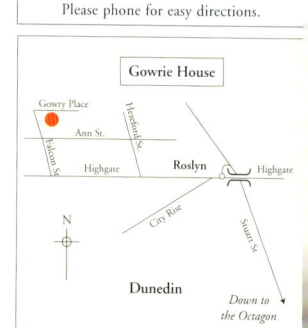

DIRECTIONS:
Please phone for easy directions.

Advance booking is recommended.

YOUR HOST: Norman Wood   Free Ph: 0800-448 563   **Dunedin**

HULMES COURT & HULMES TOO
52 Tennyson Street, Dunedin, Otago
Ph (03) 477 5319, Fax (03) 477 5310
Mobile 025-351 075
e-mail: *normwood@earthlight.co.nz*
www.hulmes.co.nz

Tariff : N.Z. Dollars	
Double	$85-175
Single	$55-95
Child	

Bedrooms	Qty
Double/Twin	11
Twin	
Single	1
Bed Size	**Qty**
Super King	
King	1
Queen/Double	10
Single	6
Bathrooms	**Qty**
Ensuite	6
Private	
Guest Share	3
Family Share	

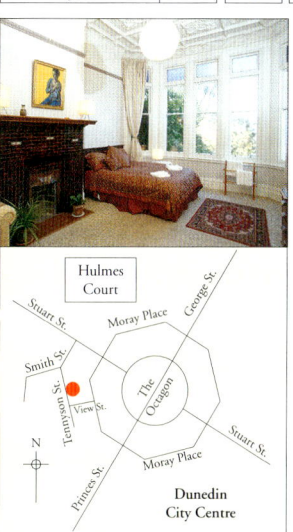

Homestay - Bed & Breakfast

Features & Attractions

- Historic: built late 1860's
- Right in centre of Dunedin
- Off-street parking
- Complimentary laundry
- Close to restaurants
- Large drawing room, open fire
- Complimentary mountain bikes and Internet access

Hulmes Court B&B is two beautiful homes only a few minutes walk from the heart of town and the Visitor Centre. Tennyson Street is quiet and we have private gardens, trees, decks and sitting areas.

The **Victoria Hulmes Court** is one of the most historic homes in Dunedin. It was built in the 1860s by the first provincial surgeon Edward Hulme who helped found the Medical School.

Hulmes Too is a large Edwardian home built next to **Hulmes Court** on the grounds of the original estate. **Hulmes Court** has a variety of rooms which cater for all tastes from the economical cute single Rose Room at $55 per night to our grand ensuite rooms in **Hulmes Too** at $175 per night.

Your host Norman owns a variety of businesses and is interested in history, philosophy, geography and has stood for parliament twice. At the same time Norman at 34 and his staff are youthful, full of energy and travel widely. We provide complimentary laundry, internet and email, BBQ, mountain bikes and off-street parking.

DIRECTIONS: Leaving the Octagon by Upper Stuart St. take the 2nd turning on the left into Smith St., then just 50m left again into Tennyson St.

Dunedin

YOUR HOSTS: **Eli and Lindsay Imlay** Ph: (03) 473 9558

PINE HEIGHTS RETREAT

431 Pine Hill Road, Pine Heights, Dunedin
Ph (03) 473 9558. Fax (03) 473 0247
e-mail: *pineheights@xtra.co.nz*
http://www.pineheights.co.nz

Tariff : N.Z. Dollars	
Double	$90
Single	$60
Child	neg.

Bedrooms	Qty
Double	1
Twin	1
Single	
Bed Size	**Qty**
Super King	
King	
Queen	1
Single	2
Bathrooms	**Qty**
Ensuite	
Private	
Guest Share	1
Family Share	

Homestay with Norwegian Flair

Features & Attractions

- *Peaceful rural views*
- *Enjoyable native bird life*
- *Relaxing three-course dinner by arrangement*
- *Cosy, comfortable, homely*
- *Only 4.5 km to city centre*
- *Handy to University and Botanical Gardens*

DIRECTIONS: Please phone for simple directions and bookings.

Relax in the comfort of our cosy home set in a tranquil rural area, where native birds are frequent visitors. Enjoy our sheltered patio and cottage garden which we love.

Absorb the peacefulness of our surroundings. Sweeping views are shared by all living and bedroom areas. It's like living in the country yet only a few minutes by car from the city centre with public transport nearby. A courtesy car is available and we have ample off-street parking.

Flexible mealtimes allow time for sightseeing in our lovely city. We enjoy meeting people and welcome you to share our home and informal lifestyle. Eli, who has lived in Dunedin for over 30 years, is Norwegian and offers a unique blend of Scandinavian and New Zealand hospitality.

Breakfast is full or continental with a wide range of choices, including fresh home-made bread and waffles. Our dinners, followed by Norwegian-style coffee are a speciality.

Children most welcome.

We will do our utmost to make your stay memorable and enjoyable.

YOUR HOSTS: Catherine & Grant Wilson   Free Ph: 0800 327 333   **Dunedin**

THE STATION MASTER'S COTTAGE

300 York Place, Dunedin, Otago
Free Ph: 0800 327 333
Mobile 025-592 732

Tariff : N.Z. Dollars	
Double	$150
Single	$90
Child	

Bedrooms	Qty
Double	2
Twin	1
Single	

Bed Size	Qty
Super King	
King	
Queen	2
Single	2

Bathrooms	Qty
Ensuite	
Private	
Guest Share	1
Family Share	

Accepted: VISA, MasterCard, Diners, American Express

Self-contained Luxury Boutique Accommodation

Features & Attractions

- *Central City location*
- *Tranquil garden setting*
- *Fine linen, fresh flowers*
- *Large luxury bathroom*
- *Historic Luxury Cottage*
- *Self-contained & exclusive*
- *Romantically furnished*
- *850 m from Octagon*

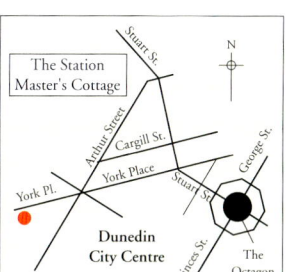

DIRECTIONS:
From the Octagon travel up Stuart St., turn left into Cargill St., then left to Arthur St. At the traffic signals travel up York Place to "The Station Master's Cottage".

Imagine a romantic historic cottage in a tranquil private garden in the city, built in 1878 for Dunedin's first station master, William Popperwell and his wife Elizabeth, extensively renovated and luxuriously furnished with fine linen and dreamy beds. Central heating, fresh flowers and a hearty breakfast. 10 min. walk to the best cafés, restaurants, bars, shops, Central City Octagon, Art Gallery and Otago University.

Self-contained, serviced accommodation. Three beautifully appointed bedrooms, large luxury bathroom, country kitchen, dining room and lounge sitting room.

The complete cottage will always be yours exclusively.

Delightful Boutique Accommodation for 1 - 6 persons, oozing the charm, comfort and ambience of past times...

| YOUR HOSTS: Margaret and Alan Dunbar | Ph: (03) 489 6131 | **Mosgiel - Dunedin** |

Stranalyth Gables

Rapid No 193, Riccarton Road,
RD 2, Mosgiel near Dunedin
Ph (03) 489 6131, Fax (03) 489 6131

Tariff : N.Z. Dollars	
Double	$85
Single	$55
Child	half price

Bedrooms	Qty
Double	2
Twin	2
Single	
Bed Size	**Qty**
Super King	
King	
Queen	2
Single	4
Bathrooms	**Qty**
Ensuite	
Private	1
Guest Share	1
Family Share	

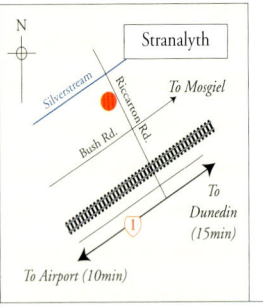

Farmstay - Bed & Breakfast

Features & Attractions

- 10 min. from Dunedin Airport
- 10 hectare property
- Lambs, sheep & calves
- River rafting close by
- Dunedin City 15 minutes
- Good fishing in Taieri River
- 3-course evening meal available
- 3 golf courses nearby

DIRECTIONS:
On SH 1 20km south of Dunedin, turn right into Riccarton Road. **Stranalyth** is at Rapid No 193 on the left

Come and enjoy a country life-style with us on our 10-hectare property, where we fatten lambs and graze sheep and calves. We are semi-retired and have hosted tourists for 10 years. You are invited to share our warm and comfortable home and enjoy the spacious garden. Great hospitality is always assured. Our farm is situated a comfortable 10 min. drive from Dunedin Airport and just 3 kilometres off State Highway One. Bus, airport or train transfers can be arranged. In the small town of Mosgiel, only 5 km from the farm, you will find good shopping facilities. The city of Dunedin is just 15 minutes drive away. Close by is the Taieri River, well known for its excellent fishing, and the more adventurous can take up the challenge of rafting on it. There are also tennis courts, and 3 golf courses nearby. With prior notice we would take pleasure in providing you with a 3-course evening meal at $20 pp. Our interests include all sports, gardening, interior decorating, the Lions Club and meeting people. Arrive at **Stranalyth** as a tourist and leave as a friend.

YOUR HOSTS: **Helen and Ken Spittle** Ph: (03) 418 1385 **Balclutha - South Otago**

Balcairn
80 Blackburn Road,
Hillend 2 RD, Balclutha
Ph (03) 418 1385. Fax (03) 418 4385
e-mail: *balcairn@xtra.co.nz*

Features & Attractions
- *500 acre sheep, deer and beef working farm*
- *Farm tours available*
- *Superb farmland views*
- *Catlins Reserve nearby*
- *Dinner by arrangement*

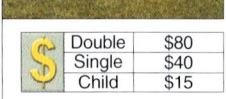

Farmstay Bed & Breakfast

Double	$80
Single	$40
Child	$15

Bedrooms	Qty
Double	1
Twin	1
Single	
Bed Size	**Qty**
Double	1
Queen	1
Single	2
Bathrooms	**Qty**
Ensuite	
Private	1
Guest Share	
Family Share	

Come and experience life on a New Zealand working farm. You can join in whatever farm activity is happening on the day or enjoy a farm tour. While in this area, a trip down the south east coast on the Southern Scenic Route through the Catlins Reserve allows you to see yellow-eyed penguins, seals, porpoises, waterfalls and caves. Or a trip into the Historic Gold Mining and fruit growing areas of Central Otago is well worthwhile.

With prior notice and booking we could arrange a tour of these areas for you. If you wish, fishing, golf and tennis could be arranged or perhaps you would prefer to enjoy the quiet, peaceful surroundings of life in the country. We are located 22 km from Balclutha and can arrange to pick-up guests from the bus or train in Balclutha or Milton and from Dunedin Airport which is only 60 km away. Children are most welcome.

DIRECTIONS:
Please phone for easy diections.

Sheep farming in Otago.

Balclutha - South Otago YOUR HOSTS: **Trish and Alan May** Ph: (03) 415 9268

ARGYLL FARMSTAY

Rapid No 246, Clutha River Road,
Clydevale No 4 RD, Balclutha
Ph (03) 415 9268, Fax (03) 415 9268
Mobile 025-318 241
e-mail: *argyllfm@ihug.co.nz*

Tariff : N.Z. Dollars	
Double	$80
Single	$45
Child	neg.

Bedrooms	Qty
Double	1
Twin	1
Single	
Bed Size	**Qty**
Super King	
King	
Queen	1
Single	2
Bathrooms	**Qty**
Ensuite	
Private	
Guest Share	1
Family Share	

Farmstay
Bed & Breakfast

Features & Attractions

- *Peaceful rural views*
- *Extra option of jet boat or fishing trip on Clutha River*
- *Experience farming life*
- *Homestyle 3 course meals avail.*
- *Swimming pool*
- *Experienced fishing guide*
- *Farm tour/deer, cattle, sheep*

Trish and Alan welcome guests to our comfortable country home with large garden, swimming pool and beautiful views of green pasture and river flats.

We farm 530 acres, running 800 deer, 150 cattle and 1000 sheep. Guests would be welcome to tour our farm or join the family at their daily farming tasks.

Argyll Farm is situated on the banks of the Clutha River that provides guests with a unique opportunity to enjoy several recreational pastimes. We offer guests the extra option of a Jet Boat Ride or Fishing Trip on the Clutha River in our commercial boat Blue Mountain Jet.

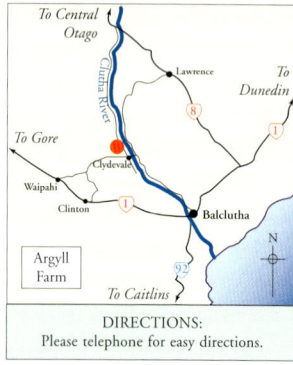

Alan is an experienced fisherman who enjoys sharing his knowledge of our local rivers. We are centrally located for visitors travelling to the Catlins, Queenstown or Te Anau. We enjoy meeting people and we hope to make your stay a comfortable, relaxing and memorable experience.

DIRECTIONS:
Please telephone for easy directions.

YOUR HOSTS: **Dorothy and Tom Affleck** Ph: (03) 207 2865   **Eastern Southland**

BLACKHILLS FARMSTAY
192 Robertson Road, North Chatton, RD Gore
Postal: RD 3. Gore, Southland
Ph/Fax (03) 207 2865
Mobile 025-209 1563

Features & Attractions

- Superb views
- 3-course dinner $25 pp
- Farm tour/sheep & cattle
- 6 fishing rivers within 30 min.
- Sports facilities in Waikaka
- Your comfort, our concern

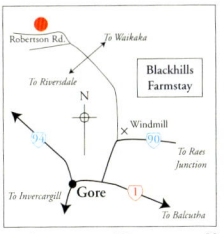

Double	$80
Single	$40
Child	$20

Farmstay Bed & Breakfast

Our sixty-year-old home – which has been renovated to give us a generous, comfortable living area – is situated on our 360 ha intensive sheep farm on a ridge above Waikaka River. You may have dinner with us, or if you prefer only bed and breakfast. A farm tour is avilable and as our family becomes more independent, we like to share time with guests. Venture off the main road and enjoy warm hospitality, superb views and the refreshment of a quiet rural visit.

DIRECTIONS: Turn off SH1 just north of Gore onto SH90. Turn left at Waikaka Valley corner, marked by church and windmill, follow sign posts to Waikaka until T-junction (approx. 10km). At T-junction turn left, then first right onto gravel – Nicolson Road. Proceed 4 km, veering right at each intersection. We live on Robertson Road, the last kilometre is a steep hill - just 20 minutes from SH 1.

Bedrooms	Qty
Double	1
Twin	1
Single	
Bed Size	Qty
King	
Queen	1
Single	2
Bathrooms	Qty
Ensuite	
Private	
Guest Share	1
Family Share	1

YOUR HOSTS: **Jean and David McRae** Ph: (03) 208 0662   **Gore - Southland**

MCRAE HOMESTAY
143A Broughton Street, Gore
Ph (03) 208 0662. Fax (03) 208 0662

Features & Attractions

- Warm home with attractive garden
- Dinner by arrangement
- Great fishing & golf close by
- Delightful family pet
- Use of laundry
- Easy walk to town

Homestay Bed & Breakfast

Double	$80
Single	$40
Child	half price

We are from farming background. David's interests are trekking and rugby. Jean enjoys gardening and golf.

Gore is ideally situated two hours from Queenstown also two hours from Dunedin.

The rivers close by are world-renowned for great trout fishing. We invite you to come, rest a while and take time out to smell the roses. We have a Bichon Frise dog "Bobby Mac", who is visitor-friendly. You are welcome to have dinner with us – $25pp. Prior notice is required.

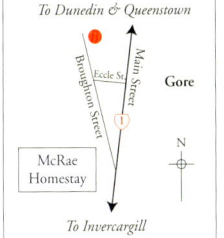

Advance bookingis recommended.

Bedrooms	Qty
Double	1
Twin	
Single	2
Bed Size	Qty
King	
Double	1
King/Single	2
Bathrooms	Qty
Ensuite	
Private	1
Guest Share	
Family Share	1

Wyndham - Southland

YOUR HOSTS: **Beverly and Doug Smith**

Ph: (03) 206 4840

Smith's Farmstay

365 Wyndham-Mokoreta Road,
No. 2 RD, Wyndham, Southland
Ph/Fax (03) 206 4840, Mobile 025-286 6920
email: *beverly@smithsfarmstay.co.nz*
www.smithsfarmstay.co.nz

Tariff : N.Z. Dollars		
	Double	$80-100
	Single	$50
	Child	neg.

Bedrooms	Qty
Double	2
Twin	1
Single	
Bed Size	**Qty**
Super King	1
King	
Queen	1
Single	4
Bathrooms	**Qty**
Ensuite	1
Private	
Guest Share	1
Family Share	

Smith's Farmstay

Fisherman's Retreat - Farmstay

Features & Attractions

- *Genuine sheep farm experience*
- *Close to "Maple Glen" garden*
- *Hand knitted jerseys - pure NZ wool*
- *Beautiful "Catlins" area close by*
- *Trout fishing 5 km*
- *Quiet, peaceful surroundings*
- *Dinner by prior arrangement*
- *Garden and craft tours*

Beverly and Doug assure you of a warm welcome to their modern farm house and 172-hectare sheep farm. We are situated on the hills, 4 km from Wyndham, giving a panoramic view of the Southland Plains and the mountains beyond. The Mataura, Mimihau and Wyndham Rivers, renowned for brown trout, are a short 5 km away.

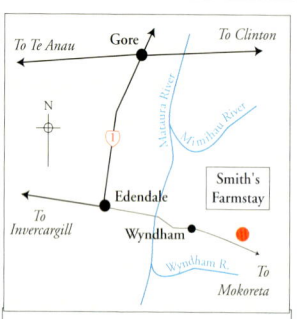

DIRECTIONS:
Drive to Wyndham: only 4km from Wyndham on the Wyndham Mokoreta Rd. Smith's Farmstay sign at gate.

Doug is a keen experienced fisherman and will be only too happy to share his knowledge of these rivers with you. Beverly, a qualified nurse, enjoys cooking, floral art, gardening and hand knitting with pure wool. Enjoy comfortable surroundings and genuine home cooking, including preserved fruits, jams, home-grown meats and vegetables. Special diets available. Packed lunches can be supplied for a small charge. Laundry facilities if required. You are most welcome to join us for an evening meal, but prior notice is required. Meal $25 pp., children under 12 years negotiable. We love sharing Christmas Day with guests, prior booking required. Tour of the farm, feeding lambs, calves and hens when in season. We have one friendly cat. We enjoy meeting people and both are of a friendly disposition with a sense of humor. Long stayers most welcome!

YOUR HOSTS: Margaret and Alan Thomson   Ph: (03) 230 4798   **Invercargill - Southland**

SOUTHERN HOME HOSPITALITY
Rimu Rural No. 375
R.D.1, Invercargill, Southland
Ph/Fax (03) 230 4798
e-mail: *home-hosp@hotmail.com*

Features & Attractions
- Warm hospitality
- Peaceful garden setting
- Fabulous meals
- Gateway to Fiordland
- Excellent golf courses
- Invercargill City

Country Homestay

Double	$90	
Single	$50	
Child	$25	

Bedrooms	Qty
Double	1
Twin	1
Single	

Bed Size	Qty
King	
Queen	1
Single	2

Bathrooms	Qty
Ensuite	
Private	1
Guest Share	1
Family Share	

Welcome to our warm and comfortable home surrounded by colourful gardens. We are semi-retired, graze cattle and sheep, enjoy meeting people, love to cook, home baking a speciality, all meals prepared from fresh produce and vegetables from our large garden. We are enthusiastic golfers, with many courses nearby. Invercargill City has historic buildings, lovely parks and gardens, interesting museum with live Tuatara, prehistoric lizard, Anderson Park, Art Gallery, famous trout fishing rivers within easy reach. Have dinner with us and share an evening of relaxation and friendship. "We look forward to having you visit us." – Margaret and Alan. Gateway to Catlins, Stewart Island, Fiordland and Queenstown.

DIRECTIONS: **From Invercargill** travel appr. 7 km towards Dunedin, turn right at Clapham Rd. (towards large green building with red roof), turn left, then right over railway line. Travel straight ahead for 4 km. A.J. Thomson is written on mailbox - Rural No. 375. **From Dunedin** turn left at Longbush Road South, turn right at crossroads - we are 1 km on right.

YOUR HOSTS: Jocelyn and Russell Dore   Ph: (03) 234 8732   **Riverton - Southland**

93 TOWACK HOMESTAY B & B

93 Towack Street, Riverton,
Southland
Ph (03) 234 8732, Fax (03) 234 8732

Features & Attractions
- Peaceful private garden setting
- Studio unit with spa bath
- Golf course & walking tracks
- Harbour & sea views
- Walk 5 minutes to restaurants and shops

Homestay Bed & Breakfast

Double	$60-120	
Single		
Child		

Bedrooms	Qty
Double	3
Twin	
Single	

Bed Size	Qty
King	
Queen/Double	3
Single	

Bathrooms	Qty
Ensuite	1
Private	
Guest Share	1
Family Share	

We would like to welcome you to Riverton, a seaside retreat. Relax and enjoy our peaceful private garden setting with excellent river and harbour views. We are within walking distance of the beach, bush walks, shops and cafés. The house has three spacious downstairs bedrooms. The bathroom has a bath and separate shower. Upstairs is a private studio unit with spa bath and superb views. Handy facilities are available. If you are looking for a relaxing stay at the seaside, Riverton is the place to be. We look forward to meeting you.

DIRECTIONS: Only 30 min. drive from Invercargill on the Southern Scenic Route. Drive over the bridge, turn left and look for the yellow **93 Towack B&B** sign.

Owaka - The Catlins

YOUR HOSTS: Gay and Arch Maley **Free Ph: 0800 105 134**

KEPPLESTONE-BY-THE-SEA
9 Surat Bay, Owaka, The Catlins
Ph (03) 415 8134. Fax (03) 415 8137
Mobile 021-251 3710
e-mail: *kepplestone@xtra.co.nz*

Features & Attractions
- Sandy beach & Hooker Sealions
- Close to penguins and falls
- Gourmet meals available
- Separate guest house
- Royal Spoonbills
- Special diets catered for

Beachstay Bed & Breakfast

Double	$65/90
Single	$50
Child	

There are NO strangers here, only FRIENDS we have not met. Situated 100 m from beach, with hooker sealions basking there. Close to all The Catlins scenery, waterfalls, walks, Royal Spoonbills. Private yellow eyed penguin viewing and tours, with Catlins Natural Wonders. Delicious breakfasts, with lots of homemade goodies. Organically grown vegetables from our own garden, served with fabulous meals. Special diets catered for with every care taken. Chip and Putt course on property and golf course 3 kms. Proud to be members of HOSTLINK, your personalised guide to New Zealand.

Directions:
Follow signs "towards" Pounawea, at golf course go "across" bridge and turn right to Newhaven and Surat Bay Road (3 kms metal) first house on left.

Bedrooms	Qty
Double	2
Twin	1
Single	
Bed Size	**Qty**
King/Single	1
Queen	1
Single	2
Bathrooms	**Qty**
Ensuite	2
Private	
Guest Share	
Family Share	1

Owaka - The Catlins

YOUR HOSTS: Alma and Fin McRae **Ph: (03) 415 8128**

BARRS FALLS
389 Barrs Falls Road, Owaka, Catlins
Ph (03) 415 8128, Fax (03) 415 8128
e-mail: *barrsfalls@catlins-nz.com*

Features & Attractions
- Quiet, peaceful surroundings
- Handy to Catlins scenic spots
- Comfortable home
- Great sea and farm views
- Wildlife nearby
- Golf, bowling, fishing close

Our Farm

Farmstay Bed & Breakfast

Double	$55-60
Single	$40
Child	$10

Bedrooms	Qty
Double	1
Twin	1
Single	
Bed Size	**Qty**
King	
Double	1
Single	2
Bathrooms	**Qty**
Ensuite	1
Private	
Guest Share	
Family Share	1

Our comfortable home is set in peaceful garden surroundings on our 385 hectare sheep and cattle farm, 5.5 km from Owaka. You will be able to take a leisurely stroll in the evening down to "Barrs Falls" waterfall in the reserve and enjoy the glow-worms and native bush and birds. A variety of wildlife is within easy travelling distance, for example 15-20 minutes to Nugget Point Lighthouse to view Hooker Sea Lions, seals and yellow-eyed penguins. Walking tracks, golf and bowling clubs and an excellent museum are added attractions. There are two dairies providing meals and takeaways, the local pub and the popular restaurant/bar the "Lumberjack". We hope you will join us in this beautiful unique area of New Zealand. Laundry, folding cot and high chair facilities available.

YOUR HOSTS: Michael and Cheryl Blair   Ph: (03) 415 8094   **The Catlins**

GORGE STREAM COTTAGE
2057 Tahakopa Valley Road, RD 2, Owaka
Tahakopa, Catlins Region
Ph/Fax (03) 415 8094, Mobile (025) 301 394
e-mail: *hosts@gorgestream.co.nz*
www.gorgestream.co.nz

Tariff : N.Z. Dollars

	Double	$225
	Single	$175
	Child	neg.

Bedrooms	Qty
Double	2
Twin	
Single	

Bed Size	Qty
Super King	2
King	
Queen	
Single	

Bathrooms	Qty
Ensuite	
Private	1
Guest Share	
Family Share	

**Exclusive Self-contained
Self-catering Luxury Cottage**

Features & Attractions

- *Hunting, fishing, mountain biking on site*
- *Thoroughly modern luxury interior*
- *Striking views in all directions*
- *Indonesian hand-carved teak wood furniture*
- *Ideal for the long stay*
- *Catlins activities nearby*
- *Secluded and private*
- *Off the beaten track*

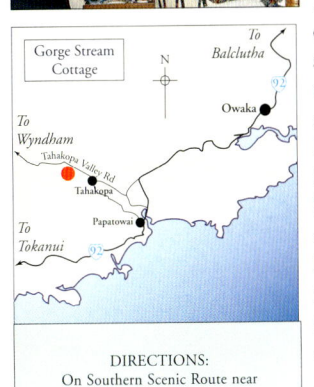

DIRECTIONS:
On Southern Scenic Route near Papatowai, turn north-west onto Tahakopa Road. and go 19 km.

Nestled in the heart of the Catlins and Tahakopa Valley and close to the beach, **Gorge Stream Cottage** is a luxurious cottage surrounded by beautiful gardens, pond, wildlife, river, stream and views to the native bush in every direction. Even though the cottage is off the beaten track, it is close to all the activities in the Catlins and an hour from Invercargill and Stewart Island. A partial list of activities in the Catlins: two golf courses, Catlins Woodstock, ocean fishing trips, four waterfalls, cliffs, beaches, surfing, tramping and walking paths, bird watching, dolphin watching, Catlins Coastal Rainforest Park, eco-tours by licensed guides, horse trekking on the cliffs and beaches, river fishing, Catlins Forest Park, Yellow-eyed penguins, New Zealand fur seals, Hooker sea lions, Elephant seal. The cottage office boasts modern communication with the outside world, e-mail, fax, internet, Sky TV satellite, as well as a fold-out sofa sleeping 2 people. Tariff includes all linens, full breakfast provisions and well stocked pantry for all cooking needs. Minimum two-night stay.

Tokanui - South Catlins

YOUR HOSTS: Betty and Pete Lyders Ph: (03) 246 8804

ALSTED FARMSTAY

173 Neill Road, Tokanui
Ph (03) 246 8804. Fax (03) 246 8804

Features & Attractions

- *Handy to the beautiful Catlins*
- *Quiet, peaceful, no traffic noise*
- *Dinner $25 pp by arrangement*
- *Wake up to bird song*
- *Farm tour optional*
- *20min. to trout fishing*

Double	$90
Single	$55
Child	$25

Farmstay Bed & Breakfast

Bedrooms	Qty
Double	1
Twin	1
Single	
Bed Size	**Qty**
King	
Queen/Double	1
Single	2
Bathrooms	**Qty**
Ensuite	
Private	
Guest Share	1
Family Share	

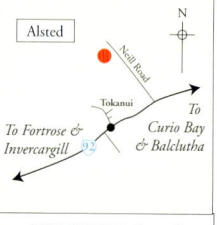

DIRECTIONS: Just off Southern Scenic Route at Tokanui. Turn at Neill Rd. 1km east of Tokanui. We are 2km uphill, rapid No 173

Welcome to our 650 hectare sheep and cattle farm. We offer rest and relaxation, warm hospitality, tasty home-cooking and a base to explore. Our home is centrally heated, has electric blankets on all beds and is just off the Southern Scenic Route in a peaceful garden setting overlooking farmland and Tokanui Village. From farm hills we have great views of Foveaux Strait towards Stewart Island and inland to the Takitimu Mountains. We are centrally located to the Catlins scenic area, petrified forest, Hectors Dolphins, trout fishing in the Mataura and Waikawa Rivers, challenging golf course, Waipapa Lighthouse and the rugged southern coast. Dinner may include local seafood, home-grown meat and fresh vegetables.

With our family grown up, we enjoy our grandchildren, meeting people, various sports and local history and travel.

Stewart Island

YOUR HOSTS: Philippa and Ian Ph: (03) 219 1394

PORT OF CALL

Leask Bay Road, PO Box 143, Stewart Island
Ph (03) 219 1394, Fax (03) 219 1394
Mobile 025-244 4722
e-mail: *info@portofcall.co.nz*
www.portofcall.co.nz

Features & Attractions

- *Stunning views*
- *Courtesy transfers*
- *Meals by arrangement*
- *Birdlife and bush surroundings*
- *Sixth generation Island family*
- *Water taxi - customised trips*

Boutique Coastal Accommodation

Double	$200
Single	$130
Child	

Bedrooms	Qty
Double	1
Twin	
Single	
Bed Size	**Qty**
Super King	1
Queen/Double	
Single	
Bathrooms	**Qty**
Ensuite	
Private	1
Guest Share	
Family Share	

From its cliff top site, overlooking Halfmoon Bay and Foveaux Strait, is Port of Call, new home of hosts Philippa and Ian. Giving you the ultimate in home-away-from home accommodation for the discerning traveller. Surrounded by native bush attracting varied birdlife. Walk two minutes to Harrolds Bay or walk on to Acker's Point Light House. The walk into Halfmoon Bay is 15 to 20 minutes.

Philippa and Ian run Stewart Island Water Taxi, Ian is a paua diver, having 20 years experience in waters surrounding Stewart Island. Being from an Island family he is happy to share his local knowledge and assist in planning daily excursions if needed. We have on the property two historic houses, sheep, goat, ducks, plus a very friendly family dog. We are in our 30s with no children at home, enjoy travel and have a great love for the Island. Come and enjoy pure nature in a tranquil and relaxed environment.

The Translated Travellers' Pages

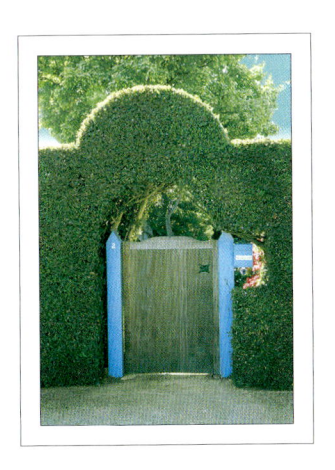

Herzlich Willkommen!

ようこそ！

歡迎！

Einführung

"Lernen Sie das wahre Neuseeland kennen - die Neuseeländer selbst"

Bed & Breakfast in Neuseeland heißt Sie herzlich willkommen!

Eine überaus große Auswahl an Übernachtungsmöglichkeiten erwartet Sie in der Welt von "Bed & Breakfast" (private Übernachtung inclusive Frühstück) - vom einfachen Landhaus bis zum stattlichen Familiensitz. Überall werden Sie auf freundliche, aufgeschlossene Neuseeländer treffen. Manche von ihnen haben die Tradition des Gastgebens im Lauf der Jahre zu einer regelrechten Kunst entwickelt, auf die sie besonders stolz sind. Sogenannte "Homestays", "Farmstays", Gastehäuser oder "Boutique"-Unterkünfte - sie alle fallen unter den Begriff "Bed & Breakfast". Hier lernen Sie das wahre Neuseeland kennen: die Neuseeländer selbst.

- Ob Lehrer, Farmer oder ein pensionierter Angestellter, ob Künstler, Obstbauer, Heilpraktiker oder Schriftsteller, die Palette ist reichhaltig. Zum angenehmen Abenteuer kann die Übernachtung beispielsweise in einer Fischerlodge oder auf einer Schafsfarm im Hochland werden. Warum lernen Sie nicht nebenbei ein wenig reiten oder weben oder fühlen Sie sich einfach wie zu Hause in einem "Homestay" oder "Countrystay" in der Stadt oder auf dem Land. Die Neuseeländer sind bekannt als warmherzige Gastgeber, Sie werden sich überall willkommen fühlen und unvergeßliche Reiseerinnerungen mit nach Hause bringen.

Einführung

Was Sie erwarten können

Bed & Breakfast in Neuseeland ist bekannt für guten Service. Die Unterkünfte sind sauber, verfügen über bequeme Betten und bieten ein gutes, reichliches Frühstück an. Natürlich steht Ihr Wohlbefinden an erster Stelle. Ihre Gastgeber werden Ihnen gerne bei der Planung Ihrer weiteren Reise behilflich sein. Die Gastgeber wissen am besten darüber Bescheid, was die jeweilige Region zu bieten hat. Nutzen Sie diese unbezahlbaren Informationen aus erster Hand.

Was man von Ihnen erwartet

Ihre Gastgeber werden alles versuchen, Ihnen den Aufenthalt so angenehm wie möglich zu machen. Vergessen Sie jedoch bitte nicht, daß Sie in den meisten Fällen in Privathäusern zu Gast sein werden. Bedenken Sie auch die scheinbar unwichtigen Dinge. Es empfiehlt sich beispielsweise, um einen Hausschlüssel zu bitten, bevor Sie abends länger ausbleiben. Falls Sie ein Ferngespräch führen wollen, ist es besser, zuerst den Tarif abzuklären. Sagen Sie bitte auch so bald wie möglich Bescheid, wenn sich Ihre Ankunft verspäten sollte. Ein wenig Rücksichtnahme Ihrerseits wird so dazu beitragen, daß alle Beteiligten die Zeit auf eine angenehme Weise verbringen.

Praktische Hinweise

Besonders während der Sommersaison können Sie unnötige Enttäuschungen vermeiden, wenn Sie Ihre Unterkunft im voraus buchen. Es empfiehlt sich auch, die Gastgeber einen Tag vor Ihrer Ankunft anzurufen, um die Buchung zu bestätigen und die ungefähre Ankunftszeit mitzuteilen. Einige Bed & Breakfast Häuser bieten einen Abholdienst von Bus, Bahn oder Flughafen an - dieser Service ist oft im Preis mit eingeschlossen. Sagen Sie auch bitte rechtzeitig Bescheid, wenn Sie bei Ihren Gastgebern zusätzlich zur Übernachtung gerne ein warmes Abendessen hätten.

Bed & Breakfast Kategorien

Bed & Breakfast

Bed & Breakfast ist der Oberbegriff für alle Unterkunftsarten, die ein bequemes Bett, ein reichliches Frühstück und persönlichen Service im Preis einschließen. Während Ihres Aufenthalts werden Sie aufs Freundlichste von Ihren Gastgebern betreut.

Homestay

"Homestay" ist eine sehr beliebte Bed & Breakfast Variante. Sie wohnen in Privathäusern, die Gastgeber sind aufgeschlossen und freundlich und werden alles ihnen Mögliche tun, damit Sie sich "ganz wie zu Hause" fühlen nach dem Motto: "Sie kommen als Fremde und gehen als Freunde."

Countrystay

"Countrystays" sind Bed & Breakfast-Unterkünfte in ländlicher Umgebung. Sie wohnen meist in nächster Nähe von dem, was Sie am typischen Landleben so schätzen. Ob Sie wandern gehen wollen, angeln oder einfach nur die unbeschreibliche Natur pur genießen wollen, hier können Sie sich abseits vom Großstadtstreß in aller Ruhe erholen.

Farmstay

Wenn Sie echtes neuseeländisches Farmerleben hautnah genießen wollen, dann sind Sie im "Farmstay" gut aufgehoben. Üblicherweise können Sie bei der Farmtour mit auf die Weiden gehen und beim Füttern der Farmtiere mit dabei sein. Das Frühstück wird meistens mit der Familie zusammen eingenommen. Viele Farmstays bieten Vollverpflegung an.

Bed & Breakfast Kategorien

Guesthouse/Inn

"Guest Houses" sind meistens Häuser, die eine größere Zahl von Gästen beherbergen, aber trotzdem eine persönliche Note aufweisen. Manche haben mehrere Aufenthaltsräume und einen speziellen Frühstücksraum. "Guest Houses" bieten im allgemeinen kein warmes Abendessen an.

Boutique Accommodation

Der Begriff "Boutique" soll Ihnen sagen, daß es sich hier um ganz besonders schöne Bed & Breakfast-Übernachtungsmöglichkeiten handelt: eine geschmackvolle Inneneinrichtung, stilvolle Architektur oder ein romantisches Ambiente. Die Gastgeber dieser Häuser legen größten Wert auf gepflegte Gastfreundschaft.

Luxury Accommodation

Die Luxusunterkünfte bieten eine hervorragende Ausstattung, exzellentes Essen und ganz besonderen Service. Oft sind diese Häuser architektonische Glanzstücke oder sie liegen in einzigartiger Umgebung. "Luxus" steht für außergewöhnliche Unterkunft und Gastfreundschaft.

Self-contained Accommodation

Unterkünfte für Selbstversorger sind oft komplette Einliegerwohnungen oder einzeln stehende Häuschen mit eigenem Badezimmer und eigener Toilette und meistens mit Küche, Waschmaschine und Wäschetrockner. In manchen Fällen nehmen Sie das Frühstück zusammen mit der Gastfamilie ein. Es wird aber auch oftmals an die Haustür gebracht, oder Sie finden die Zutaten bereits in der Küche.

"Auf einen Blick" - Alle wichtigen Informationen

"Auf einen Blick"
Kontaktaufnahme
Wer sind die Gastgeber und wo wohnen sie? Wie kommen Sie schnell mit ihnen in Kontakt?

"Auf einen Blick"
Übernachtungspreis
Alle Preise gelten für eine Übernachtung. **Double** *ist der Preis für zwei Personen in einem Zimmer,* **Single** *der Preis für eine Person in einem Zimmer. In einigen Fällen ist zusammen mit der Buchung eine Anzahlung erforderlich. Frühstück ist im Preis mit inbegriffen (falls nicht ausdrücklich anders erwähnt).* **Alle Preise gelten in $ NZ.** *Bitte lassen Sie sich die Preise von den Gastgebern bestätigen.*

"Auf einen Blick"
Symbole für Kategorien
Mit diesen einprägsamen Symbolen können Sie Ihre bevorzugte Unterkunftsmöglichkeit schnell ausfindig machen. Dieses System ist besonders hilfreich für Reisende, die die englische Sprache nicht fließend beherrschen.

"Auf einen Blick"
Kategoriestreifen
Die Gastgeber beschreiben ihre Kategorie in ihren eigenen Worten.

"Auf einen Blick"
Besondere Details
In Stichworten die attraktivsten Details der Unterkunft und der Sehenswürdigkeiten in der Umgebung.

"Auf einen Blick"
Kleine Straßenkarte
Im weißen Kästchen finden Sie den Namen des Hauses; der rote Punkt zeigt Ihnen die genaue Position. Im grünen Kästchen finden Sie die Wegbeschreibung.

Klar und übersichtlich
Schnell zu finden: Adresse, Telefon- und Faxnummer, E-Mail und Internetadresse.

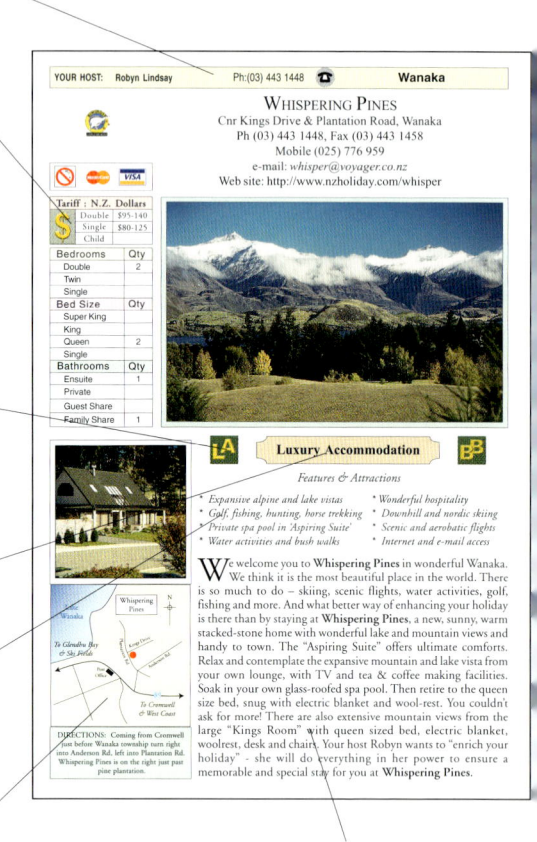

"Ein persönliches Willkommen"
Dieser Text, von den Gastgebern persönlich verfaßt, beschreibt deren Lebensstil und Interessen, die Art der Unterkunft und was Sie als Gast erwarten können.

🚭 Nichtraucher

Abkürzungen
SH – State Highway
h.p. – halber Preis
N.A. – nicht zutreffend
neg. – nach Vereinbarung
Qty – Anzahl
Tce – Terrace

Direkt buchen - Extrakosten vermeiden

Wenn Sie die Buchung selbst vornehmen, haben Sie von Anfang an persönlichen Kontakt mit Ihren Bed & Breakfast-Gastgebern in Neuseeland und vermeiden unnötige Kosten.

Wie wird dieser Reiseführer benützt – Zimmerdetails

Gästezimmer

Double = Zimmer mit Bett für 2 Personen
Twin = Zimmer mit 2 Betten für 2 Personen
Single = Zimmer mit Bett für eine Person

Bad/WC

Ensuite = Bad/WC mit Zimmer verbunden
Private = Eigenes Bad/WC, aber separat
Guest/Family Share = Bad/WC wird von Gästen oder der Gastfamilie mitbenützt.

Gästezimmer	Qty
Double	
Twin	
Single	

Bettgröße	Qty
Super King	
King	
Queen/Double	
(King-) /Single	

Bad/WC	Qty
Ensuite	
Private	
Guest Share	
Family Share	

Bettgrößen

Super King
180 x 200cm

King
165 x 200cm

Queen
150 x 200cm

Double
135 x 190cm

Single
90 x 190cm

King Single
90 x 200cm

Kategorie Symbole

- Bed & Breakfast
- Boutique Accommodation
- Countrystay
- Farmstay
- Guest House / Inn
- Homestay
- Luxury Accommodation
- Self-contained Accom. & Cottages

Gängige Kreditkarten

- Amex – American Express
- Japanese Credit Card
- VISA
- Diners
- Bankcard
- MasterCard
- Maestro
- Eftpos

Mitgliedschaft in folgenden Verbänden und Gesellschaften

- Historic Places Trust
- Hospitality Hosts
- New Zealand Association Farm & Home Hosts
- Superior Inns of New Zealand
- Auckland Home & Farmstay
- Heritage Inns of New Zealand
- Hostlink-Network of Fine Hosts
- New Zealand's Federation *of* Bed & Breakfast Hotels

Dieses Symbol versichert Ihnen einen herzlichen Kiwi-Empfang und guten, aufmerksamen Service. "Kiwihost" ist Neuseelands preisgekröntes Dienst-am-Kunden "Trainingsprogramm". Dieses Zeichen soll Ihnen zeigen, daß wir Sie überall als Kunden schätzen.

General Information

Dairies und Supermärkte

Dairies und Supermärkte

Die traditionellen "Dairies" sind kleine Läden, die meist sieben Tage die Woche von früh bis spät geöffnet haben. Sie können hier beinahe alles kaufen, was in den Supermärkten angeboten wird: Zeitungen, Zigaretten, Süßigkeiten und eine große Auswahl an Lebensmitteln. Die Preise sind etwas höher als in den Supermärkten. Dairies sind nicht nur in den Geschäftszentren sondern vor allem in reinen Wohngebieten zu finden. Einige Dairies bieten auch Postdienste an.

Alle kleinen und großen Städte haben Supermärkte. Das Angebot ist groß, und die Preise sind günstig. Normalerweise haben diese Supermärkte eigene Parkplätze oder Parkhäuser, in denen Sie gebührenfrei parken können (Manchmal ist es nötig, der Kassenzettel vorzuzeigen). Einige Supermärkte sind auch am Abend und sonntags geöffnet.

Die "Dairy" – fester Bestandteil des neuseeländischen Alltags

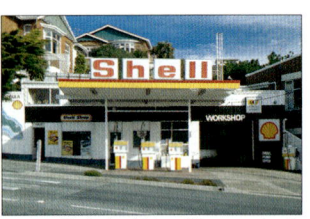

Typische, kleine Vororttankstelle

Tankstellen

In den 'Petrol' oder 'Service Stations' erhält man neben Benzin und Motoröl auch alles andere übliche Zubehör. Normalerweise haben Tankstellen keinen Reparatur- oder Inspektionsdienst. Wenn doch, dann erkennen Sie es an diesem Schild: "Mechanic on duty".
Für Reparaturen ist statt der Tankstelle sonst die "Garage" zuständig.

Visitor Information Network

Halten Sie Ausschau nach dem grünen *i* und dem "Visitor Information Network"-Zeichen. Mehr als 80 Informationsbüros stehen Ihnen in Neuseeland zur Verfügung. Die angebotenen Dienstleistungen sind vielfältig, wie etwa Reiseplanung und -beratung oder Buchungsservice für Touren und Unterkünfte.
Die Büros vermitteln Ihnen zudem eine Fülle an landeskundlichem Wissen. Speziell geschultes und qualifiziertes Personal gibt Ihnen gerne fachkundige Beratung.

Tourist Radio

"Tourist Information FM" nennt sich ein kurzes Informationsprogramm für Touristen, das rund um die Uhr gesendet wird. Für die deutsche Version stellen Sie Ihr Radio auf **100.4 FM (UKW)** ein.

Auch die **"New Zealand Automobile Association"** hat Informationsbüros im ganzen Land. Den Mitgliedern ausländischer Automobilclubs stellen diese Straßenkarten, Reiseführer und Reiseinformationen zur Verfügung. Die gebühren- freie Telefonnummer ist 0800 500 444

Neuseelands Naturschönheiten

Eindrucksvolle Gegensätze und landschaftliche Vielfalt

Neuseelands Landschaft ist so unterschiedlich und abwechslungsreich wie die Neuseeländer selbst. Kein anderes Land auf der Erde vereint eine solche landschafliche Vielfalt auf so kleinem Raum. Überall in Neuseeland findet man den "Native Bush", die ursprüngliche Buschlandschaft mit ihren immergrünen Bäumen und Sträuchern. Auf der Nordinsel können Sie die riesigen, exotischen Kauribäume bewundern. Rotorua, im Zentrum der Nordinsel, lockt mit seinen heißen Quellen, Geysiren und Tümpeln mit brodelndem Schlamm. Heiße Thermalquellen finden Sie auch in mehreren anderen Regionen. Neuseeland hat die erstaunliche Zahl von 13 Nationalparks in denen Sie eine kaum berührte Natur in all ihrer atemberaubenden Schönheit genießen können.
Die "Southern Alps", die Gebirgszüge der Südinsel, bieten ein Naturerlebnis ganz besonderer Art. Sie sind berühmt für ihre imposante Größe, ihre Gletscher, Seen und kilometerlangen, zerklüfteten Felsen, die steil ins tiefe Wasser der neuseeländischen Südwestküste abfallen. Der berühmteste der vielen Fjorde im Süden ist der Milford Sound. Man kann ihn entweder mit dem Auto oder zu Fuß erreichen. Ein Tip: Der "Milford-Track" gilt als der "allerschönste Wanderweg der Welt". Im ganzen Land finden Sie Gewässer in allen nur erdenklichen Variationen: Wasserfälle, reißende Gebirgsbäche, breite Ströme, Sandstrände und felsige Küstenstreifen.

South Island West Coast Native Bush

Waitangi Golf Course - einer der vielen ausgezeichneten neuseeländischen Golfplätze.

Neuseelands weitläufige, wenig besiedelte Natur bietet sich als idealer Ort für die verschiedensten Sportarten an. Sie können hier bergsteigen, Golf spielen, segeln und alle möglichen Wintersportarten betreiben. Die Neuseeländer gehen besonders gerne angeln oder auf die Jagd – kein Wunder, denn Fische und Wild sind in großer Zahl vorhanden. Die Neuseeländer lieben alles, was man in der freien Natur unternehmen kann, und die Naturlandschaft Neuseelands eignet sich auch ganz hervorragend dazu, sportlichen und geselligen Beschäftigungen im Freien nachzugehen.

Praktische Reiseinformationen - Straßenverkehr

Ständig wechselnde Landschaften machen das Autofahren in Neuseeland zur wahren Fahrfreude

Straßenverkehr

Das Autofahren ist in Neuseeland meistens ein echtes Vergnügen. Die Landstraßen und Autobahnen sind im allgemeinen in sehr gutem Zustand und die Neuseeländer sind auch hinter dem Steuer hilfsbereit und höflich. Trotzdem empfehlen wir Ihnen, die folgenden Zeilen durchzulesen, bevor Sie in Neuseeland Auto fahren.

Der "New Zealand Road Code" listet Neuseelands Verkehrsregeln auf. Er ist gegen eine kleine Gebühr bei der "Land Transport Safety Authority" (LTSA) erhätlich. Im örtlichen Telefonbuch finden Sie die Adresse der jeweils nächstgelegenen LTSA-Niederlassung. Sehr hilfreich ist die Broschüre *"Driving Safely in New Zealand"*, die Sie umsonst bei der LTSA bekommen können. Sie enthält auch eine deutsche Übersetzung.

Die Broschüre *"Budgets Führer durch den Straßenverkehr in Neuseeland"* mit ausführlicher Beschreibung, ist sehr zu empfehlen. Es gibt sie in allen Budget Rental Car Niederlassungen.

Praktische Informationen - Straßenverkehr

Einige Grundregeln fürs Autofahren

Linksverkehr: Es wird nicht jedem leichtfallen, sich ans Linksfahren in Neuseeland zu gewöhnen. Nehmen Sie sich Zeit und muten Sie sich nicht zu viel auf einmal zu.

Höchstgeschwindigkeit: Auf Land- oder Schnellstraßen (open road, motorway) im allgemeinen 100 Stundenkilometer.

In Ortschaften und Städten 50 Stundenkilometer, achten Sie jedoch auf Verkehrsschilder (**linke** Straßenseite!), die eine geringere Höchstgeschwindigkeit vorschreiben.

Verkehrsschilder und Straßenkreuzungen:
Stopp: Vorfahrt gewähren.

Vorfahrt gewähren: Langsam fahren, bremsbereit sein und dem Verkehr von links oder rechts Vorfahrt gewähren. Auch beim Linksabbiegen dem entgegenkommenden Verkehr Vorfahrt gewähren.

Sicherheitsgurte:
Der Fahrer und alle Fahrzeuginsassen müssen Sicherheitsgurte tragen/bzw. Kleinkinder in Kindersitzen sein.

Wenn Sie ein wenig abenteuerlustig sind, werden Sie in Neuseeland mit atemberaubenden Eindrücken belohnt.

Introduction

ニュージーランドの家庭生活を実体験！

～ニュージーランド・B＆Bへのお誘い～

ニュージーランド人は、旅行者に対する心暖まる、フレンドリーなもてなしを誇りとする国民として知られています。この「ニュージーランド風のもてなし」をじかに体験できるのが、Bed & Breakfast（ベッド・アンド・ブレックファースト、B＆B）です。これは一般のホテルとは一味ちがった、アット・ホームなサービスを身上とする宿泊施設の総称で、その具体的な中身はいろいろです。宿泊の場所でいうと、町中の一軒家・コッテージ・釣り場のロッジ・高原の牧場・乗馬や機織りの学校・お城（！）といった具合に多岐にわたっています。実際の名称としては、Guest House（ゲスト・ハウス）、Inn（イン）、Boutique Accommodation（ブティック・アコモデーション）、Countrystay（カントリーステイ）などがあります。また、安いものから高くて豪華なものまでありますので、予算に合わせて選ぶことが可能です。B&Bのホスト（host, オーナー）は現役の教員・農家・芸術家・信仰療法家・作家、さらにはもと医師や弁護士など、実に多彩です。ホストの中には、単に話好き、という人から、専門的なサービスを提供する人まで、さまざまです。B&Bは、「本物の」ニュージーランドを体験するのに恰好の機会といえます。ホストと、趣味や仕事の話などで盛り上がるのも楽しみのひとつではないでしょうか。

皆様の旅行が楽しく、思い出深いものとなりますように……

Introduction

WHAT TO EXPECT

きれいな部屋、寝心地のよいベッド、おいしくて量もたっぷりの朝食、真心のこもったもてなし…ニュージーランドの Bed & Breakfast は、サービスの水準が高いことで知られています。さらに、ホストからは、その地域や周辺の見どころに関する詳しい「生の情報」を得ることができます。お客様の興味・関心をホストにお伝えください。ホストは皆様の旅行がすばらしいものとなる手助けができることを願っています。

― 宿泊者の心得

WHAT IS EXPECTED OF YOU

ホストは、お客様が楽しく思い出深いひとときを過ごすことができるよう、最大限の努力をしていますが、お客様の側にも配慮いただきたい点があります。それは、B＆Bは、基本的には「一般家庭」に泊まる、という形式をとっているという点です。ですから、ホストやその家族にたいする「ちょとした」気配りが大切です。たとえば、夜、帰りが遅くなる場合には、余裕をもって事前にその旨を伝えておき、「合鍵」を受け取っておくとか、電話を使用する際には、あらかじめ料金の確認をしておく、などです。こうした心遣いが、B＆Bでの滞在を成功させるカギなのです。

WHAT TO DO – HINTS

B&B 宿泊の貴重なチャンスを逃さないためには、予約するのが一番です。（特に真夏は込み合います。）予約されましたら、到着の前日にホストに予約の確認をし、到着予定時刻を伝えておくことをおすすめします。ホストの中には、coach (コーチ、長距離バス)・飛行機・列車の発着場からの無料送迎サービスを行っている人もいます。また、到着日の夕食を希望される場合には、前日または前前日に、その旨をホストに伝えておきましょう。

Bed & Breakfast Categories

ベッド・アンド・ブレックファースト B&B

一泊・朝食付きの宿の総称です。快適なベッドと、たっぷりの朝食、それにホストの暖かいおもてなしを存分にお楽しみください。

ホームステイ H

ごく一般の家庭で、ホストによる身近なもてなしを受けながら宿泊するものです。ホストは人と出会うのが好きで、宿泊客をまるで自分の家にいるような、和やかな雰囲気にしてくれます。宿泊客の皆様が、初めて会った時には「見知らぬ他人」でも、別れるときには「親しい友人」となることを、ホストは心得ているのです。

カントリーステイ C

Homestay と同様、一般の家庭に滞在するものです。Countrystay の特徴は、場所が「いなか」にある点です。都会とはちがった、ニュージーランドの一面をじかに体験できます。

ファームステイ F

ニュージーランドの農業について理解を深めたい、という人には理想的な機会です。動物たちと身近に接しながら、農場での生活を経験していきます。牧場内のツアーを行っているところもあります。通常、朝食はホストの家族とともにとります。場所柄、近所にレストランなどがないため、多くのFarmstay では昼食や夕食も出されます。

Bed & Breakfast Categories

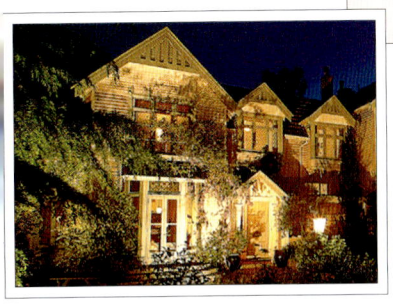

G ゲスト・ハウス

通常、規模が比較的大きく、他のB&Bの施設に比べ、より多くの宿泊客を泊めることができる施設ですが、B&Bならではの、フレンドリーなもてなしは変わりません。複数のラウンジや、朝食室が用意されているところもあります。夕食は出されないのが普通です。

BA ブティック・アコモデーション

特色ある家屋を用いたB&Bです。長い年月が醸し出す気品、優雅さ、ロマンス － Boutique Accommodationは、宿泊客の皆様をそうした雰囲気の中に包んでくれます。この雰囲気をいかに盛り上げるかが、ホストの腕のみせどころです。

LA ラクシャリー・アコモデーション

最高の立地条件のなかにある宿泊施設で、施設内外はさまざまな魅力でいっぱいです。豪華極まる設備や食事、それに群をぬいたハイ・クオリティーのサービスが特徴です。

SC セルフコンテインド・アコモデーション

宿泊者のための独立した入口・バスルーム・ラウンジを含むのが普通です。独立した台所や洗濯質室が用意されているところもあります。宿泊施設は、一軒家のなかの一区画として存在する場合と、別棟の建物として存在する場合とがあります。朝食はホストの家族とともにとる場合、宿泊施設まで届けられる場合、朝食の材料が宿泊所に用意されており、宿泊者が自分で用意する場合とさまざまです。

How to use this guide – "at a glance"

"at a glance"
  イージー・コントロール・パネル
  ホストの氏名・所在地・連絡先など。

"at a glance"
  ここに表示されているのは、一泊あたりの料金です。**Double**（ダブル）は、一部屋を2名で使用した場合の料金です。**Single**（シングル）は、一部屋を1名で使用した場合の料金です。予約の際に deposit（ディポジット、料金の一部前払い）が必要なところもあります。特に明記のない場合、料金には朝食代が含まれています。**料金の表記は、すべて「NZ ドル」です。**料金に関する詳しい内容は、直接ホストまでおたずねください。

"at a glance"
  カテゴリー・シンボル
  おさがしの B&B のタイプがすぐに見つかるよう工夫されたマークです。お役立てください。

"at a glance"
  カテゴリー・パネル
  該当する B&B のカテゴリーの、ホスト自身による定義・説明。

"at a glance"
  フィーチャーズ＆アトラクションズ
  宿泊施設およびその周辺のみどころのご紹介。

"at a glance"
  ロケーション・マップ
  宿泊施設の位置が赤丸で示されています。白のかこみの中に施設の名称が記されています。行き方の説明が追加で示されている場合もあります。

クリアー・アドレス・ディーテールズ
宿泊施設の所在地・電話番号・Fax 番号・e-mail アドレス・インターネット・ホームページのアドレスといった、大切な情報はこちらをご覧ください。

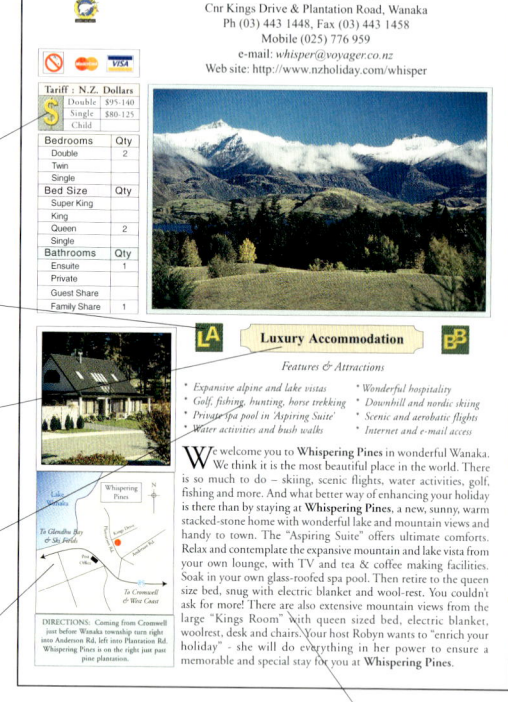

パーソナル・ウォーム・ウェルカム
ホストから読者へのひとことです。宿泊施設の特徴や、ホストの人柄・ライフ・スタイルといったものを垣間見ることができます。

No Smoking

Cnr – Corner: コーナー「角」
h.p. – half price: ハーフ・プライス「半額」
N.A. – not applicable: ノット・アプリカブル「該当項目なし」
neg. – negotiable: ニゴーシャブル「交渉可」
Qty – Quantity: クウォンティティ「数量」
Tce – Terrace: テラス

宿泊予約申し込みは、B&B のホストに直接なさいますと、ホストとそれだけ早くから知り合うことができ、また中間業者を通した場合にかかる、さまざまな手数料を省くことができるので有利です。

ガイドのてびき － 客室・設備に関する記述について

Bedrooms
- Double = 二人用ベッドがある部屋
- Twin = 一人用ベッドが２つある部屋
- Single = 一人用ベッドが１つある部屋

Bathrooms
- Ensuite = 寝室に隣接
- Private = 各宿泊客専用
- Guest Share/Family Share = 他の宿泊客またはホストの家族と共用

Bedrooms	Qty
Double	
Twin	
Single	

Bed Size	Qty
Super King	
King	
Queen/Double	
(King-) Single	

Bathrooms	Qty
Ensuite	
Private	
Guest Share	
Family Share	

Bed Size
- Super King — 180 x 200cm
- King — 165 x 200cm
- Queen — 150 x 200cm
- Double — 135 x 190cm
- Single — 90 x 190cm
- King Single — 90 x 200cm

ガイドのてびき － カテゴリー・シンボル

- **B B** Bed & Breakfast
- **B A** Boutique Accommodation
- **C** Countrystay
- **F** Farmstay
- **G** Guest House / Inn
- **H** Homestay
- **L A** Luxury Accommodation
- **S C** Self-contained Accom. & Cottages

ガイドのてびき － お支払可能なクレジット・カードについて

- Amex – American Express
- Japanese Credit Card
- VISA
- Diners
- Bankcard
- MasterCard
- Maestro
- Eftpos

ガイドのてびき － B&B が提携している協会・団体について

- Historic Places Trust
- Hospitality Hosts
- New Zealand Association Farm & Home Hosts
- Superior Inns of New Zealand
- Auckland Home & Farmstay
- Heritage Inns of New Zealand
- Hostlink-Network of Fine Hosts
- New Zealand's Federation of Bed & Breakfast Hotels

このマークは、ニュージーランド流の暖かく、フレンドリーで、質の高いサービスを保証するものです。Kiwi Host（キウイ・ホスト）は、我が国をリードする顧客サービス・トレーニング・プログラムです。

General Information

Dairies and Supermarkets

Dairy（デアリー）は、ニュージーランドに古くからある、形態の店で、日本の「コンビニ」にあたります。早朝から夜遅くまで、年中無休での営業が普通です。パン、ミルク、新聞、菓子類、それに日用の食料品といったものがここで手に入ります。営業時間が長いことと、立地の良さの関係で、通常、supermarket よりも値段が少々高く設定されています。小さな町の Dairy などでは、郵便業務を行っているところもあります。

ほとんどの都市や町には Supermarket（スーパーマーケット）があります。Supermarket では、日本のスーパーと同様、食料品をはじめ、さまざまな商品を、手ごろな値段で手に入れることができます。たいていの場合、無料駐車場付きですが、これは「買い物客専用」ですので、退場の際、レシートの提示を求められることがあります。ほとんどが毎日の営業です。

ニュージーランドの日常生活には欠かせないデアリー。

Petrol Stations

（ペトロール・ステーション）
service station（サービス・ステーション）ともよばれ、日本の「ガソリン・スタンド」にあたります。普通、自動車のメンテナンスや修理といったサービスは行っていません。そうしたサービスは、garage（ガレージ、自動車修理場）がある店で行っています。

Visitor Information Network （ビジター・インフォメーション・ネットワーク）

緑のイタリック体の文字 'i' が Visitor Information Centre (ビジター・インフォメーション・センター、観光案内所)の目印です。

Visitor Information Centre は、ニュージーランド国内に８０ヶ所以上あります。そこでは専門のスタッフが、旅行の予約、ツアーや宿泊先の案内など、幅広い情報・サービスを提供しています。

Tourist Radio

Tourist Information FM は、観光地のほとんどで受信・聴取することができます。ここでは、一日 24 時間、旅行者に役立つ情報を提供しています。英語による放送は、88.2 FM で行っています。

New Zealand Automobile Association （ AA）は、

ニュージーランド国内各地に支部をおき、地図やガイドブックをはじめ、旅行者むけの各種の情報をその会員に提供しています。お問い合わせは、フリーダイヤル 0800 500 444 で常時受け付けています。

Natural New Zealand
バラエティに富んだニュージーランドの自然

ニュージーランドは北島、南島ともに、**多種多様** の 地形から成り立っています。あまり広いとはいえない、国土のなかで、これだけバラエティに富んだ風景が望める国は他にないといっても過言ではありません。このニュージーランドの「多様性」に彩りを添えるのは、心のあたたかさと極めて友好的 な 国民気質で 知られる、 ニュージーランド人自身に他なりません。

北島、南島とも、常緑の native bush（野生のかん木の茂み）が各地で見受けられます。北島には、巨大な Kauri tree（カウリマツ）から なる エキゾチックな 林もあります。また、北島の中心部にある Rotorua（ロトルア）近 辺には、温泉・間欠泉・ boiling mud pool（ボイリング・マッド・プール、お湯 のかわりに泥が沸き立っている 温泉）といったものがあります。治療効果の認められた温泉は 北・南の 両島で見つけることができます。文明に汚されていない、ありのままの 自 然 や 景色 にあふれた 国立公園を 訪 れる人はみな、そのすばらしさに感動を覚えずには いられな いでしょう。

南島は雄大な自然の景観が売り物です。連なる 山々、氷河、湖 、見渡す限り続く海岸線、さらには、前人未到の山地を背景に ウェスト・コーストに 鋭い 切り込みを入れるフィヨルド…どれを取ってもその 素晴らしさには 驚嘆するばかりです。フィヨルドのなかでも、最も有名なのが、 Milford Sound（ミルフォード・サウンド）で、こちらは「世界で最も美しい 遊歩道」として名高い Milford Track（ミルフォード・トラック）、または一般道 からのアクセスが可能です。

ニュージーランドは、「水」に関わる景観も豊富 です。壮大な滝、大 河川、 大小の 湖 、サーフィン・ビーチ、ごつごつとした 岩からなる 海岸線 など、よりどりみどりです。

ニュージーランドには、良質のゴルフ場がたくさんあります。上の写真は、Waitangi（ワイタンギ）のゴルフ場。

こうした， ニュージーランドの豊富な自然は、 さまざまな アウトドア・アクティビティの機会を人々に提供してくれます。登山、スキー、ゴルフ、ヨット、それにさまざまなウィンター・スポーツがこの 国では盛んです。また 狩猟や フィッシングにも最適の環境が用意されています。 ニュージーランド人は全般的にスポーツを愛する国民です。そのおかげで、こうした、休暇を過ごすための環境が 万全に 整えられているのです。

| On the Road | Practical Travel Information |

NZを車でドライブ。変化に富むすばらしい景色は、最高のご褒美をドライバーに与えてくれる…

On the Road （路上で）

自動車旅行は、ニュージーランドのすばらしい景色を存分に楽しむ方法の一つです。路面の状態はおおむね良好ですが、皆様自身と他のドライバーの安全のため、以下に挙げる資料を事前にぜひお読みください。

The New Zealand Road Code (ザ・ニュージーランド・ロード・コード、ニュージーランド道路法規)は、法にかなった正しい運転のマナーについて述べたもので、Land Transport Safety Authority（ランド・トランスポート・セーフティ・オーソリティ：日本の「陸運局」のような機関）で手に入ります。最寄りのLTSAの支部の所在地は、電話帳に載っています。また、*Driving Safely in New Zealand* という小冊子も有用な資料です。これは英語・日本語・ドイツ語のセクションに分かれており、LTSAで無料で配布しています。

Budget's Guide to Safe Driving in New Zealand も貴重な資料です。これはBudget Rental Car（バジェット・レンタル・カー）の各支店で手に入ります。

| Practical Travel Information | On the Road |

Driving: Some Basic Points（運転時の基本的マナー）

Keep Left: ニュージーランドは日本と同様、左側通行です。

Speed Limit: 高速道路や山道などで、特に制限速度の標識のないところ、およびこの標識があるところでは、制限速度は時速100キロメートルとなります。町中では、基本的に制限時速は50キロですが、場合によってはそれよりも低いところもありますので、常に標識に注意が必要です。

Road Signs at Intersections（交差点における標識）：
Stop: 必ず停止し、左右および対向車（直進および右折車）に注意を払って車を再発進させてください。ニュージーランドは、日本と逆で右折車優先（左折車ではない）です。

Give way（他方向の車優先）：徐行して、左右から来る車、および対向車に注意しながら進みます。特に、対向車が右折、自分が左折の場合には、相手が優先となりますので注意が必要です。

Seatbelts: 車に乗っている者は、ドライバーに限らず、また前部座席・後部座席にかかわらず、すべて（大人も子供も）シートベルトをすることが法により義務づけられています。

介紹

"體驗真正的紐西蘭—它的民族"

歡迎來到紐西蘭多樣化的旅店住宿簡介

紐西蘭的住宿，由小屋到別墅，從經濟單位到豪華大宅，您都會享受到在一個親切友善且好客的環境中居住。有多種不同的住宿方式：家庭住宿、農莊住宿、旅客之家、小客店、豪華旅店、鄉村住宿等等，他們一律提供給您一張溫暖的床以及香噴噴的西式早餐。這些都能讓您親身感受到紐西蘭的生活，認識居住在這裡的居民。您更可選擇嗜好與自己相似的家庭住宿，例如：老師、農夫、退休的專業人士、園藝專家、畫家、作家等等，住宿在他們的家，彼此交換心得，同時可享受獨特真誠的招待，體驗在漁村、郊外綿羊、海外之家的生活。不管是旅館或多樣化的家庭住宿，除了種類多之外，還充滿了紐西蘭獨特的友善及好客，不論您選擇那一種住宿，您將都是一位貴賓，盡情享受生活，讓日後有個難忘的回憶。

介 紹

期望什麼？

在紐西蘭床鋪及早餐享有標準服務的聲譽，住客會有最清潔、舒適的床，多種選擇熱烘烘早餐，及主人樂意友善的招待。除此之外，主人也會給於您居住地區的詳細資料。他們樂意幫您安排您在本地的旅遊計劃。他們豐富的經驗能增添您居住的樂趣。

對您的期望？

主人家會為您做任何的事，讓您享受一個難忘的停留。可是，請記得無論如何您只是一個客人。所以，請您注意一些事，例如，如果您晚歸的話，要向主人索取大門鎖匙，或當您要打長途、國內、本地電話時，應先詢問主人才可使用電話。請讓主人家知道您將夜歸。您處身置地的設想，會使您及主人都感到滿意。

給予您的建議

事先訂好一間房間，以避免屆時沒房間的失望，尤其在夏天時。除外，在您出發的前一天致電到主人家確定您訂好的房間及讓他們曉得您幾時會抵達。有些主人提供接送服務，如果您有需要的話。如果您需要他為您準備午餐的話，也請您早一、兩天前通知主人。

床鋪及早餐系列

床鋪及早餐 BB

床鋪及早餐是所有不同種類住所的代稱,供您選擇。除外,在您居住時間,主人更會給予您親切友善的招待,讓您有賓至如歸之感。

古典大屋 H

在床鋪及早餐系列中,古典大屋的建築物具有古典氣息、整齊美觀、寧靜浪漫,是適合喜歡這類型的您來居住,主人將這些建築物的特質保持得非常好,確保您最佳的享受。

鄉村居住 C

鄉村居住類似家庭住宿。您將居住於私人家庭中,慢慢地認識及接觸鄉村迷人的風景。許多鄉村住宿都靠近著名的旅遊風景區,能讓您最方便認識這些地方。

農場住宿 F

如果您選擇在農場居住,通常會由農場主人一家人接待您。如有需要,可為您安排參觀農場的行程,好讓您更加了解農場,您將跟農場主人一家人共同享用早餐;晚餐必須在事先通知,農場也將會為您準備,因為農場附近沒有餐館。

床鋪及早餐系列

G 旅客之家

旅客之家通常能容納較多的旅客。雖然如此，主人仍會給您友善親切的招待。旅客之家可能會有數間的客廳及餐廳。旅客之家不常提供晚餐給住客。

BA 家庭住宿

家庭住宿是最普遍的住宿方式，居住在溫暖、友善、好客的家庭中。主人喜歡認識不同的人，且樂意讓您有"家"的感覺，讓您曉得，您剛來的時候雖是一個陌生人，當您要離開時卻是以朋友的身份離開。

LA 豪華大宅

豪華大宅代表了一流的設備，上等的餐飲和超水準的服務，許多此類住宿都有各自的特色，給予您額外一流的享受，它們代表了優越的住宿。

SC 私人住宿

此居住方式，通常包括了，私人的走道、浴室及客廳。它可以是一個家庭中隔出來的一部份或是一整間小屋。早餐可在主人家享用，也可送到您的門口或餐室。

如何使用這本指南 —"瀏覽一瞥"

容易聯絡的範圍
您的旅店老闆;無論是何人,身在何處,都能迅速與他們取得聯絡。

明確的地址
明確的地址,應包括住宿的地址,電話和傳真號碼,電子郵件地址與網址。

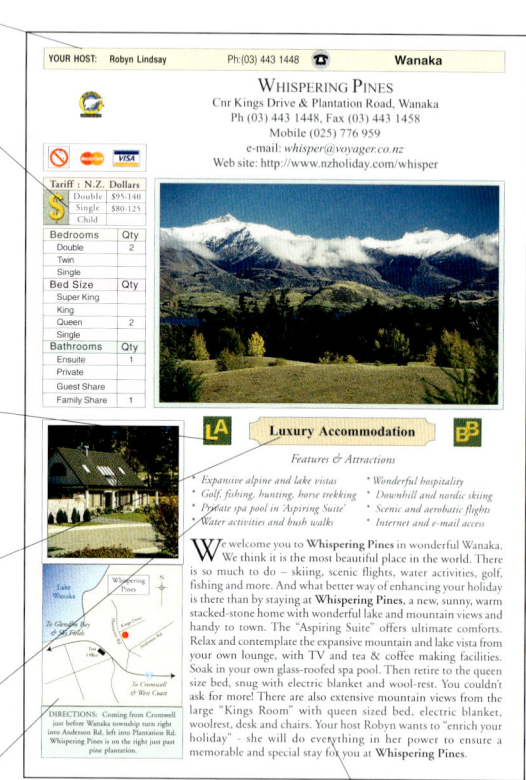

價目表
價目表上的金額,表示住宿一晚的住宿費。雙人(Double)表示兩人合用一間房間的價錢。當您預定房間時,您可能要預付訂金。價目表上的價錢通常包括早餐,除非有特別註明不提供早餐。全部價錢都以紐幣計算。請與旅店老闆確定住宿明細資料。

各種住宿的代表符號
設計這些容易辨認的符號,是為了方便您預約訂房,對於不太熟悉英文的遊客們,這是絕對有幫助的。

住宿種類
旅店老闆會為您詳細介紹住宿種類。

地區特色及焦點
您住宿的四周環境以及您住宿區域的特色與焦點,都會為您列出。

區域地圖
您所住宿的地點,在地圖上將以紅點標示。旅店的店名,也會在地圖上刊出。通常為配合找尋,也都有方向圖來確認正確方向。

"一項特別及溫暖的歡迎"
通常歡迎詞是由旅店老闆親自設計。有關店內設備以及獨特的住宿方式,都會有清楚的說明。

No Smoking

縮寫
Cnr—角落
h.p.—半價
N.A. —無此設備
Qty—可磋商
Tce—陽台

直接預約—省錢

與紐西蘭"床與早餐"
旅店系列的老闆直接預約住宿,
您從一開始就會省了許多
不必要的附加費用。

如何使用這本指南 — 客房資料

房 間

Double = 一或二張床提供兩人住宿的房間
Twin = 提供二張床給兩人住宿的雙人房
Single = 提供一張床給單人住宿的單人房

浴 室

Ensuite = 浴室在您的房間內
Private = 提供您個人專用的浴室
Guest Share/Family Share = 公共浴室，必須與其他家庭或住客共同使用。

Bedrooms	Qty
Double	
Twin	
Single	
Bed Size	**Qty**
Super King	
King	
Queen/Double	
(King-)Single	
Bathrooms	**Qty**
Ensuite	
Private	
Guest Share	
Family Share	

床的尺寸

Super King *180 x 200cm*
King *165 x 200cm*
Queen *150 x 200cm*
Double *135 x 190cm*
Single *90 x 190cm*
King Single *90 x 200cm*

如何使用這本指南 — 代號種類

- **B** Bed & Breakfast
- **BA** Boutique Accommodation
- **C** Countrystay
- **F** Farmstay
- **G** Guest House / Inn
- **H** Homestay
- **LA** Luxury Accommodation
- **S** Self-contained Accom. & Cottages

如何使用這本指南 — 旅店老闆接受信用卡付款

- Amex – American Express
- Japanese Credit Card
- VISA
- Diners
- Bankcard
- MasterCard
- Maestro
- Eftpos

如何使用這本指南 — 協會

- Historic Places Trust
- Hospitality Hosts
- New Zealand Association Farm & Home Hosts
- Superior Inns of New Zealand
- Auckland Home & Farmstay
- Heritage Inns of New Zealand
- Hostlink-Network of Fine Hosts
- New Zealand's Federation of Bed & Breakfast Hotels

這個商標就是保證您是受本地人所歡迎的，以及獲得親切友善的服務。Kiwi Host 是紐西蘭顧客服務訓練計畫的得獎者，我們確信我們對於您的重視，與您對於我們的肯定。

實際旅遊資訊———道路駕駛

在紐西蘭的道路上駕駛，令您心情愉悅，
並且享受真正迷人的景色…

在道路上駕駛

在紐西蘭不但有怡人的風景，舒坦的道路，再加上樂於助人及禮貌週到的紐西蘭人，會讓您享受到駕駛的真正樂趣。雖然如此，為了您本身及其他駕駛者的安全，我們希望您能花一點時間(此地的紐西蘭人會耐心的等候您)在您尚未開動車子以前，請參閱以下事項：

"紐西蘭道路使用規則"是教導您如何正確及合法地在紐西蘭駕駛的一本指南。

您可以低價在交通局買到這本駕駛指南。您也可以在電話簿獲取交通局的地址。在交通局中，您也可以免費索取德文及日文版的"紐西蘭安全駕駛"的小冊子。

此外，另有一本名為"在紐西蘭的預算與安全駕駛指南"，您可以在"預算"租車公司的辦公室，獲得這本英文、德文、日文及中文不同版本的小冊子。

實際旅遊資訊──道路駕駛

駕駛：一些基本規則

靠左：當我們在紐西蘭駕駛時，是必須靠左行駛。外國遊客開始時可能會帶給您困擾，因此，我們建議您花些時間來適應及計劃您的旅程。

車速：一般來說，在快速道路最高車速為100公里/小時。在市區或鄉鎮中，最高車速50公里/小時。有時也會有例外，所以，請注意位於道路左邊的路標，因為它會正確地指示您駕駛的速限。

在交叉路口的路標：

停止 STOP：請立刻在馬路黃色停止標線前停車，讓路給所有的車輛。

讓路 GIVE WAY：請減低您的車速。如果有車輛由左或右向您靠近，請停車讓路給所有的車輛。但當您準備左轉時，您也必須停車讓路給對面來車。

安全帶：駕駛者及所有乘客(大人/小孩)──包括後座乘客，都必須繫上安全帶，或使用合格的嬰兒安全配備。

Thanks and Acknowledgements

Special thanks to all of these friends who gave help and reassurance when deadlines loomed and spirits were low:

Christine Buess, for production assistance.
Tim Cornelius, famous Dunedin graphic artist.
James Kirkus-Lamont, for production assistance.
Joshua and Matthew Newman, photographers.
Julia Stroud, fastest typist in Dunedin.

Scanning by *Norm & Marion Alford at Scanning Services Port Chalmers, Dunedin, nitefly@clear.net.nz*

Translations

German translation by *Uli Newman.*
Japanese translation by *Yoshi Isoyama at Transla NZ, PO Box 8069, Dunedin, New Zealand. isoyama@xtra.co.nz*
Mandarin (Chinese) translation by *Stephen Liu at Asian Communication Company Ltd., Dunedin, New Zealand.*

Photographs:

Destination Northland. *Pgs 4, 24, 25, 32; E-Mail: northland@xtra.co.nz*
"Hartridge Bed & Breakfast". *Pg 16 vintage car.*
New Zealand Post. *Pg 22 (envelopes), E-Mail: cschelp@nzpost.co.nz*
"Parua House". *Pg 9*
Tourism Dunedin. *Pg 229; E-Mail: visitor.centre@dcc.govt.nz*
Tourism Nelson. *Pgs 142; E-Mail: info@tourism-nelson.co.nz*
Tourism Rotorua. *Fly Leaf and Pg 80, E-Mail: marketing@tourism.rdc.govt.nz*
Tourism Wairarapa. *Pgs 19, 80, 114,117; E-Mail: tourwai@xtra.co.nz*
Tourism Waitaki. *Pg 153, E-Mail: oamvin@nzhost.co.nz*
West Coast Tourism. *Pg 24, E-Mail: tourismwc@minidata.co.nz*
University of Otago Photographic Services. *Pg 202*

Alphabetical Index of Listings

93 By the Sea, *New Plymouth* 97
93 Towack Homestay, *Riverton* 233
A Room With A View, *Napier* 102
Airport Pensione, *Auckland* 56
Al & Julie's Homestay, *Owhango* 98
Albany Country Home,
    Albany - Auckland 48
Albergo Hanmer, *Hanmer Springs* 162
Alloway, *Dunedin* 220
Almond Cottage, *Nelson* 142
Alraes Lakeview Homestay, *Rotorua* 79
Alsted Farmstay, *The Catlins* 236
Althorpe, *Nelson* 139
Amberley Bed & Breakfast,
    Devonport – Auckland 50
Amersham House,
    Parnell – Auckland 51
Anchorage Bed & Breakfast,
    Russell 38
Anderson's Alpine Residence,
    Stratford 98
Arapiki, *Nelson* 143
Arcadia Lodge, *Russell* 37
Ardara Lodge, *Kaikoura* 163
Ardern's Fine Accommodation,
    Waiheke Island – Auckland 58
Argyll Farmstay,
    Clydevale – Balclutha 230
Arles, *Wanganui* 107
Aspiring Images Homestay, *Wanaka* 189
Atanui, *Port Chalmers – Dunedin* 219
Atawhai Homestay, *Nelson* 145
Awapiriti, *Murchison* 153
Balcairn, *Hillend – Balclutha* 229

Balconies Bed & Breakfast,
    New Plymouth 97
Ballindalloch,
    Culverden – Canterbury 163
Barrs Falls, *Owaka – The Catlins* 234
Bay View Bed & Breakfast, *Nelson* 140
Bayview Manly B&B,
    Whangaparaoa – Auckland 48
Beach Abode,
    Ahipara – Northland 30
Beachfront Farmstay,
    Karamea – West Coast 152
Beaumere Lodge, *Hamilton* 66
Bellbird Cottage,
    Lake Hawea – Wanaka 186
Belvedere Homestay,
    Warkworth – Sandspit 47
Birdhaven, *New Plymouth* 96
Black Fir Lodge,
    Lower Hutt – Wellington 120
Blackhills Farmstay,
    Waikaka – Gore 231
Bloomfields Bed & Breakfast,
    Christchurch 173
Blythcliffe, *Akaroa – Canterbury* 177
Brackenhurst, *Oruanui – Taupo* 83
Braebyre,
    Pauatahanui – Wellington 119
Bridesdale,
    Ladies Mile – Queenstown 203
Brookers Bay Olive Grove,
    Whananaki – Northland 42
Buchanan's of Devonport,
    Auckland 50

Alphabetical Index of Listings

Burnard Gardens,
 Waikanae – Kapiti Coast 113
Bush Creek Health Retreat,
 Queenstown 205
Bush Haven Cottage,
 Okere Falls – Rotorua 75
Campbells B&B, *Queenstown* 206
Carrickfergus,
 Harihari – West Coast 159
Castlewood, *Dunedin* 221
Catley's Homestay, *Taupo* 89
Cavendish House,
 Lyttelton – Christchurch 175
Channel Vista, *Whangarei* 44
Charlemagne, *Tauranga* 70
Charmwood, *Blenheim* 150
Chelsea House, *Whangarei* 43
Chester Le House,
 Richmond – Nelson 138
Cill Chainnigh, *Dunedin* 222
Clover Downs Estate,
 Kaharoa – Rotorua 77
Cockle Bay Homestay,
 Howick – Auckland 54
Cornucopia Lodge,
 Eskdale – Napier 100
Cosy Cat Cottage, *Whitianga* 62
Cosy Kiwi Bed & Breakfast,
 Te Anau 214
Cotswold Cottage, *Thames* 59
Cotswold Lodge,
 Katikati – Bay of Plenty 68
Country Patch,
 Waikanae – Kapiti Coast 112

Craidenlie Lodge, *Hokitika* 157
Croydon House B&B Hotel,
 Christchurch 168
Dahlia Cottage,
 Ross – West Coast 159
Deacons Court, *Dunedin* 223
Deer Pine Lodge,
 Ngongotaha – Rotorua 78
Devondale House,
 Belfast – Christchurch 164
Doone Cottage, *Motueka Valley* 135
Driftwood,
 Wakatipu – Queenstown 211
Drumduan, *Atawhai – Nelson* 146
Edgewater , *Seatoun – Wellington* 126
Emandee Farm B&B,
 Paradise Valley – Rotorua 82
Eskview Heights, *Napier* 101
Estuary Bed & Breakfast,
 Mapua – Nelson 136
Ethridge Gardens, *Timaru* 185
Fairleigh Garden Guest House,
 Harewood – Christchurch 165
Fairlight River Lodge, *Paihia* 34
Fairviews, *Taupo* 89
Fernbrook, *Kerikeri – Northland* 30
Fishers Above the Beach,
 Howick – Auckland 55
Five Mile Bay Homestay, *Taupo* 95
Flower Haven, *Waipu – Northland* 46
Francesca's Homestay,
 Seatoun – Wellington 125
Froggy Cottage,
 Greytown – Wairarapa 116

Alphabetical Index of Listings

Garden Vineyard Homestay,
 West Melton – Canterbury 179
Glen Foulis,
 Waianakarua – Oamaru 218
Glen Haven Bed & Breakfast,
 Oamaru 218
Glen Sheiling,
 Katikati – Bay of Plenty 68
Glendale, *Takaka – Golden Bay* 133
Gorge Stream Cottage,
 Tahakopa – The Catlins 235
Gowrie House, *Dunedin* 224
Graelyn Villa, *Whangarei* 43
Greatstay, *Riccarton – Christchurch* 166
Green Gables Deer Farm,
 Methven – Mid Canterbury 180
Halcyon Heights, *Whitianga* 63
Harbour Lights Guesthouse,
 Whitianga 62
Hartridge House,
 Mapua – Nelson 137
Havenlee Homestay,
 Westport – West Coast 154
Heriot House B&B, *Dunedin* 223
Hiburn Farmstay, *Cromwell* 197
Homestay Wellington,
 Ngaio – Wellington 121
Horopito Lodge, *Ohakune* 99
House of Glenora,
 Picton – Marlborough 148
Hulmes Court, *Dunedin* 225
Hulverstone Lodge,
 Avondale – Christchurch 169
Hunt's Homestay, *Wanaka* 188

Il Casa Moratti Homestay,
 Whangamata – Coromandel 64
Jarvis Farmstay,
 Pakaraka – Bay of Islands 40
Jensen's Homestay, *Taupo* 90
Jervois Road Bed & Breakfast,
 Taradale – Napier 104
Kahilani Farm, *Ngongotaha – Rotorua* 81
Kapiti Vistas,
 Waikanae – Kapiti Coast 111
Karaka Point Lodge,
 Karaka Point – Picton 149
Karamana Homestead, *Coromandel* 61
Kauri House Lodge,
 Dargaville – Northland 46
Kepplestone, *Owaka – The Catlins* 234
Kimeret Place,
 Mapua – Nelson Region 138
Kinloch Lodge, *Kinloch – Taupo* 84
Kleynbos Bed & Breakfast,
 St. Martins – Christchurch 171
Kooringa, *Acacia Bay – Taupo* 86
Kotiri Lodge, *Taupo* 92
Kowhai Lodge,
 Mossburn – Southland 213
Lake Wanaka Home Hosting,
 Wanaka 190
Lakeside Bed & Breakfast,
 Okere Falls – Rotorua 75
Larch Hill Bed & Breakfast,
 Queenstown 208
Larchwood Lodge,
 Dublin Bay – Wanaka 187
Larkhall, *Palmerston North* 108

Alphabetical Index of Listings

Lavender Towers,
 Avonhead – Christchurch 166
Lewood Farm Park,
 Okaihau – Bay of Islands 41
Little Blue House,
 Te Anau – Fiordland 215
Locarno Gardens Apartment,
 St. Martins – Christchurch 172
Lochinver Homestay, *Taupo* 90
Lynmore Homestay, *Rotorua* 82
Mahana Country Homestay,
 Motueka – Nelson 136
Mapledurham,
 Richmond – Nelson 141
Markbeech Homestay,
 Papamoa – Bay of Plenty 71
Matai House,
 Hataitai – Wellington 123
Matai Lodge,
 Whataroa – South Westland 161
Matangi Oaks, *Hamilton* 67
Mataura Valley Station,
 Garston – Southland 212
McRae's Homestay,
 Gore – Southland 231
Menteith Country Homestay,
 Lincoln – Christchurch 176
Meychelle Manor,
 Kirwee – Canterbury 178
Minarapa, *Oruanui – Taupo* 83
Monterey Lodge,
 Hawea Flat – Wanaka 188
Mountain View Bed & Breakfast,
 Auckland Airport 56

Mynthurst Farmstay,
 Waipukurau – Hawkes Bay 105
Naumai Otaki Gracious Lady,
 Otaki – Kapiti Coast 111
Ngongotaha Lakeside Lodge,
 Ngongotaha – Rotorua 80
Oakridge Lake Wanaka, *Wanaka* 191
Oban, *Takaka – Golden Bay* 133
Okuru Beach Bed & Breakfast,
 Haast – South Westland 161
Omahu House,
 Remuera – Auckland 53
Operiki, *Wanganui* 107
Ounuwhao B&B Homestead,
 Russell 36
Paeroa Lakeside Homestay,
 Acacia Bay – Taupo 87
Panorama Homestay,
 Sumner – Christchurch 174
Papamoa Homestay,
 Papamoa – Bay of Plenty 72
Pariroa Homestay,
 Acacia Bay – Taupo 85
Parklands Lodge, *Wanaka* 192
Parnassus Farm & Garden,
 Huntly – Hamilton 65
Paroa Homestay, *Greymouth* 155
Parua House, *Whangarei* 45
Pataka House, *Taupo* 91
Patons Rock Homestay,
 Takaka – Golden Bay 134
Perenuka Farm,
 Te Anau – Fiordland 216
Pine Heights Retreat, *Dunedin* 226

Alphabetical Index of Listings

Piners Homestay, *Greymouth* 156
Plaisted Park Homestay, *Hunterville – Rangitikei* 106
Pleasant Point Homestay, *Pleasant Point – South Canterbury* 184
Pohutukawa Farmhouse, *Matata – Whakatane* 73
Port of Call, *Leask Bay – Stewart Island* 236
Quartz Reef Creek, *Cromwell* 198
Queenstown House, *Queenstown* 207
Raemere Homestead, *Kerikeri – Bay of Islands* 31
Reomoana, *Mahia Peninsula* 95
Rhododendron Lodge, *Blenheim* 150
Richlyn, *Taupo* 93
Rivendell Lodge, *Fairlie – South Canterbury* 183
River View Lodge, *Westport – West Coast* 154
RiverPark, *Paihia – Bay of Islands* 33
Riversong, *Nelson* 144
Ro Nali, *Palmerston North* 109
Roevyn Homestay, *Nelson* 145
Rossendale, *Hokitika – West Coast* 158
Saltaire, *Island Bay – Wellington* 127
Sandtoft, *Papamoa – Bay of Plenty* 72
Sealladh, *Orakei – Auckland* 52
Seaview Homestay, *Seatoun – Wellington* 124
Shakespeare House, *Te Anau – Fiordland* 215

Shalimares, *Khandallah – Wellington* 122
Smith's Farmstay, *Wyndham – Southland* 232
Southern Home Hospitality, *Invercargill – Southland* 233
Southey Manor, *Greytown – Wairarapa* 116
Southshore Homestay, *Southshore – Christchurch* 172
Squires Bed & Breakfast, *Wanaka* 193
Stafford Villa, *Birkenhead Point – Auckland* 49
Stornoway Lodge, *Havelock South – Marlborough* 147
Stranalyth Gables, *Mosgiel – Dunedin* 228
Taiparoro House 1882, *Tauranga* 69
Tamar Vineyard, *Rapaura – Blenheim* 151
Tapua, *Te Anau – Fiordland* 214
Tarata Homestay, *Stoke – Nelson* 143
Tatu Orchards, *Waiuku – Auckland Region* 59
Te Mata Bay Homestay, *Thames Coast* 60
Te Moenga, *Acacia Bay – Taupo* 88
Te Wanaka Lodge, *Wanaka* 194
Teichelmann's Bed & Breakfast, *Hokitika – West Coast* 158
Temasek House, *Wanaka* 195
Ten on One Home/Farmstay, *Kaikohe – Bay of Islands* 39

Alphabetical Index of Listings

Terracotta Lodge,
 Carterton – Wairarapa 115
The Ambers, *Greytown – Wairarapa* 117
The Brae,
 Geraldine – South Canterbury 182
The Fantails,
 Levin – Horowhenua 110
The Grange, *Christchurch* 169
The Hermytage,
 Dannevirke – Hawkes Bay 105
The Historic Stone House,
 Queenstown 206
The Inn at 670,
 Lake Hayes – Queenstown 202
The Old' Ferry Hotel,
 Lower Shotover – Queenstown 204
The Palms B&B, *Tauranga* 71
The Pillars, *Bonshaw Park – Taupo* 94
The Rocks Homestay,
 Punakaiki – West Coast 155
The Station Master's Cottage,
 Dunedin 227
The Summer House,
 Kerikeri – Bay of Islands 32
The White House, *Whitianga* 63
Tide Song, *Whangarei* 44
Tirohanga Farmstay,
 Opotiki – Bay of Plenty 74
Tokarahi Homestead,
 Tokarahi – North Otago 217
Top O' T'ill,
 Hataitai – Wellington 122
Top of the Hill, *Brookby – Auckland* 57
Trelawn Place, *Queenstown* 209

Twinpeak, *Napier* 103
Twin Waters Lodge,
 Collingwood – Golden Bay 132
Twynham at Kinloch,
 Kinloch – Taupo 85
Tyrone Deer Farm,
 Methven – Canterbury 181
Villa 121,
 Merivale – Christchurch 167
Villa 536, *Mt. Eden – Auckland* 51
Villa Amo, *Cromwell* 197
Villa Casablanca, *Paihia* 35
Villa Sorgenfrei, *Queenstown* 201
Wai-Tui Lodge,
 Kerikeri – Bay of Islands 31
Waingaro Palms, *Huntly – Waikato* 65
Walnut Grove, *Cromwell* 199
Wanaka Springs Lodge, *Wanaka* 196
Wapiti Park Homestead,
 Harihari – South Westland 160
Whatamonga Homestay, *Picton* 148
Whispering Pines,
 Mangaroa – Wellington 118
Whitfords Country Villa,
 Howick – Auckland 55
Willow Lodge, *Christchurch* 170
Willowbrook,
 Arrowtown – Queenstown 200
Windsor Heights, *Queenstown* 210
Woodbery Lodge B&B,
 Hamurana – Rotorua 76
Woodlands, *Remuera – Auckland* 52
Yeoman's Lakeview Homestay,
 Acacia Bay – Taupo 91